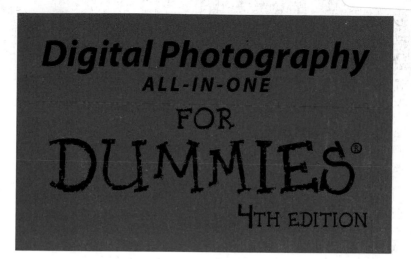

Digital Photography
ALL-IN-ONE
FOR
DUMMIES®
4TH EDITION

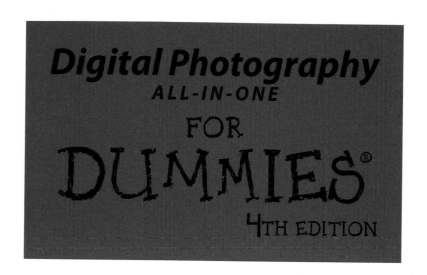

Digital Photography
ALL-IN-ONE
FOR
DUMMIES®
4TH EDITION

by David D. Busch

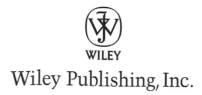

WILEY

Wiley Publishing, Inc.

Digital Photography All-in-One For Dummies®, 4th Edition

Published by
Wiley Publishing, Inc.
111 River Street
Hoboken, NJ 07030-5774

www.wiley.com

Copyright © 2009 by Wiley Publishing, Inc., Indianapolis, Indiana

Published by Wiley Publishing, Inc., Indianapolis, Indiana

Published simultaneously in Canada

For general information on our other products and services, please contact our Customer Care Department within the U.S. at 800-762-2974, outside the U.S. at 317-572-3993, or fax 317-572-4002.

For technical support, please visit www.wiley.com/techsupport.

Wiley also publishes its books in a variety of electronic formats. Some content that appears in print may not be available in electronic books.

Library of Congress Control Number: 2008939186

ISBN: 978-0-470-40195-8

Manufactured in the United States of America

10 9 8 7 6 5 4 3 2 1

WILEY

About the Author

As a roving photojournalist for more than 20 years, **David D. Busch** illustrated his books, magazine articles and newspaper reports with award-winning images. He's operated his own commercial studio, suffocated in formal dress while shooting weddings-for-hire, and shot sports for a daily newspaper and Upstate New York college. His photos have been published in magazines as diverse as *Scientific American* and *Petersen's PhotoGraphic*, and his articles have appeared in *Popular Photography & Imaging, The Rangefinder, The Professional Photographer*, and hundreds of other publications. He's currently reviewing digital cameras for CNet and *Computer Shopper*.

When About.com recently named its top five books on beginning digital photography, occupying the number one and two slots were this book and *Mastering Digital Photography*. His other 80 books published since 1983 include best-sellers like *Digital SLR Cameras & Photography For Dummies, The Nikon D70 Digital Field Guide, The Official Hewlett-Packard Scanner Handbook*, and *Digital Photography For Dummies Quick Reference*.

Busch earned top category honors in the Computer Press Awards the first two years they were given (for *Sorry About The Explosion* and *Secrets of MacWrite, MacPaint and MacDraw*), and later served as Master of Ceremonies for the awards.

Dedication

I dedicate this book, as always, to Cathy.

Author's Acknowledgments

Thanks to Wiley Publishing for the continued innovation that has helped keep this book fresh and up-to-date. Key personnel include Steve Hayes, Senior Acquisitions Editor; Pat O'Brien, Project Editor; and Heidi Unger, Copy Editor.

Technical Editor Michael D. Sullivan added a great deal to this book in addition to checking all the text for technical accuracy. A veteran photographer (in the military sense of the word!), he began his photo career in high school where he first learned the craft and amazed his classmates by having Monday morning coverage of Saturday's big game pictured on the school bulletin board. Sullivan pursed his interest in photography into the U.S. Navy, graduating in the top ten of his photo school class. Following Navy photo assignments in Bermuda and Arizona, he earned a BA degree from West Virginia Wesleyan College.

He became publicity coordinator for Eastman Kodak Company's largest division where he directed the press introduction of the company's major consumer products and guided their continuing promotion. Following a 25-year stint with Kodak, Sullivan pursued a second career with a PR agency as a writer-photographer covering technical imaging subjects and producing articles that appeared in leading trade publications. In recent years, Sullivan has used his imaging expertise as a Technical Editor specializing in digital imaging and photographic subjects for top selling books.

Publisher's Acknowledgments

We're proud of this book; please send us your comments through our online registration form located at www.dummies.com/register/.

Some of the people who helped bring this book to market include the following:

Acquisitions, Editorial, and Media Development

Project Editor: Pat O'Brien

Acquisitions Editor: Steve Hayes

Copy Editor: Heidi Unger

Technical Editor: Michael Sullivan

Editorial Manager: Kevin Kirschner

Editorial Assistant: Amanda Foxworth

Sr. Editorial Assistant: Cherie Case

Cartoons: Rich Tennant
(www.the5thwave.com)

Composition Services

Project Coordinator: Erin Smith

Layout and Graphics: Stacie Brooks, Reuben W. Davis, Melissa K. Jester, Christin Swinford, Christine Williams

Proofreaders: Caitie Kelly, Linda Quigley

Indexer: Palmer Publishing Services

Publishing and Editorial for Technology Dummies

    Richard Swadley, Vice President and Executive Group Publisher

    Andy Cummings, Vice President and Publisher

    Mary Bednarek, Executive Acquisitions Director

    Mary C. Corder, Editorial Director

Publishing for Consumer Dummies

    Diane Graves Steele, Vice President and Publisher

    Joyce Pepple, Acquisitions Director

Composition Services

    Gerry Fahey, Vice President of Production Services

    Debbie Stailey, Director of Composition Services

Contents at a Glance

Table of Contents

Introduction

The future of photography is in your hands, and it's becoming all digital! Not since the 19th century, when photographers had to be artisan, craftsperson, artist, chemist, and public relations expert rolled into one, has so much of the photographic process been entirely in the control of the person taking the picture. Now you can compose and view the exact picture you're going to take by using your camera's full liquid crystal display (LCD) screen. Review the picture an instant after pressing the shutter. If your computer is nearby, you can upload it seconds later, view a super-large version on your display, crop it, enhance it, and then make your own sparkling full-color print — all within minutes!

When you go digital, you never need to buy film or wait while your photos are processed in a lab. You decide which images to print and how large to make them. You can display your digital photographic work framed on your wall or proudly over your fireplace. You can make wallet-size photos, send copies to friends in e-mail, or create an online gallery that can be viewed by relatives and colleagues over the Web.

And if alchemy is in your blood, you can transform the simplest picture into a digital masterpiece by using an image editor. Correct your photos, delete your ex-brother-in-law from a family portrait, or transplant the Eiffel Tower to the seashore.

Digital photography gives you the power to take pictures on a whim or to create careful professional-quality work that others might be willing to pay for. The choices are all yours, and digital photography puts all the power in your hands. All you need is a little information about how to choose and use your tools and how to put them to work. That's what you'll find within the pages of this thick, comprehensive, all-in-one guidebook.

The most exciting aspect of digital photography is how rapidly the technology is changing to bring you new capabilities and features that you can use to improve your pictures. Today, digital cameras with 4-megapixel (mp) or less resolution are difficult to find except in photo-capable cell phones — and some cell phones offer 10-megapixel or more resolution! Even the leanest digital camera you're likely to find in stores will have 5–6 megapixels of resolution. I've tested models in this range that cost less than $150! You'll find 7-megapixel and 9-megapixel cameras for $500 or so, and 10-megapixel models are widely available for quite a bit less than $1,000. Digital single-lens reflex cameras (dSLRs) with interchangeable lenses are available from companies like Nikon, Canon, Olympus, and Sony if you're willing to pay top dollar.

Adobe Photoshop has bumped up the image-editing ante with lots of new capabilities of interest to digital photographers, and even inexpensive applications like Adobe Photoshop Elements have more features than you could find in the most powerful image editor four or five years ago. Your new hardware and software tools make working with digital images easier while giving you important new capabilities.

About This Book

This book, now in its fourth edition, has been updated to include all the latest technology and gadgets available to the digital photographer. It is written for the person who has a good grasp of using a computer and navigating an operating system and has at least a cursory knowledge of the operation of a digital camera. It would help if you have some familiarity with an image editor, such as Corel Paint Shop Pro, Corel Photo Paint, or Adobe's Photoshop or Photoshop Elements. It is intended to be a comprehensive reference book that you can read cover to cover or reach for when you're looking for specific information about a particular task.

Wherever I can, I sneak in a useful tip or an interesting technique to help you put digital photography to work for your project needs.

If you have some knowledge of conventional photography, this book will help you fine-tune your capabilities. If you know very little about photography, there's help for you here, too. One large chunk of the book — Book III — is devoted to tips on the most popular genres of photography, from close-up and sports photography to travel photography and shooting for publication. Check out the helpful section on getting the best composition. If you're puzzled over what equipment to buy, look to the sections on choosing cameras, photo accessories, and related equipment, such as printers and scanners.

What's in This Book

This book is broken down into mini-books, each covering a general topic. Each mini-book comprises chapters, each covering a more specific topic under the general one. Each chapter is then divided into sections, and some of those sections have subsections. I'm sure you get the picture.

You can read the book from front to back, or you can dive right into the mini-book or chapter of your choice. Either way works just fine. Anytime a concept is mentioned that isn't covered in depth in that chapter, you'll find a cross-reference to another book and chapter where you'll find all the details. If you're looking for something specific, check out either the Table of Contents or the index.

The Cheat Sheet at the beginning of the book provides helpful information you'll use often. Tear it out, tape it to your monitor, and don't forget to say, "Thanks." (You're welcome.)

And finally, you get pictures. Lots of them. Many of these pictures illustrate good photo techniques as well as traps to avoid. You'll find examples of the kinds of pictures you can take right away and maybe a few that you'll want to strive to equal or exceed.

This book contains seven mini-books. The following sections offer a quick synopsis of what each book contains.

Book I: Building Your Digital Photography Studio

This section is your digital photography short course, providing all the information on a variety of topics that you really need to know to get started. This book helps you choose the right camera, whether it's your first digital camera or the one you're dreaming about as a replacement for your current model. You'll read all the facts on resolution, lens settings, storage, and accessories. One chapter shows you the requirements for setting up a PC for digital photography. The good news is that you probably already have everything you need in your computer. I'll give you some advice on some recommended upgrades that can make your system work even better with digital images.

Book II: Using Digital SLRs

This book provides a concise overview of the tools and capabilities you'll find in the latest digital SLR cameras. You find out why these cameras can do things that their non-SLR counterparts cannot and how to use those features to improve your photography.

Book III: Taking Great Pictures

This is the meat of the book for veteran and aspiring photographers alike. Each of the six chapters is devoted to a different kind of photography. You'll see the basic rules for composing great photos — and when to break them. You'll discover the secrets of close-up photography and how to make pleasing portraits of individuals and groups.

Whether shooting for publication is part of your job description or just a goal, you'll find tips on how to take publishable photos and how to market them. I also include chapters on sports and action photography as well tips on travel photography.

Book IV: Basics of Image Editing

This book is your introduction to image editing, providing general tips on what you can — and can't — do with popular image editors such as Paint Shop Pro, Corel PhotoPaint, PhotoImpact, or Adobe Photoshop and Photoshop Elements. You'll see the capabilities of these programs, discovering the full range of tools at your disposal.

Book V: Editing with Adobe Photoshop and Photoshop Elements

This book goes into a little more detail on the use of the two most popular image-editing programs: Adobe Photoshop (favored by professionals) and Adobe Photoshop Elements (an inexpensive younger sibling that has lots of power but is still easy to use). You discover the power of making selections, brush away problems in your digital photos, correct your colors, and apply special effects with filters.

Although this book is not a complete guide to Photoshop, you'll find lots of good information you can use right away to try out your digital photo-editing muscles. (For tons of in-depth coverage, read *Photoshop CS4 All-in-One Desk Reference For Dummies,* by Barbara Obermeier [Wiley].)

Book VI: Restoring Old Photos

Continue your study of Photoshop and Photoshop Elements with this book, which shows you how to restore old photos and make some common repairs to your digital images. Read chapters on scanning in print images, tips for working with slides and negatives, and some common fixes for vintage photos.

Book VII: Printing and Sharing Your Digital Images

Your digital photos are going to be so good that you won't be able to keep them to yourself. This book provides more information on printing your photos and shows you ways to share your pictures over the Internet. You'll become more comfortable with your printer's capabilities, discovering all the things that you can do with photos online, whether it's showcasing your pictures among your friends and colleagues or making photo greeting cards, T-shirts, or other gift items.

Conventions Used in This Book

Digital photography knows no operating system limits. All digital cameras and many software applications work equally well on a PC and a Macintosh. To that end, this book is cross-platform. Understandably, some differences do crop up, particularly in the chapters that deal with image editing. In this book, Windows commands are given first, followed by Mac commands, like this:

Press Enter (or Return on the Mac) to begin a new line.

Occasionally, text will be specific to one platform or another. Commands listed often involve using the keyboard along with the mouse — for example, "Press Shift while dragging with the Rectangular Marquee tool to create a square," or "Alt+click (Option+click) the eyeball to redisplay all layers."

When you see a command arrow (⇨) in the text, it indicates that you should select a command from the menu bar. For example, "Choose Edit⇨Define Custom Shape" means to click the Edit menu and then choose the Define Custom Shape option.

Although this book was written based on the latest digital cameras and the newest software (such as Photoshop Elements 7), if you're still bouncing around with earlier versions, you can still glean valuable info. You might just have to poke around a little more to find a tool or option that has moved — and of course, the topics covering new features won't be applicable. But hey, seeing the cool new features might just be the impetus you need to go out and upgrade!

Icons Used in This Book

While perusing this book, you'll notice some icons in the margins beckoning you for your attention. Don't ignore them; embrace them! These icons point out fun, useful, and memorable tidbits about digital photography, plus facts you'd be unwise to ignore.

This icon indicates information that will make your digital photography experience easier. It also gives you an icebreaker at your next cocktail party. Whipping out, "Did you know that many digital cameras can focus down to within an inch of an object?" is bound to make you the center of conversation.

This icon is a reminder of things that I want to *gently* re-emphasize. Or I might be pointing out things that I want you to take note of in your future digital photography excursions.

The little bomb icon is a red flag. Heed these warnings, or else your camera or image editor might show its ugly side.

This icon points out info you don't necessarily need to know. If you're interested in getting more technical, however, you'll find such information interesting.

Where to Go from Here

If you want your voice to be heard, you can contact the publisher of the *For Dummies* books by visiting www.dummies.com, by sending an e-mail to customer@wiley.com, or by sending snail mail to Wiley Publishing, Inc., 10475 Crosspoint Boulevard, Indianapolis, IN 46256.

And, of course, the very next place to go is to the section of this book that covers your favorite topic. Go ahead and dive right in.

Book I
Building Your Digital Photography Studio

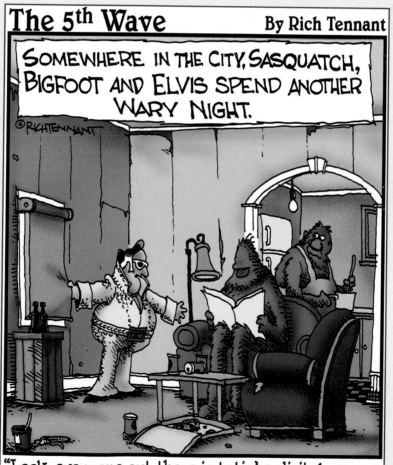

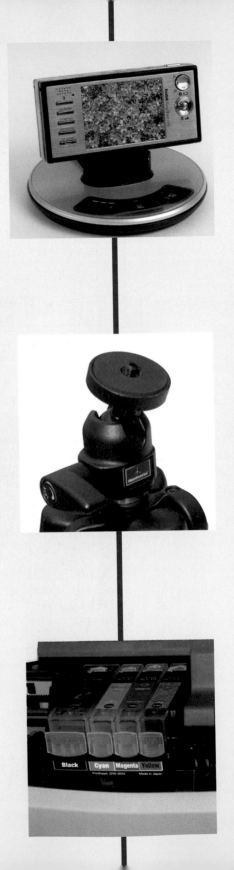

*I*n this book, I show you how to assemble a suitable digital photography arsenal, with explanations of all the key features of the weapons at your disposal, including camera equipment, computer gear, printers, and cool accessories like tripods, electronic flashes, and (if you're going the digital SLR route) add-on lenses.

I also give you in-depth explanations of key features, including zooms, viewfinders, storage options, and whether you really do need a gazillion megapixels of resolution. You'll find out how to set up your computer, transfer pictures from your camera to your hard drive, and archive your photos effectively for posterity. I also show you how a few accessories can make a dramatic difference in the quality of your photos.

Chapter 1: Choosing the Right Camera

In This Chapter

✓ **Key components of digital cameras**

✓ **Evaluating lens requirements**

✓ **Understanding sensors and resolution**

✓ **Selecting exposure options**

✓ **Finding a camera that's easy to use**

✓ **Understanding your computer's memory and storage needs**

*C*hoosing the right digital camera has gotten a lot more exciting recently! The traditional "point and shoot" camera has become much more sophisticated, with more features and better image quality than snapshooters could have dreamed of only a few years ago. At the same time, the digital single lens reflex (dSLR) cameras — the ones that have interchangeable lenses and show you an optical and (in many cases) an optional electronic preview image through the same lens that takes the picture — have dipped under the $600 price point and are nosing around the $500 neighborhood, making them a reasonable choice for many more serious amateur photographers. You no longer have to be a photography fanatic to enjoy and use an incredibly sophisticated dSLR.

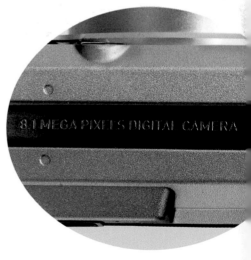

Affordable 10-megapixel (and up) cameras provide sharper, better pictures without busting your wallet. Digital cameras — both the point-and-shoot and dSLR varieties — are becoming smaller and easier to use and are packed with special features. This is a great time to choose a digital camera, whether you're a snapshooter or a dedicated photo hobbyist.

Yet, selecting the right digital camera isn't as daunting a task as it might appear to be on the surface, even with the increased number of features and options to choose from. Most of the leading vendors of digital equipment produce fine products that take great pictures. It's really hard to go wrong. All you need is to do a little homework so that you're aware, when you make your purchase, of the features you need — and features you don't need. The vendors write their brochures and ad copy so that those who don't sort out features and benefits ahead of time might think that every single feature is essential.

Trust me: They're not. For instance, the ability to shoot several pictures consecutively, each using different color settings to make sure that one picture is perfectly color-balanced, might sound cool, but it's not something many people need every day. But if you find yourself constantly taking pictures under varied lighting conditions and color accuracy is very important to you, a feature like that might be a lifesaver. Only you can decide for sure.

The key is having the upfront information you need to wisely choose the camera that has the largest number of your must-have features — and a nice sprinkling of nice-to-have features — at a price you can afford. In selecting a camera, there are six main things to consider, which are

- Lens requirements
- Viewfinder options
- Sensor resolution
- Exposure controls
- Storage options
- Ease of use

This chapter looks at each of these considerations, plus others, in detail, with a brief mention of the newest digital SLR cameras (which are covered more exhaustively in Book II). Although much of the information can help you select a camera, you can also find some basic explanations of digital camera nuts and bolts that will be helpful as you take pictures. If you ever wanted to know what shutter speeds and lens openings do, this is your chance.

Choosing a Camera Category

Digital cameras fall into several different categories, each aimed at a particular audience of buyers, as well as particular kinds of applications for them. The major types are listed next.

Web cams

Web cams are low-cost (often less than $30) TV cameras that can supply low-resolution (640-x-480 or 320-x-200/240-pixel), full-motion images that can be transmitted over the Internet, put on Web pages, or attached to e-mails.

Most can also capture low-resolution still images. They're fun to use and essential for things like videoconferencing, online video chats, or Internet video phone calls. You'll find them built into many laptops and available as an accessory for desktop computers.

These cameras frequently have no removable storage, no controls, and lenses that don't zoom and may not even have a facility for changing focus. Only a few years ago, they made a good first camera for kids or a spare digital camera, but today that function is more likely to be found in the cell phones that virtually every person in the country seems to carry constantly. Web cams aren't covered in this book because most don't have the kind of image quality and capabilities required for serious photography.

Camera phones

Camera phones are cellular phones with photo capabilities — which includes virtually every cell phone on the market these days, right on up to Apple's iPhone and other "smart" 3G (third generation) cell phones that can make calls, cruise the Web, handle your appointments, and take still and video pictures — seemingly at the same time! Many multipurpose cell phones are capable of 2-megapixel or better resolution that exceeds the picture quality available from some $500 digital cameras from only a few years ago. In Japan, cell phones with cameras built in have practically vaporized the demand for one-time-use film cameras. Folks who sometimes forget to take their digital cameras with them wouldn't be caught dead without their cell phones, so they're always ready for the kind of spur-of-the-moment photography that single-use cameras have traditionally served.

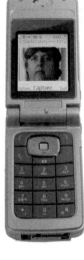

I have one in my own cell phone, shown in Figure 1-1, and I find it useful for sending photos to family members along with a text message on the order of "Is this what you wanted me to pick up on the way home?" They can also be handy for note-taking (say, to document the various steps of a science experiment). However, most phone cams aren't flexible enough for the most serious kinds of digital photography, but I expect that to change within five years. I truly believe that, eventually, there will be just two main classes of digital cameras. We'll have the cell phone point-and-shoot models, which will resemble current snapshot cameras, and we'll also be using digital single-lens reflex cameras priced at $400 and up when we're doing "serious" photography.

Figure 1-1: Web cams and phone cams are fun, but they aren't quite ready for prime time.

I'm not covering these useful (but specialized) devices in this book (even though I own and use one myself), nor cameras built into other products, such as personal digital assistants (PDAs). None of them are intended for use as a primary camera.

Point-and-shoot models

These entry-level digital cameras (see Figure 1-2), priced at $100–$200, offer 6 to 12 megapixels of resolution (although it's becoming very difficult to find a 6-megapixel camera in stores), simple lenses (usually with zoom), and autoexposure. I recently tested a 10-megapixel camera with a 3X zoom lens that could be purchased for $169! Clearly, even the most basic point-and-shoot cameras are gaining resolution and features almost faster than we can keep track. This kind of camera is an excellent choice for someone looking for a basic camera with few manual adjustments, and for casual shots that will be enlarged no more than about 5 x 7 inches. Point-and-shoot digital cameras have a built-in flash, some sort of removable storage (usually a Secure Digital or SD memory card), and a zoom lens that magnifies the image from 3X to 5X or more. Expect automatic exposure and no manual controls.

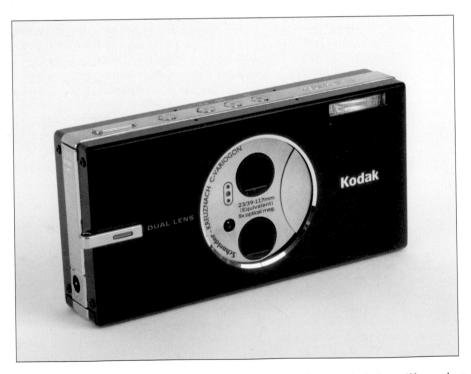

Figure 1-2: A typical point-and-shoot camera will have basic features, including a 3X zoom lens.

Intermediate models

Priced in the $200–$500 slot, intermediate digital cameras have 10- to 14-megapixel resolution, a 5:1 or 8:1 or better zoom lens, and Secure Digital (SD), xD, or, sometimes, CompactFlash storage. Many have close-up focusing, burst modes that can snap off seven or more frames in a few seconds, and they have some manual controls. The average snapshooter would be very happy with a camera in this category and would be satisfied with the few tweaks that can be made to add a little creativity to selected photos. Look for at least a few special options, such as different exposure modes, close-up focusing, or manual controls.

Advanced consumer models

In the $500–$800 range, you can find deluxe digital cameras (like the one shown in Figure 1-3) with roughly 10 to 14 megapixels of resolution, decent 8:1 to 18:1 zoom lenses, lots of accessories, optional exposure modes, and a steep learning curve. These cameras are easy to operate, so the average snapshooter can use them with a little training and practice. Yet, they are also versatile, with features like electronic viewfinders and manual settings, that serious photographers can invoke for those special picture-taking situations. These are aimed at those who want some special features, extra resolution, or a longer zoom lens. Many provide *two* LCD viewfinders: the traditional back-panel display and a second, electronic viewfinder (or EVF) inside the camera that provides a dimmer, but still SLR-like view. You'll find plenty of add-on accessories, such as wide-angle and telephoto attachments, filters, external flash units, and more in these cameras, along with lots of optional exposure modes, customizable settings, and other (potentially confusing) features. Advanced consumer cameras usually require a session or two with the instruction manual to master all their capabilities, but they have few limitations.

Prosumer digital SLR models

The prosumer dSLR, shown in Figure 1-4, is the fastest growing breed of digital camera, originally created in 2003 when Canon introduced the Digital Rebel for $999 (with lens), and other vendors, including Nikon and Pentax, followed. In price, there is some overlap with the prosumer non-SLR cameras. However, the true SLR type offers interchangeable lenses and other features found in the traditional advanced-amateur favorite.

These are the models that photo buffs and even professional photographers favor. The avid photographer doesn't countenance much in the way of compromises and is willing to spend the $500 to $1,800 sticker price for these cameras in order to get the advanced features. Pros find them useful as backup cameras, even if the lowest priced models aren't quite rugged enough to take the beating that professional equipment is subjected to.

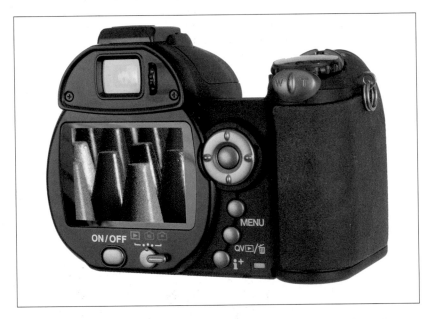

Figure 1-3: Advanced consumer models may offer both a back-panel LCD and a second EVF display seen through a viewing window.

In addition to their interchangeable lenses, these cameras are prized for their ultra-fast responses. They have virtually no *shutter lag* (the delay between when you press the shutter release all the way and when the picture is actually taken) and can crank out 2.5 to 8 pictures per second for action sequence photography. They can be purchased just as a camera body alone (in case you already own compatible lenses, perhaps for an older film camera) or in a kit that includes an inexpensive but serviceable zoom in the

18mm–55mm or 18mm–70mm range. Expect a minimum of 8 to 14 million pixels to shoot with, plus a lot of extra weight to lug around compared to point-and-shoot cameras.

You get automatic and manual focus, multiple automated exposure modes, plus manual shutter speed and lens opening settings if you want them. The key differences between high-priced prosumer digital SLR cameras and professional digital SLR cameras is resolution (pro models have 12 to 24 megapixels or more), speed (pro cameras can usually snap off digital pictures at a 5-to-11-pictures-per-second clip; some prosumer models may be limited to 3 pictures per second), and ruggedness.

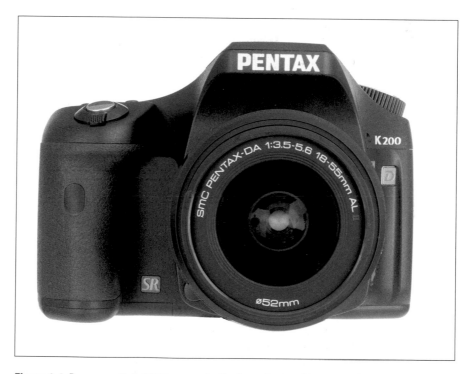

Figure 1-4: Prosumer digital SLR cameras offer interchangeable lenses and other advanced features.

Professional models

Professional-quality digital SLR cameras used to cost $5,000 and (way) up and had 6–14 million pixels of resolution. Today, you can still pay around $5,000 or more for a pro camera (without lens), and resolutions now go up to 24 megapixels, but some very fine professional-worthy models are available for a few thousand dollars less, too. The manufacturers of the top-end cameras are feeling the pressure of competition from the sub-$1,000 digital SLRs, so you can expect prices to drop even further as features proliferate. However, professional photographers will continue to pay a premium for these cameras because they frequently operate more quickly, allowing the pro to grab shot after shot without pausing for breath.

They're rugged, too, which means they can withstand the harsh treatment pros often subject their equipment to (not because they're mean, but because they're *working*). If you can't do it with one of these, it can't be done. You can fit standard interchangeable lenses to them while retaining all the sophisticated autoexposure and autofocus modes.

As I mention earlier, one feature pros demand is speed. If you use a pro camera, you'll see just how this speed is applied. With lesser cameras, there is often a tiny time lag while the autofocus system locks in; with pro cameras, this interval is hard to detect. With a pro camera, such as the one shown in Figure 1-5, you can usually snap off pictures as quickly as you can press the shutter release, or else trigger the *motor drive* (continuous shooting) mode. You may be able to snap off 5 to 11 pictures per second for as long as you like, or at least until the storage media fills up. That can be a long time because pro digital cameras usually accept humongous storage options, such as 4GB (or larger) memory cards.

Some pro dSLR cameras (as well as prosumer models) with interchangeable lenses boost the effective magnification of your lenses as well because the sensors are smaller than the nominal 24-x-36mm 35mm film frame. A 35mm lens or zoom setting has the same field of view as a normal lens on a film camera. A 105mm portrait lens becomes a longer telephoto. However, some of the latest professional cameras from both Canon and Nikon have a true 24-x-36mm sensor and can use lenses at their marked focal lengths.

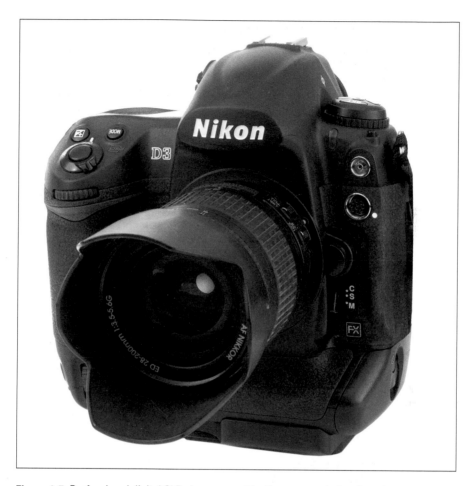

Figure 1-5: Professional digital SLRs have rugged bodies, extremely fast focusing and shooting, as well as high resolution.

Examining the Parts of a Digital Camera

If you're very new to digital cameras, you might be wondering what all those buttons, LEDs, and windows are for. Here's a quick introduction to the key components of the average non-SLR digital camera. Not every camera will have all these features, and some will have additional features not shown in Figures 1-6 and 1-7.

✓ **Shutter release:** Pressing this button halfway locks exposure and focus; press all the way to take a picture.

✓ **Control buttons:** Miscellaneous control buttons might turn on/off close-up mode, automatic flash, or other features; set picture quality; or activate the self-timer.

✓ **Shooting mode dial:** Most cameras use this button or dial for changing among different scene modes (such as Night, Portrait, or Sports), adjusting automatic or manual exposure choices, selecting Movie mode, or switching into close-up mode.

✓ **Microphone:** This captures audio for movie clips and voice annotations; it can even activate a sound-triggered self-timer.

✓ **Focus-assist light:** This is an auxiliary illumination source that helps the camera focus in dim lighting conditions.

✓ **Electronic flash:** This provides light under dim conditions or helps fill in dark shadows.

✓ **Optical viewfinder:** This window, which doesn't show exactly the same view that the lens captures, is for framing and composing your picture.

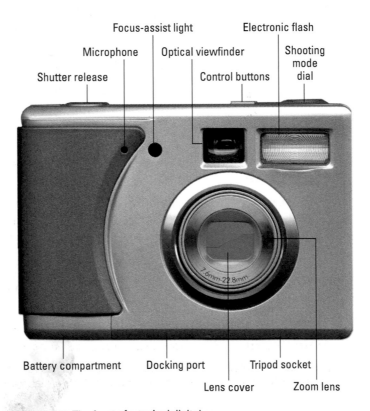

Figure 1-6: The front of a typical digital camera.

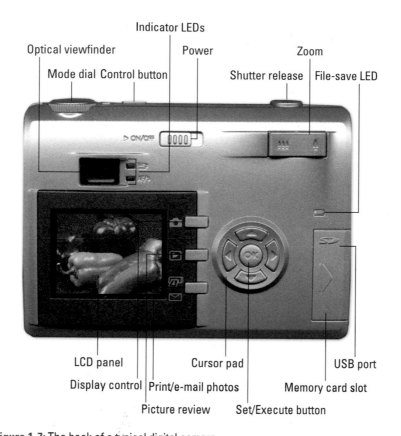

Figure 1-7: The back of a typical digital camera.

✔ **Zoom lens:** This magnifies and reduces the size of the image, taking you closer or moving you farther away.

✔ **Lens cover:** This protects the lens when the digital camera is turned off.

✔ **Tripod socket:** This allows you to attach the camera to a firm support, such as a tripod or monopod, plus other accessories, such as an external flash bracket.

✔ **Docking port:** Some cameras have a special dock that can be used to transfer photos, recharge the batteries, make prints, or perform other functions.

✔ **Battery compartment:** This contains the cells that power the camera.

✔ **Power switch:** Here is where you turn the camera on or off.

✔ **Indicator LEDs:** These indicators show status, such as focus and exposure, often with green and red go/no go LEDs (light-emitting diodes).

✔ **LCD (liquid crystal display) panel:** This shows the sensor's view of an image before exposure, shows preview images after exposure, and displays status, photo information, and menus.

✔ **Display control/Menu button:** This controls the amount of information shown on the LCD and produces menus. Some digital cameras have multiple buttons for recording menus, setup menus, and special functions.

✔ **Picture review:** Press this button to review the pictures you've already taken.

✔ **Print/e-mail/share photos:** Some digital cameras allow printing directly from the camera to compatible printers or marking pictures for printing or e-mailing later.

✔ **Cursor pad:** Use this to navigate menu choices. Many digital cameras use the cursor buttons to activate frequently accessed features, such as flash options, macro mode, exposure value adjustments, and a self-timer.

✔ **Set/Execute button:** Press this to activate a feature or set a menu choice to the current selection.

✔ **Memory card slot:** This accepts digital memory cards.

✔ **USB port:** Use this to connect your camera directly to your computer or to a printer via a USB cable.

✔ **File-save LED:** This light usually flashes or lights up to indicate that an image is currently being saved to the memory card.

✔ **Power zoom control:** Press this to zoom the lens in and out.

Evaluating Your Lens Requirements

The lens and the sensor are the two most important parts of any digital photographic system. The lens gathers the light from your scene and focuses it onto the sensor, which transforms the light into something that can be stored permanently and viewed as a picture after digital processing.

Sharp lenses and high-quality sensors lead to technically good images; poor lenses and bad sensors lead to poor photos. Indeed, in one sense, most of the other components of a camera are for your convenience. Theoretically, you could mount a simple lens on one end of an oatmeal box, focus it on a sensor affixed to the inside of the other end of the box, and make an exposure by covering and uncovering the lens with a dark cloth. Of course, a digital version of this science fair project would require some additional electronics to handle the captured signal, but such a system could work.

When you're choosing a digital camera, the first thing to concentrate on is the lens furnished with it. You probably don't need to go into as much detail as I'm going to provide, but understanding the components of a camera lens does help you use your optics as much as it helps you choose them. The major things you need to know fall into four simple categories:

- **The optical quality of the lens itself:** Just how sharp is the piece of glass (or, these days, plastic)? The better the lens, the better it can capture — *resolve* — fine details. In most cases, the optical quality of digital camera lenses marches in lockstep with the price of the camera and the resolution of the sensor. Even at the low and medium ends of the price spectrum, digital cameras have good-quality lenses that usually can resolve a lot more detail than the 6- to 8-megapixel sensor can capture.

Camera vendors have been mass-producing lenses like these for film cameras for decades. At higher price levels, lenses have better-quality optics, which are necessary to keep up with the detail-capturing capabilities of 8- to 10-megapixel (and higher) sensors.

- **The amount of light the lens can transmit:** Some lenses can capture larger amounts of light than others, generally because they have a greater diameter that can transmit more light. This factor, called *lens speed*, is a bit more complicated than that. Think of a 1-inch-diameter pipe and a 2-inch-diameter pipe and visualize how much more water (or light) the wider pipe can conduct; now you're thinking in the right direction. Lens speed, in part, controls how low of a light level you can take pictures in. If you take many pictures in dim light, you'll want a *faster* lens. I look at this factor in greater detail later in this chapter.

- **The focusing range of the lens:** Some lenses can focus closer than others. The ability to get up close and personal with your subject matter can be very important if your hobbies include things like stamp or coin collecting or if you want to take pictures of flowers or bugs. Indeed, close-focusing can open whole new worlds of photography for you, worlds you can explore in more detail in Book III, Chapter 2.

- **The magnification range of the lens:** Virtually all digital cameras have a zoom lens, which allows you to vary the amount of magnification of the image. You might be able to take your basic image and double it in size (a 2:1 zoom ratio), triple it (a 3:1 zoom), or magnify it 12X or more (a 12:1 zoom). The zoom range determines how much or how little of a particular subject you can include in an image from a particular shooting distance. As you might expect, the ability to zoom enhances your creative options significantly. At the widest settings (wide-angle settings), you can take in broad sweeps of landscape, whereas in the narrowest view (telephoto), you can reach out and bring a distant object much closer.

Understanding How Lenses Work

You don't need to have a degree in optical science to use a digital camera, but understanding how lens openings (*f-stops*) and some other components work can help you use those components more effectively.

Lenses consist of several optical elements made of glass or plastic that focus light in precise ways, much like you focus light with a magnifying glass or with a telescope or binoculars. The very simplest lenses, like those used on the least expensive digital cameras, are *fixed focal length* lenses, usually comprising just three or four pieces of glass. That is, the elements can produce an image only at a single magnification. You find these in the simplest point-and-shoot cameras that have no zooming capabilities. There aren't many of these around, but I did run into a camera with no "real" zoom recently: an extra-compact model that used a 3:1 digital zoom as a substitute for optical zooming capabilities.

Most digital cameras have zoom lenses, which have very complex optical systems with 8, 10, 20, or more elements that move in precise ways to produce a continuous range of magnifications. Zoom lenses must be carefully designed to avoid bad things, such as stray beams of light that degrade the image bouncing around inside the lens. For that reason, when choosing a digital camera with a zoom lens, you need to pay attention to the quality of the image. All 4:1 zooms are not created equal; one vendor might produce an excellent lens with this range, whereas another might offer a lens that is less sharp. Among digital cameras with similar or identical sensors, lens quality can make the biggest difference in the final quality of an image. You'll discover how to select the best lens for your needs as we go along.

You can get a top-quality lens and still save some money if you know how to interpret digital camera specifications. Many vendors share lenses and sensors among similar models in their product lines. I tested two cameras from the same manufacturer that had identical resolution and lens specifications, but one model was more compact, was outfitted with a rechargeable battery, and included rubber gaskets that made it water resistant. (It also cost $100 more!) A penny-pinching photographer who doesn't mind a tiny bit more bulk, is willing to use AA batteries, and doesn't plan any photography in rain showers could buy the less expensive version and save enough money to buy some extra memory cards or other accessories.

Magnifications and focal lengths

Comparing zoom ranges of digital cameras can be confusing because the exact same lens can produce different magnifications on different cameras. That's why you usually see the zoom range of a digital camera presented either as absolute magnifications or in the equivalents of the 35mm camera lenses that the zoom settings correspond to.

Optical zoom versus digital zoom

Non-SLR digital cameras have two kinds of zooming capabilities: optical and digital. *Optical zoom* uses the arrangement of the lens elements to control the amount of magnification. Usually, optical zoom is the specification mentioned first in the camera's list of features. *Digital zoom* is a supplementary magnification system in which the center pixels of an image are enlarged using a mathematical algorithm to fill the entire image area with the information contained in those center pixels.

Digital zoom doesn't really provide much in the way of extra information; you could zoom in on an image in your image editor if you like. However, digital zoom is a way of turning a 4:1 zoom into an 8:1 (or better) zoom lens even if the results aren't as good as those you'd obtain with a true optical 8:1 zoom. I tend to discount digital zoom capabilities when buying a camera because I want the sharpest picture possible, and many of the digital zoom pictures I've taken have looked fuzzy and pixelated. The feature doesn't cost you anything, and you can usually switch it off so you won't accidentally grab a digital zoom picture by mistake.

Zoom range doesn't relate to lens quality. You'll find excellent 4:1 zooms and average 4:1 zooms. However, the longer the zoom range, the more difficult it is to produce a lens that makes good pictures at all zoom settings. You should be especially careful in choosing a lens with a longer zoom range (8:1 or above); test the camera and its lens before you buy. However, lenses from the major manufacturers (Canon, Sony, Nikon, Fuji, and so forth) are all generally quite good.

Until the advent of digital cameras, figuring the magnification of consumer camera lenses was relatively easy because, in recent years, most consumer (and the workhorse professional) film cameras used a standard film size — the 35mm film frame — which measures a nominal 24mm x 36mm. Some cameras also used Kodak's now-discontinued Advanced Photo System (APS) film format, which produced images in three different configurations.

The magnification of any particular lens with a standard film size is easily calculated by measuring the distance from the film the lens must be positioned to focus a sharp image on the film. (This is the focal length of the lens.)

By convention, in 35mm photography, a lens with a 45–50mm focal length is considered a *normal* lens. (The figure was arrived at by measuring the diagonal of the film frame; you can calculate the focal length of a normal lens for any size film or digital camera sensor by measuring that diagonal.)

Lenses with a shorter focal length, such as 35mm, 28mm, 20mm, or less, are described as *wide-angle* lenses. Those with longer focal lengths (such as 85mm, 105mm, or 200mm) are described as *telephoto* lenses. We've lived happily with that nomenclature for more than 75 years, since the first 35mm camera was introduced. Wide-angle and telephoto images are shown in Figure 1-8.

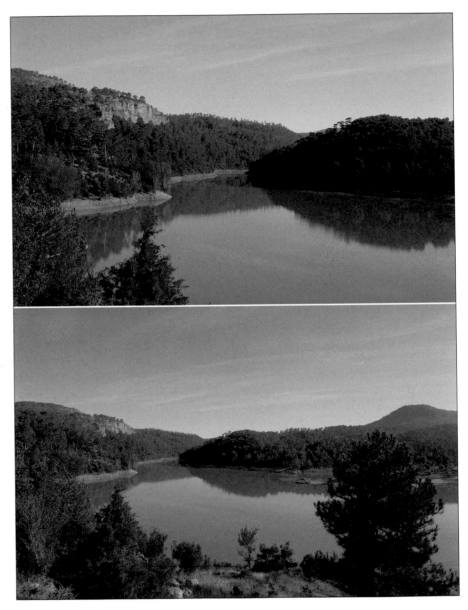

Figure 1-8: Telephoto (top) and wide angle shots (bottom) provide different perspectives on a subject.

Then came the digital camera, and all the simple conventions about focal lengths and magnifications went out the window. For good and valid technical reasons, most digital camera sensors do not measure 24mm x 36mm. You wouldn't want a sensor that large (roughly 1" x 1.5") anyway in a compact digital camera because the camera would have to be large enough to accommodate it. In addition, as with all solid-state devices, the larger a device such as a sensor becomes, the more expensive it is to manufacture. Sensors that are as large as the full 35mm film frame are available for an increasing number of digital SLR cameras, which means the magnification effect I'm about to describe doesn't apply for those models.

Most sensors for non-SLR cameras are more likely to measure, say, 16mm x 24mm or less. Even the larger digital camera sensors might be no bigger than about 38mm x 38mm. So, a normal lens on one digital camera might be 8mm, whereas another normal lens on another camera might be 6mm. A 4:1 zoom lens can range from 8mm–32mm or 5.5mm–22mm. What a mess! How can you compare lenses and zoom ranges under those conditions?

Camera vendors have solved the problem by quoting digital camera lens focal lengths according to their 35mm equivalents. If you're already familiar with 35mm camera lenses, that's great. If you're not, at least you have a standard measurement to compare with. That's why you often see digital camera zoom ranges expressed as "35mm–135mm equivalent (roughly 4:1)" or some similar expression. You can safely use these figures to compare lenses in your quest for the perfect digital camera.

Because digital camera lenses have such short focal lengths in the first place, most models tend to be deficient in the wide-angle department. Expect to see most digital cameras with no better than a 35mm–28mm wide-angle equivalent. That's barely acceptable because 35mm isn't very wide. If you really need a wide field of view, consider a wide-angle attachment that fits on the front of your lens.

What focal length (equivalents) do you look for? Your preferred range will depend on what kind of photos you want to take. If you shoot architecture or indoor photos, you'll want the shortest focal length possible. An alarming number of digital cameras seem to have settled on a 38–39mm (equivalent) focal length as their widest setting. There are several reasons for that. First, a lens with that meager wide-angle field of view is easier to design (and usually more compact) than one with a broader perspective.

In addition, a lens with a particular magnification will have a longer telephoto effect if you're starting from a base focal length that's narrower to begin with. Consumers tend to get more excited about long telephotos than they do about wider wide angles, even though both perspectives have an important place. Table 1-1 shows how a 4:1 zoom lens gains a more impressive telephoto "look" when the vendor snips millimeters from the wide-angle portion of the range.

Wide angles and digital SLRs

A digital SLR with interchangeable lenses doesn't make the wide-angle problem go away. Remember that if your SLR has a sensor that's smaller than what is called *full-frame size,* the focal length of any lens you attach will be magnified. If your camera's "magnification" factor is 1.6x, a super-wide 18mm lens (or zoom setting) is instantly transformed into a moderately wide 28mm lens. Extreme wide angles can be expensive in the first place, so you might be crushed when you discover that your expensive piece of glass that qualifies as an ultra-wide angle on a 35mm camera provides you with a rather ordinary wide-angle view when mounted on a digital camera.

If wide-angle photography is important to you, look for a digital SLR with a full-frame sensor or purchase a lens that has been designed specifically for digital photography. A wide lens for a 35mm camera costs as much as it does because it must cover a full 24mm x 36mm film frame evenly. When a lens designer is creating optics that will be used with sensors that are smaller than the traditional film frame, the lens can have a wider view, be more compact, and still provide an image that is sharp over the entire surface of the sensor.

Although one of the attractions of digital SLRs is the ability to recycle a photographer's existing stable of lenses, the major vendors are all introducing lenses specifically for digital cameras that do a better job, cost less, and provide improved fields of view. I look at this in more detail in Book III.

Table 1-1	4X Zoom Lenses (35mm Equivalents)
Minimum Focal Length	*Maximum Focal Length*
28mm	112mm
32mm	128mm
35mm	140mm
38mm	152mm

Hey, wouldn't you prefer a 152mm medium telephoto over a 112mm short telephoto? You would until you find yourself with your back up against the wall trying to take a picture of an entire (albeit moderately small) room and discover that your 4X zoom lens would give you no more than the field of view of a 38mm lens. You might be happier with a lens that has a wider minimum focal length but which accepts a telephoto attachment for those times when you really need to reach out and touch something.

Lens apertures

The *lens aperture* is an adjustable control that determines the width of the opening that admits light to the sensor. The wider the aperture, the more light that can reach the sensor, making it possible to take pictures in dimmer light. You can think of an aperture as the pupil of your eye. When it's bright outside, your pupils contract (and you squint), letting in less light. When it's dim, your pupils dilate.

A narrow aperture reduces the amount of light that can reach the sensor, letting you avoid overloading the imaging device in very bright light. These lens openings are used in tandem with *shutter speed* (the amount of time the sensor is exposed to the light) to control the exposure. (I explain more about exposure later in this chapter.) Your digital camera needs a selection of lens apertures (*f-stops*) so that you can take pictures in a broad range of lighting conditions.

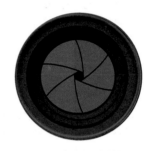

F-stops aren't absolute values; they're calculated by measuring the actual size of the lens opening as it relates to the focal length of the lens, using a formula that I won't repeat here. The easiest way to visualize how f-stops work is to imagine them as the denominators of fractions. Just like $1/2$ is larger than $1/4$ or $1/8$, f/2 is larger than f/4 or f/8. The relationship is such that as the amount of light reaching the sensor is doubled, the f-stop increases using an odd-looking series of numbers: f/2 is twice as large as f/2.8, which is twice as large as f/4, and so on through f/5.6, f/8, f/11, f/16, and f/22 (which is just about the smallest f-stop you'll encounter in the digital realm). Figure 1-9 shows a lens opening that's partially closed down.

Figure 1-9: Lens opening, f-stop, aperture — all mean the doorway that light passes through to the sensor.

If you're taking photos in automatic mode, you don't need to know what f-stop you're using because the camera selects it for you automatically. Your digital camera probably displays the f-stop being used, however, either in the viewfinder or on an LCD panel, and the information can be helpful. See Figure 1-10 and just remember these things:

- ✔ The larger the f-stop (the smaller the number), the more light that is admitted (*faster*). An f/2 lens (small number, large f-stop) is a fast lens, whereas one with a maximum aperture of f/8 (larger number, smaller f-stop) is *slow*. If you need to take photos in dim light, you want to buy a camera with a fast lens.

- ✔ The smaller the f-stop (larger the number), the more of your image that is in sharp focus. (More on this later.)

- ✔ As the f-stops get smaller (larger number), exposure time must be increased to let in the same amount of light. For example, if you take a photo at f/2 for one-half second, you need to double the exposure time to one full second if you *stop down* (reduce the aperture) to f/4. I look at exposure a little later, too.

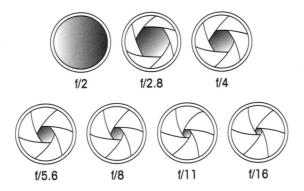

Figure 1-10: As the f-stop gets larger (the number gets smaller), more light is admitted.

Typically, you'll find that among non-SLR digital cameras, the *speed* or maximum aperture of camera lenses is smaller than is common among 35mm film cameras, and the range of available apertures is more limited, too. For example, even an inexpensive snapshooter 35mm film camera might have an f/1.9 lens (pretty fast), and serious photographers with 35mm SLRs probably own f/1.4 or faster normal and wide-angle lenses. Although zoom lenses usually have smaller maximum apertures, in the 35mm film world, f/2.8–f/3.5 are common numbers.

In the digital camera realm, things are a bit different primarily because the very short focal lengths of the lenses are more difficult to design with large lens openings. So don't be alarmed if your favorite digital camera has an f/4 or f/5.6 maximum aperture. You might even find that the lens is labeled f/4–f/5.6 because the effective widest opening can vary as a lens is zoomed in and out. A lens might have an f/4 opening when zoomed out to 38mm but only f/5.6 at its maximum telephoto setting of 152mm. (In most cases, as the focal length increases, the lens opening itself moves along with the optical glass, so the opening is farther away from the sensor and looks smaller.)

To make things really interesting, your digital camera lens might have only a limited number of different f-stops available for manual selection, perhaps f/4, f/5.6, and f/8, or maybe none at all. You won't miss the lack of f-stops: Modern electronic shutters are fast enough to provide the proper exposure without smaller lens openings. Further, in 35mm photography, smaller lens openings have been used to increase the range of sharpness (called *depth-of-field*). As you can read in Book III, Chapter 2, though, the short focal length of non-SLR digital camera lenses usually means that just about everything is sharp, anyway.

Focus range

The *focus range* of a digital camera is simply how close it can be from a subject and still create a sharp image. Digital cameras vary in their close-focusing (also called *macro*) capabilities. If you want to photograph flowers, hobby collections, items for sale on eBay, or anything else up-close, you want to make sure that your camera is up to it. Close focus can vary from model to model. Some vendors deem anything less than about a foot as macro capability. Other cameras take you down to half an inch from your subject. Here are some things to consider when evaluating focus range:

- ✓ **There's such a thing as too close.** When you get to within a few inches of your subject, you'll find that the subject is difficult to light. The camera itself can cast shadows and keep sufficient light from reaching your subject. You'll find more about lighting close-ups in Book III, Chapter 2.

- ✓ **Some lenses don't allow close focus at all zoom settings.** You might want to step back a foot and zoom in to get the best view of your subject. However, some lenses don't allow automatic (or even manual) focus at longer zoom settings. Some restrict macro capabilities to mid-range or wide zoom settings.

- ✓ **Close focusing is tricky.** You want to make sure your digital camera includes automatic macro-focusing capabilities so that you don't have to focus manually when shooting up tight to the subject.

- ✓ **Keep attachment friendliness in mind.** If your favorite digital model doesn't have sufficient built-in macro options, see whether you can attach close-up lenses to the front of your lens. Not all digital cameras can accept screw-on attachments of this type.

Exposure controls

Because light levels vary, digital cameras must vary the amount of light reaching the sensor. One way to do that is to change the f-stop, as described earlier in this chapter. The second way is to alter the length of time that the sensor is exposed to the light. This is done either electronically or with an actual mechanical device — a shutter — that opens and closes quickly to expose the sensor for a set period — the *shutter speed*.

Like f-stops, shutter speeds are the denominators of fractions. The larger the number, the less light reaches the sensor. Typical shutter speeds include 1/60, 1/125, 1/250, 1/50, and 1/1000 of a second. Your digital camera read-out might show them as 60, 125, 250, 500, or 1000 because the numerator is always 1. However, a recent trend has been to include the numerator anyway to avoid confusion with longer shutter speeds, which are whole numbers. Otherwise, you'd have no way of telling whether an 8 in the view-finder means 1/8 second or 8 seconds.

Cameras (chiefly film models) that use mechanical shutters might have only exact intervals, although most film cameras have electronic shutters these days. Electronic shutters aren't limited to fixed incremental values and can provide you with any actual interval from a few seconds through 1/2000 (or sometimes even 1/4000) of a second. The traditional shutter speed values are useful only when calculating equivalent exposures.

For example, suppose a basic exposure were 1/250 of a second at f/16 (which is a typical exposure for a digital camera in bright daylight). If you wanted to stop some fast-moving action, you might want your camera to switch to 1/500 of a second to freeze the movement with the shorter exposure time. (You can find out more about stopping action in Book III, Chapter 5.)

Because you've cut the amount of light in half by reducing the shutter speed from 1/250 to 1/500 of a second, your camera needs to compensate by doubling the amount of light admitted through the lens. In this example, the lens is opened up from f/16 to f/11, which lets in twice as much illumination.

Usually, all this happens automatically, thanks to your digital camera's handy autoexposure modes, but you can set these controls manually on some models if you want. It's probably a better idea to choose a different autoexposure mode (described later) that gives you the flexibility you need. Sometimes, you'll look at an image on your LCD review screen and decide that the picture is too dark or too light. A digital camera's autoexposure modes can take care of this, too. When shopping for a digital camera, you'll want to look for the following exposure options.

Plus/minus or over/under exposure

With these modes, you can specify a little more or a little less exposure than the ideal exposure that your camera's light-measuring system determines. These adjustments are called *exposure values* (EV for short) or *exposure compensation*, and most digital cameras let you fine-tune exposure +/– about 2EV, using half- or third-stop increments. The most conveniently designed cameras have the EV adjustment available from one of the main buttons on the camera, such as the up-cursor key. Beware of cameras that make you wend your way into the menu system to make an EV adjustment. Fortunately, after it's set, the EV setting "sticks" so that you can continue to take pictures in the same environment with the modified setting.

Full autoexposure

With this option, your digital camera selects the shutter speed and lens opening for you by using built-in algorithms, called *programs*, that allow it to make some intelligent guesses about the best combination of settings. For example, on bright days outdoors, the camera probably chooses a short shutter speed and small f-stop to give you the best sharpness. Outdoors in dimmer light, the camera might select a wider lens opening while keeping the shutter speed the same until it decides to drop down to a slower speed to keep more of your image in sharp focus.

Some digital cameras have several autoexposure program modes (sometimes called *scene settings*) to select from, so if you're taking action pictures and have chosen an action-stopping mode, the camera tries to use brief, action-stopping shutter speeds under as many conditions as possible. These program modes are different from the aperture/shutter-preferred modes described next because they frequently include other factors in their adjustments. They might have names like Sports, Night, Night Portrait, Landscape, Fireworks, or Portrait. I used a camera with a scene setting called Cuisine (I kid you not), which (after a little digging) I discovered also increased the sharpness and color richness of the picture to supposedly make food pictures look better. Some cameras have both an Auto (A) and Program (P) setting.

Aperture-preferred/shutter-preferred exposure

These options let you choose a lens opening (aperture-preferred) or shutter speed (shutter-preferred). The camera automatically sets the other control to match. These settings might be indicated by A or S markings — commonly, Av and Tv (Time value). For example, by choosing shutter-preferred, you can select a short shutter speed, such as 1/1000 of a second, and the camera locks that in, varying only the f-stop.

Unlike the programmed modes described in the preceding section, if your camera finds that the selected shutter speed, for example, can't be mated with an appropriate aperture (it's too dark or too light out), it might not take a photo at all. I've run into this at soccer games when I've set my camera to an action-stopping shutter speed, but clouds dim the field so much that even the largest lens opening isn't enough to take a picture. Figure 1-11 shows an action shot taken with the camera set on shutter priority.

Full manual control

With this option, you can set any shutter speed or aperture combination you like, giving you complete control over the exposure of your photo. That means you can also completely ruin the picture by making it way too dark or much too light. However, complete control is good for creative reasons because seriously underexposing (say, to produce a silhouette effect) might be exactly what you want.

Other factors to consider

In addition to exposure options themselves, you must consider other factors when evaluating the exposure controls of your dream digital camera. Here is a quick checklist of those you should look out for:

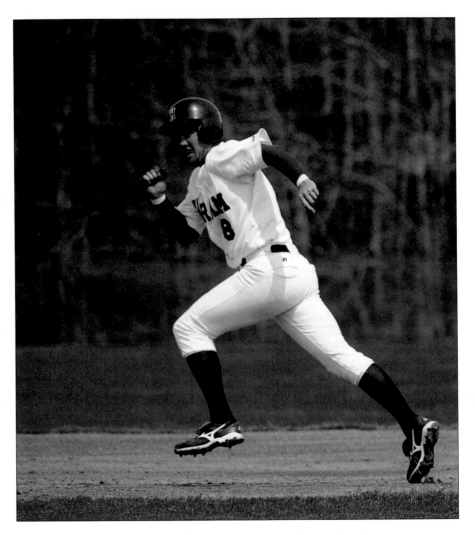

Figure 1-11: Choosing shutter priority lets you select an action-stopping shutter speed.

> ✔ **Sensor sensitivity:** Like film, sensors have varying degrees of sensitivity to light. (For film, this is its *speed.*) The more sensitive the sensor is, the better it can capture images in low light levels. Most digital cameras have a sensitivity that corresponds roughly to that of ISO 50 to ISO 100 film (so-called *slow* film), and the specs often use that terminology. Many cameras let you specify the sensitivity, increasing from the default value of, say, ISO 100 to ISO 400 or even ISO 800 (fast) to give you a "faster" camera. (ISO stands for International Organization for Standardization, a group that defines benchmarks for a wide variety of technologies, not just photography.)

Unfortunately, upping the ISO rating usually increases the amount of random fuzziness — *noise* — in the image. It's like turning your radio up really loud when you're driving a convertible with the top down. The wind flying past your ears tends to cancel out some of the audio information that your too-loud radio produces. Increasing the ISO boosts image information while increasing background noise in the image. If you plan to shoot many pictures in very dim light, any camera you buy should be tested first to see whether ISO settings can be set manually. Then check how noisy the pictures become when you increase the sensitivity.

✔ **Measurement mode:** Just how does your digital camera's exposure system measure the light? Sometimes it measures only the center of the picture (which is probably your subject anyway); sometimes, it might measure the entire frame and average out the light that the sensor sees. You don't always want the camera to measure the light the same way. Measuring a center spot sometimes produces the most accurate reading. Other times, such as when the scene is evenly lit, an averaging system works best. On still other occasions, say, when there is a lot of sky in the photo, you might want the camera to measure only the light in the lower half of the picture.

Many cameras have multiple exposure modes that allow you to choose what part of the image is measured. One clever exposure system I've used works in conjunction with the camera's automatic focus, selecting the part of the image that is in sharpest focus to calculate the exposure.

✔ **Compensation systems:** Many exposure systems can sense when a picture is *backlit* (most of the light is coming from behind the subject) and add exposure to make the subject brighter. Sophisticated cameras can analyze your scene and choose an exposure mode that best fits each individual picture, compensating for potential trouble spots in the photograph. Or the camera might have an override to the exposure system, allowing the sensor to receive more light from backlit subjects when you choose to activate it.

✔ **Manual exposure:** If you're seriously interested in photography, you'll want at least the option of setting exposure (both f-stop and shutter speed) manually so you can custom-tailor your exposure to the artistic effect you're trying to achieve.

Selecting Your Resolution

The best lens can't produce any more sharpness than the sensor used to capture its information. For that reason, the resolution of most digital cameras is the specification most people use to choose their equipment. They want a 10-megapixel camera or a 12-megapixel model or maybe a 14-megapixel camera. They figure (with some justification) that the more pixels they have, the more features the vendor packs into the camera. After all, you can expect a 12-megapixel camera to have a decent zoom lens, lots of exposure control choices, close focusing, and all the other goodies, right?

Most of the time, that's true. The sensor is usually the most expensive part of any digital camera, so if you're building a camera that's going to cost $600 anyway, you might as well load on the other goodies to justify the price. However, as sensors get less expensive, you'll see cameras with (supposedly) equivalent sharpness with widely varying feature sets. For example, I've used cameras in the 10-megapixel range that cost as little as $169 (and had sparse lists of features to match) and others with the same nominal resolution that cost $800 and were chock-full of advanced capabilities.

And even when dealing with sensors, all pixels are not created equal. For one thing, the *true* resolution of a sensor is likely to be somewhat less than you might think. Take a sensor measuring 3456 x 2592 pixels. You'd think that such a sensor could image about 9 million different details. Bzzzt. Wrong answer! That would be possible only if the camera were designed to capture an image only in black and white.

In practice, the sensor has to capture red, green, and blue pixels. With current sensors, each pixel can capture only one particular color, so those 9 million pixels are actually divided into red-sensitive pixels, green-sensitive pixels, and blue-sensitive pixels. If the pixels were divided evenly, you'd wind up with three, 3-megapixel sensors — one each for red, green, and blue — rather than the 9-megapixel sensor you thought you had.

However, the pixels aren't divvied in that way. Because our eyes are more sensitive to green light than to the other colors, sensors typically divide their pixels unevenly: 50 percent are green, 25 percent are red, and 25 percent are blue. That's done by alternating red and green on one line, and green and blue on the next, as shown in Figure 1-12.

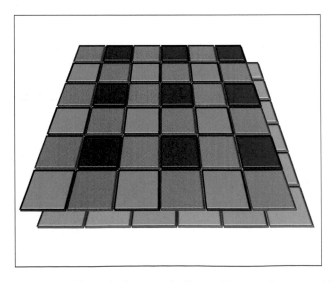

Figure 1-12: The typical sensor pixel is sensitive to red, green, or blue light.

Your camera's brain examines the picture and calculates (or *interpolates*) what the red and blue values probably are for each green-sensitive pixel position, what the green and blue values are for each red-sensitive pixel position, and the likely green and red values for each blue-sensitive pixel.

Other digital cameras use technologies that are a little different — or a lot different. For example, Sony has offered a sensor that captures what it calls RGB+E (for emerald) light, producing what it describes as color fidelity that is closer to human color perception, with more life-like rendering of blue, blue-green, and red hues. Another vendor, Foveon, produces a sensor like the one offered in the Sigma DP1 that has separate layers for red, green, and blue light, as shown in Figure 1-13, so that each pixel is capable of capturing any color light without interpolation.

Beyond the capture scheme used, other factors affect sensors. Some sensors are more sensitive than others, and other factors make a particular sensor not perform as well as another one with the same number of pixels. For example, some sensors don't register some colors well or have pixels that bright light can easily overwhelm.

When choosing a digital camera, you want to choose one with the resolution you want. If possible, compare the pictures taken with each camera under consideration to see whether that resolution is being put to good use.

When it comes to megapixels, you can estimate the resolution you require with these guidelines:

- **Low *res* (short for *resolution*):** If you're shooting pictures intended for Web display, for online auctions, or for pictures that either won't be cropped or enlarged much, you can get by with a lower-resolution camera in the 6- to 8-megapixel range.

- **Medium res:** If you often need to crop your photos, want to make larger prints, or need lots of detail, you want at least an 8- to 10-megapixel camera.

- **High res:** If you want to extract small portions of an image, make 8-x-10-inch prints or larger, or do a lot of manipulation in an image editor, you want a 10- to 14-megapixel (or more) camera.

Most digital cameras allow shooting in a reduced mode, so if you own a high-resolution camera, you can still shoot in low resolution to pack more images on your digital film or to reduce file sizes on your hard drive. Resizing images is rarely a good idea, even with a good image-editing program, so you usually want to shoot at the resolution you intend for your finished photo. Resize later, if you want, but keep your full-size version for printing, just in case.

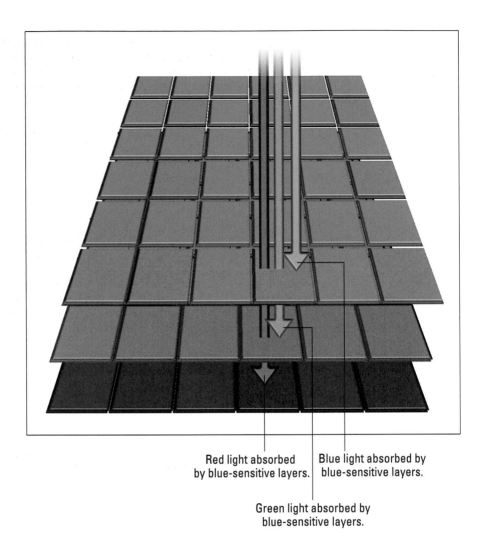

Red light absorbed
by blue-sensitive layers.

Blue light absorbed by
blue-sensitive layers.

Green light absorbed by
blue-sensitive layers.

Figure 1-13: The Foveon sensor has separate layers for each color of light.

The mode in which your camera stores the image on your digital film can affect the final resolution of your image, too. Digital cameras usually store photos in a compressed, space-saving format known as *JPEG* (Joint Photographic Experts Group). The JPEG format offers reduced file sizes by discarding some information. In most cases, a JPEG file is still plenty good, but if you want to preserve all the quality of your original image, you might want to set your camera to store in a *lossless* image format (that is, one that doesn't discard any image information when compressing the file), such as TIFF, or RAW. You might be able to choose from different JPEG quality levels, too.

Expect these alternate formats to eat up your memory card storage quickly. One of my digital cameras can store 200 images on a particular low-capacity digital film card in JPEG format but only 150 in RAW and 40 in TIFF. TIFF and RAW also take more time to store on the film card, too, so they're not a good choice when you're shooting sports or other sequence-type photos.

Some cameras generally label their resolution choices with names such as Large, Medium, Small; Standard, Fine, Superfine, Ultrafine; and so forth. These terms can vary from vendor to vendor.

Choosing Your View

Generally, you want what you see to be what you get, but that's not always the case with digital cameras. That's because the viewfinders available are usually a compromise between what works best and what can economically be provided at a particular price level. In the digital photography realm, the solution has long been to provide you with two viewfinders per camera, each with its own advantages and disadvantages. In a non-SLR camera, you usually find

- A **color LCD display screen** on the back of the camera, which you can use to preview and review your electronic images.

- An **optical viewfinder,** which you can peer through to frame and compose your image. Some digital cameras with large LCDs don't have optical viewfinders at all.

Some cameras have two LCDs: one on the back in the traditional location, and a second one inside the camera and visible through an optical system. This variety is an *electronic viewfinder* or EVF. None of these are ideal for every type of picture-taking application.

LCD viewfinders

In a non-SLR, the liquid crystal display, usually measuring 2–3 inches diagonally, shows an electronic image of the scene as viewed by the sensor. Digital SLRs can't preview images on their LCD by default because the mirror, shutter, and other components get in the way of the sensor until the moment of exposure. They must use a special *live view* mode. On the one hand, that's good because you can view more or less the exact image that will be captured. It's also not so good because the LCD screen is likely to be difficult to view, washed out by surrounding light, and so small that it doesn't really show what you need to see. That's especially true with a digital camera that lacks an optical viewfinder and is used in the traditional camera-held-at-arms'-length mode.

Moreover, the backlit LCD eats battery power. I've used digital cameras that died after 20 minutes when the LCD had depleted their rechargeable batteries. Luckily, some digital cameras let you specify that the LCD is turned on only when composing a picture or only for a few seconds after a picture is taken (so that you can quickly review the shot).

Although sometimes not at their best in bright daylight, LCDs are better in more dimly lit conditions. Some third parties offer LCD hoods that fit over the back panel of the camera to shield the LCD from direct illumination. If you mount your camera on a tripod and make sure all the light is directed on your subject, an LCD is entirely practical for framing, focusing, and evaluating a digital image (even outdoors, if you use one of those protective hoods.)

As you shop for a digital camera, check out the LCD under a variety of conditions to make sure it passes muster. Here are some things to look for:

- **Brightness controls:** Many cameras include a brightness control that allows you to increase the brightness of the LCD to make it easier to view in full sunlight, or decrease the brightness indoors to use less battery juice. A related factor is whether the LCD automatically "gains up" by amplifying a dim image to provide a usable view when it's very dark.

- **Swivel mount:** The LCD doesn't have to remain fixed rigidly to the back of the camera. Some swivel and rotate, allowing you to point the camera in one direction and move the LCD so that you can easily view it at an angle, as shown in Figure 1-14. (Alternatively, the part of the camera with the lens can swivel while the part with the LCD remains in place.)

- **Resolution and size:** Ultracompact digital cameras often have tiny LCD displays, sometimes as small as 2 inches (measured diagonally), and others have more generous 3-inch LCDs. The size of the LCD and the number of pixels it contains will partially determine how easy it is to preview your image. Some may have as few as 80,000 pixels; others may have 230,000 pixels or more. Guess which is easier to view!

- **Display rate:** Some digital cameras update their LCD images more efficiently, so the view is smooth even when the camera or your subject is moving. Others offer blurry images or ghost trails that make it difficult to view images in motion.

- **Vanishing images:** What happens when you press the shutter release? Does the image instantly freeze as soon as you start to press the button but before you actually take the picture? If so, what you saw might not be what you get because your subject matter might have changed in the time between the initial press and the actual photo. Or does the LCD go completely blank, leaving you with no clue about what you're shooting? Ideally, the LCD should display a real-time image right up until the instant before the picture is taken.

✔ **Accurate viewpoint:** Believe it or not, even though an LCD viewfinder's display is derived from the same sensor used to make the exposure, the LCD might not display 100 percent of the sensor's view. Instead, it might trim a little off the sides, top, and bottom, and show you 80 to 90 percent of the actual picture. That's not good when you're carefully composing a photo to make the most of your pixels, particularly with lower-resolution cameras that don't have pixels to spare.

✔ **Real-time corrections:** Some cameras have live *histograms* — graphs that show the distribution of the tones in the image — that can be viewed on the LCD and used to correct exposure manually while you shoot. These are all non-SLR types, of course. With a dSLR, a histogram is visible only after the exposure.

✔ **Accurate rendition:** I've found that some LCDs don't let you evaluate just how good (or bad) your picture is because they provide an image that's more contrasty, or brighter, or with more muted colors than the actual digital picture. You don't want to reshoot a picture because you *think* it looked bad on the LCD, or worse, make a manual exposure or other adjustment to correct a defect that appears only on the LCD and not in the finished photo.

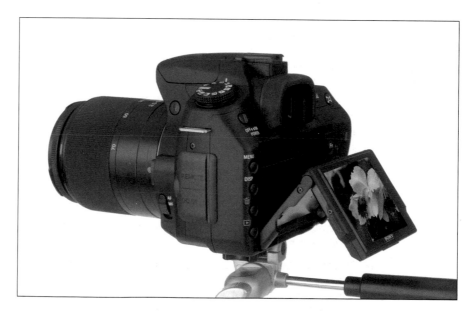

Figure 1-14: Swiveling LCD screens and a "live view" preview mode are handy features when using a tripod.

Optical viewfinders

Some digital point-and-shoot cameras and all dSLRs offer the option of an optical viewfinder, which is bright and clear, uses no power, and lets you compose your image quickly. However, optical viewfinders in point-and-shoot cameras have problems of their own, most notably *parallax*. Parallax is caused by the difference in viewpoint between your camera's lens and the optical viewfinder. They don't show the same thing.

If the optical viewfinder happens to be mounted directly above the camera lens, its view will be a little higher than that of the lens itself. This becomes a problem chiefly when shooting pictures from relatively close distances (3 feet or less). Such a viewfinder tends to chop off the top of any subject that is close to the camera. Optical viewfinders usually have a set of visible lines, called *parallax correction lines,* which you can use to frame the picture. If you keep the subject matter below the correction lines, you can avoid chopping off heads. Of course, you get *more* of the lower part of your subject than you can view.

Parallax becomes worse when the optical viewfinder is located above and to one side of the lens. In that case, a double set of parallax correction lines is needed to help you avoid chopping off both the top and the side of your subject. Yuck! Here are some things to look for in optical viewfinders:

- ✔ **Magnification:** I get to use dozens of digital cameras in a year, and one of the first things I notice is the difference in magnification of the optical viewfinders. Put the camera up to your eye, and you might see a tiny image floating off in the distance, with the details of your scene barely discernible. Other cameras provide a big view that makes it easy to frame and compose your photo.

- ✔ **Parallax correction:** As I mention earlier, optical viewfinders might not accurately frame the image when you move in close to your subject. The position of the viewfinder window can have an effect: If the viewfinder is directly above the lens, the side-to-side view will be accurate, but you might cut off the top of your subject if the camera doesn't provide parallax correction. If the viewfinder is immediately to the side of the lens, your problems will involve accidentally cutting off the side of your subject. Some viewfinders are both above the lens and to one side, as shown in Figure 1-15, which can produce parallax problems in both directions.

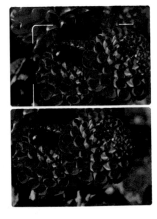

Figure 1-15: Parallax correction lines help you avoid chopping off heads, or worse.

✔ **Accurate viewpoint:** As with LCD screens, the optical viewfinder might not show everything you're framing, with some image area clipped off the top, bottom, or sides.

✔ **Diopter adjustment:** Eyeglass wearers might want an optical viewfinder that offers adjustment for common prescriptions so the camera can be used without wearing glasses.

✔ **Extended eyepoint:** The *eyepoint* is the distance your eye can be from the viewfinder's window and still see the entire view. Some viewfinders mandate pressing your eye up tightly against the windows. Others let you back off a few millimeters, which is handy when you want to be able to see *around* the camera to monitor the whole scene (and not just what appears in the viewfinder) or prefer to wear your glasses while using the camera (and are thus not able to get close to the window because the glasses get in the way).

✔ **Readouts:** What information is available within and around the optical viewfinder? Some cameras show nothing but the unadorned image. Others have framing or parallax correction lines or perhaps a faint grid to help you line up the image. Perhaps some camera status indicators appear in the viewfinder, too, such as a flash-ready LED, within the field of view or located just outside the viewfinder window where it can be detected by the eye.

Electronic viewfinders (EVFs)

Some affordable cameras are available with hybrid viewfinders that work like optical viewfinders (that is, you put your eye up to a window to view your subject) but that use an electronic display to show you the image. These LCDs are much like the LCDs found on the backs of cameras, but because they are automatically shielded from extraneous light, they are much easier to view. Because they form an image by using the signal from the sensor, when compared with optical viewfinders, they offer a potentially more accurate and SLR-like picture-taking experience. You'll find this viewfinder most often in so-called "super zoom" cameras, which include a non-interchangeable lens with a 12:1 to 18:1 magnification ratio, and both a camera-back LCD and internal LCD electronic viewfinder.

Poorly designed EVFs can be a pain to use, so you'll want to examine the view through any camera so equipped before you sink your money into one. Here are some of the considerations to think about:

✔ **Magnification:** EVFs can suffer from the same viewfinder magnification issues as optical viewfinders. Because you'll be composing and (in some cases) focusing manually via the internal LCD, make sure your view is as large and sharp as possible.

✔ **Extended eyepoint:** Just as with optical viewfinders, you might not be able to (or want to) press your eyeball up to the viewfinder window, so an EVF with an extended eyepoint is a plus, particularly with eyeglass wearers.

- ✔ **Readouts:** Compared with optical viewfinders, EVFs usually contain a lot of information, including status readouts, grids, focus and exposure area indicators, and so forth. Make sure you can turn off these distracting elements when you don't want to see them.

- ✔ **Swivel mount:** Some eyepieces for EVFs can swivel 90 degrees to allow taking pictures from especially low or high angles. I find this capability handy when I have the camera mounted on a tripod at about waist level and I don't want to crouch down to look through the viewfinder.

- ✔ **Resolution and size:** The LCDs in EVFs typically have more detail than their camera-back counterparts. Vendors have raised the bar on EVF resolution, with at least one offering a full megapixel display on its top-of-the-line camera. These high-resolution electronic viewfinders are easier to see to discern detail and more reliable when used for focusing.

- ✔ **Display rate:** EVFs can have ghost images, too. A brand-new feature on some models is so-called *smooth mode*, which refreshes the EVF image 60 times a second (about twice as fast as normal), providing an especially good preview of your photo.

- ✔ **Vanishing images:** Obviously, the EVF can't provide a continuous image because the sensor's view must be collected and captured at the instant the photo is taken. During that interval, the image might freeze on-screen or vanish entirely. Some cameras switch into *high-gain mode* under dim lighting conditions, in which the image signal is amplified to provide better viewing, sometimes offering only a fuzzy or black-and-white view in that mode. Better cameras give you an accurate, full-color preview up until the exact moment the photograph is taken.

- ✔ **Accurate viewpoint:** EVFs don't always display 100 percent of the sensor's view, either. The best show at least 92–99 percent of the actual picture area in the viewfinder.

- ✔ **Accurate rendition:** As with any LCD, the image you see might not be exactly like your final photograph, but the results should be close.

SLR viewfinders

And there's always the single-lens reflex (SLR) camera, which shows you (more or less) the exact image the sensor sees through the lens via an optical system. It's done with mirrors (really). In the most common configuration, you view the subject through the lens by using an image bounced off mirrors and (sometimes) a glass prism. When you take the picture, the mirror moves out of the way to expose the sensor. You lose sight of the image for a fraction of a second, but film SLR users have been tolerating that inconvenience for decades.

Both general types of SLR viewfinders use a mirror to bounce light upward, where it then reflects off a series of surfaces until the final image (erect and nonreversed from left-to-right) is viewed through an optical window.

Less-expensive cameras use a series of mirrors (often called a *pentamirror* because of the five total surfaces in the structure), and more costly models use a solid glass prism, called a *pentaprism*. The latter provides a brighter, higher-contrast image that looks better and is easier to use for viewing and focusing. However, pentamirror viewfinders can also be very good, particularly if you don't compare them directly with models using a pentaprism. The light path for an image viewed by a pentamirror/pentaprism viewing system is shown in Book II, Chapter 1.

REMEMBER

Regardless of what optical or SLR viewing system you use, if you wear glasses and want to shoot without them, you want to make sure your camera either has built-in eyesight (diopter) correction to adjust for your near-/far-sightedness or can be fitted with corrective lenses matched to your prescription. This vision correction enables you to get your eye close enough to the viewfinder to see the whole image. Some viewfinders make it difficult for those wearing glasses to see through the optical system because a bezel or other part of the viewfinder prevents the glasses from getting close enough.

No Flash in the Pan: Determining Your Lighting Needs

Your digital dream camera's electronic flash capabilities (or lack of them) should be on your list of things to evaluate before you make a purchase decision. Not every photo is possible using existing light. Even if there is plenty of light, you might still want to fill in those inky shadows with an electronic flash. Your camera's built-in flash features are definitely something to consider.

Most digital cameras have a built-in flash unit that can be turned on or flipped up or swung out or otherwise activated when you want to use a flash — or when the camera decides for you that the flash is required. (Usually, a tip-off is a flashing red light in your viewfinder or next to it. Time to flip up that flash!)

You should be aware that most flash units are good only over a particular range. If you've ever seen a fan stand up in the balcony at a Bruce Springsteen concert and take a flash picture of the Boss from 100 feet away, you'll understand just how limited flash is at long distances. Some units are so feeble that they can only illuminate subjects 2 to 12 feet away. Others have special settings to spread the flash illumination for wide-angle shots or tighten it up for telephoto pictures. You may need to purchase an add-on flash to add some lighting power to your repertoire.

Here are some features to look for in an electronic flash:

✔ **Auto-on:** It's useful to have a flash that can be set to flash only when it's needed. Some cameras require you to flip up the flash to use it. Others build the flash into the body of the camera in such a way that the flash can be used anytime.

- **Autoexposure:** An electronic flash can sense the amount of light reflected back from the subject and turn itself off when the exposure is sufficient.

- **Red-eye prevention:** Some flashes can be set to produce a short preflash just before the picture is taken. That causes the subjects' irises to contract, reducing the possibility of the dreaded red-eye effect. Alternatively, the preflash can fool your subjects into thinking that their ordeal is over and produce some priceless weird expressions.

- **External flash capabilities:** At times, you want to use an external flash, either in concert with or instead of your camera's built-in flash. See whether your camera has either a built-in flash-sync socket or a *hot shoe* that you can use to mount an external flash and connect the camera to the flash.

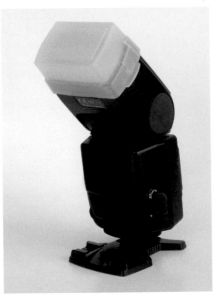

Figure 1-16: External flash units add power and flexibility to your lighting repertoire.

Many digital cameras require that you use only a particular brand of flash to retain the automated exposure features or (in some cases) to avoid frying your camera's flash triggering circuit with too much voltage. If you're thinking of using a slave sensor to trigger the flash, make sure that it can be used with your camera. The preflash of some cameras will set off the slave unit. Figure 1-16 shows an external flash unit fitted with a diffusing dome to soften the illumination.

A Dozen Exotic Digital Camera Features

After automobile manufacturers introduced heated seats and the Global Positioning System (GPS) for their luxury cars, everyone wanted them, so the designers had to come up with other high-end features, like holographic rearview mirrors and rocket-powered ejection seats. Digital camera vendors are in a similar race to develop features that are similarly too-cool-for-school. (Believe it or not, some high-end cameras can use GPS to record the camera's current geographical location when each picture is taken!) Here are some of my favorite features that are exotic now but probably won't be exotic by the time you purchase your next camera:

✓ **Sound-activated self-timers:** I had a ball playing with a new camera that could be triggered by sound. Just set the audio sensitivity, go get in the picture yourself, and shout, "Cheese!" No more racing to beat the self timer or ending up with a photo showing you holding your camera's infrared (IR) remote control.

✓ **Ultra-fast shutter speeds:** At least one camera has a shutter speed of 1/16,000 of a second. You might need a supernova as your illumination source, but you can stop the fastest action with this baby.

✓ **Image stabilizers:** Several cameras offer internal stabilization that cancels the effects of shaky hands or the blur induced by the high magnification of a telephoto lens. My favorite are the cameras that automatically move the sensor in time with your camera jiggles.

✓ **Night shot capabilities:** Digital camera sensors are inherently sensitive to IR illumination, so vendors like Sony provide enhanced night photography capabilities by taking advantage of this sensitivity.

✓ **Infrared photography:** Many cameras have a device called a *hot mirror* to filter out infrared light but allow flipping this filter out of the way or leaving enough remaining IR sensitivity to allow you to take interesting weird-tonal infrared pictures.

✓ **Predictive focus:** Slow autofocus is the bane of digital cameras, which is why I was glad to see the introduction of high-end models smart enough to figure out where focus *should* be set ahead of time when you're photographing subjects for which the focus changes rapidly.

✓ **Enhanced movies:** Traditionally, digital cameras have been able to shoot only short video clips (perhaps 15–30 seconds) at abysmal resolutions (some no better than 320 x 240 pixels) and not necessarily with sound. That's changing with the latest crop. Some recent digital cameras are virtual camcorders, letting you grab VHS-quality clips for as long as your digital memory card holds out. Make sure your card is a capacious one because digital video can eat up a megabyte a second!

✓ **Unlimited burst mode:** I loved using an advanced digital camera that uses a technique called *pipelining* to keep the images flowing onto the memory card at high speed (when used with a high-speed card). I managed to take more than 150 3.3-megapixel resolution photos in a row at around 4 frames per second (fps) before my 256MB memory card filled up. Set to a lower resolution, I took 1,500 shots in a little more than five minutes. My finger got tired before this ultra-fast camera started slowing down. Think how well you can analyze your golf swing with a camera like this!

✓ **Panorama photography:** A growing number of digital cameras have cool panorama capabilities that make it easy to shoot a series of pictures that can be automatically stitched together in your computer. You find out more about panorama photography in Book III, Chapter 6.

✔ **Two-in-one shot:** Don't have a tripod but want to get in the photo yourself? Some cameras let you take a picture of the background, have someone else take a picture of you, and then merge the two shots automatically.

✔ **Underwater photography:** I once purchased a Nikonos underwater film camera specifically so I could take surfing photos at Huntington Beach, California. (I wasn't surfing; I was *photographing* surfers.) Now, anyone with a digital camera and an inexpensive underwater housing offered for Canon and other models can take pictures in, around, and under the sea. Digital cameras are much better than my old Nikonos: You get to see exactly what you shot right away, so you can jump back in and do it over until you get it right.

✔ **Time-lapse photography:** Thirty or forty years ago, the big thing was time-lapse photos of flowers opening and paint drying. Today, every television show includes a sunset-to-sunrise time-lapse sequence to demonstrate that time marches on. Whether you have some flowers you want to watch opening or you need to document a construction project, digital cameras with time-lapse capabilities can snap off a picture every few seconds or every few hours, depending on how you set them. This is a great feature that's fun to play with.

Checking Out Ease of Use

Usability is one of the most important factors to keep in mind when choosing a camera. The sharpest lens, the most sophisticated sensor, and the most advanced features are all useless if you can't figure out how to operate the stupid camera! I've owned digital cameras that absolutely could not be used without having the manual at hand. Even common features were so hard to access that I sometimes avoided taking certain kinds of pictures because activating the feature took too long.

Today, even digital cameras that most resemble their film counterparts bristle with buttons, command dials, mode controls, menus, and icons. That's not necessarily a bad thing. What is evil is an interface that's so convoluted that even advanced users might have problems. You might have to wade through nested menus to change the autofocus or exposure control mode. Switching from aperture priority to shutter priority can be a pain. Something as simple as changing from automatic focus to manual focus can be difficult, particularly if you don't make the switch very often and forget which combination of buttons to press.

Ease of use varies greatly, depending on which sets of features are most important to you. A camera that one person might find a breeze to use might be impossible for another person to manage simply because a particular must-have feature is hard to access.

I urge you to try out any digital camera that you're seriously considering buying before you plunk down your money. A camera's feature set, the vendor's reputation, or recommendations of a friend won't tell you how the camera will work for you. Hold the camera in your hand. Make sure it feels right — that its weight and heft are comfortable to you. Be certain your fingers aren't too large or too small to handle the controls. Can you see through the viewfinder?

If possible, take the camera for a test drive, borrow a similar camera from a friend or colleague, or at least shoot some photos in the store. Can you find the features you use most? Can you figure out the menus and buttons? Is the camera rugged enough to hold up under the kind of treatment you'll subject it to?

As much as I like buying by mail order or over the Internet, a digital camera is too personal a tool to buy from specifications lists and photos. If you're reading this book, you're probably serious enough about digital photography that you'll be spending a lot of time with your camera — and probably will spend more than you expected to get the camera you really want. Make sure it really is the one you want by giving it a thorough workout.

Is Your Computer Ready?

You might be ready for digital photography, but is your computer up to the task? The good news is that virtually any computer of recent vintage probably has the horsepower and features you need to work with the digital images that you capture with a camera or scanner.

Even so, the differences between a computer that's good and one that's good enough can be significant. Your system might be exceptional, or it might be the exception. You probably don't want to work with the minimal system possible even if you'd rather invest your money in a better digital camera. (I know, if faced with the choice of a new, superfast computer and a digital single lens reflex, I'd choose the camera every time.)

This chapter helps you develop your own checklist of recommended hardware, shows you how to upgrade to make your work even easier, and offers tips on setting up your computer to make working with digital images a breeze.

In this chapter, I cover only the main equipment options for setting up a computer for digital photography editing and storage. You can find information on equipment used to transfer images between your camera and computer in Book I, Chapter 2.

Choosing a Computer Platform

Hardware wars, revisited. Macs versus PCs. Why are we even having this conversation? Is it because of the cute commercials on TV featuring the sublime John Hodgman and everyman Justin Long? Or, have we been enchanted by the newer ads from Microsoft with Jerry Seinfeld?

Well, it wasn't my idea. Windows Vista has managed to make using a personal computer less fun at the same time that Steve Jobs and his crew decided to revitalize the always-cool, but pricey, Mac. The Macintosh became more competitive with the PC, arousing the interest of even dedicated Windows PC operators. Anyone weary of the monthly "Patch Tuesday" updates that plague Windows computers or anyone who covets the stylish and common-sense design of the Mac is now taking a serious look at the computer arena's "other" platform. That's become especially true with the introduction of Macintosh software that lets you install Microsoft Windows XP or Vista on the new Intel-based Macs and boot either operating system (OS).

Of course, digital photography, graphics work in general, and multimedia production were the key arenas in which the Macintosh versus PC battle never died out. In most other areas, Windows-based systems have taken over the desktop, with Macs relegated to specialized or oddball applications. Apple keeps coming up with compelling hardware, interesting computer designs, and lots of quirky but cool applications (GarageBand, anyone?), but those computer troops solidly camped in the Windows realm usually take notice of what's going on only when those cute Macintosh commercials interrupt prime-time TV.

Not so in the digital photography world. Visit any newspaper or magazine that relies on digital cameras, and you'll find Macs. Drop in to any professional digital photographer's studio, and you'll see a brawny Macintosh perched on the desktop. Talk to the top Photoshop users in the country. Most of them are using Macintoshes, too, either exclusively or in tandem with a Windows box.

Indeed, for a long time the only logical choice for most photographers has been the Macintosh. The decision was along the lines of selecting a 35mm Nikon or Canon film SLR for photojournalism or a Sinar view camera for studio work: a no-brainer. Although I don't have hard figures, my gut feeling is that Macs outnumber PCs in many imaging-production environments. In the rest of the business world, the figures are reversed, except on television, where anyone shown with a laptop computer is always using an Apple PowerBook.

By and large, the latest Macintoshes provide enough muscle for virtually any still-image work, particularly when equipped with dual processor chips (which provide extra speed with applications designed to work with multiple CPUs) and gigabytes of memory. No photographer need be ashamed of driving a properly equipped Mac.

In the digital photography world, Macs are not only viable but are often the system of choice. However, in some cases, you might not have a choice — maybe you already own a computer or need to use a particular system to remain compatible with friends and colleagues.

Yet, if you aren't locked into a particular platform and operating system, should you be using a Macintosh or a Windows computer? If you want a definitive answer, I'd say, "It depends." (Which isn't very definitive, is it?) Each platform has its pros and cons. Here is a summary of some of the things you should consider:

- ✓ **The bandwagon effect:** If you plan to make your living (at least in part) from digital photography, you need to learn two things: how to use a Mac and how to perform image magic with Photoshop. Both skills are expected to be part of your résumé. Jump on the bandwagon while you can. On the other hand, Windows proficiency is expected for most jobs outside imaging. Unless you're a full-time graphics professional, you might have to learn to wear two hats.

- ✓ **Ease of use:** The Macintosh is generally acknowledged to be a bit easier to learn and somewhat easier to use for many tasks. Of course, the Macintosh system's vaunted ease of use has been subverted over the years as Apple has tried to catch up with Windows systems. (For example, if you want to stick with the Mac's sublimely simple single-button mouse, you must augment it by holding down the Control key while clicking to reproduce the Windows two-button mouse's right-click option. You can also reprogram certain Macintosh mice to provide the same results.) If you're just starting out in computing and don't want to climb a steep learning curve, the Mac is your computer.

- ✓ **Software compatibility:** Not all applications are available for both Mac and PC. Most key applications are offered for both, including the Photoshop image editor in both Mac and Windows incarnations; the StuffIt archiving tool; browsers such as Netscape and Internet Explorer; and business applications such as Microsoft Office. Plus, Microsoft is now offering Virtual PC for the Macintosh, making it possible to run Windows XP and Windows applications under Mac OS X on many different Macs. Boot Camp does the same thing for the latest Intel-based Macintosh models. But if you must be totally compatible with Windows, you still need Windows.

- ✓ **The cost factor:** Macs have generally been more expensive than PCs, although the cost difference has decreased over the years. Even so, with powerful Pentium systems available in bare-bones configurations for $500 or so, even the least expensive Mac capable of image editing still costs a bit more. In the Mac's favor, however, most peripherals and add-ons, such as memory, hard drives, DVD devices, monitors, and so forth, cost the same whether you're purchasing them for a Mac or a PC.

- **Hardware reliability:** Reliability is a double-edged sword. Macs are wonderfully crafted machines, a beauty to behold when you dismantle one, and filled with high-quality components. The insides of some of the assembly-line-built PCs have a decidedly industrial look, and if you examine the parts, you might find a mixture of known brand-name pieces and *what's this?* components. On the other hand, if something does break on your PC, you can run down to the local MegaMart and buy a new floppy drive, a CD burner, and maybe some memory off the shelf next to the cell phone batteries. My local *grocery store* carries these items. Macs also use many off-the-shelf components, but some specialized parts for your Mac might be harder to come by, and it's unlikely you'll know how to replace them anyway. So, even assuming the Mac is more reliable than the average PC, is that always an advantage?

- **Operating system reliability:** Trust me, Macs do crash, especially when Apple is making a transition, as it did from Mac OS 9.x to OS X or from the current version of OS X to the next one. Early versions of a Mac OS can crash and burn as spectacularly as any Windows release. On the other hand, Mac users don't add hardware or new applications at the same clip as Windows users, who seem to be constantly trying this new utility or that, applying the monthly patches Microsoft issues for its software and OS, and doing other fiddling that can lead directly to the Blue Screen of Death (BSOD).

  Anyone who swears his or her Windows installation never crashes is probably using Windows XP with Service Pack 3 rather than Windows Vista, never runs more than two or three applications at once, and avoids installing new software more often than once every six months. I'm an exception to that rule: I haven't had a crash in more than a year on my XP computer. As long as I hide behind my firewall, don't use Internet Explorer, and am careful about what Web sites I visit, I'm able to run my antique installation of Windows with no crashes. Still, if avoiding crashes is on your holiday gift list, the Mac still has the edge. This may eventually change as virus-happy hackers turn their attention to producing viruses and ill-behaved applications that exploit the weaknesses that exist in Mac OS.

- **Technological superiority and coolness:** If owning a computer that looks like a Tensor lamp or is built into an LCD screen is your cup of tea, and you like the idea of having cool stuff before anyone else, you really, really need a Macintosh. The most exotic hard drive interfaces (from SCSI in the '80s to FireWire in the '90s) came to the Mac first, along with flat-panel displays, DVD burners, and other radical innovations that turned out to be a little (or a lot) before their time.

Hardware differences aside, the most visible differences between Macs and PCs (after you get past transparent, multicolored cases and eye-catching design tricks) stem from the two competing operating systems. Only a few years ago, before Mac OS X and Windows Vista were introduced, a dual-barbed joke was circulating, implying that the current version of Windows was almost identical to the Macintosh operating system of 1984. But of course, the same observer noted, the *current* Mac OS was also almost identical to the Macintosh operating system of 1984. The more things change, the more they stay the same.

The gibe is no longer true. Windows has been transformed into Windows XP, which is the most stable, easiest-to-use operating system Microsoft has ever offered (which is probably why Microsoft discontinued it in mid-2008), even if it does still resemble some of the older versions of Mac OS. Windows Vista has some things going for it, too, and there are millions of happy owners running that operating system. As long as you have the leading-edge hardware needed to run Vista smoothly, and are willing to put up with its quirks (such as the tendency to ask for confirmation every time you try to install/remove/change something), Vista can work well.

At the same time, Mac OS is completely different, too. Mac OS X is now a thinly disguised version of Unix, which is both good news and bad news. Unix is more stable than the OS 9.x and earlier versions that preceded it, but Mac-Unix has some underlying complexities (including — horror of horrors — a command-line interface if you want it) that didn't intrude themselves on Macintosh users in the past.

Windows of any type has its advantages and disadvantages. One advantage is that it's almost universally available and has the broadest range of widely used applications written for it. One disadvantage is that Windows still forces you to do things the Microsoft way when you'd really rather do them your own way. For example, Windows is fond of setting up your network the way it likes (I had to change the network Workgroup name I'd been using for eight years because Vista didn't like it), bludgeons you into using Internet Explorer for some tasks (such as Windows Update) even if you prefer Firefox or some other browser, and has a tendency to coerce you into using the Windows Media Player for everything and anything.

Mac OS, on the other hand, lets you do things your own way quite easily. Would you prefer that your digital camera application be installed on your secondary hard drive rather than the one you first installed it on? Just drag it to the new hard drive; there's no need to uninstall it and reinstall it as you must do with Windows.

Although you probably won't choose a computer based on the operating system, these things are nice to know.

What Equipment Do You Need?

Digital cameras themselves make few demands on a computer system, of course. The real drain on your system is running your image-editing program and storing your images for editing or archival purposes. Make no mistake, image editing is among the most demanding types of work you can lay on a computer, so before you start down this road, you'll want to know about the minefields that lie along the way. If you want the flying short course, the ten most important things you'll need to consider are

- ✔ Memory
- ✔ More memory
- ✔ Even more memory
- ✔ Adequate local storage (a fast, big hard drive. Or two.)
- ✔ A fast microprocessor
- ✔ Archival storage
- ✔ Advanced video display capabilities (maybe two monitors)
- ✔ Other peripherals, such as digitizing tablet and pen devices
- ✔ A little more memory
- ✔ More RAM than you thought you'd ever need

The rest of this chapter examines each of these needs thoroughly.

Determining How Much Memory You Need

If you noticed that I listed memory five times in the preceding top ten list, there's a reason for that. Memory makes everything else possible. A fast, big hard drive is also important because it gives you room to work with your current project's files and can substitute for RAM (memory) when you finally do run out. But nothing can replace memory when decent performance is your goal.

You can finish reading the rest of this section if you want to know the hows, whys, and how muches of memory, but I can give you a two-word recommendation that will let you skip ahead, if you want:

Two gigabytes!

That much RAM will cost you very little, perhaps less than a hundred dollars; it's the most RAM the most recent version of Photoshop (and the most prevalent versions of Windows) can use, and it will solve most of your problems. We now continue with the technical portion of our program (for those of you who aren't skipping ahead).

I can't emphasize this point enough: When you're working with images, you must have, as a bare minimum, at least six to ten times as much RAM as the largest image file you plan to work with on a regular basis. With inexpensive 8-megapixel cameras now available for a few hundred dollars, many digital photos in their native RAW format can be huge, requiring 180–600MB of RAM for each image you want open at once. If you're working with more reasonably sized 4MB images but need to have ten of them open at one time, you still need tons of memory to do the job.

Without sufficient RAM, all the bucks you spend on a super-speedy microprocessor are totally wasted. Your other heavy-duty hardware is going to come to a screeching halt every time you scroll, apply a filter, or perform any of a number of simple functions. That's because without enough RAM to keep the entire image in memory at once — plus your image editor's Undo files (basically copies of the image in its most recent states) — your computer is forced to write some or all of the image to your hard drive to make room for the next portion it needs to work with.

Digital photography can produce some large images, too, especially if you're working with a serious camera in the 8- to 14-megapixel range and choose to save your files in the highest-quality mode. An 18MB image is fairly common these days, so you should be prepared with as much RAM as you can cram into your computer.

Most systems have two to four memory slots, which can each hold a 256–2024MB memory stick. Loading your computer with 2 to 4GB of memory is not at all outlandish and is relatively inexpensive. You can purchase that much memory for a few hundred dollars. Any Mac or PC with 1GB of RAM is hopelessly underequipped for digital photography. Beefing up your memory can be the least expensive and most dramatic speed enhancement you can make.

Choosing Local Storage

Your graphics powerhouse is only as fast as its narrowest bottleneck, so you should pay special attention to that looming potential roadblock I just mentioned: your mass storage subsystems. You need one or more big hard drives for several reasons:

✔ **To keep as many images as possible available for near-instant access:** A large hard drive enables you to store all of your current projects — plus many from recent months — all in one place for quick reference or reuse. With a large hard drive, you can store a vast library of your own photographic clip art, too, and avoid having to sort through stacks of archive DVDs.

✔ **To provide working space for your current projects:** You'll want *scratch* space — space on your hard drive — to store images that you probably won't need but want to have on hand just in case. Alternate versions of images eat up more space as you refine your project. Image editors such as Photoshop also need spare hard drive space to keep multiple copies of each image you're editing.

✔ **To let you store additional applications:** Good bets are panorama-generating programs, a second or third image editor for specialized needs, utility programs, extra plug-in programs, and so forth.

In the recent past, your hard drive storage options were limited to internal hard drives in one of two categories: fast, expensive hard drives using a Small Computer System Interface (SCSI; *SKUZ-zee*) or inexpensive, slow hard drives using the Enhanced Integrated Drive Electronics (EIDE) interface or ATA (Advanced Technology Attachment). Today, the technologies have converged. SCSI drives are no longer used very much, except for specialized applications, such as file servers, where the SCSI interface's ability to address many drives simultaneously comes in handy. Fortunately, ATA drives have graduated to the new SATA (Serial ATA) interface and, in the process, have gotten much, much faster. These SATA drives can be installed internally or configured as external hard drives that link to your computer via FireWire or Universal Serial Bus (USB.) There are also connections that allow you to use SATA drives over the speedy eSATA (external serial ATA) interface.

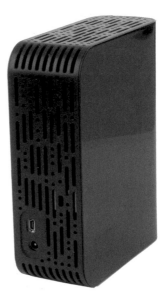

Although most computers are fitted with one or more internal hard drives, you may be limited in the size and number of such drives you can add. Some computers can accommodate four ATA and two SATA internal drives, but it's more common for newer computers to offer only two ATA attachments (with one dedicated to a CD/DVD reader/writer.) External hard drives can allow connecting a virtually unlimited number of storage devices. So, with external hard drives, you're no longer limited to the number of disk drives you can cram into your computer's housing. These disks, such as the one shown in Figure 1-17, link to your computer using an IEEE 1394 (FireWire) or USB 2.0 interface.

Figure 1-17: This external drive allows adding 500GB or more of storage to your computer.

The advantage of external storage is that you can install and remove FireWire and USB 2.0 drives without opening your computer's tower, and you don't need to worry about how to fit them in the case. You can also easily move such an external drive from computer to computer.

Archiving and Backing Up

Digital photos can fill even the largest hard drive faster than Yankee Stadium on Bat Day. Your graphics powerhouse needs open-ended storage that is relatively cheap and reliable and that provides near-online (permanent storage) access speeds.

Zip disks (R.I.P.)

Zip disks became a part of popular culture, almost turned into a generic term, and threatened to replace the floppy disk before $40 CD and DVD burners killed them off. Today, you see Zip disks only in old spy movies in which a secret agent copies crucial data while a bar graph on the computer display shows the progress.

Today, solid state "thumb" or "jump" drives do the same thing more cheaply and plug right into your USB port.
(The latest spy movies show the agents using a thumb drive, but the bar graph remains maddeningly slow because the need for suspense hasn't been eliminated by the pace of technology.)

CD-Rs and CD-RWs

CD-R and CD-RW discs have a bit more credibility in this arena because you can cram a useful 700MB on a CD that can cost as little as a nickel. You still wouldn't want to back up your 160GB drive to 200 CD-RW discs (even though the media itself might cost you only $20), but it's entirely practical to archive your digital photos on this media if you are using a camera with no more than 5 or 6 megapixels of resolution. For cameras that produce larger files, even CDs don't have much capacity.

DVDs

DVDs have become a more viable long-term storage medium, even though the basic one-layer DVD barely holds the contents of a 4GB memory card. (And those of us with higher-resolution cameras can fill up a 4GB card *very* quickly; on a recent trip, I snapped roughly 4GB of photos every day for ten days running.) Depending on how many layers are used, DVDs can store up to 50GB or more each.

The cost of DVD burners is coming down, and this medium should become more popular when the industry settles on a single, standard format. In a world with DVD-ROM, DVD-RAM, DVD+RW, and DVD-RW, the best plan is to buy a DVD burner that supports them all. For the highest capacities, you'll need to use Sony's blue-laser Blu-ray discs, which come in 25GB and 50GB versions. The discs are expensive ($20 each and up as I write this) and Blu-ray disc writers are several times more expensive than a basic DVD reader/writer. But costs will drop dramatically during the life of this book.

Visually Speaking

When I am upgrading computers, I lavish the most attention on the trio of components I interface with directly all day, every day, usually for long periods of time. For efficiency and sanity's sake, you should insist that these pieces of equipment be only the very best available, and don't change them capriciously. So, I've used the same keyboard and wireless mouse for a long period of time, with multiple computers. And, I pay special attention to the third component set: the monitor and its accompanying video card.

For digital photographers, your display and video card are two of the most important components in your system. You need a video card with 64–128MB of fast memory (or more) so that you can view 24-bit images with 16.8 million colors at resolutions of up to 2048 x 1536 (or more) on a 19- to 24-inch monitor. A combination like that enables you to examine your photos closely, array several large images side by side, and view pictures at a size very close to their printed size. Here are some specific recommendations:

- Unless you also play computer games, you don't need to spend hundreds of dollars on video cards with video accelerators so powerful that they require their own fans. Instead, sink your funds into a video card with enough RAM to display images at high resolution. Think 2-D instead of 3-D.

- Consider buying a dual-head video card capable of displaying separate images on two different monitors. You'll find that most serious Photoshop users and digital photographers work with two monitors (at least). One monitor can contain your image editor, and another can display a Web browser or another application. Or you can move Photoshop's palettes to the second monitor to make more room for your images.

Another trick is to use different resolutions for each monitor, say 1920 x 1440 on one for a high-resoution display, and 1024 x 768 for a larger view on the second monitor. If a Web page is hard to read on my main display, I often just slide it over to the second monitor at 1024 x 768 for a closer view. Figure 1-18 shows a dual monitor setup in the Windows Display control panel.

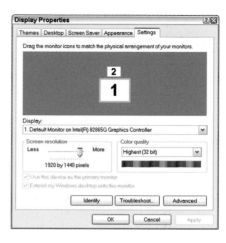

Figure 1-18: Dual monitors can be set up in your Control Panel.

✔ Two video cards can also give you dual monitor capabilities. When I upgraded most recently, I purchased an "obsolete" 64MB PCI video card for about $40 and installed it in tandem with my system's built-in card. I then purchased a 17-inch monitor with multiple rebates for a net cost of $49. For less than a C-note, I was in dual monitor heaven.

✔ Check out the monitor you buy in the store before you purchase it. You'll be staring at it all day, so you want a sharp image that you can live with.

✔ If you've been using CRT monitors for awhile, expect a surprise when you go to replace your display. Traditional tube-based monitors are becoming hard to find and are being replaced wholesale with LCD monitors. That's not good news for the budget-minded because LCD displays are still a bit more expensive than the CRT type, and the cheapest models are *not* suitable for image editing. The cheap-o models have colors that aren't accurate, they don't offer an easy way to calibrate them, and their fixed resolution may not be fine enough for image editing.

Of course, on the plus side for LCDs, you can tuck one of these flat beauties onto the most confined desktop or even hang one on the wall. And they don't require geometry (shape), convergence (alignment of the electron guns), or focus adjustments. They're easier on the eye, emit no radiation, use as little as ten percent of the power of a tube-based display, and are not affected by electromagnetic fields.

Look for an LCD with a high contrast ratio (700:1 to 1000:1 is good), with the resolution you need. A 20–21-inch LCD should offer 1920 x 1200-pixel resolution. You don't want to edit images on a 1280 x 960-pixel display. Also find one with a DVI interface so you can connect to your video card's digital connector rather than analog link.

Chapter 2: Getting Your Pictures from the Camera to the Digital Darkroom

In This Chapter

✓ Connecting the camera to the computer

✓ Using various connections and memory cards or disks

✓ Moving your images from camera to digital darkroom

✓ Understanding your organizational options

✓ Choosing the right tools to organize and store your photos

✓ Keeping your treasured photos safe

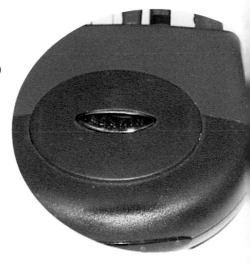

*W*hen you take pictures with a conventional film camera (remember those?), you end up with a roll of exposed film that must go to a photo lab (or the minilab at your local drug store) for processing and printing using special chemicals and darkroom equipment. When you get the prints back a few hours or days later, you get to see how your pictures turned out. Often, a fair number of pictures end up in the trash, and you keep the rest. If you want extra prints or enlargements of the good shots, it's back to the lab to order reprints.

One of the great things about digital photography is that you don't have to process and print every single image you shoot. Most digital cameras let you preview your images right in the camera, so you know immediately how you did. And you can discard the obvious blunders and bloopers before anyone else sees them. What remains are the pictures you want to print.

With digital photography, there's no need to go to a photo lab to get prints from your pictures, although many still avail themselves of that option because of the convenience and cost-per-print advantages. But, if you're in a hurry and want to fine-tune your digital photos, the darkroom and lab are as close as your own computer. But unlike conventional photography, there's no roll of exposed film to send off for processing. Instead, you move your digital pictures from your camera to your computer by copying the image files from one device to the other.

How you do that depends on the features of your camera (and to a lesser extent, your computer). This chapter first addresses the various camera-to-computer connections you're likely to encounter and then describes the process of transferring images from camera to computer.

Making the Connection between Camera and Computer

Before you can use your computer as a digital darkroom to process and print pictures from your digital camera, you must get your picture files out of the camera and into the computer. After you save the images as files on your computer's hard drive, you can manipulate them with the image-editing software of your choice and print them on your printer. Books IV and V describe the basics of editing images and working with Photoshop products to do so.

Some printers are capable of accepting images directly from a digital camera and printing them without going through an image-editing program or other software on your computer. These use the PictBridge standard, which was created for printing from digital cameras to printers by using a direct connection, without the need of a PC. Different vendors can make the camera and printer; all devices that support the PictBridge specification (and the number is growing all the time; check your camera manual) should work fine with any other device that conforms to the standard.

Several technologies for transferring pictures from your camera to your computer are available. The range of options might seem confusing, but you don't need to worry about most of them because a given camera rarely supports more than one or two options.

In general, the image-transfer technologies fall into three broad categories:

- **Wired connections:** A USB cable, like the one shown in Figure 2-1, enables you to transfer picture information from the camera to the computer. The communication between your computer and your camera is similar to that between your computer and other peripheral devices, such as printers, scanners, or external modems. I discuss wired connections in the following section.

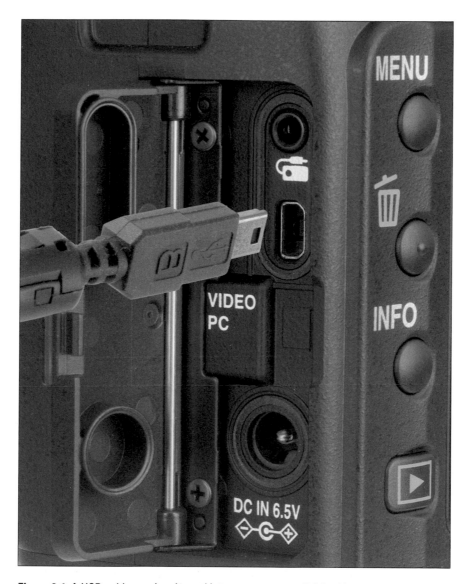

Figure 2-1: A USB cable can be plugged into your camera to link it with your computer.

✓ **Wireless connections:** In the future, more digital cameras will use wireless transfer to beam pictures directly to a computer or printer. Today, you'll find such connections chiefly on high-end digital SLRs and a few consumer cameras, including new Kodak EasyShare models, and cameras that use Bluetooth technology.

✔ **Removable media: The** camera stores picture data on a memory card that you can remove from the camera and then insert into a drive, slot, or reader on your computer. This process is like saving files to a floppy disk and then moving the disk to another computer and accessing the files there. For information about different types of removable media, see the later section, "Memory cards."

Getting Wired

When you look at the back (or, often, front) of a typical computer, you see a variety of sockets and ports in different shapes and sizes. Some of them probably have cables attached that lead to assorted peripheral devices, such as your mouse and your printer. Camera manufacturers have standardized the USB (Universal Serial Bus) port as the all-purpose connection for digital cameras. The original USB 1.1 port (with up to 12-megabits-per-second transfer rate) has already been supplanted by the faster USB 2.0 version now found on new computers. USB 2.0 is 40 times faster than the original, at up to 480 megabits per second. Cameras and other peripherals will work with either type, although at a slower speed when connected to a USB 1.1 port.

An even faster version, USB 3.0, which is 10 times speedier at 4.8 *giga*bits per second transfer, is expected to be available in products introduced in 2009 and 2010.

Even at current speeds, USB connections can move data faster than the older serial and parallel connections. Because USB connections are also *hot swappable,* you can safely plug in and unplug USB cables without shutting down your computer. You can also expand the number of USB ports available by adding a hub (a small box with multiple USB ports) or a device that has extra USB ports built in, such as a keyboard or monitor. Then, you can plug your camera or other USB device into the added ports, just like the USB ports on the back of your computer. Your hub may need a power adapter to run some equipment. Some gear works from the unadorned port, drawing power from your computer, but others require more juice.

Some older computers might not have USB ports built in. You can upgrade most of those computers with a relatively inexpensive add-in card to provide the needed USB ports.

The USB port is a small, flat, rectangular socket approximately $^3/_{16}$ x $^1/_2$ inch. You usually find at least two of them on the back of your computer, clearly marked with the special symbol shown in the margin. USB ports might also be available on the front of the computer, on a USB hub (like the one shown in Figure 2-2), or on a keyboard or other device that has a built-in hub.

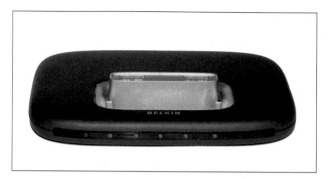

Figure 2-2: A powered USB hub allows connecting many different peripherals at once.

You can use any of these ports to connect your camera to the computer. USB is also used to link stand-alone and internal card readers (discussed in the "Transferring Images from Camera to Computer" section later in this chapter) to your computer.

To hook up your camera, follow these steps (with your computer turned on):

1. **Plug one end of the cable into the USB port on your camera.**

   The USB connector is often hidden behind a small door on your camera. It's sometimes a squared-off, D-shaped socket, approximately $^1/_4$ x $^5/_{16}$ inch. If your camera includes a standard USB port, you can use a standard USB cable, which has a rectangular plug on one end and a square plug on the other. However, most digital cameras now use a smaller mini-USB connection called *mini-A* to save space. Additional connectors such as mini-B, micro-A, micro-B, and micro-AB are found in a few cameras and devices such as PDAs and cell phones. If that's what you have, you will need to use the special cable supplied with your camera if it's not a standard mini-A USB connector.

2. **Plug the other end of the cable into the USB port on your computer or USB hub.** (The computer connection is a standard plug, called Type A.)

3. **Insert the camera manufacturer's driver disc into your computer if prompted to do so.**

   Windows automatically recognizes when a new device is added to a USB port. The first time you connect your camera to the computer, Windows versions prior to Windows XP and Vista might need to load drivers supplied by the camera manufacturer in order to access the camera. Mac OS also recognizes new peripherals when plugged in.

4. **Use the camera manufacturer's software (or other file-management software) to transfer image files from the camera to the computer.**

FireWire

FireWire connections (formally known as IEEE 1394) are an alternative to USB connections. Like USB, FireWire transfers data faster than serial and parallel ports and is hot-swappable. You can also connect multiple FireWire-equipped devices to the computer. FireWire connections are a standard feature on all Macintosh computers built in the last few years. FireWire is also available for PCs, but built-in FireWire on a PC is only now becoming common (USB does most of what Windows users need to do).

You might need to purchase and install an add-in card for your PC if your camera needs a FireWire connection.

Currently available in FireWire 400 and FireWire 800 varieties, the implementations are sensibly named for their maximum transfer rates of about 400 and 800 megabits per second, respectively. Additional versions, with speeds of up to 6.4 gigabits per second, are planned to compete with USB 3.0 in the future.

FireWire isn't common on digital still cameras; you encounter it more frequently on digital video cameras. But because some digital video cameras can capture still images as well as digital video, I guess that qualifies them as digital photography devices.

The FireWire port is a small, rectangular socket that looks similar to a USB port. The FireWire port is a little fatter than a USB port, however, so there's no chance of mistakenly plugging a FireWire cable into a USB port or vice versa.

Follow these steps to connect your camera to your computer via a FireWire port:

1. **Plug one end of the cable into the FireWire port on your camera.**

   The FireWire connector is often hidden behind a small door on your camera and is identified with the symbol shown in the margin. If your camera uses a special cable configuration to save space, you need to use the special cable that came with your camera.

2. **Plug the other end of the cable into the FireWire port on your computer.**

3. **Insert the camera manufacturer's disc into your computer if prompted to do so.**

   Like USB, Windows and the Mac automatically recognize when a new device is added to a FireWire port and will prompt you for a disc if it needs to load drivers supplied by the camera manufacturer in order to access the camera.

4. **Use the camera manufacturer's software (or other file management software) to transfer image files from the camera to the computer.**

Riding the (infrared) light wave

An IrDA (Infrared Data Association) port enables you to transfer computer data from one device to another by using pulses of infrared light instead of a physical wire. The process is similar to how most TV remote controls send channel and volume adjustment instructions to the TV. Infrared connections are slow and not very reliable, but those drawbacks are countered by the convenience of not having to poke around the back of your computer every time you want to make a connection or deal with wires that get tangled and lost.

An IrDA port looks like a small, dark red (nearly black) lens or window. You find them on some digital camera models from Kodak and Hewlett-Packard, and on a few printers and laptop computers, but rarely as standard equipment on a desktop computer. If your computer doesn't have an IrDA port, you can purchase an adapter that will probably connect to your computer via a cable to one of the standard serial or USB ports.

To use an IrDA port to transfer pictures to your computer, follow these steps (with your computer turned on):

1. **Turn on your camera and set it for infrared data transfer.**

   Use the camera's controls to select the infrared data transfer mode. Each camera model is different, so refer to your camera's instructions for details.

2. **Position the camera's infrared port so that it points toward the infra-red port on your computer.**

   Although it's possible to make an infrared connection from several feet away, you generally get better results when the two infrared ports are close together (just a few inches apart). Ensure that no obstructions are between the two IrDA ports and that no bright lights (such as sunlight from a nearby window) are shining on the infrared sensors.

3. **Use the camera manufacturer's software on your computer to start transferring picture data.**

Transfers with teeth (blue)

No, Bluetooth is *not* used exclusively by nerds you encounter as they walk around seemingly talking to themselves. Some computers and printers have Bluetooth adapters that can be used to accept images from Bluetooth-enabled devices (which these days are mostly cell phones). To transfer images from your device, you must first "pair" your two Bluetooth components so they recognize each other. Then follow the instructions that came with your camera and computer or printer to make the exchange.

Memory Cards

The kind of storage your digital dream camera uses will never be a factor in making your selection (unless it's a truly odious choice, and that's a matter of personal taste). The days of the digital cameras that used floppy disks and other oddball media are long gone. Today, all digital cameras use one (or more) of the following options. (The first four are shown in Figure 2-3.) I describe them in more detail in the next section.

- **Secure Digital (SD): Among non-SLR cameras,** the SD format is by far the most popular memory card format. These postage-stamp-size cards, which allow manufacturers to design smaller cameras, are available in roughly the same capacities as CompactFlash, and they cost about the same.

- **CompactFlash (CF):** CompactFlash is the second-most-favored format in the United States. Although physically larger than SD, CompactFlash cards are still very small and convenient to carry and use. As larger capacities are introduced, they usually appear in CF format first. They are the most popular memory card format for digital SLRs, although Nikon, Canon, and other vendors have switched to SD cards for their entry-level dSLRs.

- **xD and mini-xD:** The xD and mini-xD formats are smaller than Secure Digital, and they're supported by fewer vendors (currently only Olympus and Fuji). Although it's wise to avoid getting stuck using a Betamax format when everyone else has converted to VHS, you're safe in choosing a camera using an xD variant. The vendors are important enough that even if the format eventually fails, you should be able to purchase memory cards for as long as your camera works. Indeed, because memory cards are typically used over and over forever, the cards you purchase with your camera or shortly thereafter are likely to serve you throughout your camera's useful life. In addition to mini-xD, there is an even smaller version called micro-xD, about the size of the fingernail on your little finger, which is used in the tiniest MP3 players. I don't expect to see these used in digital cameras any time soon.

- **Sony Memory Stick:** About the size of a stick of gum, Sony's Memory Sticks are useful because you can also use them with other devices, such as MP3 players. They're not going to replace CompactFlash, though. Sony has had an unfortunate tendency to flip around among memory choices for its digital camera, and it didn't stop when the Memory Stick was introduced. It's now available in Memory Stick (up to 128MB sizes), Memory Stick Pro (larger capacities), Memory Stick Duo (a smaller version that needs an adapter to fit memory card readers outfitted for Memory Sticks), and most recently, Memory Stick Pro Duo. Whew!

✔ **Mini hard drives:** For a long time, mini hard drives were your only option when you needed more than a gigabyte of storage. Today, these mini drives have been entirely supplanted by CompactFlash cards in the same form factor that are faster, more rugged, and have higher capacities. I'm mentioning this storage option only as a historical note for those who may encounter them on the used market.

✔ **CD-R/RW:** Sony, in its never-ending quest to change its digital camera media options annually, actually tried out both floppy disks and mini-CD-R and CD-RW discs for its digital cameras. Although not really a bad idea, because the media was relatively inexpensive, this option never caught on because digital camera memory requirements eventually exceeded the capacity of mini-CDs. Sony seems to have settled into an ever-changing Memory Stick groove now and offers CompactFlash storage for its digital SLR cameras.

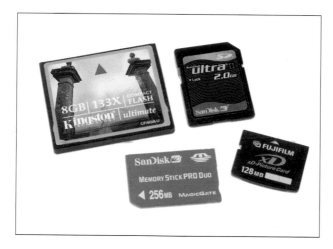

Figure 2-3: Clockwise from top left: CompactFlash, Secure Digital, xD, and Sony Memory Stick Pro Duo.

The following points give you some insight on inserting, removing, and accessing files on cards (which can be a trickier endeavor than you might think):

✔ To remove a memory card of any type from your digital camera (or computer), just press the eject button next to the card slot (for some kinds of cards) to pop the card loose from its connection. Then you can grab the end of the card and pull it out of its slot. Other kinds of cards pop out automatically when you press them.

✔ To insert a memory card into a laptop computer, card reader, or digital camera, insert the card connector-edge first into the slot. Slide the card all the way in and press it firmly but gently to seat the connectors along the edge of the card. If the card won't go all the way into the slot, it's probably upside down. Flip it over and try again.

✔ After you insert the memory card into your computer, you should be able to access it as a virtual disk drive. You can use your normal file-management techniques to copy and move image files from the memory card to your computer's hard drive.

Windows XP, Windows Vista, and Mac OS X usually recognize your digital memory card in a card reader or when you connect your camera and will pop up a dialog box like the one shown in Figure 2-4. You can choose one of the actions available, including copying the files to your computer and erasing them from the memory card when finished. Some applications, such as Photoshop Elements, come with a utility that recognizes a memory card and performs the transfer under your direction. I explain image transfer in detail later in the "Transferring Images from Camera to Computer" section in this chapter.

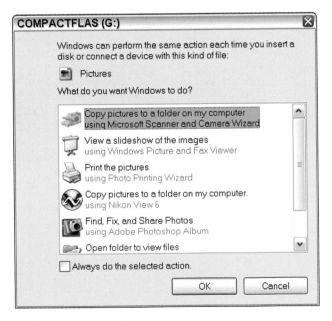

Figure 2-4: Your computer may recognize when a memory card is inserted and offer to make the transfer for you.

CompactFlash cards

CompactFlash cards, like the one shown at upper left in Figure 2-3, are used as removable memory in a dwindling number of other devices, but their primary application is for image storage in digital cameras. They provide a much smaller and more efficient form of removable memory than PC cards (which I discuss a bit later).

At about 1¹/₂ inches square, a CompactFlash card isn't much larger than a postage stamp, and it's just a little thicker than a credit card. Still, there's room for two rows of holes for connector pins along one edge. All CompactFlash cards are physically about the same size (there are Type I and a thicker Type II variety), but they can have various memory capacities ranging from 4MB (generally no longer available) to 16GB or more. A higher-capacity version seems to come out every few months. As I write this, 32GB and 48GB CF cards are already available, but they currently are more expensive, on a per-byte basis, than 16GB and smaller cards.

Digital memory cards might be offered in various speeds, such as *standard*, *high-speed*, *40X*, *Ultra*, and *Extreme*, depending on the nomenclature used by the vendor. The faster, more expensive media are able to store images more quickly. Unless you're shooting sequences and don't want to wait even a short time between pictures, standard media will probably do the job for you. Some newer digital cameras that provide a high-speed burst-photo mode require these higher-performance digital cards to function as advertised, however. With CompactFlash memory cards now being offered in 133X, 150X, and 300X speeds, there's no telling where the speed race will end. The fastest CompactFlash cards conform to the new UDMA (Ultra Direct Memory Access) specification. While the super-speediest cards may provide little advantage when taking pictures, you'll find that you can download images from them to your computer much more quickly when equipped with a compatible high-speed card reader.

For tips on removing, inserting, and accessing files on CompactFlash cards, see the bulleted list in the preceding section.

Secure Digital/MMC cards

Secure Digital (SD) cards and the identically sized but less flexible MultiMediaCard (MMC) are still other memory card formats similar to CompactFlash. Secure Digital cards are a format that has swept the industry in a relatively short period of time because the smaller size (roughly ⁷/₈ x 1¹/₄ inches) of the SD card allows designing smaller cameras. One key difference between MMC and SD cards is that the Secure Digital version allows encryption of the files to prevent tampering. They also offer higher performance and thus are preferred over MMC cards for digital cameras.

Using a Secure Digital card for image storage is essentially the same as using a CompactFlash card except that the card itself is slightly smaller, which means that the sockets in the camera and the card reader must be made to fit the Secure Digital card. The Secure Digital format is not interchangeable with the other formats. Indeed, the latest SD cards larger than 2GB in size use a new specification SDHC (Secure Digital High Capacity), and work only in cameras designed to be compatible with SDHC (all newer digital cameras are).

Memory Stick

The Sony Memory Stick is one more form of memory card, functionally similar to the CompactFlash and Secure Digital cards. Sony uses the Memory Stick in several of its high-end, point-and-shoot digital cameras and also in digital video cameras, music players, and so on, which means that you can move your Memory Sticks between devices and use them for storing pictures, music, and other files. Sony has switched to CompactFlash for its digital SLRs, but offers a CF-to-Memory Stick adapter if you want to use your current Memory Sticks.

The basic Memory Stick (which is no longer used in current digital cameras) is about the size of a stick of chewing gum and comes in capacities of 32 to 128MB. The newer Memory Stick Pro offers higher capacity but is not backward-compatible with earlier devices that used the original Memory Stick. There is also the half-sized Memory Stick Pro Duo. The latest versions can be purchased in sizes up to 4GB.

Several models of Sony laptop computers include a built-in Memory Stick slot so that you can use the laptop computer to access the contents of your Memory Sticks. You can also use a card reader similar to the card readers for CompactFlash and Secure Digital cards to access Memory Sticks from your desktop computer. The card reader attaches to your computer via USB cable.

Here are some pointers for removing, inserting, and accessing files on a Memory Stick:

- To remove a Memory Stick from your digital camera (or card reader), press the eject button next to the slot to pop the stick loose, grasp the exposed end of the stick, and slide it out of its slot.

- To insert a Memory Stick into the camera (or card reader), insert the stick into the slot in the direction of the arrow marked on the surface of the stick. The arrow and a clipped corner help you orient the stick properly. The stick goes into its slot in only one way. Push the stick in firmly but gently to seat it properly.

✔ Like the other memory cards, after you insert a Memory Stick into the card reader attached to your computer, you can access and manipulate the files on the stick as if they were located on a virtual disk drive. Copy, move, and erase the files using your normal file management tools.

The Memory Stick includes an Erasure Prevention Switch that lets you protect the contents from accidental erasure. Make sure the switch is in the Off position when you want to record images onto the stick in your camera or erase files in the card reader.

CompactFlash cards, Secure Digital cards, Memory Sticks, and the like are often called *digital film* because inserting a memory card into a digital camera is analogous to loading a conventional camera with a fresh roll of film.

SmartMedia cards

SmartMedia cards have faded almost completely from the scene and exist today only as memory options for older digital cameras. They are similar to CompactFlash cards but in an even smaller package, and they are limited to only 128MB capacity. Unless you have a very old digital camera, you won't be using one of these.

Mini-CD

To combat the problem of the limited capacity of floppy disk drives (used in some very early Sony digital cameras), Sony built some digital cameras with a mini-CD drive in place of the floppy disk drive. The camera actually includes a CD burner to record picture data onto mini-CDs, which are smaller-diameter versions of standard CDs. A standard CD-ROM drive can read the mini-CDs, and because CD drives are standard equipment on almost all computers, the mini-CD enjoys the same universal accessibility as floppy disks. The downside is that the mini-CDs aren't readily available for purchase like floppy disks or even memory cards are.

Microdrive

The Hitachi or Seagate Microdrive is a tiny hard drive that's a little thicker than the standard CompactFlash card but otherwise the same. Such drives are also available from other sources, including Seagate. If your camera is equipped with a CompactFlash Type II slot, you can use the Microdrive. The Microdrive has in the past been less expensive than solid-state CompactFlash cards of the same capacity, but that is no longer true. They have been available in sizes up to 8G or more. Using the Microdrive is just like using a standard CompactFlash card except that because it is actually a miniature hard drive, it must be handled with more TLC than a CompactFlash card.

Digital memory cards might be offered in various speeds, such as standard, high-speed, 40X, ultra, and extreme, depending on the nomenclature used by the vendor. The faster, more expensive media are able to store images more quickly. Unless you're shooting sequences and don't want to wait even a short time between pictures, standard media will probably do the job for you. Some newer digital cameras that provide a high-speed, burst-photo mode require these higher-performance digital cards to function as advertised, however. With memory cards now being offered in 133X, 150X, and 300X speeds, there's no telling where the speed race will end. The fastest cards conform to the new UDMA (Ultra Direct Memory Access) specification. While the super-speediest cards may provide little advantage when taking pictures, you can download images from them to your computer much more quickly when equipped with a compatible high-speed card reader.

Transferring Images from Camera to Computer

As the previous section shows, different digital cameras offer different tools for connecting the camera to your computer. It might be a direct connection, such as a cable from the camera to a port on your computer, or it might be an indirect connection, such as a memory card that you can remove from the camera and then insert into a reader or drive attached to your computer.

Card-reader adapters are available for your computer, or may be built into the computer itself. These adapters enable you to read and manipulate the contents of a CompactFlash card. The card reader is usually a small, external device, like the one shown in Figure 2-5, that attaches to your computer via a FireWire or USB, cable. Sometimes, a card reader for your computer comes with the camera. If not, you can purchase one from most computer supply stores for less than $30. PC card adapters are also available. The adapters enable you to access your CompactFlash cards via a PC card slot in a laptop computer. However, most newer laptops have their own readers built in for the most common digital memory card sizes.

After you make the connection between your camera and your computer, you might have a few more options available regarding what software you use to transfer pictures from the camera connection to your computer. Most digital camera manufacturers supply a program with the camera that is designed to handle the task, but you might also have the option of transferring pictures to your computer via image-editing software or your computer's normal file management utilities.

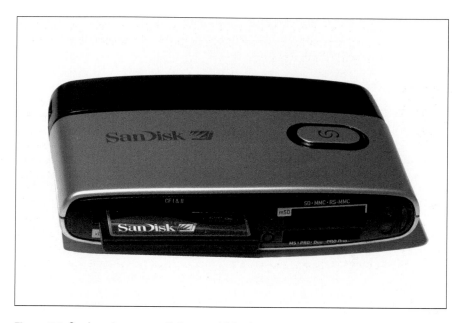

Figure 2-5: Card readers generally have multiple slots that accept every kind of memory media used in digital cameras.

Transferring pictures using camera utility software

Windows XP, Windows Vista, and Mac OS X can recognize memory cards or cameras and offer to transfer your photos for you, using a dialog box like the one shown in Figure 2-4. However, you'll often prefer to use the utility software provided with your digital camera because such software frequently has additional features, such as the ability to edit your photos after you transfer them.

Just about every digital camera on the market today ships with a disc containing software designed specifically to transfer pictures from the camera to your computer. Often, the software has a number of other features as well, but its main purpose is to allow you to use your computer to access the pictures you shot with your camera.

The details of the installation and use of the software accompanying the various digital cameras vary as much as the cameras themselves. Covering all the different programs in detail in this book is not possible, but the general process goes something like this:

1. **Make sure the camera (or card reader) is connected to the computer and is turned on.**

    This ensures that the software can find the camera/card reader connection if the installation searches for it.

2. **Insert the disc that came with your camera into your computer's disc drive and launch the installation utility (if it doesn't start automatically).**

   The software disc is usually a CD, and the installation routine usually starts automatically a few seconds after you insert the disc into your computer. However, if the installation doesn't start automatically, you can usually get things going by using Windows Explorer to double-click a file icon labeled Setup or Install. You can probably find the file in the root folder of the drive where you inserted the disc. With Macs, click the program's icon on the Desktop.

3. **Follow the on-screen instructions to install the software.**

   A couple of mouse clicks to accept defaults are all it usually takes.

4. **Start the camera utility software.**

   Sometimes the utility software sits in the background and waits for your camera to be connected. Then it pops up automatically and goes to work. Adobe Photoshop Elements' Photo Downloader program is shown in Figure 2-6. If nothing happens, double-click the Desktop icon that the installation program added or look for the new addition to your Windows Start menu. If the camera or card reader is connected and turned on when you start the program, it will usually find your camera automatically. In some cases, you might need to help the program locate the camera by choosing a command such as File⇨Connect and selecting the appropriate location in a dialog box.

5. **Click an icon or menu command to view the image files on the camera or removable media.**

   Here's where the different software programs really go their own way. There is usually an icon or menu command that you can use to display a list of picture files on your computer. You might even be able to preview the pictures as *thumbnail* (small) images.

6. **Select the picture files you want to transfer and click an icon or menu command to begin moving the files to your computer.**

   Again, the details vary greatly in the different programs, but there is usually a prominent icon that you can click to start the transfer process. If you don't see an obvious icon, check the File menu for a command such as Import. As the files are transferred, a progress indicator usually shows what's going on. Elements' Photo Downloader progress bar is shown in Figure 2-7.

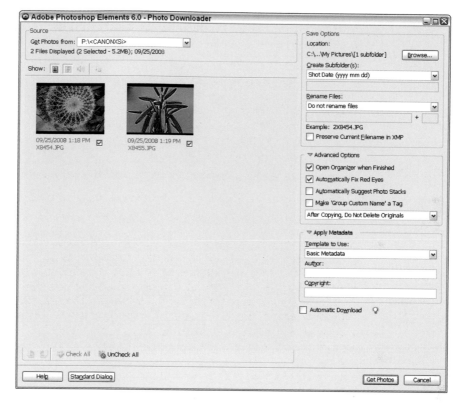

Figure 2-6: In Photoshop Elements, select the images you want to download in the Photo Downloader window.

The same utility program that enables you to transfer pictures from your camera to your computer often includes features that enable you to edit or manage your image files. You can also erase pictures from your camera's memory after transferring them to your computer so that you have room to shoot more pictures with the camera.

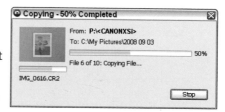

Figure 2-7: As your photos download to your computer, a bar indicator will show the progress of the transfer.

After you transfer the images to your computer, you can view, edit, and print them using any appropriate program on your computer. Windows' and Mac OS X's built-in utilities are sufficient for basic viewing and printing, but you'll undoubtedly want to use more capable programs for most image-editing tasks.

Copying files to your hard drive

Perhaps the simplest and most straightforward way to move pictures from your camera to your computer is to treat them like any other computer file. You simply use your standard file-handling utilities to copy, move, and delete the image files. This is the technique you use with most forms of removable media, and you can often use it with direct camera connections via USB or FireWire as well.

The biggest advantage of this approach is that you don't need to deal with a specialized program in order to access your pictures. Instead, you use familiar tools, such as Windows Explorer and the Open dialog boxes, in your favorite programs.

In order for this technique to work, your computer operating system (Windows or Mac) must be able to access your camera or card reader adapter as part of the computer's file system. Fortunately, that's exactly how most memory card readers and many cameras (most cameras that connect via USB or FireWire) work. They appear to your computer as virtual disk drives, and you can read, write, and erase the files on those devices just like you can files on your hard drive or floppy disk (if your computer has one).

To transfer pictures from your camera to your computer, you can use any of the same techniques you would use to move files from one disk drive to another. The only exception is the extra steps needed to connect a virtual drive (your camera or card reader) to the computer. The following steps summarize the process for the Windows environment. (Similar techniques work for Mac OS.)

1. **Connect the camera or card reader to your computer and turn it on.**

   After a moment or so, Windows displays a message box saying that it has found new hardware and is installing the necessary software drivers. An icon appears in the system tray portion of the taskbar next to the clock.

2. **If prompted to do so, insert the manufacturer's disc containing drivers for your camera or memory card reader.**

   You only need to do this the first time you attach your camera or card reader to the computer.

3. **Open Windows Explorer and navigate to the virtual disk drive representing your camera or card reader.**

   You can double-click the Computer or My Computer icon on your desktop to open an Explorer window and then double-click the appropriate drive icon to display the contents of the camera memory or the memory card in your card reader. Look for a new drive letter that doesn't correspond to one of the standard disk drives installed in your system.

The name of the drive might be the brand name of your computer or card reader.

4. **Open another Windows Explorer window and navigate to the folder where you want to store the picture files from your camera.**

   Be sure to position the two Explorer windows on your desktop so that you can drag and drop between them.

5. **Drag and drop one or more files from the first Explorer window onto the second window.**

   That's all it takes to copy pictures from your camera to your computer. If you copy them in this way, you'll need to delete them from the memory card if you no longer want them there.

Of course, after you connect your camera (or the memory card from your camera) to your computer as a virtual disk drive, you can use all the standard Windows tools and techniques to manage your picture files. The default action for a drag and drop is to copy the files to their new location. However, if you click and drag with the right mouse button instead of the normal left button, Windows displays a contextual menu that gives you the option to move the files instead of copying them. The Move command copies the files to their new location and then erases them from the old location in one step. You can also return to the first Explorer window and erase the picture files from your camera memory in a separate operation.

After you finish transferring pictures from the camera to your computer, don't forget to disconnect the camera properly. To do so, you need to right-click the Safely Remove Hardware icon in the system tray, and in the dialog box that appears, choose to unplug, eject, or stop the device. Then, select the camera from the list in the dialog box that appears next and click the Stop button to tell Windows that you want to disconnect the device. Windows displays a confirmation message, after which you can physically disconnect the camera and its cable from the computer. With a Mac, you should drag the camera's icon to the Trash before disconnecting your camera.

Importing images into image-editing software

The normal sequence of events is to use your camera's utility software to transfer one or more picture files from your camera to your computer. Next, you launch your favorite image-editing software and open the image file to make some adjustments before finally saving or printing the picture. However, several image-editing programs can do the transferring for you, which shortens the whole process.

If Windows recognizes your camera or card reader as a mass storage device (and most such devices that connect to the computer via USB and FireWire are), the device and all the files on it appear to Windows just like any other disk drive. Consequently, you can open a picture for editing in your image-editing program by simply selecting it in the program's Open dialog box. The only thing you have to do is make sure the camera is connected and turned on (and recognized by Windows) before you attempt to open files in the photo editor.

Macs operate in the same way, recognizing your camera or card reader and offering to open the photos in iPhoto.

To transfer images from your camera directly to your image-editing software, you first need to tell the program what camera you use and where to find it. Make sure that the camera manufacturer's software has been installed and is operating properly on your computer and then configure your image-editing software to access images from the camera. The setup process varies in the different programs, but the following steps are typical:

1. **Connect your camera to the computer and turn it on.**

2. **Choose File⇨Import⇨Digital Camera⇨Configure (or an equivalent command) in your image-editing program.**

   The program usually opens a dialog box, but it might present a submenu instead.

3. **Select your camera and (if necessary) the port where it's connected; then click OK to close the dialog box.**

After you configure your image-editing software, you can use it to access images from your camera. Here's how:

1. **Connect your computer to the camera and turn it on.**

2. **Choose File⇨Import⇨Digital Camera⇨Access (or an equivalent command) in your image-editing program.**

   A dialog box appears, giving you access to the images stored on your camera. This is usually a subset of the camera manufacturer's access software.

3. **Select the image or images you want to open in the image-editing program and then click the button or choose the command to begin the transfer.**

   The software transfers the selected pictures from your camera to the image-editing software.

4. **If the image-editing software doesn't return to the foreground automatically, click its taskbar button.**

    The selected images appear in the image-editing program window, ready for you to begin working with them.

Organizing Your Photos

When it comes to taking control of your photo organization, you have a few different approaches to choose from. Your personality, your computer, and your access to the Web all dictate your choice. Here are some approaches to consider:

- ✔ Setting up a file structure on your computer
- ✔ Working with software that makes it easy to organize and store your images and view them through a special interface
- ✔ Organizing and storing your images in an online gallery

What do I mean about your personality influencing your choice of organization tools? If you're a very organized person who enjoys straightening out closets and dresser drawers, always knows where the remotes are, and always puts things away after using them, using the file-management tools already on your computer might appeal to you.

If, on the other hand, you aren't too tidy and often forget where you left your glasses or your keys, you might prefer either using software that organizes things for you or posting your images to an online gallery. The tidy person might like these latter approaches as well.

Using your computer's file-management tools

You already have some great tools for organizing your images, and the tools have been on your computer all along. If you're running Windows XP or Vista, you have Computer or My Computer and the Windows Explorer right there at your fingertips. If you're using a Mac, you can use the file-management tools that you've already been using to create folders on your desktop or hard drive.

Using these tools requires devising some sort of filing system — one or more folders that will help you categorize your images. You might start with one called Photos and create subfolders called, perhaps, Family Photos, Vacation Pictures, and Scanned Vintage Photos. You can create folders on your computer for groupings that fit the pool of images you have. After you create the folders, all you have to do is move your images into the appropriate folders and remember the folder names when you store new images in the future.

Using Windows Explorer to store and organize your photos

Working with folders under Windows is pretty basic but deserves a review in the context of organizing your digital image files. To create folders to store your images by using Windows Explorer, follow these simple steps:

1. **Choose Start⇨Programs⇨Windows Explorer in Windows XP, or Start⇨Computer in Vista.**

   You can also right-click the Start button and choose Explore from the context menu using either XP or Vista

2. **When Windows Explorer opens, click the C: drive icon.**

   If there's a plus sign next to the icon, click that plus sign to display the folders currently on the drive. If there's a minus sign next to the icon, that means you can already see all the folders.

   The Windows Explorer window is divided into two panes: the Folders pane on the left and the Content pane on the right (see Figure 2-8). When you click a drive or folder in the Folders pane, that drive's or folder's contents are displayed in the Content pane. This two-sided display makes it possible to drag items from one folder to another simply by displaying the source (where the content is now) and target (where you want the content to be) folders in separate panes.

   If you don't see the Folders pane, you can open it either by choosing View⇨Explorer Bar⇨Folders or by clicking the Folders button on the toolbar.

3. **If there's a folder (such as My Pictures) that you want to use as the basis for your image organization, click it. If you want to start a new folder for your photos, choose File⇨New⇨Folder from the menu bar.**

   If you go the New Folder route, a New Folder appears in the Content pane, with its temporary name highlighted, waiting for you to type its real name. (See Figure 2-9.)

4. **If you go the New Folder route, give your new folder a name and press Enter to confirm it.**

With a folder created to house some or all of your photos, you can begin to place them in a single location. You can also make subfolders in that main folder to categorize your photos. For example, if you have a Photos folder, you can create a Vacation Photos subfolder and a Baby Pictures subfolder to keep those two, distinct photo subjects separate. Figure 2-10 shows just such a folder system.

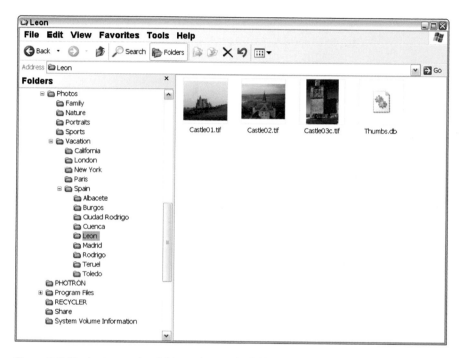

Figure 2-8: Navigate your hard drive to locate the folder you want to use.

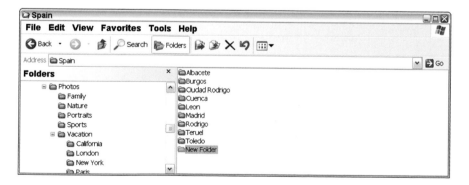

Figure 2-9: Create a new folder if necessary.

To create subfolders of the main folder, simply click the main folder to select it (on the left side of the screen, in the Folders pane), and repeat Steps 3 and 4 from the preceding steps list. You're going to use the File⇨New⇨Folder command to create a new folder, but because you're in an existing folder when you do it, the new folder appears inside the active folder.

The process is like taking one of those green hanging Pendaflex folders and putting one or more manila folders in it. The green folder represents the main Photos folder, and each of the manila folders is the same as the subfolders you create to categorize your photos. You can create as many subfolders as you want, and even create subfolders within subfolders. The folder hierarchy can become as complex as you want or need it to be, but be careful not to make managing files so cumbersome that the process becomes confusing when you need to place an image in the right folder.

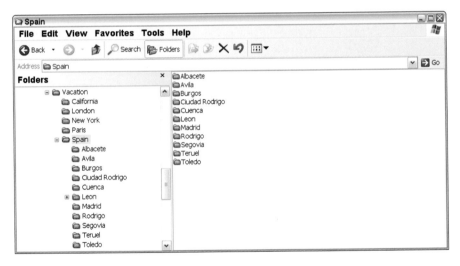

Figure 2-10: Here's a typical folder system for organizing images.

You can also use My Computer to find your images. It works much like Windows Explorer. Insead of a two-paned window, however, you have separate windows for each drive and folder on your computer. The command for creating new folders is the same (File⇨New⇨Folder), but you have a visually different environment in which to work when creating and using your folders. Figure 2-11 shows the main My Computer window, displaying the C: drive, D: drive, E: drive, and other computer components.

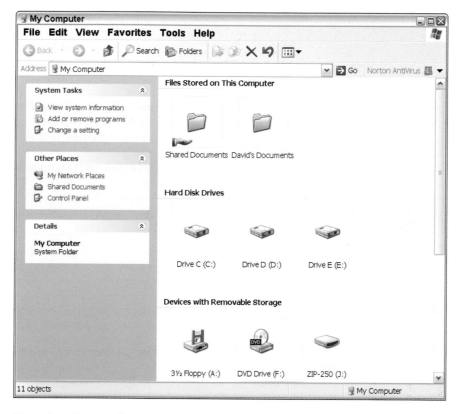

Figure 2-11: You can also use My Computer to navigate your hard drive.

If you don't need to categorize your photos by subject, consider creating folders that separate your photos by date. You can have a separate folder for individual years, months, or weeks, depending on how prolific a photographer you are.

Organizing your photo images on a Mac

If you're using Mac OS, you can easily create folders to store your photos and other digital images. You can choose to store them on your hard drive or make them quickly accessible from your desktop.

To create a new folder in OS X, follow these steps:

1. **Choose File⇨New Folder from the menu bar.**

   A folder called *Untitled Folder* appears on the desktop. You can also press Shift+⌘+N or Control-click the desktop and choose New Folder from the context menu that appears.

2. **Give your folder a short yet relevant name that will make it easy to find the folder in the future.**

3. **You can leave the folder on the desktop or open your hard drive and drag the folder there.**

If you store the folder on the desktop, it is quickly available at any time, but you also make it quickly available to anyone using your computer. If you don't want people poking around in your photos, store the new folder somewhere on your hard drive other than the desktop.

4. **If you want folders within the folder you just created, open the folder, then repeat Steps 1 through 3 to create the subfolders.**

You can duplicate an existing folder by choosing File⇨Duplicate. Or, drag the existing folder to a new location on the same hard drive while holding down the Option button; this approach makes a copy of the original folder and leaves the original where it was.

Using photo album software

Setting up a series of folders to store and categorize your images is easy enough. To view them after they're stored, however, you either have to open them in the software you used to edit/retouch them or use the generic software that came with your computer to see the images. If you find that inconvenient (and you probably will, especially if you like to look at and work with your images frequently or to view them side by side), you'll probably be glad to know that several great photo album applications are on the market. These applications enable you to view one, two, or several of your images at the same time, all in one easily navigated workspace.

Figure 2-12 shows a group of photos viewed through a typical album program. Similar programs are often furnished with cameras and software bundles from other vendors.

Want more? Do a search at your favorite search site for *"Photo Album Software."* (Use the quotation marks to make sure the search engine uses the full phrase.) You can also check Web sites, such as www.buy.com and www.amazon.com, where you can do similar searches for the photo album software each site has to offer.

Your criteria for actually selecting photo album software is a personal thing. You may prefer ease of use and not care if you don't get a lot of fancy functionality. If you want a lot of bells and whistles, you may not mind if the product is a little more complicated to use. Some photo album software serves as both an organizational tool and a vehicle for creative display of your photos, and some just does the latter job. If you already have a system for organizing your images, you may not need software that does double duty.

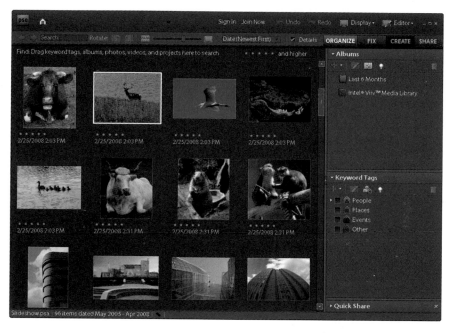

Figure 2-12: Album software makes it easy to organize, find, and retrieve your images.

You can download and test many photo album products for free (with a time or number-of-uses limitation), making it possible to test-drive two or more products before plunking down any cash and making a commitment. It pays to shop around if you plan to use this software frequently. ThumbsPlus is available for evaluation at www.cerious.com/download.shtml. Other popular album applications include ACDSee and Apple iPhoto (for the Mac).

Look for these features when choosing photo album software:

- ✔ Ability to categorize and classify each photo, using built-in or custom-designed categories.

- ✔ Provision for adding your own captions and other annotations.

- ✔ Search capabilities, so that you can locate all the images classified as Vacation pictures by using keywords such as *beach* and *2008*.

- ✔ Sorting abilities, so that you can permanently or temporarily arrange your photos by filename or other criteria. (These features go hand-in-hand with search capabilities.)

- ✔ Features for uploading from your local album to your own Web space or picture-sharing services, such as SmugMug (www.smugmug.com), Flickr (www.flickr.com), or PBase (www.pbase.com).

✔ Viewing capabilities that include looking at single photos and arranging them into slide shows.

✔ Simple image-editing features such as cropping, resizing, and rotating, so that you can make small changes to your pictures without firing up your image editor.

Using online galleries

You probably already e-mail photos to friends, sending the images as message attachments that the recipients must open to view. Then, your recipients can save any images they want to keep on their hard drives. There may be a better way to share your images, assuming you don't mind having your images posted on the Internet, by using online galleries to display your photos. This section is an overview of using online galleries. SmugMug, Flickr, and PBase, mentioned earlier, are three of the best.

The online approach to image distribution has some great advantages and some drawbacks. Check out the advantages first:

✔ You can avoid the hassle of having to e-mail photos to lots of different individuals because you're placing all your photos on one Web site. All you have to do is let people know to check the site for your images. This makes it possible to share images that are larger than some e-mail services can handle. (Many services have a 2MB limit.)

✔ You can share more images with more people. Anyone with an Internet connection can view the images without owning any special software — other than a browser, which people need to surf the Web anyway.

✔ You have yet another relatively protected repository for your images. If you lose the original files, you can download them from the online gallery.

Possible disadvantages — and only you can decide if they are real disadvantages — are as follows:

✔ Your photos are on the Web, and, unless you use the provider's privacy provisions, anyone can view them. This can expose you and your family to people with whom you would not normally share your vacation, holiday, and other personal photos. You have to be careful about posting photos that show your house number, last name, or any other identifying information.

✔ Most online galleries charge a fee for providing space on their site for your photos. The fees are usually reasonable, but compared to e-mailing photos, which is free (you're already paying to have e-mail anyway), the cost may be more than you're willing to pay.

To find an online gallery to post your photos, you can search online for *"Online Galleries."* You'll see quite a few that are devoted to actual artists (and this may be of interest if you are an artist) and some that are for the general public to use. If you add *"+free"* to the search criteria, you'll ferret out those sites that offer the space for free or that will let you test their services for free or for a limited time.

Archiving and Backing Up Photos

Not all your photos will require instant, easy access. Vacation photos from the past — especially if you visited a not-too-exciting place — may be a waste of valuable hard-drive real estate. But what if you don't want to delete those infrequently viewed images? There's no reason to make rash decisions; you can simply archive the ones you don't need to access quickly or frequently. If a photo is valuable to you on some level in the long run but you don't imagine wanting to look at or print it within the foreseeable future, just save it to disc — a CD or DVD, or store it on external hard drives or an online archiving service.

Backing up your best shots

First, because you've already organized your photos (assuming you've read the beginning of this chapter), you should already have your photos categorized and know which ones are especially dear to you. These cherished shots need to be backed up, stored in some way, in order to protect them from anything that can happen to your computer or your photo albums (printed or electronic).

Your backup options are simple.

✔ **Store the photos on a spare hard drive.** External hard drives are becoming the most popular backup medium because they hold many, many more images than even the highest-capacity removable media, including 50GB Blu-ray disks. Plug-in external hard drives that connect to your USB or FireWire ports may cost less than $100, and they can make a large-capacity, relatively inexpensive backup system. External hard drives in sizes of 500GB or less can cost less than $100 and will hold tens of thousands of images. I purchased a 1TB (1000 gigabyte) external drive for my own backup purposes, and there are 1.5TB (1500 gigabyte) and larger for those who truly shoot *lots* of photos. You can unhook the drive and store it in a safe place when you're not actually using the images you've backed up. Of course, hard drives are prone to failure (eventually), and even an extra external drive shouldn't be used as your only backup destination. Prices are so low that it's now feasible to buy two external drives and back up to both!

✔ **Write them to a disc using a CD or DVD burner.** This method enables you to store up to 800MB on a single CD, or almost 5GB on a conventional DVD. Even higher capacities are available from dual-layer DVDs and Blu-ray discs. If your computer already has a burner in it or attached to it, all you need is a package of writeable CDs or DVDs. The discs are so inexpensive, you can make two copies. To be 100-percent safe, you should plan on copying your important discs to fresh media every few years. Even good-quality CDs and DVDs can "fade" over time. Also plan to copy your media to whatever new kind of storage replaces CDs and DVDs five or ten years down the road. You don't want to end up with "antique" discs and no way to access them!

✔ **Store them online.** Many Web sharing sites also can provide you with a sort of backup for your images. It's best to use these as a secondary backup (sort of as a backup to your backup) because there's no guarantee how long these services will be around!

Using CD-R and CD-RW

In these days of 10- and 12-megapixel point-and-shoot cameras, 800MB CDs seem woefully inadequate. You'd need three of them to copy all the files from even a relatively small 2GB memory card. But CDs still have an advantage over older magnetic media, such as floppy and Zip disks (remember them?), which could be ruined by exposure to magnets, heat, cold, sunlight, water, and rough handling: CDs are pretty stable. Other than breaking or scratching them, you can't really hurt them. They might fade on their own after a very long period of time, but it won't be your fault! Studies have shown that CDs are actually more stable than DVDs as the years speed by, although DVD permanence is sure to improve as the technology matures.

Although DVDs are the new standard, the old CD format still has a lot of life left in it. Here's a refresher course in CD media:

✔ Writeable CDs come in two types: CD-R and CD-RW. CD-Rs can be written to (the R stands for Recordable), but only once. CD-RWs can be written to and erased, and written to again.

✔ You can use a CD-R or a CD-RW like a floppy or Zip disk by using a mode called Packet Writing. In that mode, you can copy files or groups thereof to the CD. However, you can't interrupt the writing process as you can with a floppy or Zip disk, and the process takes a bit longer.

✔ Commercial CDs (like the discs that contain software or audio tracks) are pressed from a mold. CD-Rs and CD-RWs are marked with a laser, creating spots that represent data (in binary form). CDs are virtually indestructible (unless you crack, break, or severely scratch them) and can withstand a sunny day in the car or a night below freezing in that same glove box. Even so, CD-Rs and CD-RWs shouldn't be exposed to direct sunlight or extreme heat, although they are less vulnerable to such conditions than older magnetic media.

DVD storage

DVD burners have largely replaced CD-only burners in most computers. Indeed, the older single-layer, 4.8GB DVD drives are being phased out by double-layer drives that can record 8.5GB of data and Blu-ray discs that can store 25 and 50GB of information.

For the digital photographer, plain-old 4.8GB DVD drives make a lot of sense until the technology settles down more. For one thing, single-layer DVDs cost much less than half what dual-layer blank discs sell for and only a fraction of what you must pay for a Blu-ray disc. And you can be assured that your dual-layer or Blu-ray drive will read your old single-layer discs when you do migrate. Like CDs, DVDs also come in more than one variety:

✔ DVDs (the prerecorded kind) come with stuff prewritten to them. You can view what's on them, but you can't erase and then rewrite to them.

✔ DVD+R and DVD-R discs (note the use of the plus and minus signs) can be written to only once. The plus/minus varieties are separate formats, but most drives and burners can read both types. The -R version can be slightly more compatible with some television DVD players.

✔ DVD+RW and DVD-RW discs can be written to, erased, and written to again.

✔ DVD+/-RW burner/players can play DVD discs and play or write to DVD+/-R and DVD+/-RW discs.

If your older computer has a DVD player in it, that doesn't mean you can write to DVDs; it simply means you can play them. To write to a DVD, you need the burner version.

✔ DVD dual-layer discs use a dual-layer compatible drive or player.

Off-site storage for maximum safety

If your photos are so precious that you'd be devastated if anything happened to them, or if they're important for legal, financial, or other compelling reasons, don't risk losing them to a fire or burglary. You can store your archives off-site in one of three ways:

✔ Use a bank safe-deposit box.

✔ Use a safe located in a secure storage facility.

✔ Keep one of two archive copies with a friend or family member.

If you save your precious images to a CD or DVD, you can make two sets and store one set off-site, selecting one of the aforementioned places based on the level of security you need. The bank could burn down, but the safe-deposit boxes are usually in or near the vault and are protected from very high temperatures, even in the event of a fire. If you keep a safe in a paid off-site storage space, the place is likely to be fireproof or protected by sprinklers and video cameras, so it's probably more secure than your home. If neither of these is an option, find a friend or relative you trust and give the extra set to him or her.

Chapter 3: Picking Up Some Accessories

*T*ypical point-and-shoot digital cameras have everything you need to take great pictures, right? And they're not really very expandable because they usually have a nonremovable lens, built-in flash, close-up capabilities, and other features that you might normally purchase as accessories. What more could you want?

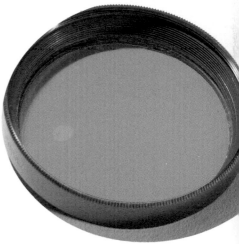

A lot. One of the most diabolical things about photography is that as you use the capabilities of your camera equipment, you always find even more interesting things you could do if you just had *this* accessory or *that* gadget. Even the most basic point-and-shoot digital camera can do more things if you have a sturdy tripod to mount it on. You can get into the picture yourself, steady the camera for interesting long exposures at night, or use the tripod's rock-solid foundation to help you take sharper close-up pictures.

If your digital camera is a little more advanced and has a long zoom lens, there will come times when you wish you had an even *longer* zoom. Discovering ways to use your digital camera's built-in flash effectively can make you yearn for a bigger, better external flash that can pump out the light needed to take pictures at a greater distance.

When the accessory bug really hits you, you'll start searching for previously unknown add-ons to help you do things you didn't even know could be done. You'll even think up ways in which having a second digital camera can help you (as a spare, as a smaller camera to keep constantly at hand, and so forth). After you become serious about photography, accessory-itis is sure to strike. I say this from the viewpoint of someone who currently owns more than a dozen single lens reflex (SLR) cameras, a clutch of digital cameras, some 15 lenses, eight or nine flash units, and a closet-full of close-up attachments, filters, and other add-ons.

Don't fight it. Enjoy your incurable addiction. You can have a lot of fun playing with your accessories, and most of them don't cost all that much, anyway. They help you shoot better pictures, too. This chapter highlights some of the most common and most needed accessories for digital photography.

Getting Support from Tripods

A *tripod* is a three-legged stand, like the one shown in Figure 3-1, designed to hold your camera steady while a picture is composed and taken. Although a tripod might be a little cumbersome to carry along, at times, you'll find one indispensable. Here are some of the things a tripod can do for you:

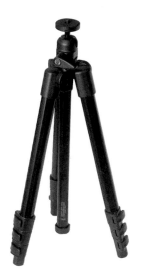

Figure 3-1: Get the support you need from a tripod.

✔ **Hold the camera steady for longer exposures.** You need a longer shutter speed to capture an image in dim light.

✔ **Hold the camera steady for photos taken at telephoto zoom settings.** Telephoto settings do a great job of magnifying the image, but they also magnify the amount of vibration or camera shake. Even tiny wobbles can lead to photos that look like they're out of focus when they're actually just blurry from too much camera movement. A tripod can help eliminate this sort of blur.

If pictures keep ending up fuzzy when the camera's set for its maximum telephoto zoom setting, it's more likely that the problem is camera shake than a poor autofocus mechanism. At long zoom settings, most digital cameras often switch to a slower shutter speed. The slower shutter speed coupled with the telephoto's magnification of the tiniest bit of camera shake leads to a photo that appears out of focus. It's not that the picture is out of focus at all; it's just that the camera has been vibrating too much. If your camera or lens has a built-in anti-shake (vibration reduction/image stabilization) feature, turn it on. If you don't have that feature or still experience blur caused by camera motion, mounting the camera on a good, sturdy tripod is the best cure for this problem. You can turn your image stabilization off while using the tripod.

Getting multiple shots with a tripod

Here's a trick that shows you just how useful a tripod can be. Multiple shots can be merged to solve difficult lighting situations because using a tripod also allows multiple images from exactly the same camera position. This is important because it can help the photographer correct problems with lighting that's too contrasty.

Many times, a scene is lit in such a way that the difference between the brightest white and the darkest black is greater than the sensor can handle. When this happens, pictures end up with areas that are solid white or solid black and have no detail in them.

When circumstances permit, pros correct this by taking more images of exactly the same scene with the camera mounted on the tripod. The first image is exposed so that the highlights are properly exposed; the second image is exposed so that the shadows have detail. *Hint:* When in doubt, take one picture that's a

little overexposed and one picture that's a little underexposed. (One setting above what the camera recommends and one setting below what the camera recommends would be a good rough estimate.) Some cameras have this capability built-in, usually called *auto exposure bracketing.*

Back at the computer, the two images are merged in an image-editing program such as Photoshop so that the combined image carries detail throughout the picture. Using this technique might stretch your comfort zone with both your computer and your camera, but it can also help you improve many photos, such as scenics, that can be taken with the camera mounted on a tripod. You can always take an extra shot at the setting the camera recommends so that you still have the shot you'd have gotten anyway. That's one of the nice things about digital cameras; you don't have to worry about wasting shots!

✔ **Hold the camera in place so you can get in the picture, too, by using your digital camera's self-timer feature.** This way, you only have to worry about how you look as you make a mad dash into the picture. (Some cameras offer an infrared remote control to trigger the shutter and avoid the mad dash; but you'll still need to mount the camera on a tripod or other support.)

✔ **Allow for precise positioning and composition so that you can get exactly the image you want.** This is especially important if you want to take multiple shots from the same spot, and it's also useful if you're experimenting with filters or trying different lighting ideas.

✔ **Hold the camera for multipicture panoramic shots that you stitch together into one photo in your image editor.** I discuss panoramas in greater detail in Book III, Chapter 6.

✔ **Hold the camera for close-up photography.** I discuss close-ups in Book III, Chapter 2

Because most modern digital cameras are fairly lightweight, you won't have to carry a massive tripod like many pros do; just be sure the tripod is strong enough to keep the camera steady. Beware of the models that claim to go from tabletop to full height (roughly eye-level at five feet or more); odds are that they sway like a reed when fully extended. If you have one of the new, low-cost digital SLR cameras like those available from Canon, Nikon, Olympus, Sony, and Pentax, you might need a slightly heftier tripod because these models, although small for a dSLR, are a bit heavier than the run-of-the-mill digital point-and-shoot camera.

Types of tripods

Tripods come in several types of materials, styles, and sizes. Pro units are capable of handling heavy cameras and extending 5 to 6 feet high. These tripods are made of wood, aluminum, or carbon fiber and can cost anywhere from a couple hundred dollars to a thousand dollars or more. You probably don't want one of these. Your ideal tripod is probably a compact model made of aluminum. Here are the common types of tripods:

- **Less expensive units:** May range in size from 1 to 5 feet tall and cost just a few dollars to a hundred dollars or more.

- **Full-size models:** These range from 4 to 6 feet tall (or even larger) when fully extended and might have from two to four collapsing sections to reduce size for carrying. The more sections, the smaller the tripod collapses. The downside is that the extra sections reduce stability and provide more points for problems to develop.

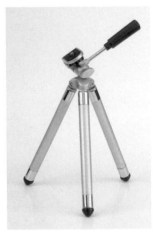

- **Tabletop or mini-tripods:** These are promoted as lightweight, expandable, and easy to carry, which they are. They can be small enough to carry around comfortably. They're also promoted as sturdy enough for a digital SLR, but they probably aren't unless set to their lowest height. Most can handle a point-and-shoot digital camera, however. If used on a tabletop or braced against a wall with a small digital camera, these units do a decent job. They come in handy in places where there's not enough room to use a full-size tripod. Figure 3-2 shows a typical tabletop tripod, which stands just 8 inches tall.

Figure 3-2: Tabletop tripods work great on tabletops!

To use a mini-tripod against a wall, brace it against the wall with your left hand while pressing your left elbow into the wall. Use your right hand to help stabilize the camera while tripping the shutter. Keep your right elbow tight against your body for added stability.

✔ **Monopods:** While not exactly a tripod (a monopod has only one leg), a monopod helps reduce camera shake. These single-leg, multi-segment poles, like the one shown in Figure 3-3, about double the steadiness of the camera.

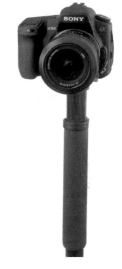

Don't use a monopod around some protected buildings, such as museums and government facilities, because monopods resemble guns from a distance.

✔ **Hiking stick monopods:** Another option is a combination hiking stick/monopod. If you do a lot of hiking, these can be very worthwhile. Although not as sturdy or stable as a high-quality monopod, these hybrids can work quite well with the typical small digital camera.

Figure 3-3: Monopods provide a more compact means of support for heavier cameras, like this digital SLR.

Most of them have a wooden knob on top that unscrews; a quarter-inch screw mates with the camera's tripod socket. (Check to make sure your digital camera has one; not all models do.) Mount the camera on the hiking stick, brace the bottom of it against your left foot, pull it into your body with your left hand, and gently squeeze the shutter release button.

You can find excellent tripods and monopods from Bilora, Bogen, Benbo, Gitzo, Lenmar, Slik, Sunpak, and Smith Victor at your photo retailer.

Scrutinizing tripod features

Not all tripods are made alike, so I encourage you to take a close look at how the tripod you're thinking of purchasing is put together. The following subsections are a rundown of what to look for.

Locking legs

All collapsible tripods offer some way of locking the legs in position. Most common are rings that are twisted to loosen or tighten the legs in place. Some manufacturers use levers instead. When buying a tripod, check this part closely. Remember, every time you want to fully extend or collapse the tripod, you're going to have six or more of these locks to manipulate. A good tripod lets you open or close all the locks for one leg simultaneously when the legs are collapsed, as shown in Figure 3-4. (Cover all three rings or levers at the same time with your hand and twist; they're all released, and then with one simple movement, they're all extended. This also works in reverse.)

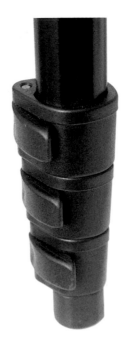

Range of movement

Some tripod legs can be set to a right angle from the camera mount. This feature can be handy if you're working on uneven ground, such as a hiking trail.

Figure 3-4: Grip all three locks to open or close them simultaneously.

Extra mounting screws

Some tripods offer an extra mounting screw on one of the legs. Hypothetically, this is useful, but its use is rare enough that I wouldn't choose one tripod over another for this. A more useful extra is a reversing center column post, available on better tripods, that can accept a camera on its low end (for ground-level shots) or that has a hook that holds a weight or camera bag. Placing extra weight on a tripod makes it steadier for longer exposures, so this capability is very useful.

Heads

A *tripod head* is the device that connects the camera to the tripod legs. On inexpensive models, these are often permanently attached. On better quality models (although not necessarily expensive ones), they are removable and can be replaced with a different type. There are quite a few styles of tripod heads. Many tripod heads that offer a *panning* capability (the ability to spin or rotate the camera on its horizontal axis) also offer a series of 360 markings to help orient the camera for panoramas. Here are some of the types of tripod heads to consider:

- **Pan/tilt heads:** These allow you to spin the camera on one axis and tilt it on another. These are generally the cheapest and most labor intensive because you have to make adjustments to multiple levers to reposition the camera.

- **Fluid, or video, heads:** These usually have a longer handle that extends from the head. Twist the grip to loosen it, and you can pivot and tilt the camera simultaneously.

- **Joystick heads:** Similar to the fluid or video head, this type has a locking lever built into a tall head. By gripping the lever and head and squeezing, you can pan and tilt the camera quickly and easily. These were designed and marketed for 35mm cameras, but they don't work particularly well for these cameras because they're subject to creep. Basically, *creep* occurs when you reposition your camera on a tripod head, lock it, and then notice the camera move a little as it settles into the locked position. Creep can be a very annoying problem with any tripod head, but the joystick models seem to have more trouble with it.

For a smaller digital camera, these heads might be a better choice simply because these cameras weigh so much less.

- **Ball heads:** These are probably the most popular style with pro photographers because they provide a full range of movement for the camera with a minimal number of controls to bother with. This type of tripod head, shown in Figure 3-5, uses a ball mounted in a cylinder. The ball has a stem with a camera mount on one end, and when the control knob is released, you can move your camera freely until reaching the top of the cylinder. A cutout on one side of the cylinder allows the stem to drop down low enough for the camera to be positioned vertically. Ball heads range in price from just a few dollars to $500 or more. The best ones don't creep at all, which is why photographers pay so much for them.

Checking out tripod alternatives

Several other items on the market are also worth considering for those who need to travel light. A tried and true classic for supporting bigger camera/lens combinations is the beanbag. Whether you use the basic beanbag that you tossed around as a kid or the one specially designed for photography, by putting the bag on a wall or car roof and then balancing the lens on the bag, you can maneuver your equipment easily while letting the wall or car take the weight of the lens.

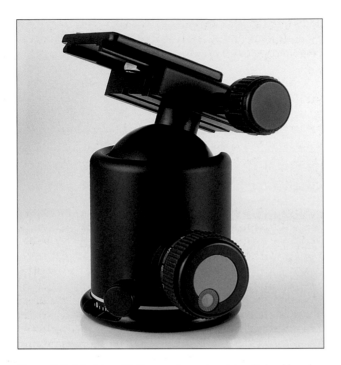

Figure 3-5: A ball head is the most popular style of tripod head for still photography.

You can also find a number of clamp-like devices coupled with the quarter-inch screw necessary to attach them to your camera's tripod socket. You then clamp the camera to a tree limb or fence post or any other solid object, and *voilà!* Instant tripod. (Don't add water.)

These camera-holding clamps range from a modest C-clamp device for just a few bucks up to the Bogen Super Clamp system (which you can find at www.bogenphoto.com). The basic Super Clamp costs around $30. The basic C-clamp style should do the job for travelers using a shirt-pocket-size digital camera. Those working with one of the larger, digital SLR cameras might want to consider a Super Clamp. A local camera store can probably help you out.

Making Good Use of an Electronic Flash

Because available light (more commonly known as *available darkness*) is undependable, digital photographers should consider carrying an accessory flash unit. Although most digital cameras have some sort of built-in flash capability, these don't produce a very powerful light. The built-in flash unit is usually good only for a range of up to about 8 feet or so, which isn't always enough.

Accessory flash units do more than just provide extra light when it's too dark to shoot without it. Although I cover accessory lighting more thoroughly in Book III, Chapter 3, here are some situations in which an accessory flash is useful:

- **Fill flash:** Is your subject standing in the shadows while another part of the scene is brightly lit? If you rely on your camera's light meter, you'll either get a properly exposed subject and overexposed area where the light was too bright or an unrecognizably dark subject and an okay scene. Using an accessory flash lets you balance the light throughout the scene by exposing for the bright area and using the flash to light up the shadows.

- **Painting with light:** Suppose you want to take a picture of a building or other large structure, and it's pitch dark out. One technique for handling this situation is known as *painting with light*. Set your camera on a tripod or something equally solid and then pull out your accessory flash unit. Set your digital camera to its bulb (B) or time (T) exposure setting if it has one — or if not, then use the longest exposure (shutter speed) possible. While the shutter is open, use your flash to light up sections of the building one section at a time. Here's where the true wonder of the digital camera comes in: You can check your photo as soon as you're done taking it. Although film photographers have been using this technique for years, they've always had to wonder whether they got it right until they got their prints back or saw their negatives in the darkroom.

- **Macro, or close-up, photography:** Getting in close requires lots of light simply because as the camera gets closer to its subject, the area of sharp focus — *depth of field* — diminishes. Using your external flash helps provide enough light to allow an aperture setting for greater depth of field. The external flash also provides more even illumination for your subject.

It's best if you use a setup that allows your flash unit to operate while it's off the camera because lighting your subject from the side brings out more detail than lighting from straight ahead. Some flash units, such as ring lights, are specifically designed for macro photography. (I take a look at ring lights a little later in this chapter.)

- **Bounce flash:** Many accessory flash units include a tilt/swivel head that lets you point the unit toward a reflective surface instead of right at your subject. By bouncing the flash off the surface and toward your subject, you create softer light and shadows than you would if the flash was directed straight at your subject. Some include a built-in card or deflector that can help you direct the bounce light, as shown in Figure 3-6.

Bouncing a flash unit this way weakens its effective output because the light has to travel a greater distance to reach the subject. This isn't a problem if the surface is reasonably close, but distance matters. Beware of cathedral ceilings!

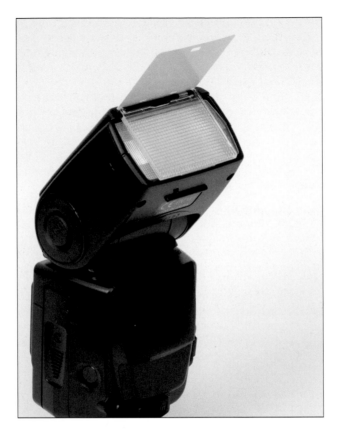

Figure 3-6: An external flash unit's light can be bounced off any available surface.

✔ **Multi-flash:** It's possible to use multiple inexpensive flash units to create a flattering lighting setup. By positioning these flashes properly, you can either create a nicer informal portrait lighting setup or distribute the lights well enough to evenly illuminate an entire room.

Built-in flash units can also speed the camera's battery drain tremendously. Because they're positioned right above the lens, the built-in strobes are also a prime cause of *red-eye*. This is a reddish tinge in human pupils (greenish or yellowish in many animals). Red-eye is particularly difficult to prevent when photographing (with flash) young children. An accessory flash can help reduce this effect because you can position it farther from the lens than a built-in unit.

Many higher-end digital cameras offer some method of triggering an accessory flash unit, either by a cable connection or via a *hot shoe* — the device on a camera that holds an external flash and provides an electronic connection to the camera. Many amateur and advanced amateur digital cameras, however, offer no such provision. The answer in this case is a *slaved flash* (a flash that's triggered by the burst of light emitted by another electronic flash unit) specifically designed for digital cameras (which I discuss in more detail in the next section).

Types of electronic flash units

There are as many different electronic flash units available as there are digital cameras. The following subsections provide a quick rundown of the kinds you'll want to consider.

Before buying flash equipment of any kind, be sure it works with your camera. Flash units can be triggered via the camera's hot shoe, by electronic slaves, by wireless radio triggers, and via several different types of cables. Some cameras can use a generic, old-fashioned connection called a *PC cable* (not named for a personal computer but for the Prontor-Compur shutters of the early film cameras that used this connection). These cables are inexpensive and work with any camera that has a PC connection, but all they do is trigger the flash unit.

A camera's manufacturer makes another type of cable, known by several different designations (TTL and E-TTL, for example); this proprietary type is designed specifically for the manufacturer's cameras (sometimes for just one segment of its camera line) and no other, although these cables do work with third-party flashes. The advantage to these types of flash cords (which are much more expensive than PC cords) are that they allow the camera and flash unit to communicate with each other so that the camera can turn the flash's output off when it determines proper exposure is reached.

Small, light minislaves

Minislave units are electronic flash devices with built-in remote triggering, and they're designed to help augment the camera's built-in flash unit. They're generally useful for adding a little extra dimension to your lighting and as a way of filling in background areas. These units are slaved to fire when another flash unit goes off. Such photographic slaves are photoelectric sensors designed to trigger a flash unit when another flash is fired within the sensor's field of view (in the case of a digital camera, when the camera's built-in flash fires). These slave-triggering circuits are sold as independent units that you can attach to existing flash units, or the circuitry can be built right into a flash.

Hot shoe mount flashes

These are more powerful than both the minislaves and the camera's built-in flash units. They might or might not offer a tilt or swivel capability. Some camera systems (usually higher-end digital cameras) offer a cable that hooks up to the camera's hot shoe (shown in Figure 3-7) and allows the flash to communicate with the camera's electronics while being positioned in ways the hot shoe mount won't permit. The advantage to these cables over slaves is that they usually permit the camera/flash combo's full range of capabilities. (Some cameras are set to turn off the flash as soon as the correct exposure is reached, whereas a slaved flash will continue pumping out light as set.)

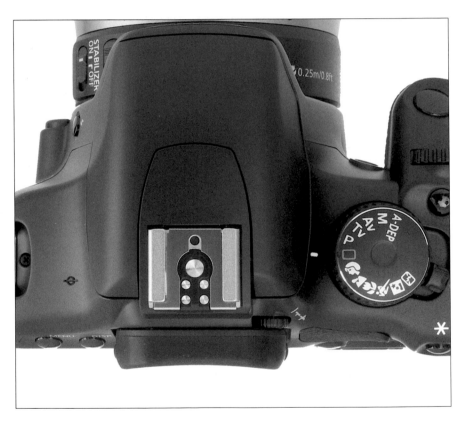

Figure 3-7: External flash units slide onto your camera's accessory or "hot" shoe.

Professional flash models

While you probably won't be venturing into this territory, you might want to know that professional flash units tend to be the manufacturer's most powerful and most advanced models. They have lots of features, including built-in slave capabilities and the ability to work with wireless remote systems. In many cases, they're also capable of taking advantage of the digital camera's lack of a true mechanical shutter at higher shutter speeds. This means the flash can be used with faster shutter speeds than those used with film cameras. In addition to the manufacturer's flash models, dedicated flashes offered by third-party manufacturers also work with many existing camera systems.

Many third-party flash units and lenses are reverse-engineered to work on major brand-name cameras. Sometimes, this equipment might not work with later equipment made by your camera's manufacturer. If a third-party flash causes damage to your camera (and today's highly electronic cameras can be susceptible to damage from improper voltage discharge), the camera manufacturer might not repair the damage under warranty.

What to look for in a photographic slave flash

A basic *slave unit* is a small device designed to mate with the flash unit's hot shoe or other connection. The slave (good ones have on/off switches) triggers the flash when another flash unit is fired. A slave has its own hot shoe foot (to mate with stands designed for such things or the L-bracket described in a few paragraphs) and a quarter-inch tripod socket in its base so that you can screw it onto an extra tripod.

Wireless or radio slaves also exist. These are significantly more expensive (although I paid just $75 for my radio unit), but they're worth it when other photographers and their accompanying flashes are in the vicinity. A regular photoelectric slave doesn't care that it's been triggered by the wrong photographer's flash unit; it simply does its job. Wireless triggers work via radio signals, not light. These devices generally offer multiple frequencies to minimize the likelihood of another photographer triggering them.

A standard photographic slave won't work properly with a digital camera because most prosumer and amateur digital cameras emit a preflash (to help the camera make some internal settings), which triggers earlier slave designs prematurely. If you're interested in a slaved flash unit, make sure it's designed to work with a digital camera. Nissin, an electronics firm, makes a flash unit known as the Digi-Slave flash. You can find about a half-dozen different units, ranging all the way up to a pro unit. Check out SR, Inc. (at www. srelectronics.com), for pictures and descriptions of the models available.

Although the slaved flash doesn't help reduce the drain on the camera's battery, the more powerful light still helps improve photos. The photographer also gains the ability to position the light higher up from the lens (usually slightly to the right or left as well) to reduce the likelihood of red-eye and provide a more pleasing effect. Generally speaking, setting the camera's exposure system to automatic can handle the increased flash okay; if you're not satisfied with the result, switch to your camera's aperture priority mode (which allows you to choose the f-stop while the camera selects the shutter speed) and experiment! The exception is with close-up photos, where overexposure is likely. Dialing in a correction (usually a reduction of about two f-stops) through the camera's exposure compensation system solves this problem.

An electronic flash unit without power is an expensive paperweight. With the exception of the portable studio lighting kits, which require electrical outlets, electronic flashes usually require AA batteries, although the smallest might take AAAs instead. Rechargeable batteries generally are an inexpensive option, although they tend to recycle (recharge the flash unit) more slowly than alkaline batteries do. PC cables and manufacturer flash cords malfunction (take care not to crimp them), so for important trips, carry extras (especially if you're going overseas, where it might be hard to find a replacement). Some rechargeable batteries also tend to lose their charge faster than alkaline batteries when stored.

Lighting/flash accessories

Depending on your shooting requirements and how much weight you can afford to carry, some accessories out there can help improve your photography. Here's my list of possibilities:

- **Brackets:** A nice complement to the accessory flash route is an L-bracket flash holder. This device mounts to the camera via the tripod socket and has a flash shoe at the top of the L, where you position the flash. In addition to providing a secure hold for the flash unit, the L-bracket tends to provide a steadier grip for the camera.

- **Background cloths/reflectors:** Garden enthusiasts interested in photographing flowers can bring swatches of colored cloth large enough to serve as a background for a shot of a plant or bloom. Black is a good all-purpose color, whereas red, green, and blue complement common flower colors. Another helpful item is a collapsible reflector; camera stores sell small ones, or you can pick up ones designed as sun blockers for car windows. These reflectors can kick some sunlight back into the shadow areas to help create a more pleasing image. For the most serious flower photographers, a *ring light* or circular flash unit that mounts in front of the camera lens provides an even, balanced light for flower close-ups. A Digi-Slave flash ring light unit can be configured for many amateur and prosumer digital cameras.

Choosing a Camera Bag

Depending on the size of a digital camera and the accessories accompanying it, a camera bag or pouch could be a necessity. For just the basics — a small camera, extra batteries, extra memory cards, and a lens cleaning cloth — a simple fanny pack does the job and leaves room for hotel keys, money, and identification.

A more serious photographer who's carrying a larger digital camera needs more space. A larger camera bag might be the answer, but for the active traveler, there are some interesting options. Because camera bags are especially useful for traveling photographers, I've included a longer description of the options and features in Book III, Chapter 6, which deals with travel photography.

Acquiring Other Useful Devices

Gizmos. Gadgets. Thing-a-ma-jigs. Many of these items don't fall into any particular type of category, except that they do something useful. Some are quirky but cool, such as little shades that fasten onto the back of your camera and shield your LCD readout screen from the bright sun. Others are serious working tools, like the add-on battery packs described in an upcoming section. Photographers love gadgets, and you'll find lots of them for digital cameras. Here are a few of the most practical.

A filter holder

A helpful device I especially like is a filter holder engineered by the Cokin company (www.cokin.com) and sold by most camera outlets. One Cokin holder, designed for cameras that can't accept filters, mounts to the base of the camera via the tripod socket. This adapter allows the use of Cokin's square filters and circular filters (see Figure 3-8), which slide right into the adapter to provide a variety of effects and corrections. Note, however, that you could achieve many of the same results in an image-editing program. To those who are more comfortable tweaking things on the computer, filters aren't important. But, if you're new to computer photo editing, relying on traditional filters might be easier.

You can always take one shot with a filter and one without and then try to tweak the filterless shot to look like the filtered one. This process can help you figure out how to get the most from your image-editing software.

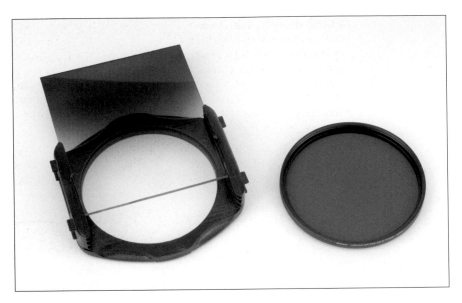

Figure 3-8: Cokin filter holders attach to the front of your lens and accept square and round slide-in filters.

Filters

Filters, those glass disks that can be screwed onto your camera's lens, are a popular accessory. Here are some of the different kinds of filters you can buy and play with:

- **Warming:** Some filters produce what photographers refer to as a *warming effect*. This filter can help make up for the lack of color in midday light and tries to add some reddish-orange color to the scene. Usually, these are coded in the 81 series (as in 81A, 81B, and 81C). At the camera store, just ask for a warming filter.

- **Cooling:** These do just the opposite of the previous type. They add blue to the scene to reduce the reddish-orange color. These fall into the 82 series for daylight conditions.

- **Neutral density:** Another type of filter reduces the amount of light available. These neutral density (ND) filters (*neutral* because they have no color, and *density* because they block light) come in handy for things such as achieving the spun-glass effect from moving water. The filter blocks an f-stop's worth of light or more, making a slower shutter speed possible and increasing the blur of the moving water. You can use ND filters to operate at a wider aperture to blur the background in portraits, too.

- **Neutral density, take two:** Sometimes a photographer wants to photograph a street scene without cars driving through the photo. By stacking neutral density filters, it's possible to create such a long exposure that no cars are in the scene long enough to register in the image. Obviously, a camera support of some sort is required. (**Hint:** The ground's pretty stable, too, unless you're visiting California.) Having a camera capable of extremely slow shutter speeds is also necessary. A neutral density filter is shown in Figure 3-9.

- **Split neutral density:** Another version of the neutral density filter is a split neutral density design. This filter provides half neutral density and half clear filtration, preferably with a graduated transition from the light-blocking half to the clear half.

  The main use for a split ND filter is for occasions when half the scene is brighter than the other. The most common example of this is a bright sky against a significantly darker foreground. This condition is typical of midday lighting conditions.

- **Polarizers:** Polarizing filters can reduce the glare bouncing off shiny surfaces in your photos. Simply attach the filter and view the image through your LCD. Rotate the polarizer until the glare disappears. Polarizers can also help deepen the contrast of the sky from certain angles.

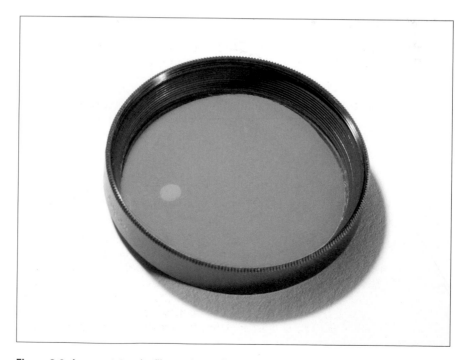

Figure 3-9: A neutral density filter reduces the amount of light reaching the sensor.

A second camera

Sooner or later, you'll think about buying a second camera — say, when you're ready to leave on that vacation of a lifetime. A small, inexpensive digital camera doesn't cost much, and if the primary camera fails, it might prove worth its weight in gold, photographically speaking. Shop for one — or borrow one — that uses the same type of batteries and storage medium as your primary camera, if possible. The extra camera can also entice a spouse or child into sharing your love of photography.

Second cameras are easy to come by. Every time I upgrade to a new digital camera, the old one gets passed down to a family member or kept in reserve as a spare camera. My old 3.3-megapixel Nikon Coolpix 995 was great in its day, but it became a backup when I upgraded to an EVF model with a super-sharp 8:1 zoom lens. Then digital SLRs came along and eventually I ended up with a Nikon D300 as a "main" camera and the incredible, super-compact Nikon D60 as an everyday backup.

Cleaning kits

You'll also often need a good cleaning kit. An inexpensive microfiber cleaning cloth is great for cleaning optics, but first use a blower to blow any dust particles from the lens. You can then hold the lens near your head, fog the lens with your breath, and gently (very gently) wipe the lens with the cloth. Canned (pressurized) air also does a good job of blowing dust and dirt off the camera, but make sure the can is held level, or solvents from the aerosol might contaminate the lens.

Damp or dusty conditions call for more serious efforts. Protect your camera inside heavy-duty plastic freezer or sandwich bags while inside the camera bag, thus reducing exposure to dust and moisture. Keep the little packets of silica that come with electronic equipment and place one or two of these in the camera bag to eat up moisture, too. The following section provides more detailed information about dealing with extreme weather conditions and bags and containers for protecting gear. (Call it the difference between shooting at a dusty ball field on a windy day versus shooting in a windstorm in the desert.)

If you have a digital SLR, you might need a special cleaning kit for removing dust from your sensor. Something as simple as a bulb air blower may work, or you might need to buy a kit containing a brush and swabs for liquid cleaning.

Waterproof casings and housings

Extreme conditions call for better protection for your camera. Better yet, photography in wet weather, or even underwater, can be fun, too. Waterproof casings that still allow for photography are available from several companies, including ewa-marine (`www.ewa-marine.de`). These are useful for both underwater photography (careful on the depth, though) and above-the-water shots when you're sailing or boating. Keep in mind that salt spray is very possibly the single worst threat to camera electronics. Make sure your camera casing provides good protection against wind and salt spray.

Another option for those who want to shoot in wet conditions often is a new underwater digital camera. The SeaLife ReefMaster underwater digital camera series (`www.sealife-cameras.com`) comes in a waterproof housing and works both on land and underwater. The cameras, which can be purchased for as little as $400, produce 3.3- to 5-megapixel images, and they save you the trouble of trying to find a housing to fit an existing digital camera. The cameras also have an LCD that works underwater and a fast delete function to make it easier to operate underwater.

For serious underwater enthusiasts, heavy-duty Plexiglas housings now exist for small digital cameras. These housings are available for a wide range of digital cameras and may be found for as little as a couple hundred dollars.

Battery packs

One of my digital cameras uses a lithium-ion (Li-Ion) rechargeable battery that's good for a couple hundred shots. Unless you're involved in a serious photographic project or leave home on vacation, a single battery (plus one spare) might be all you need. However, that same camera can be fitted with an add-on battery pack that fits under the camera body and holds two more of the same model Li-Ion batteries (increasing the shooting capacity to nearly 600 shots). More importantly, the accessory battery pack accepts standard AA batteries, which the camera itself does not.

You'll find an add-on battery pack like this extremely useful for those shooting sessions that involve treks into backcountry far from AC power. Or if you're on vacation, you might be unable to recharge your digital camera's batteries until you check into your next hotel, so the additional juice might be handy. If you need an accessory battery pack, you probably also need a charger that works on multiple voltage settings (so it can be used overseas) or with an automobile connector so that you can recharge your batteries on the road.

Book II
Using Digital SLRs

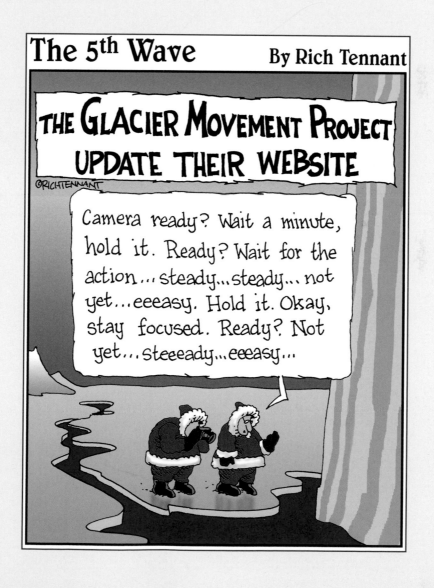

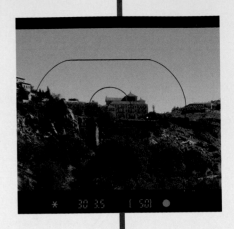

$\mathcal{B}$e honest: If you're really serious about digital photography as a hobby, you probably turned to this book first because digital single-lens reflexes (dSLRs) have, in a few short years, become the dream camera of almost every photo enthusiast. Those point-and-shoot cameras are great to slip into a pocket or purse for spur-of-the-moment pictures, but dSLRs are really where the action is among photo hobbyists.

So, if you're the type who loves to be on the bleeding edge of technology, this book's three chapters will help slake your dSLR-knowledge thirst. I show you exactly why these cameras can do things that other types of picture-shooters (both film and digital) cannot. I'm even up-front with explanations of a few things that dSLRs can't do (and why you shouldn't care). I help you figure out how to manage a dSLR's controls to select the right focus mode, as well as choose between aperture-priority, shutter-priority, programmed exposure, or one of those intriguing Scene modes. I explain the differences between prime lenses and zooms and how to select an add-on lens that gives you the most flexibility without sacrificing image quality. This book is a concise introduction to an exciting camera technology.

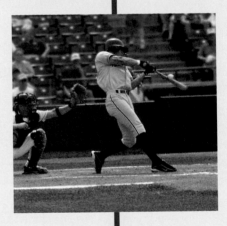

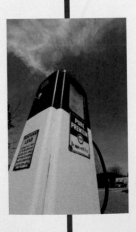

Chapter 1: The Digital SLR Advantage

In This Chapter

✔ **A half-dozen advantages of digital SLRs**

✔ **Six downsides that are ancient history**

✔ **How dSLRs really work**

✔ **Dealing with quirks**

The digital single-lens reflex (dSLR) camera is replacing point-and-shoot models for all photography beyond simple snap-shooting. Certainly, pocket-sized digital cameras are useful as carry-anywhere picture takers for unplanned and spur-of-the-moment shooting. But now that dSLRs are available in ultracompact packages for ultra-low prices, serious photographers seem unwilling to settle for anything else. Virtually everything you can do with a traditional digital camera, you can do with a dSLR — faster, with more creative options, and usually with a better picture.

Working with what most amateur photographers used to consider the high end of the digital photography equipment realm won't make you a better photographer. But upgrading to a dSLR will probably make you a *happier* photographer, particularly after you've mastered all the new controls and features these cameras offer.

As you may (or may not) know, single-lens reflex cameras are film or digital picture takers that use mirrors and/ or prisms to give you a bright, clear optical view (not a TV-like LCD view) of the picture you're going to take, using the same lens that is used to take the picture. Best of all, that lens can be *taken off* (it's *interchangeable*) so you can substitute another lens that brings you closer to your subject, offers a wider view, or maybe focuses down close enough to see the hungry look in the eye of a praying mantis. Is that cool, or what?

Whether you already own a dSLR or you're thinking of buying one, this chapter and the two that follow are your introduction to the exciting features of these top-of-the-digital-food-chain cameras. If you want to find out more, check out my book *Digital SLR Cameras & Photography For Dummies,* but everything you really *must* know right off the bat is in this book.

Six Great dSLR Features

All digital SLRs have six killer features that make your job as a photographer much easier, more pleasant, and more creative.

A bigger, brighter view

The perspective through a dSLR's viewfinder is larger and easier to view than what you get with any non-SLR's optical window, back-panel LCD, or internal electronic viewfinder (EVF). With a dSLR, what you see is almost exactly what you get (or at least 95 percent of it), although you might need to press a button called a *depth-of-field preview* if you want to know more precisely what parts of your image are in focus. The dSLR's viewfinder shows you a large image of what the lens sees, not a TV-screen-like LCD view. (See Figure 1-1.) If you have your heart set on using an LCD, many of the latest digital SLRs from Canon, Nikon, Olympus, Sony, and Pentax offer a feature called Live View, which displays the actual sensor view on the LCD prior to taking the picture. And as with any digital camera, you can still review the picture you've taken on your dSLR's LCD after it has been captured. (See Figure 1-2.)

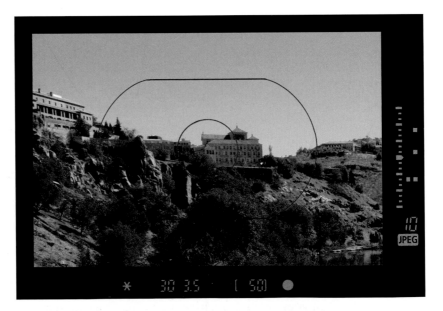

Figure 1-1: A dSLR viewfinder gives you a big, bright view of your scene for easy composition and focus.

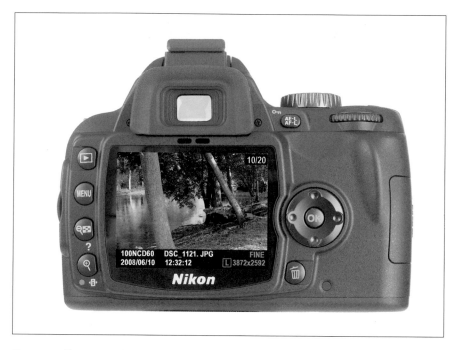

Book II
Chapter 1

The Digital SLR Advantage

Figure 1-2: You can review your image on your dSLR's screen after it has been captured.

Faster operation

Any non-SLR digital camera suffers from something called *shutter lag*, which is a delay of 0.5 to 1.5 seconds (or more) after you press the shutter release all the way but before the picture is actually taken. Lag is a drag when you're shooting sports action or trying to capture a fleeting expression on the faces of your kids. A dSLR responds to your command to shoot virtually instantly and can continue to take pictures at a 3 to 5 frames-per-second clip (or even faster). Try *that* with a non-SLR camera! All functions of a dSLR camera, from near-instant power-up to autofocus to storing an image on your memory card, are likely to operate faster and more smoothly with a dSLR than with other types of digital cameras.

Lenses, lenses, and more lenses

Certainly, many non-SLR cameras are outfitted with humongous zoom lenses with 12X to 18X zoom ratios. A typical superzoom range is the equivalent of 35mm to 420mm on a full-frame digital or film camera. Yet, these lenses don't do everything. Only a digital SLR, which lets you pop off the lens currently mounted on your camera and mount another one with different features, has that capability. Non-SLR digital cameras rarely offer wide angle views as broad as the equivalent of 24mm to 28mm. Digital SLR lenses commonly offer views as wide as 10mm. You'll also want a dSLR if you need to focus extra-close or want a *really* long telephoto. The lenses offered for dSLR cameras are often sharper, too. For many photographers, the ability to change lenses is the number-one advantage of the digital SLR.

Better image quality

You'll find non-SLR digital cameras today with 8 to 14 megapixels of resolution. (There are even *camera phones* with resolution in that range.) But a good-quality dSLR will almost always provide better image quality than a traditional digital camera of the same or *better* resolution. Why? Because the dSLR's sensor has larger pixels (at least 4 to 5 times larger than the typical point-and-shoot camera's), which makes them more sensitive to light and less prone to those grainy artifacts we call *noise.* A 10-megapixel dSLR usually provides better images with less noise at a sensitivity setting of ISO 800 than a 10-megapixel non-SLR camera at ISO 400.

Camera-like operation

The workings of a non-SLR digital camera have more in common with a cell phone than with a traditional film camera. If you don't like zooming by pressing a button, visiting a menu every time you want to change a setting, or fine-tuning focus with a pair of keys, you should be using a digital SLR.

More control over depth of field

Depth of field (DOF) is the distance range in which things in your photos are in sharp focus. DOF can be shallow, which is a good thing when you want to make everything in your image other than your subject blurry, so that your subject is isolated or highlighted. Depth-of-field can also be generous, which is great when you want everything in the picture to look sharp.

Digital SLR cameras allow you to choose between shallow DOF, extensive DOF, and everything in between. Non-SLR cameras usually give you two choices when you're not shooting close-up pictures: having everything in sharp focus, and having *virtually* everything in sharp focus. You can find out more about the technical reason for this (the extra depth of field provided by the shorter focal length lenses used in non-SLR cameras) in Book III, Chapter 2. If you want to use focus creatively, a dSLR is your best choice.

Six dSLR Drawbacks That Are Ancient History

Wow, can technology change quickly in the digital camera realm! In the last edition of this book, I listed six drawbacks of digital SLRs that you probably could live with. Shazam! Two years later, all six have (mostly) bitten the dust. Not only can dSLRs do many things that non-dSLRs can't, their limitations are becoming fewer and fewer all the time. Here's a recap of those drawbacks that have now become, for the most part, ancient history:

No LCD preview? Meet Live View!

"Where's my preview?" was the number-one question asked by new dSLR owners who started out using conventional digital cameras. Because the mirror and shutter of a dSLR block the sensor from receiving light until the moment the picture is actually taken (I discuss this in more detail in the "How Digital SLRs Work" section later in the chapter), it formerly was impossible to offer a preview image prior to taking the picture. That limitation has been licked.

The leading dSLR vendors now offer a Live View feature that shows, in real time, the image being captured by the sensor. Figure 1-3 shows a Live View picture in action, with a Canon EOS Digital Rebel XSi. Most cameras offer a choice of hand-held and tripod modes; automatic focus is provided either by flipping the mirror back down for an instant prior to exposure so the normal autofocus functions can be applied or focusing of the LCD image itself.

Live View is handy for close-up photography, remote picture taking, and other situations where you want to monitor the actual image before taking the picture.

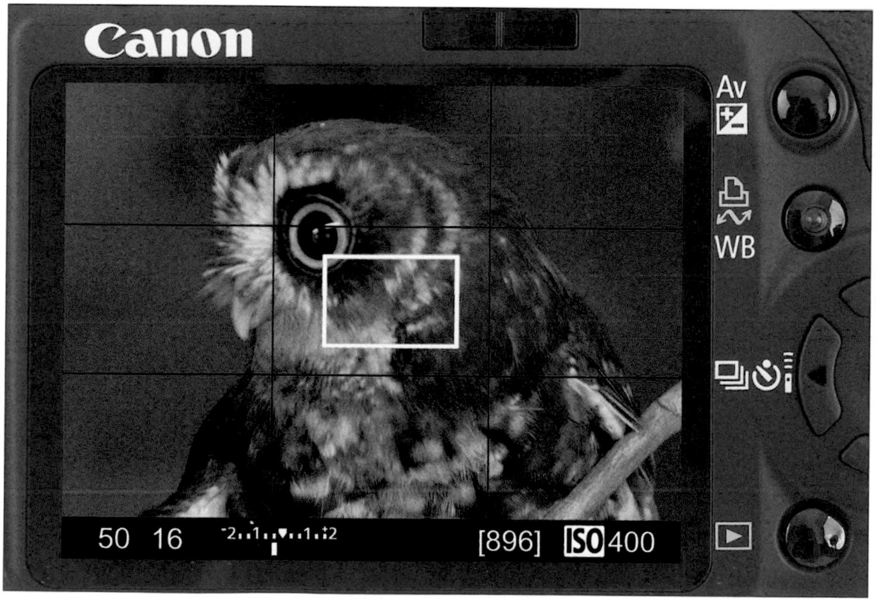

Figure 1-3: Live View allows you to preview your image on the LCD.

Limited viewing angles? No longer!

With previous dSLRs, you always had to have your eye right up to the view-finder to line up your shot. And when reviewing your pictures, you usually had to look at the back of the camera straight-on. Showing your pictures to several friends who tried to view the screen from an oblique angle was a pain.

All that's changed. You can, of course, buy add-on viewing attachments (including right-angle adapters) that can give dSLR owners a little more flexibility when composing a shot through the optical viewfinder. But the growing number of cameras that offer an LCD Live View preview, particularly those with a swiveling LCD, let you hold the camera at arms length, overhead, or down low to compose your pictures. Today's LCDs allow wider viewing angles, too, so you can glimpse your screen from off to the side — and so can your friends.

Lack of super-wide lenses? Improvements made!

If your dSLR has a sensor that is smaller than 24mm x 36mm (a 35mm film camera's full frame), the perspective of each lens is cropped by this smaller sensor size, increasing the focal length's effective field of view by 1.3X to 2X, depending on the dSLR you're using. (The focal length isn't really multiplied, however.) This factor is good news for those who want to reach out with a longer telephoto lens, but it's bad news for those who find their 20mm super-wide-angle lens has become an ordinary 26mm to 40mm moderately wide or normal lens.

In the past, super-wide-angle lenses for dSLRs were rare and expensive. But the manufacturers of digital SLRs and third-party lens vendors like Tamron, Sigma, and Tokina have come to the rescue. Extra-wide lenses are now readily available, and at somewhat lower prices. My favorite is a 10-17mm fisheye zoom lens from Tokina (by way of the Pentax optical labs). It allows me to take ultra-wide shots I never could get before.

Dirt and dust? Automatic cleaning has arrived!

Virtually all current dSLRs have automatic cleaning features, which relieve your sensor of the dust and dirt that infiltrates your camera each time you swap lenses. While this dirt is often invisible in your final photos, you'll see it in large, plain, light-colored areas of your image (such as the sky) in photos taken with smaller f-stops (which provide extra depth of field that brings the dust into sharp focus). In the past, many of us faced a weekly or monthly chore of locking open our shutters and cleaning the sensor with a blast of air, a brush, or a swab moistened with a cleaning fluid.

Today, your sensor probably shakes off that dust automatically every time you turn your camera on or off (or both.) The frequent cleaning regimen is a thing of the past. You may still need to manually dust off your sensor every six months or so, and the process induces panic the first time you need to do it, but it's really easy and will be something you need to do only rarely.

No movies? Not always!

One digital SLR from Nikon allows creating *stop motion* movies right in the camera. You can assemble your silent movie from a continuous series, edit the clip, and view it on the camera's LCD, or you can transport the mini-film to your computer. Other dSLR vendors should offer a similar feature soon.

Of course, dSLRs still can't take true motion pictures like those possible with many digital snapshooting cameras. Most point-and-shoot models can take movies with sound at TV-quality 640 x 480 pixels at 30 frames per second (fps). Although most of these cameras will never replace a true camcorder, it's handy to have this capability for spur-of-the-moment movie clips. Alas, the fastest professional dSLR is capable of snapping shots at no more than about 8 fps and would be mechanically incapable of shooting 30 fps movies even at a drastically reduced resolution. If you want real movies *and* dSLR stills, you're going to have to carry two cameras.

Too much weight and size? The gap is narrowing!

Digital SLR cameras still can't be slipped into a pocket — unless you're a kangaroo — but the smallest weigh not much more than the largest of their non-SLR counterparts. Electronic-viewfinder and superzoom cameras can be huge, too. Some dSLRs are smaller than others, and the latest from Nikon, Canon, Pentax, and Olympus are truly petite. If you want to have a camera with you at all times (and you should!), you'll need to get one of these smaller dSLR models or buy a second, ultracompact snapshooting camera as a constant companion.

How Digital SLRs Work

As you might expect, there are some differences in the way digital SLRs capture pictures. Knowing a little of the inside dope on these cameras can help you understand how best to use their features.

Like their non-SLR counterparts, digital SLRs rely on sensors composed of an array of pixels. But because the sensors are larger in a dSLR, the pixels are larger, so most 12-megapixel dSLRs produce sharper and more noise-free results than 12-megapixel non-dSLRs. Some dSLRs even outperform other dSLRs with greater resolution because of the quality of the sensors, lenses, or electronic circuitry. So, with dSLRs as with other types of digital cameras, the raw number of megapixels is only a guideline, even though more pixels is often better.

You might not actually need all that extra resolution, especially when you consider that every million pixels you stuff into a digital SLR adds up to a more expensive camera that might not actually give you better results. Those extra pixels fill up your memory cards: My first dSLR could fit 150 highest-resolution photos on a 1GB CompactFlash card; my newest requires a 4GB card for 190 photos.

In the same vein, I had to upgrade my hard drive to store those larger images and switch from CD to DVD and external hard drives for archiving. Those bigger photo files take longer to transfer from my card reader to my computer, and I needed more RAM and a faster processor to edit them in my image editor. The demands of multiple megapixels probably won't dissuade you from buying that advanced camera you've been lusting after, but you should keep the equipment requirements of your upgrade in mind.

You'll find that the components of a dSLR are very similar to what you find in the generic digital camera I describe in Book I, Chapter 1. To recap, digital SLRs include the following parts (shown in Figure 1-4):

- **Lens:** This optical component captures light and focuses it on your sensor. Usually, a lens on a digital camera is of the *zoom* variety, which can change focal lengths at your command to provide more or less magnification of the image. However, with a dSLR, the lens may also be a fixed focal length or *prime* lens. (See Book II, Chapter 3 for more information.) Digital SLR lenses are removable and interchangeable.

- **Aperture:** This opening inside the lens can be adjusted to allow more or less light to reach the viewfinder and sensor. Non-SLR cameras may offer only a very limited number of apertures (or *f-stops*), sometimes only one in addition to the maximum aperture (the largest lens opening available). Lenses for dSLRs usually include a full range, from the largest (often f/2.8 or larger) to the smallest (frequently f/22 or smaller).

- **Viewing system:** Non-SLR cameras may have an optical window to supplement the back-panel LCD that provides an image of what the sensor sees. As I mention earlier in this chapter, older dSLRs have no such LCD preview but instead use a mirror that bounces the light received from the lens to other mirrors or to a prism for inspection through what is called an *eye-level viewfinder.* This system requires some mechanism for flipping the mirror out of the way when the picture is taken, plus a ground-glass or plastic focusing screen that the reflected image is formed on. Newer dSLRs offer an option called Live View that provides a real-time preview of the image that will be taken.

- **Shutter:** Non-SLR cameras usually control the length of the exposure with an electronic shutter, which briefly sensitizes the sensor and then turns it off. Digital SLRs, too, often use an electronic shutter for the very briefest shutter speeds, usually those no longer than 1/180 to 1/500 of a second — the slowest electronic shutter speed varies from dSLR to dSLR. But these cameras also use a mechanical shutter located just in front of the sensor (at the *focal plane)* that exposes the sensor for a period of time by opening a curtain that travels over the surface of the sensor, followed by a second curtain that makes the same trip to cover the sensor back up. This focal plane shutter handles exposures from 30 seconds or longer down to 1/180 to 1/500 of a second (depending on the camera).

✔ **Sensor:** All digital cameras use a sensor, as described in Book I, Chapter 1. Digital SLR sensors are larger, more sensitive to light, and produce less noise at a given sensitivity setting.

✔ **Storage:** A digital SLR has very fast internal memory, called a *buffer,* which accepts each image (actually, a series of images, enabling your dSLR to take one picture after another). Like other types of digital cameras, the dSLR also has a removable memory card, usually a CompactFlash, SD, or xD Picture Card, that stores the images as they are written from the buffer.

**Book II
Chapter 1**

**The Digital SLR
Advantage**

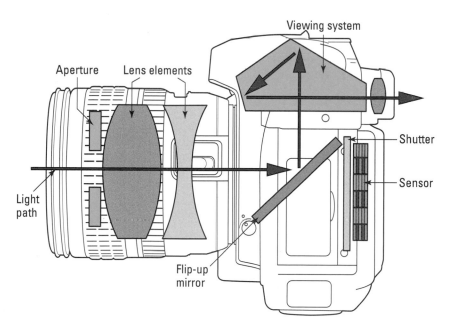

Figure 1-4: Parts of a digital SLR.

The size and speed of your digital camera's buffer and the writing speed of the memory card determine how many pictures you can take in a row. Digital point-and-shoot cameras generally let you take between 5 and 30 shots consecutively and in continuous bursts of about 2.5 to 8 frames per second. When your buffer fills, the camera stops taking pictures. However, as the buffer fills, the dSLR will simultaneously write some of the pictures to your memory card, freeing up space for more pictures. So, a faster memory card (they are measured in relative speed, such as 40X, 80X, 133X, and 300X) allows you to take more pictures consecutively, making your camera's built-in buffer that much more effective.

Managing dSLR Quirks

Earlier in this chapter, I describe the differences between a dSLR and a non-SLR camera. Whether you call them quirks, idiosyncrasies, or foibles, most of these differences, like the faster operation and lack of shutter lag, are advantages that you can benefit from. Others, such as lack of an LCD preview if you have an older dSLR, are things you must simply get used to. But other dSLR quirks command a bit of your attention. The three most demanding idiosyncrasies are detailed in the following sections.

Noise about noise

If you date back to the film era, you might recall that film came in various speeds or sensitivities, represented by ISO ratings. (ISO is the name chosen by the International Organization for Standardization, but it isn't an acronym.) You probably purchased an ISO 200 film for everyday use, perhaps a slower ISO 100 product when you wanted a less grainy picture or because you believed these films provided better quality. If you planned to shoot under low light levels or needed fast shutter speeds, you might have purchased an ISO 400 film.

Digital camera sensitivity is measured in ISO-equivalent settings, too, but, in truth, each digital sensor has only one *actual* ISO sensitivity — usually the lowest setting available for that camera. This minimum ISO setting varies from ISO 50 to about ISO 200, depending on the camera. All other ISO settings are created by amplifying the signal captured by the sensor, so photons that were almost too dim to register are electronically beefed up to become full-fledged pixels.

Unfortunately, at the same time, non-photons are mistaken for true pixels and assigned pixel-hood even though they don't deserve it. These bogus pixels are what photographers call *noise,* and unless you *want* a grainy look to your photos, noise is usually a bad thing. Noise appears in your pictures as multi-colored flecks that look like grainy, irregular dots.

Other factors cause noise, too. If an exposure is very long, some spurious pixels can be produced, often because the sensor heats up after being sensitized for a long period (about a second or more). Some kinds of electrical interference can also produce noise in your images.

Non-SLR cameras are the worst in the noise department, which is why most snapshooting cameras do their best work at ISO 400; although a few cameras now go all the way up to ISO 1600–3200 (with mixed results). Digital SLRs have a distinct advantage. They have larger pixels, which are more sensitive to light because they have more area to capture photons. So, virtually all digital SLRs can be used at ISO 800 with little noise, and many go up to ISO 3200. The very best performers tend to be the full-frame dSLRs, such as the Canon EOS 1Ds Mark III and Nikon D3, which have the largest pixels of all.

If you're new to dSLRs, you may be unfamiliar with the possibilities of high ISO shooting and, in particular, the relative image quality your own camera produces at various ISO settings. Take the time to capture a few shots at each available setting to find out what your dSLR can and can't do.

You'll want to figure out how to use your camera's noise reduction (NR) features to reduce problems like those shown in Figure 1-5. Depending on the model you own, NR may be applied automatically to high ISO settings but be optional for longer exposures. Or your camera may have separate user-defined settings for each type of noise. Excessive noise reduction can reduce the amount of detail in your image, so you should find out exactly how to use your camera's NR features. You'll also want to find out how to apply noise reduction after the picture was taken by using software like Adobe Camera Raw, Noise Ninja, or the filter built into Photoshop.

The real dirt on sensors

It might take awhile, especially if your camera has automatic sensor cleaning, but eventually you'll get some dust on your dSLR sensor that absolutely has to be removed manually. A camera's automatic sensor-shaking cleaning can only go so far, and some kinds of dust are sticky and stubborn. Don't panic! The process isn't difficult or dangerous, but you can take steps to minimize the number of times you'll have to clean your sensor.

- **Minimize dust entry.** If you point your camera downward when changing lenses, dust particles are less likely to settle into the mirror compartment.

- **Don't provide dust with a safe haven.** Make sure the mounts of your lenses and the rear lens elements are clean and dust-free when you attach a lens to your camera.

- **Think clean.** Try to change lenses in relatively clean environments. Avoid dusty rooms or gusty outdoor locations.

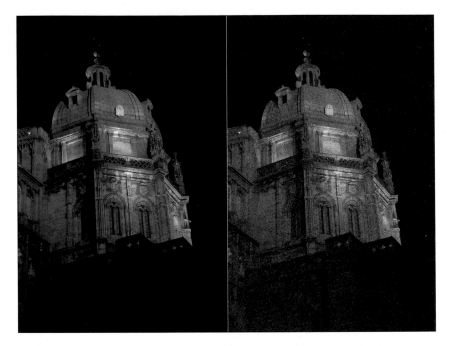

Figure 1-5: A long exposure at a high ISO (left) with noise reduction applied is not contaminated by the multicolored specks we call noise, seen in the example at right.

✔ **Minimize the time your camera is lensless.** Have your new lens ready to mount, with the rear cap off but placed loosely on the back of the lens. Then, remove the lens that's already on your camera, set it down, and immediately take the rear lens cap off the new lens. (Set it on the back of the old lens if you can do it quickly.) Then pick up the lens to be mounted and fasten it as quickly as you can. It's okay to leave the old lens naked for a few seconds if you're careful — you can always clean dust that settles on it later. The goal is to get the old lens off and the new one attached as quickly as possible.

Do a Google search for *"Sensor Cleaning"* to find extensive discussions on the various ways of cleaning digital SLR sensors. You can use specially designed bulb blowers to waft the dust off, certain types of soft brushes to remove more firmly attached particles, and moist swabs to get the really stubborn artifacts off. Don't use general-purpose products intended for cleaning lenses or your vehicle's dashboard. Your Google quest will provide

Managing dSLR Quirks **125**

all the information you need to do it right. (I also include a long discussion of the process in *Digital SLR Cameras & Photography For Dummies*.)

Going in crop factor circles

As I note earlier in this chapter, many digital SLR cameras use a sensor that is smaller than the 35mm film frame. Even so, many vendors (Olympus is a notable exception) rely at least partially on lenses that were originally designed for these full-frame film cameras. Although many digital-only lenses are being introduced, there is still a momentum of thinking of optics in terms of the 24mm x 36mm format.

That means that if you cut your teeth on 35mm cameras, the apparent focal lengths of your dSLR camera's lenses are likely to seem wrong to you. The smaller sensors cause the image to be cropped, so a 50mm normal lens becomes a mild telephoto. A 105mm portrait lens that you used to take head-and-shoulder shots with a film camera might not be such a good choice for portraits anymore. (For one thing, you'll have to take a few steps backward to keep your subject within the frame.)

Book II
Chapter 1

The Digital SLR Advantage

And, of course, your wide-angle lenses might not be so wide when cropped by your sensor. This effect is sometimes called, inaccurately, a *multiplication factor* or lens *multiplier* because the easiest way of representing the effect on the camera's field of view is by multiplying the focal length of the lens by the factor. A 100mm lens becomes a 150mm lens with a camera that has a 1.5X crop factor.

Of course, in truth, no multiplication is involved. That 100mm lens is still a 100mm lens and has the same depth of field. Your 180mm f/2.8 optic isn't magically transformed into an amazing 360mm f/2.8 super-telephoto. You could get the same effect and look by shooting a picture on a full-frame camera and then cropping it. That's why the correct terminology for this effect is *crop factor*. Common crop factors with today's dSLRs are 1.3X, 1.5X/1.6X, and 2X, as shown in Figure 1-6.

As a dSLR user, you need to become accustomed to thinking about this factor as it really is — as a crop rather than multiplication factor. That will help you better understand what is going on in your camera, although it won't eliminate all the confusion that results from trying to equate your 70mm to 200mm (actual focal length) lens with what it really is in dSLR terms. The good news is that you'll eventually get used to the crop factor and begin thinking of 30mm as a normal lens focal range and a 50mm lens as a portrait lens before you know it.

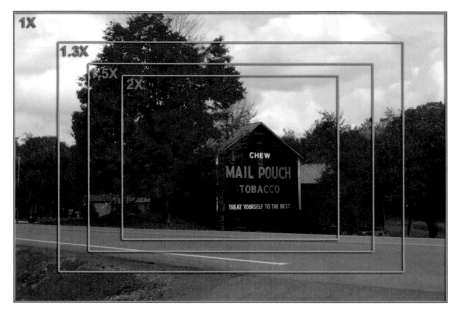

Figure 1-6: Crop factors change the effective view of your dSLR's lens.

Chapter 2: Mastering Digital SLR Controls

In This Chapter

⌐ **Dealing with exposure follies**

⌐ **Mastering focus features**

⌐ **Understanding other controls**

*D*igital SLR cameras have many more controls, buttons, dials, and options than their non-SLR counterparts. If you bought a dSLR because you wanted to take control of your photography and gain access to customization features that let you produce photos with the exact color rendition, sharpness, and focus you want, the additional layers of settings are a great thing. No other type of digital camera gives you access to so many different shooting parameters that you can use to optimize image quality or to manipulate your photos in creative ways.

Of course, if you bought your dSLR because you wanted a big, impressive-looking camera to overwhelm your friends with your photography prowess, you have some studying ahead of you. If they laugh when you sit down at the piano, they'll *really* be amused if you don't know how to tickle the keys and buttons of your shiny new dSLR!

One great thing about dSLRs is that you probably won't have to wade through menus to adjust many settings. These cameras frequently have dedicated (or multifunction) buttons for given types of settings, so all you need to do is press the button and twist a dial or thumb a cursor control. That's much faster!

In this chapter, I explain some of the key controls you use with your dSLR, with an emphasis on the more advanced things you can do with a dSLR.

Exposure Controls

Point-and-shoot cameras don't always give you much input into adjusting exposure. You point; you shoot. If you're daring, you look at the results on your LCD and, if dissatisfied, rinse, lather, and repeat (or the photographic equivalent). You have a dozen or two scene modes that can adjust exposure and some other settings based on the kind of picture you're taking (for example, Beach, Night, or Portrait). You probably also have exposure value (EV) settings that can increase or decrease the exposure a bit. A higher-end model might have aperture priority, shutter priority, and manual exposure modes.

As you'd expect, digital SLRs have the same roster of exposure controls found in even the most advanced non-SLR digital cameras (although a few dSLRs eschew the only semi-useful scene modes or trim their roster drastically to five or six basic scene options). But dSLRs give you a lot more to work with, too, because, while getting a good exposure is relatively easy, getting the *best* exposure can be tricky. For dSLR owners who are serious about photography, good is rarely good enough.

No camera can capture every tone available in a scene. The range from the darkest detailed picture elements to the brightest is called the *dynamic range,* and the goal of proper exposure is to make sure that the most important tones in an image fall into that range.

Metering modes

All digital cameras have built-in routines that let the camera read the lightness and darkness values from a range of locations (or *matrix*) in the scene and calculate the best compromise in terms of exposure. The most advanced cameras, including dSLRs, let you choose how the information is gathered and interpreted. So, your camera will offer a choice of metering modes:

- **Matrix metering:** This is usually the default mode. The camera collects information from multiple locations in the scene, which can range from a dozen or so to more than 1,000 locations, as shown in Figure 2-1. The camera's programming can use this information to guess what kind of picture you're shooting and set exposure accordingly. For example, if the matrix system determines that the upper half of your image is light and the bottom half is dark, it may decide that you're shooting a landscape and will optimize exposure so there will be detail in the foreground, allowing the sky to be a little too light, if necessary.

- **Center-weighted metering:** In this mode, the camera puts the most emphasis on the information in the center of the scene, but it takes into account the illumination in the rest of the frame. This mode is a good choice if you know your main subject will be in the middle of the frame but the other areas of the picture have some importance, too.

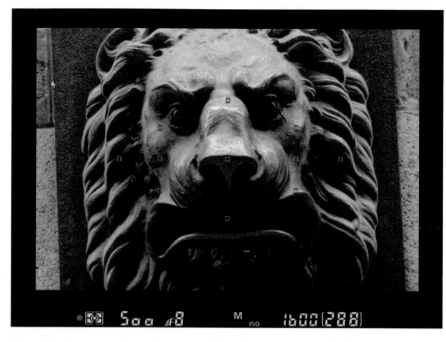

Figure 2-1: Exposure info may be gathered from a few locations or, as in this figure, from more than 1,000 invisible points arranged in a matrix.

✔ **Spot metering:** In spot mode, the camera derives its exposure setting exclusively from an area in the center of the frame. This setting is a good choice at, say, a concert, where you want to expose for the spot-lit performer and don't want the inky dark surroundings to affect the settings.

Correcting exposure

Digital SLRs have an adjustment system called EV (exposure value) compensation. (Other kinds of digital cameras often have EV settings, too, but they are sometimes buried down in the menu system.) With dSLRs, this adjustment is easy to apply: You simply press the EV button on your camera (usually it's on the top panel) and use a command dial or left/right cursor key to add more exposure (+EV) or reduce exposure (–EV) using 1/2 or 1/3-value increments. (+0.5 EV gives 150 percent of the metered exposure, +1.0 EV provides 200 percent, and so forth.)

You can determine whether to add or subtract EV by reviewing an image you've just taken on the LCD or by reviewing a picture's histogram, which can be displayed on the LCD along with the image itself. (You usually must activate this option in a menu setting.)

A *histogram* is a bar chart with 256 vertical bars spaced very closely together, usually forming a curve that looks like a mountain, with a high peak in the middle, trailing off to foothills at the left and right. All you really need to know to use a histogram is that the left side of the chart represents the darkest tones in your image, the right side represents the lightest tones, and the middle hump represents the tones in between.

Your goal is to produce a histogram in which the entire "mountain" is solidly in the center of the chart, with none of the dark tones lost at the left side or light tones at the right. If you look at a histogram of your most recent shot carefully, you can learn to add a little exposure (+EV) when the dark tones are cut off at the left side, or subtract a little (–EV) when the light tones are cut off on the right side. (See Figure 2-2.)

Other exposure adjustments

You have several other options for changing your camera's exposure setting:

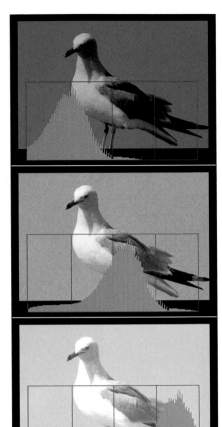

Figure 2-2: An underexposed image (top), correctly exposed image (middle), and overexposed image (bottom).

- ✔ **Scene modes:** Scene modes are the modes offered on many digital SLRs that are similar to the scene options found in other digital cameras. They set up your camera to use specific exposure options (for example, long exposures for Night scene or Night Portrait mode), set shutter speed and/or aperture preferences for action in Sports mode, as well as adjust parameters such as color richness and sharpness.

- ✔ **Exposure lock:** The exposure settings are fixed when you press a special exposure lock button or simply press the shutter release down halfway. Such a lock gives you the freedom to set exposure and then reframe the photo any way you like without worrying that the settings will change. Using a separate button has an advantage because you don't have to keep your finger on the release button.

✔ **Bracketing:** *Bracketed pictures* are a series of photos, with one taken at a particular setting, another taken at a plus setting, and another taken at a minus setting. The plus/minus factors can be exposure, color saturation, color balance, and flash exposure. Your camera might allow you to bracket more than one of these settings and in the order you choose.

✔ **Shifting equivalent exposures:** Most dSLRs allow you to choose equivalent exposures without changing the actual amount of light that reaches the sensor. For example, if the meter chooses 1/500 of a second at f/11, you might be able to flip to 1/1000 of a second at f/8 (which is the same effective exposure with a faster shutter speed for stopping action) or 1/250 of a second at f/16 (which is also equivalent but provides more depth of field).

Shooting modes

Metering modes, which I describe earlier in this chapter, are the options for collecting exposure information and calculating an exposure. *Shooting modes* tell your camera how to apply that information. These modes are the exposure options most used by dSLR owners:

✔ **Auto:** Full auto mode handles all the settings for you, with (often) no options for adjustment. This is the mode you use when you hand your camera to a passerby and ask to have your picture taken. No fuss, no muss, no options.

✔ **Programmed:** Your dSLR uses its built-in smarts to analyze your scene and recommend exposure. However, you can override the camera's selections with EV settings, equivalent exposure shifts, or other tweaks.

✔ **Shutter priority:** You choose the shutter speed, and the camera locks it in, which makes this a good choice for sports shots like the one shown in Figure 2-3. The autoexposure system keeps the shutter speed you've chosen and varies *only* the aperture to achieve correct exposure. You also see the selected aperture in the viewfinder so that you can decide when, say, the f-stop is getting a little too large for comfort and you want to accept a slower shutter speed to gain a smaller aperture. Should light conditions change enough that your selected shutter speed won't produce a correct exposure with the available f-stops, you're alerted with a LO or HI indicator in the viewfinder or, perhaps, a flashing LED.

✔ **Aperture priority:** This mode lets you choose the f-stop, letting the camera select the shutter speed needed for correct exposure. Perhaps you want a small aperture to maximize depth of field or a large f-stop to minimize it. If you notice that the shutter speed is too slow or high, you can adjust the f-stop you've dialed in to one that's larger or smaller.

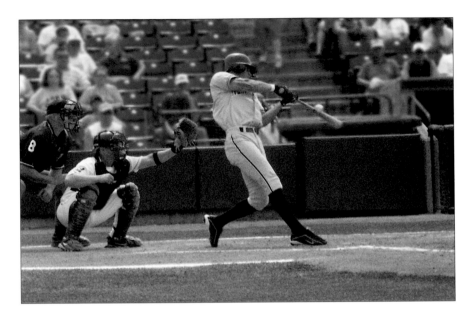

Figure 2-3: Shutter priority lets you lock in a high shutter speed to freeze action.

✔ **Manual exposure:** Use manual exposure when you want to set both the shutter speed and aperture yourself. Don't worry! You're not on your own and forced to guesstimate exposure. You can still use your dSLR's metering system to determine the correct exposure and then set it yourself — or set some other exposure entirely for a special effect.

Manual exposure is a good choice if you're using a non-automatic flash unit or an older lens that doesn't allow automatic exposure with your camera.

Focus Controls

Correct focus is important because, although you can often at least partially correct for bad exposure after a shot is taken, there isn't a lot you can do when your picture is blurred beyond recognition. Point-and-shooters actually have *less* of a problem with correct focus (in one way) than dSLR users do because the short focal length lenses on cheaper cameras render almost everything in sharp focus. Of course, that makes using selective focus (creatively placing parts of an image out of focus to emphasize other portions) more difficult, but you win some and lose some.

Digital SLRs give you back selective focus, while making it more critical to focus correctly. Fortunately, you have two ways to focus — manual focus and autofocus. Manual focus is accomplished by twisting a focus ring on the lens until the image looks sharp in your viewfinder. (Some cameras provide a viewfinder signal when you have focused correctly manually.) Automatic focus achieves the same results but with the camera deciding when the image is sharply focused. In both cases, the apparent contrast between your subject and its (relatively) blurry surroundings is used to determine that focus point.

Manual focus can be difficult when you're shooting moving objects (think sports) or are in a hurry for any reason. Our brains have a poor memory for sharpness, so it takes awhile for us to decide that the current setting is, in fact, sharper than the image we saw just a fraction of a second ago. The camera's autofocus mechanism has no problem comparing relative sharpness and can zero in on the right focus point very quickly — assuming the camera actually knows what object you *want* to be in sharp focus in the first place.

So, manual focus can be your best choice when you want to focus on a particular object that might be difficult for the autofocus system to lock in on because, say, it's surrounded by similar-looking objects or confusing backgrounds, or you want to isolate a particular subject, like the one in Figure 2-4.

**Book II
Chapter 2**

**Mastering Digital
SLR Controls**

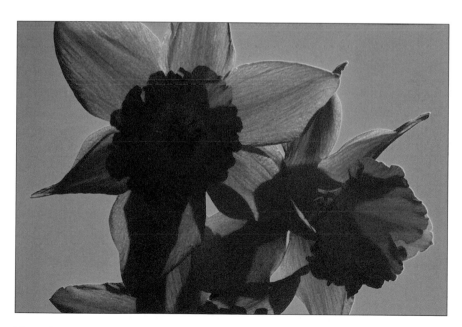

Figure 2-4: Manual focus is a good choice when you want to focus on a particular object precisely.

Automatic focus can work for you the rest of the time, particularly when you can use your dSLR's ability to choose which of several different focus zones to use. Most dSLRs have five to nine (or more) focus sensors grouped around the viewfinder screen. You can tell the camera how to use those zones or manually select a zone yourself. It's also possible to tell the camera *when* to lock in focus by using one of two common focus modes:

- **Continuous autofocus:** When you press the shutter release halfway, the camera sets the focus but continues to look for movement within the frame. If the camera detects motion, the lens refocuses on the new position. Use this option for action photography or other subjects that are likely to be in motion.

- **Single autofocus:** Press the shutter release halfway, and focus is set. It remains at that setting until you take the photo or release the button. This mode is best suited for subject matter that isn't likely to move after it has been brought into sharp focus, and for reframing a subject slightly without having the camera change the focus.

Other Controls

Your digital SLR has other controls that may be less used with other kinds of digital cameras or that are more important to dSLR owners who want optimal results. These controls include

- **White balance fine-tuning:** Digital SLRs let you fine-tune white balance (color balance) much more precisely. Instead of simply choosing a white balance from among a half-dozen preset values, you can often set the white balance based on an existing photograph, choose a specific color temperature, tweak white balance slightly toward blue or red, and measure actual white balance from a neutral surface such as a white wall or gray card.

- **ISO settings:** Digital SLRs usually let you set sensitivity in much finer increments and to much more sensitive levels (say ISO 1600 or ISO 3200) than other types of digital cameras.

- **Image compression:** Digital SLRs almost always allow you to choose from several different levels of squeezing (compressing) for JPEG image files, so you can select from large files with optimum quality and smaller files that may lose a little quality during the squishing process.

- **Camera functions:** You'll find that digital SLRs are customizable in the way the controls operate, and you might even be able to adjust what certain buttons do. You can tailor how long your LCD remains on after picture display and how many seconds of display your self-timer provides. You can also assign certain functions to particular buttons or even dictate how large the spot focus circle in the center of the viewfinder is. While some non-SLR cameras may also offer some of these customization controls, few have the extensive range found in dSLR cameras.

Chapter 3: Working with Lenses

In This Chapter

✔ **The myth of the do-it-all lens**

✔ **Choosing prime lenses or zoom lenses**

✔ **Special features you might like**

*A*ll digital cameras have lenses, of course. Digital SLR owners just have more of them to choose from. The ability to change lenses is one of the top advantages of the digital single-lens reflex camera, especially for those who want to go longer, wider, deeper, or closer or want to shoot in less light. If the lens currently mounted on your camera doesn't do what you want, just remove it and replace it with one that does (assuming you have the funds to *afford* your dream optics).

This chapter concentrates on the special things you can do with the interchangeable lenses available for dSLRs.

Optical Allusions

You'll find references to a disease called *lens lust* all over the Internet. It's that strange malady that strikes dSLR owners when they discover just how much more they could do if they just had this or that particular lens.

Unfortunately, no single lens can do every job, although a few come close. Several vendors offer an 18mm to 200mm zoom lens (one of them, shown in Figure 3-1, with camera-shake-nullifying vibration reduction built in) that covers most of the focal lengths you need for everyday shooting. But even that lens won't give you ultra-wide-angle shots or superzoom perspectives, and it won't operate well at light levels that call for a large maximum aperture (say, f/2 or f/1.4).

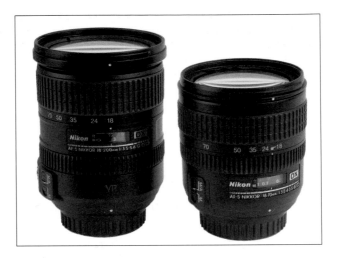

Figure 3-1: An 18–200mm lens with built-in vibration reduction (left) and a less expensive 18–70mm lens furnished with several digital SLRs as basic equipment.

So choosing the right lens is important when you want the best lens for a particular job. Here are some of the things that the right lens can do for you:

- **Shoot in low light.** The basic zooms furnished with most digital SLRs have maximum apertures of f/3.5 to f/4.5, which is much too slow to be useful in low light levels. You can choose other zooms with f/2.8 maximum apertures (although they tend to be expensive) or select a fixed-focal-length lens with an f/1.4 to f/2.0. Some of these, such as the 50mm f/1.8 lenses offered for most cameras, can be very cheap — $100 or less. But if you're able to spend a little more, you can buy 28mm, 30mm, 35mm, 50mm, or 85mm f/1.4 lenses that can shoot under very dark conditions. They'll be optimized to produce pretty good results wide open, too.

- **Shoot sharper.** You can often get better results with a special lens that was designed to produce sharper images rather than to do everything passably well. That 50mm f/1.8 lens you pick up for less than $100 just might be the sharpest lens you own. Or you might buy a close-up lens that's optimized for macro photography and produces especially sharp images at distances of a few inches or so.

- **Shoot wider.** Wide-angle lenses let you take in a broader field of view, which can be useful when there isn't room to move farther away from your subject. The lens that came with your camera probably has a field of view no wider than that of a 28mm lens on a full-frame film SLR. You can get a wider look from lenses designed to provide that extra-broad perspective with a dSLR.

- **Shoot farther.** Telephoto lenses let you bring distant objects that much closer to your camera, as you can see in Figure 3-2. The lens that came with your camera probably provides only a moderate telephoto effect, perhaps around 70mm, which, with a 1.5 crop factor, is the equivalent of a 105mm short telephoto on a full-frame 35mm film camera. Longer lenses are easy to find, fairly affordable, and fun to use when you want to reach out and almost touch something.

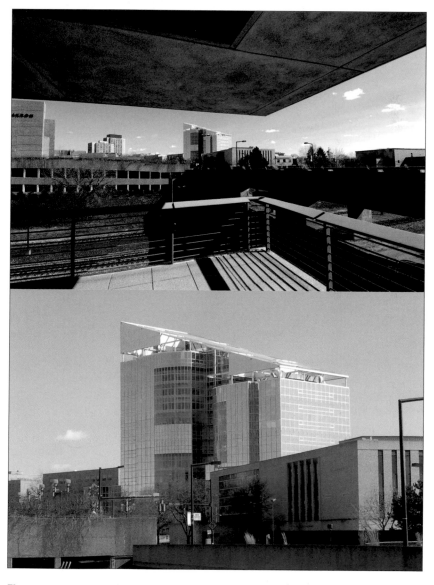

Figure 3-2: A wide-angle lens provides a broader view (top), while a telephoto lens takes you up close to your subject (bottom).

✔ **Shoot closer.** An interchangeable lens that you buy may be able to focus on subjects a lot closer to the lens, giving you valuable close-up or *macro* capabilities. Macro photography is literally a whole new world, encompassing subjects that you couldn't capture before (such as small animals or insects), as well as new ultra-close looks at familiar objects.

Primes or Zooms

Digital SLRs can use one of two basic kinds of lenses: prime lenses and zooms. *Prime lenses* are fixed-focal-length lenses, the kind that were the mainstay of photographers years ago before *zooms* (variable-focal-length lenses) became as sophisticated as they are today. Because prime lenses were the best, sharpest, and fastest optics available, it was even common for photographers to carry around two or three camera bodies, each with a different lens, to avoid having to swap lenses.

Today, zoom lenses are sharper, faster, and more practical for all-around use, but they still lag a bit behind their prime lens cousins. Your own lens kit will probably end up containing a few of each type, each suitable for a different kind of photography.

Pros for primes

Primes have their advantages. For example, if you shoot architecture, you might want a fast wide-angle lens to let you shoot interiors without a tripod or capture images from unusual angles with less lens distortion, as shown in Figure 3-3. Sports photographers might want a similar wide-angle lens for indoor sports such as basketball, mated with a fast telephoto prime lens for night football or baseball under the lights. If you plan on shooting portraits destined for display on the wall, you'll want a sharp, short telephoto lens. Prime lenses with close-focusing capabilities are great for macro work. Wide-angle prime lenses produce results that are sharp enough to enlarge to 20 x 30 inches for display as home décor.

The main drawbacks of using prime lenses is that you must buy a bunch of different lenses to cover a range of focal lengths — plus you must be willing to swap lenses whenever you need to shoot something that doesn't suit the lens currently mounted on the camera. Digital SLR owners can be leery of changing lenses often, especially when working in dusty environments, because of the danger of getting dust on the sensor.

Primes or Zooms **139**

Pros for zooms

There's a lot to like about zoom lenses, too. They are convenient and flexible, allowing you to shoot several different magnifications without moving, so you can frame your photo carefully and precisely right in the camera. That's important when you don't want to waste valuable pixels by cropping later in an image editor.

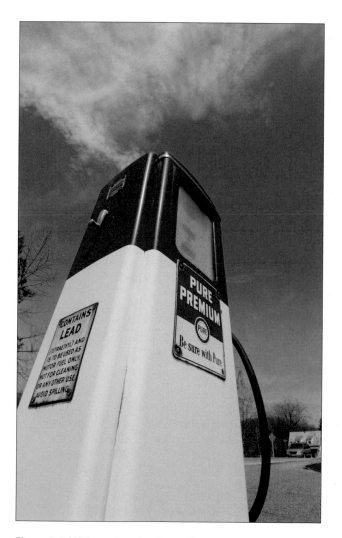

Figure 3-3: Wide-angle prime lenses let you capture photos from unusual angles.

Zooms come in several types, which I discuss in the list that follows.

- **Wide-angle zooms** have focal lengths like 10–20mm or 12–24mm. Depending on the crop factor of your camera, these offer the equivalent of 15–30mm to 18–36mm lenses on a full-frame film or digital camera. Because of the distorted looks that these super-wides can sometimes provide, they are often relegated to special situations that truly require an ultra-wide perspective.

- **Mid-range zooms** are more general purpose. These have ranges that start at 17–18mm and extend out to 55–70mm at the telephoto end. They're usually much less expensive than other types of zooms and may be furnished with your camera at an incremental cost of only $100 or so above the cost of the camera body alone. Expect the maximum aperture to shift as you zoom out; such a zoom may offer an f/3.5 opening at the wide-angle end, but only f/4.5 in the telephoto range.

- **Short telephoto to telephoto zooms** sacrifice the wide-angle end of the range to give you a telephoto reach that may extend to 200mm or 300mm. Several popular lenses go from 28mm to 200 or 300mm. The affordable models suffer from the same limited maximum aperture as the mid-range zooms.

- **Telephoto zoom lenses** cover only a telephoto range and tend to extend to much longer focal lengths. One of my favorite lenses is a 170–500mm zoom (although the same vendor also offers a very good 50–500mm version that is highly prized but much more expensive). Other popular telephoto zooms have ranges like 200–400mm. As with all very long lenses, you'd be crazy to use one of these without a tripod or other sturdy support.

- **Macro zooms** are a specialized kind of zoom lens, usually in the medium telephoto range (from about 100mm–200mm), that can focus especially close. You'll find these lenses useful outdoors for shooting small animals and insects that must be photographed from a few feet away but that require extra-close focusing. As your critter flits or hops around, you can follow him with your macro zoom while still remaining far enough away to keep him from becoming skittish. The same lens will work with non-moving objects like flowers, too.

Special Features

Some lenses have special features that let them do things that other types of lenses cannot do. Here's a summary of some of those capabilities that are common (or uncommon) among add-on lenses:

- **Image stabilization:** Referred to variously as *image stabilization* (by Canon and some other vendors . . . and me), *vibration reduction* (by Nikon and allied companies), *anti-shake* (Sony), *optical image stabilization* (Sigma), and other names, this feature operates by shifting lens elements or the sensor itself to nullify the shakiness that can result when the camera or photographer wobbles during exposure. Image stabilization can give you the equivalent of two to three shutter speed increments more steadiness, so you can shoot at 1/30 of a second instead of 1/250 of a second — or with a long telephoto, 1/250 of a second instead of 1/2000 of a second.

  Image stabilization does *not* counteract a moving subject and may actually slow down your camera a little when shooting sports. You'll still need a fast shutter speed for that kind of work.

  You'll find image stabilization in the lens only (with Nikon and Canon products), or included in the camera body (with all other vendors offering the feature). The advantage of in-lens stabilization is that it can be optimized for the particular lens. In-body stabilization is nice because it transforms every lens you own into an anti-shake component.

- **Perspective control:** These highly specialized and expensive lenses shift the lens elements from side to side and up and down to improve the perspective when photographing buildings or other subjects that converge in the distance, reducing that falling backward look that you see in the top image in Figure 3-4.

- **Close focus:** I've already described the close focusing capabilities of macro lenses. These lenses also offer improved sharpness and may include extra-small apertures (such as f/32 or f/45) to give you extra depth of field.

- **Focus control:** Some very specialized lenses lend themselves to portrait work by letting you adjust how the out-of-focus background appears in photographs in which single subjects are centered in the frame, such as portraits. The effects you get with focus control lenses are unlike those available with any other type of lens.

**Book II
Chapter 3**

**Working with
Lenses**

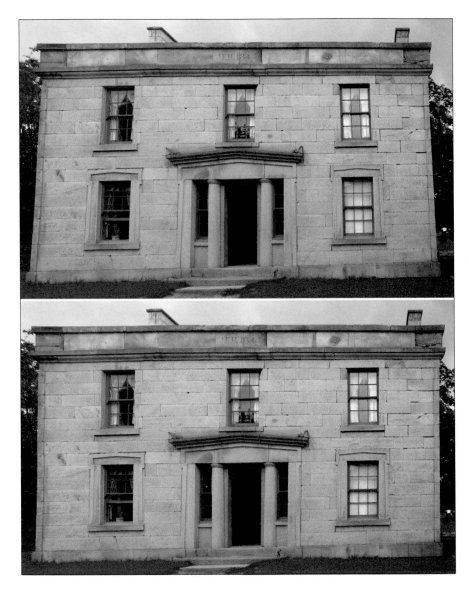

Figure 3-4: Perspective control lenses compensate for distortion from tilting the camera up to take in the top of a building.

Book III
Taking Great Pictures

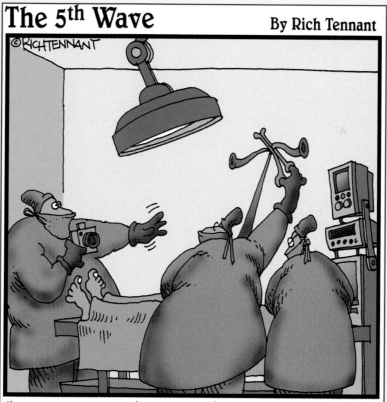

The 5th Wave   By Rich Tennant

"Ooo — wait! That's perfect for the clinic's home page. Just stretch it out a little further...little more..."

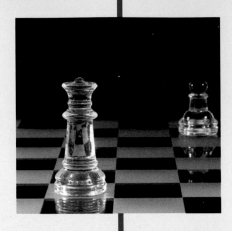

This book is the main course in your digital photography banquet, a sumptuous repast for both veteran and aspiring photographers looking to improve their photographic skills. Each of the six chapters is devoted to a different aspect of digital photography. First, I reveal the basic rules for composing great photos. Then I give you advice on when you should ignore these rules to create even more powerful images. I also provide some tips on dramatic close-up photography and the best ways to produce pleasing portraits of individuals and groups.

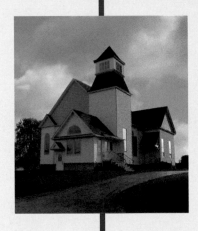

If shooting for publication is on your to-do list, you'll want to read the chapter on taking print-worthy photos, accompanied by tips on how to market your pictures. I also provide meaty chapters on sports and action photography and tips on getting good travel photos as you trot the globe.

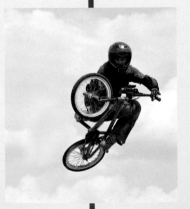

Chapter 1: Tools and Techniques of Composition

In This Chapter

- Developing a picture concept
- Centering on your main subject
- Selecting vertical or horizontal orientations
- Mastering the rule of thirds
- Using lines to draw interest
- Balancing and framing your image
- Avoiding unintentional mergers

Random snapshooting can sometimes yield lucky shots — happy accidents that look good and prompt you to say, "Actually, I *meant* to do that" (even if it wasn't the case). Some Pulitzer Prize–winning photos have resulted from a photographer instinctively squeezing off a shot at what turned out to be a decisive moment in some fast-breaking news event. However, lacking a Pulitzer-winner's intuition, most photographers end up with a larger percentage of pleasing photos when they stop to think about and plan their pictures before putting the viewfinder up to their eyes.

In this chapter, I tell you about the essentials of photo composition that set you on the road to taking great pictures. I introduce the basic elements of good composition, such as selecting what to include in and what to leave out of a well-designed photograph. You find out some basic rules, such as the rule of thirds, and most importantly, you find out when you should ignore these rules in order to get dramatic effect.

Understanding Photo Composition: The Big Picture

One difference between good photojournalists and superior photojournalists is the ability to take a newsworthy picture quickly when circumstances don't allow much time for preparation or thought. If you examine the work of these professionals, you find that even their impromptu shots are well composed. With an instant's notice, they can line up and shoot a picture that commands your attention.

The very best photos are usually not accidents; they are carefully planned and composed. That is, such pictures display good *composition,* which is the careful selection and arrangement of the photo's subject matter within a frame. I'm not suggesting you set up your camera on a tripod and wait hours — à la Ansel Adams — in anticipation of the universe settling into exactly the right arrangement. Instead, simply understanding how good composition works and keeping that in mind when you plan your photos can make a world of difference. The following list gives you an overview of how to plan and execute good photo composition:

- **Visualizing a concept for your picture:** It's important to know what you want your picture to say and who your audience is.

- **Choosing your subject matter:** This isn't as easy as it appears to be. A picture might be filled with interesting things to look at, but you must select which one should be the subject of the picture.

- **Deciding on a center of interest:** One point in the picture should naturally draw the eye as a starting place for the viewer's exploration of the rest of the image. With a center of interest, the photo becomes focused and not simply a collection of objects.

- **Picking the picture orientation:** Some subjects look best when shown in a tall, vertically oriented frame. Some look best in a wide, horizontal format. A few need a square composition. To make the most of your camera's resolution, choose an orientation when you take the photo rather than cropping it later in an image editor.

- **Establishing the distance and point of view:** These elements affect your photo's composition and are sometimes difficult to control. For example, when you're attending that World Series game, you can't easily substitute your upper-deck seats for a choice position next to the dugout (although it's worth a try).

- **Planning for action:** If your subjects are moving, you need to anticipate where they will be and how they will be arranged when you take the picture.

- **Working with the background:** Objects and textures in the background can work for you or against you. The area behind your main subject is an important part of the composition.

✔ **Arranging all within the frame:** How you accomplish arranging within the frame depends on the situation. In some situations, such as at sports events, you can't dictate how the subjects are arranged. For example, no matter how much you want an action shot of Ichiro Suzuki, the Seattle Mariners' star isn't likely to relocate to center field to accommodate your photo.

✔ **Directing the eye within the frame:** Use lines and curves to provide a guided tour of your image, directing the viewer from one portion to another to finally focus on the main center of interest. Balance the composition to keep the eye from wandering to lopsided parts of the image.

Although these guidelines for composition can help you, remember that they are only guidelines. Your instincts and creative sense will tell you when it's a good time to break those rules, grind them up into tiny pieces, and stomp them under your feet in your quest for an unusual, eye-catching picture. If you examine Picasso's earliest art, you'll see that he knew how to paint in the classical style. His legacy is based on knowing when *not* to paint according to the time-honored rules.

Visualizing a Concept for Your Picture

Take some time to visualize your photo before you begin the actual picture-taking process. You don't need to spend hours dwelling over your photo, but you need to have at least a general plan in mind before you shoot. The following sections ask — and then answer — the questions that lead you through the process of visualizing a concept for a picture.

What do you want your image to say?

Will your photo be a portrait, a sports action shot, or a scenic masterpiece? The kind of picture you want to take can affect the composition. For example, portraits of teenagers frequently include props (from skateboards to pigskins) that reflect their lifestyles. For a sports picture, you might want to get a high angle or one from a particular location to include the field of play or other elements that say, "Action!"

A scenic photo can be composed in different ways, depending on what you want the image to say. For example, a photo taken in a national park can picture the grandeur of nature with a dramatic skyline with purple mountains' majesty and amber waves of grain. On the other hand, you might be tempted to make a statement about the environmental impact of humans by focusing on trash left behind by careless visitors or perhaps desiccated amber mountain majesties and chemically tainted waves of purple grain.

**Book III
Chapter 1**

Tools and Techniques of Composition

Some of the best photographs use composition to take a stand or say something beyond the photo itself. Figure 1-1 is an example of a photo that makes a subtle statement, juxtaposing the idyllic academic setting of Kent State University in Ohio today with a stark memorial that shows where the body of a slain student fell. In one sense, it's a less graphic version of those chalk outlines you see on police shows, but it's just as effective as a reminder of a place where a human died.

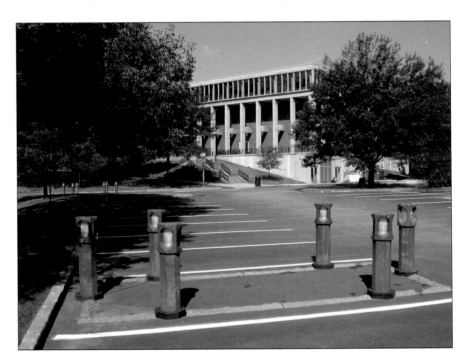

Figure 1-1: A memorial to a slain student stands out against the peaceful, tree-lined campus in the background.

Where will the image be used?

How the photo will be used can affect composition. If you plan to print the picture in a publication or enlarge it for display in a frame, you want a tight composition to maximize sharpness. If you want to use the shot on a Web page, you might want to step back to take in a little extra and crop later with your image editor because the resolution lost from cropping pixels isn't as critical for Web graphics.

Whom are you creating the image for?

You compose a photo for your family differently from a photo that your colleagues or strangers will view. Your family might like a picture better if the composition revolves around that cute new baby. Create a photo that says, "I've been to Paris," and you'll include the Eiffel Tower somewhere in the picture so your family and friends will know where you've been. Colleagues might want to see a product highlighted or the CEO shown in a decisive pose. Subject matter that's extraneous for one audience could be important for another.

Selecting a Subject and a Center of Interest

Photographs shouldn't send the person looking at them on a hunting expedition. As interesting as your subject is to you, you don't want viewers puzzling over what's the most important part of the image or perhaps conducting a vote by secret ballot to see who has successfully guessed your intent. Every picture should have a single, strong center of interest. You want to narrow down your subject matter: Rather than include everything of interest in a photo, choose one main subject. Then find secondary objects in the picture that are also interesting (giving the photo depth and richness) but that are still clearly subordinate to the main subject.

Narrowing your subject matter

Narrowing your subject matter means eliminating everything from your photo that doesn't belong there and concentrating on fewer objects that can form an interesting composition.

Find something in the photograph that the viewer's eye should focus on, thus forming a center of interest. Your center of interest is usually a person, a group, or the object you're seeking to highlight. You don't want eyes roaming around your photo searching for something to look at. Some aspect should jump out and grab your viewers' attention. If other portions of the photo compete for attention, look for ways to eliminate or minimize them.

For example, you can crop more tightly, move to one side or change your angle, ask the extraneous person to leave (your brother-in-law is a good guy; he'll understand), or physically move something to omit it from your composition. Figure 1-2 shows photos of the same goose taken from the same distance but with a clear center of interest in the second shot.

Book III
Chapter 1

Tools and
Techniques of
Composition

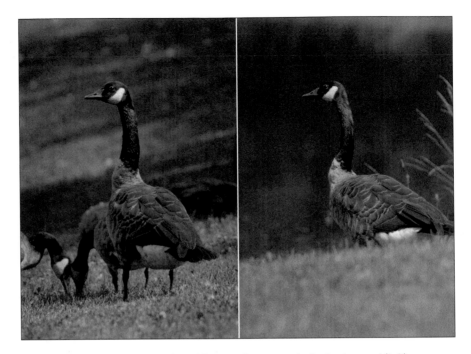

Figure 1-2: To avoid spoiling a shot with secondary geese in the background (left), wait until they move on (right) for a better composition.

One good technique when shooting groups is to plan several photographs, each using a different part of the subject matter in view. That way, each person or object can take a turn at being the center of interest, and you won't be looking for ways to reduce the competition among them.

Choosing one main subject

You can use several compositional techniques to ensure that the main subject you've selected is, in fact, the center of interest. Here's a quick checklist to follow:

- ✔ **Make sure that your center of interest is the most prominent object in the picture.** You might think of Aunt Mary as a worthy photo subject, but if she's standing next to a '60s-era minibus with a psychedelic paint job, she might not even be noticed. Large, distinctive, highly unusual, or controversial objects are likely to take on a life of their own and seize the focus of attention in your photograph.

- ✔ **See that the center of interest is either the brightest object in the photo or at least is not overpowered by a brighter object.** Gaudy colors or bright shapes in the background distract viewers from your main subject. Some elements — such as spotlights at a rock concert or a reflection of the sun on water — become part of the environment and aren't necessarily distracting. Other parts of a photo — such as a bright sail on a boat or a white automobile located behind your subject — can interfere with your carefully planned composition. Eliminate such objects, move them behind something, or otherwise minimize their impact.

✔ **Make sure that your composition has only one center of interest.** Other things in a photo can be interesting, but they must clearly be subsidiary to the main center of interest. A child seated on the floor playing with a puppy would be interesting. However, other puppies in the photo should be watching or vying for the child's interest, not off somewhere else in the photo engaged in some distracting activity. Figure 1-3 shows a photo of some flowers that are colorful, but there's no real center of interest anywhere in the photo, although the clump of blossoms at right do attract the eye in its frantic search for something to focus on.

✔ **Avoid always placing the center of interest in the exact center of the photograph.** There are many occasions when it's okay to center your subject, such as for close-ups or portraits. But most of the time, you want to move the important subject to either side and a little toward the top or bottom of the frame. Don't take the word *center* literally in all cases. Refer to Figure 1-2, shown previously, for an example of a center of interest moved to one side but still somewhat centrally located. I explain how to locate your center in interesting spots later in this chapter.

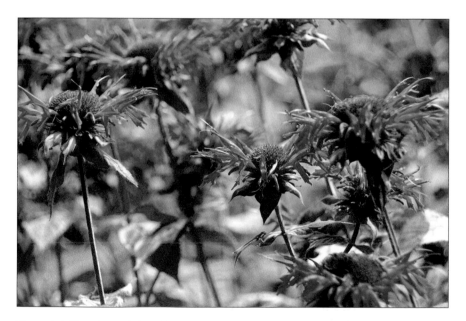

Figure 1-3: This is a bad photo because it has no true center of interest.

Using secondary subjects

Having more than one center of interest is confusing. If you really have several things of importance in a single picture, consider taking several separate photos of each and using them to tell a story. Or group them to form a single, new center of interest.

However, you can easily include (and should, in many cases) secondary points of interest that give the photograph depth and richness. A portrait of a child should concentrate on the child's face, but a favorite toy can speak volumes about what this youngster likes to do. A rock singer on stage can command your attention, but a view showing the adoring fans in the front row tells the viewer how popular the performer is. (Conversely, having a scant few bored spectators as a secondary subject can make another statement, turning the picture into a bit of visual irony.)

Successful secondary subjects are clearly subordinate to your main center of interest. You can indicate what's secondary in your image through location, brightness, or even degree of sharpness. (**Hint:** A bit of image editing can help you after the fact.)

Choosing an Orientation

The *orientation* of a photo — whether it's a wide or tall picture — affects how you look at the image. When you see a landscape-oriented photo, you tend to think of panoramas and horizontal sprawl. A vertically oriented photo, on the other hand, provides expectations of height. Most subjects fit into one of these orientations; very few photos are actually composed within a perfectly square frame. Square photos are often static and uninteresting and are usually put to work only with subject matter that suits them, such as circular objects or images that have important horizontal *and* vertical components.

Digital cameras are built with a horizontal layout because that configuration is best suited for holding in two hands held side by side. Indeed, the default orientation for digital cameras is so much easier to use that some digital SLRs have either a built in or optional *vertical grip* that makes it easier to hold the camera and trip the shutter when the camera is rotated 90 degrees.

Because of this bias, many photographers unconsciously slip into the trap of viewing every potential photo in a horizontal mode. They turn the camera only when confronted by subject matter that simply can't be photographed in any other way, such as the Eiffel Tower, a rocket that's headed skyward, or any NBA all-star.

Here are some tips that will help you decide when it's appropriate to use a vertical composition — and when you should think horizontal instead.

✔ **If you're taking pictures for a slide show or for a computer presentation, stick with horizontal pictures.** Slide-show images are seen sequentially and should all have the same basic frame that is often sized to fill up the horizontal screen as much as possible. Inserting a vertical picture might mean that the top and bottom of your photograph is cut off or appears odd on-screen.

You can still have a vertically composed picture in your slide show; just mask off the right and left sides in your image editor to produce a vertical image within the fixed-size horizontal frame. The key is to make your vertical image no taller than the short dimension (height) of a horizontal picture in the same show.

✔ **If your subject has dominant horizontal lines, use a horizontally composed image.** Landscapes and seascapes with a prominent horizon, photos of sprawling buildings or bridges, the long shopping gallery shown in Figure 1-4, many sports photos focusing on more than one team member, and the majority of four-legged animal pictures look their best in horizontal mode.

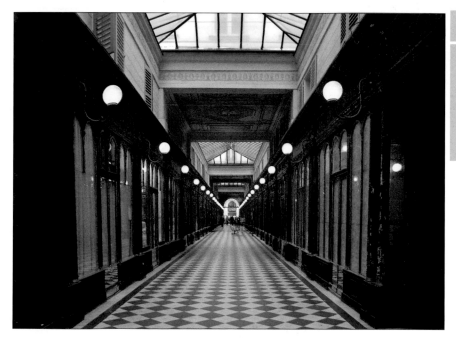

Figure 1-4: Some images look best in a horizontal orientation.

✔ **If your subject has strong vertical lines, use a vertical composition.**
The Eiffel Tower, trees, tall buildings, pictures of individuals (whether
full-length or portrait photos), and similar compositions all call for a vertical orientation, as shown in Figure 1-5, which shows a tall sculpture.

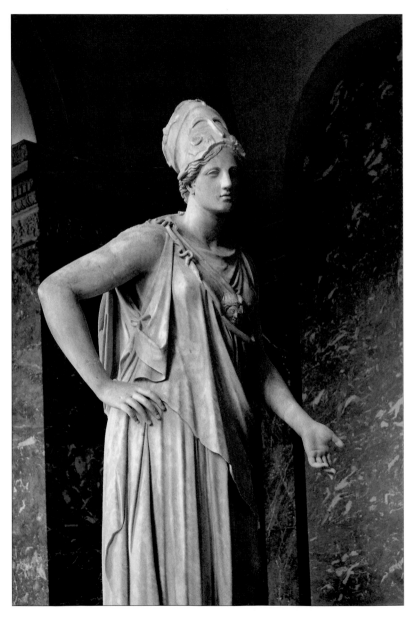

Figure 1-5: Vertical pictures are appropriate for showing human figures, height, or vertical
movement.

✔ **Use a square composition if vertical and horizontal objects in your picture are equally important and you don't want to emphasize one over the other.** A building that is wide but that has a tall tower at one end might look good in a square composition. The important vertical element at one end would keep the image from being too static. Circular images lend themselves to square compositions because the round form fits comfortably inside a square frame, as shown in Figure 1-6.

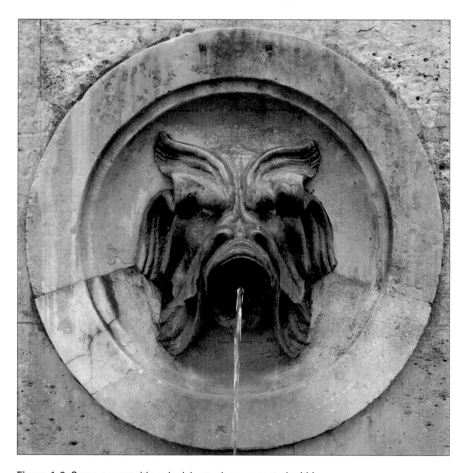

Figure 1-6: Some compositions look best when presented within a square.

Arranging Your Subjects

A basic skill in composing great images is finding interesting arrangements within the frame for your subject matter. You need to position your subjects, make sure they're facing an appropriate way, and ensure that they are well-placed in relation to the horizon and other elements of your image. Your first consideration when arranging your subject is to choose the subject's distance from the camera.

Choosing subject distance

Choosing your distance from the subject to provide the desired point of view is one of the first things to do, but it's not something you do once and then forget about. While you take pictures, constantly examine your distance from the subject and move closer or farther away if adjusting your position will improve the composition. Here's how to choose a subject distance:

- **To convey a feeling of space and depth, use a wide-angle lens or, if your back is not already up against a wall, move back.** Standing back from your subject does a couple of things. The foreground area becomes more prominent, adding to the feeling of space. You also take in more of the sky and other surrounding area, giving additional depth.

- **Make sure that your subjects don't appear too small when you're moving back; they should still be large enough to be interesting.** Moving too far back is the most common mistake amateur photographers make, as shown in Figure 1-7. If you're showing wide-open spaces in your picture, be certain that it's because you *want* to.

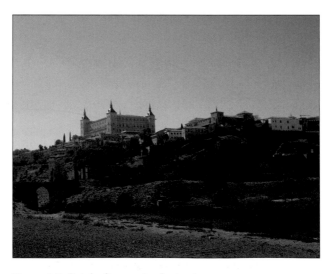

Figure 1-7: But don't move *too* far back.

✔ **For photos that emphasize a person, group of people, or a particular object, move in as close as you can.** A close-up viewpoint adds intimacy and shows details and textures of a subject that can't be seen at greater distances, as shown in Figure 1-8. A short telephoto setting is often the best route to getting closer;

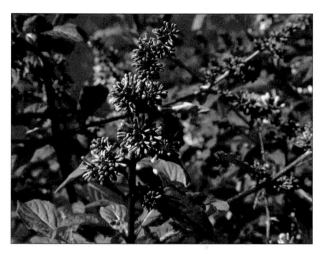

Figure 1-8: Some kinds of backgrounds can be found in nature, but avoid the cluttered background in this shot.

with a normal or wide-angle lens, you can get some apparent distortion of objects that are very close. With kids or animals, you should not only get close, but get down to their level and shoot eye-to-eye.

✔ **Move so you fill the frame completely with interesting things.** Whether you're shooting close to your subject or at a distance, your composition should not include anything that isn't needed to make the picture. Full frames mean less enlargement and sharper pictures, too!

Optimizing backgrounds

Unless you're taking a picture in the dead of night or on a featureless sand dune or snow field, you'll have some sort of background to contend with. A background can be a plus or a minus depending on how you use it in your composition. Here are some tips for making the most of your background:

✔ **Check your background to make sure that it's not gaudy, brightly colored, or busy.** The background should not be more interesting than the subject, nor should it be a distraction.

✔ **For portraits, a plain background (such as a seamless backdrop) can be effective.** A plain, featureless background can work for portraits as long is it isn't totally bland. Notice how professional photographers who pose subjects against a seamless background still use lights to create an interesting gradient or series of shadows in the background.

✔ **Outdoors, trees, grass, cloud-studded skies, plain walls, and other textured surfaces can make good backgrounds.** Such backgrounds are interesting without overpowering your subject. (Refer to Figure 1-8.)

✔ **Watch for strong lines or shapes in the background that don't lead the eye to your subject.** Straight or curved lines are good for compositions but not if they distract the viewer from your subject. Also watch out for things in the background that seem to grow out of your subjects or the borders of the image. (These are called *mergers*, discussed later in this chapter.)

✔ **Consider using *depth of field* (the amount of the image that's in sharp focus) to make your background blurry.** Figure 1-8 uses this technique to make the foliage background less distracting.

Because of how their lenses are designed, consumer digital cameras often show *everything* in sharp focus. Workarounds include using longer lens zoom settings and wider lens openings. You find out exactly what these are and more in Book III, Chapter 2.

Framing the Shot with the Rule of Thirds in Mind

The position of your subject within a picture is one of the most important decisions you make. Whether you can move the subject or objects around, change your position, or wait until everything moves to the right spot, you should constantly be aware of how your subject is arranged. Photographers often consciously or unconsciously follow a guideline called the *rule of thirds*. It's simply a way of dividing your picture horizontally and vertically into thirds. (See Figure 1-9.)

The best place to position important subject matter is often at one of the points located one-third of the way from the top or bottom and sides of the frame.

Placing important objects at imaginary junction points

Follow these steps to compose your pictures effectively using the rule of thirds:

1. **Divide the frame into thirds horizontally and vertically.**

   Above all, you want to avoid having your subject matter centered. By imagining the frame in thirds, you automatically begin thinking of those ideal, off-center positions. Your camera may have a grid you can turn on or off to use as a guideline. Check your manual.

2. **Try to have important objects, particularly your center of interest, at one of the four intersections of the imaginary lines that divide the picture. (Refer to Figure 1-9.)**

3. **Avoid having objects at the edge of a picture unless the part that isn't shown isn't important.**

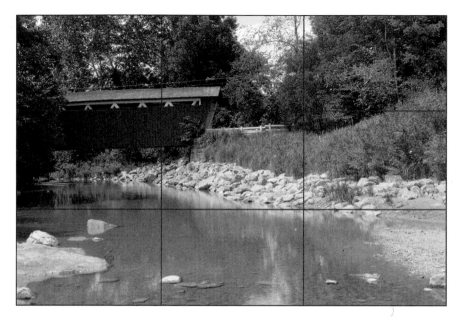

Figure 1-9: To divide your image into thirds, picture the imaginary lines shown on this image.

Book III
Chapter 1

Tools and
Techniques of
Composition

If you're taking a picture of a group of people, cropping out part of the building they're standing next to or trimming off half a tree that's not an important part of the composition is okay. But don't cut off heads!

When to break the Rule of Thirds

Sometimes, you want to break the rule of thirds. This rule has almost as many exceptions as it has good reasons to apply it, which is why the rule should be considered only a guideline. Think of the rule of thirds as a lane marker on a highway. Sometimes you want to stay within the markers; other times, like when you see an obstruction in the road, you want to wander outside the lines. (If you happen to move from the United States to the United Kingdom, you'll find that it's wise to swap sides and use the lane markers on the opposite side of the road.)

You might want to ignore this handy rule when:

- **Your main subject is too large to fit comfortably at one of the imaginary intersection points.** You might find that positioning an object at the correct location crops it at the top, bottom, or side. Move it a bit to another point in your composition if you need to see the whole thing.

✔ **Centering the image would help illustrate a concept.** Perhaps you want to show your subject surrounded on all sides by adversity or by a threatening environment. Placing the subject at one of the intersection points implies motion or direction, as if the subject were about to flee the picture entirely. However, putting the center of interest in the very center of the picture gives the subject nowhere to hide.

✔ **You want to show symmetry.** Centering a symmetrically oriented subject that's located in a symmetrically oriented background can produce a harmonious, geometric pattern that is pleasing, even if it is a bit static. If the subject makes you think of motion, a square image can even boast a bit of movement, as shown in Figure 1-10.

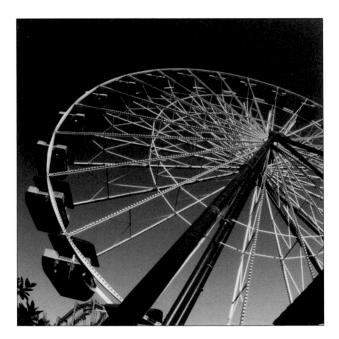

Figure 1-10: Sometimes a square picture can have an interesting geometrical arrangement.

Incorporating Direction and Movement

A photo composition creates an entire world for the viewer to explore. You don't want to destroy the illusion by calling attention to the rest of the universe outside the frame. Here's how to orient people and other objects in a picture:

✔ **If your subjects are people, animals, statues, or anything that you think of as having a front end and back end, make sure they are either facing the camera or facing into the frame rather than out of it.**

If a person seems to be looking out of a picture, rather than somewhere within it, viewers will spend more time wondering what the person is looking at than examining the actual person. The human doesn't actually have to be looking at any object in particular as long as they are looking somewhere within the picture.

✔ **If objects in the frame are moving or pointed in a particular direction, make sure they are heading into the frame rather than out of it.**

A stationary automobile, a windmill, a palm tree bent over by a strong wind, anything with a sense of direction to it should be facing into the frame for the same reason that a person should be looking into it, as shown in the action shot in Figure 1-11.

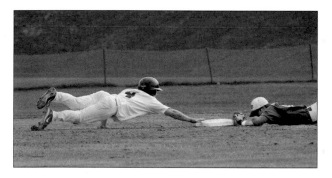

Figure 1-11: Here both subjects are headed into the frame, from opposite directions.

✔ **Add extra space in front of any fast-moving object (such as a race car) so that the object has somewhere to go while remaining in the frame.**

If an object is moving, having a little more space in the frame in front of it is best so that the viewer doesn't get the impression that it's on its way out of view.

Using Straight Lines and Curves

After you have the basics out of the way, progressing to the next level and creating even better compositions is easy. All you need to know is when to apply or break some simple rules.

One of the elements of good composition is a bit of surprise. Viewers like to see subjects arranged in interesting ways rather than lined up in a row.

Lines within your image can help your compositions by directing the eye toward the center of interest. The lines don't have to be explicit; subtle shapes can work just as well. Try these techniques:

✔ **Look for straight lines in your image and try to use them to lead the eye to the main subject area.**

Some lines are obvious, such as a fence or a seashore leading off into the distance. These kinds of lines are good when you want a dramatic composition, like the one in Figure 1-12, which includes multiple sets of diagonal lines.

✔ **Find diagonal lines to direct the attention to the center of interest.**

Diagonal lines are better than straight lines, which are static and not particularly interesting.

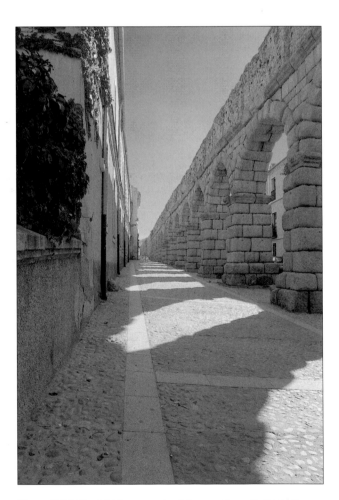

Figure 1-12: Straight lines can lead the eye through the picture.

✔ **Use repetitive lines to create an interesting pattern.**

Repetitive lines could be multiple lines within a single object, such as the grout lines in a brick wall. Repetitive lines could also be several different parallel or converging objects, such as a road's edges, the centerline of the road, and the fence that runs along the road. Strong repetitive lines can become a pleasing composition in themselves, like the ones in Figure 1-12.

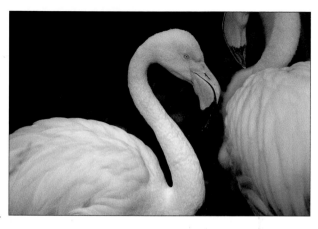

Figure 1-13: Curved lines form graceful, more harmonious pointers for the eyes.

✔ **Curved lines, which are more graceful than straight lines, can lead the viewer from one portion of the composition to another.**

Curving roads are a good example of arcs and bends that can contribute to a composition. Other graceful curves include body parts of living things, such as the necks of flamingos, as shown in Figure 1-13.

✔ **Look for shapes within your composition to add interest.**

Three objects arranged in a triangle make a picture more interesting than if the objects form a square shape. Your eye naturally follows the lines of the triangle toward each of the three points, or apexes, whereas squares or rectangles don't point anywhere. Instead of posing groups of people in rows and columns, stack them in interesting arrangements that make shapes the viewer's eye can explore. Figure 1-13 uses two flamingos to create an interesting set of repeating curved shapes that almost form a heart.

Balancing an Image

If you place every element of interest in a photograph on one side or another, leaving little or nothing to look at on the opposite side, the picture is unbalanced, like a seesaw with a child at one end and no one on the other. The best pictures have an inherent balance that makes them look graceful.

To balance your image, arrange objects so that anything large on one side is balanced by something of importance on the other side. This is not the same as having multiple centers of interest. A group of people arrayed on one side need only be balanced out by having a tree or building on the other. Or a chess piece queen can be balanced by other pieces on the opposite side of the image, as shown in Figure 1-14.

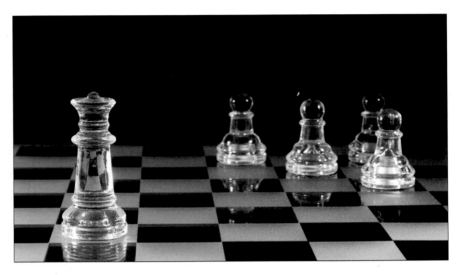

Figure 1-14: Other elements of the photo can balance the composition.

You can balance objects in two ways:

- **Symmetrical balance:** Have the objects on either side of the frame be of roughly similar size or weight.

- **Asymmetrical balance:** Have the objects on opposing sides be of different size or weight.

Framing an Image

Photo prints are frequently put in physical frames for a good reason: A border defines the picture's shape and concentrates attention on the image within the frame. You can use the concept of framing to provide an attractive border inside of your pictures by using these tips:

✔ **In the foreground, look for obvious framing shapes in which you can place your composition.**

You won't easily miss the most readily apparent frames: doorways, windows, arches, and space between buildings. These have the advantage of being a natural part of the scene, like the cliffs in Figure 1-15, and not something you contrived in order to create a frame. In this illustration, the cliffs at the left side of the image partially frame the ocean inlet at right.

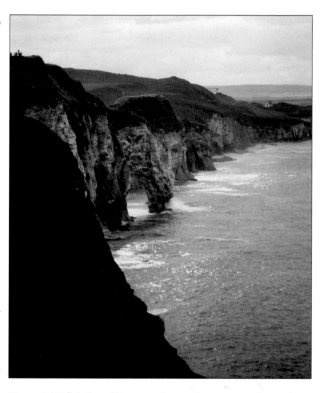

Figure 1-15: Existing objects can be used to create a frame for your photo.

✔ **Frame the shot by changing position until foreground objects create a border around your image.**

Find a curving tree branch and back up until the scenic view you want to capture is wrapped in its leafy embrace. Climb inside something and use an opening as a frame.

✔ **Place your frame in the foreground.**

Shapes in the background that delineate your image don't make an effective frame. You want something that appears to be in front of your subject matter, just like a real frame would be.

✔ **Use a frame to create a feeling of depth.**

A flat-looking image can jump to 3-D life in a frame. Usually, you want to have the frame and your main subject in focus, but you can sometimes use an out-of-focus frame to good effect.

Book III
Chapter 1

Tools and
Techniques of
Composition

✔ **Use a telephoto lens setting to compress your frame and your subject; use a wide-angle lens setting to add distance between the frame and your main subject.**

With a telephoto lens, however, you have to be especially careful to keep the frame in focus.

What's That Tree Doing Growing Out of My Head?

Mergers are the unintentional combining of portions of an image. With our stereoscopic vision, our eyes and brain distinctly separate objects that are farther apart. Other visual clues let us keep objects separate, such as the relative size of the objects compared with our knowledge of their actual size. For example, we know that a tiny human is located in the distance whereas another human in the same field of view who appears to be four times as large is simply closer. However, viewed through the one-dimensional perspective of a camera lens, it's easy for objects that we know to be distinct to merge into one.

We've all seen photographs of hapless photographic subjects posed with what looks like a telephone pole growing out of their heads. Sometimes, the merger is with a border of the image or a simple joining of two objects, as in Figure 1-16, in which the penguins at right appear to share a body. This mistake is easier to make than you might think — and easy to avoid. Follow these steps:

1. **When composing an image, look behind the subject at the objects in the background. Then, examine the borders of the image to look for things "attached" to the edges.**

   By concentrating, you can see how the background and foreground will appear when merged in your final photograph.

   Sometimes it helps to close one eye while viewing the scene.

2. **If an unwanted merger seems likely, move the subject to either side or change your position slightly to eliminate the juxtaposition.**

Like the other rules discussed in this chapter, you can ignore the antimerger guideline (even if you aren't a captain of industry looking to build a giant conglomerate). Keep in mind that you can creatively use mergers to make humorous photographs. You just might want that forest ranger to appear to have a tree growing out of his or her head.

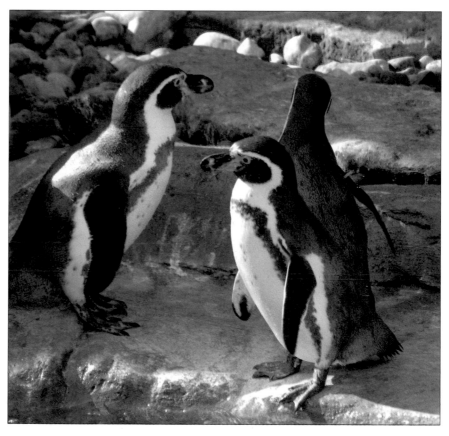

Figure 1-16: A two-headed penguin at right? No, just an unwanted merger.

Chapter 2: Close-Up Photography

In This Chapter

- ✔ Mastering the jargon
- ✔ Previewing the fun of macro photography
- ✔ Choosing your location
- ✔ Assembling the necessary equipment
- ✔ Taking that photo
- ✔ Digital single-lens reflexes and close-ups

*O*ne area that has really benefited from the digital camera revolution has been close-up, or *macro,* photography. Digital cameras of any sort make close-up pictures easy. Even the most basic point-and-shoot camera can focus close enough for a great macro shot, with many of them zeroing in on subjects only a few inches from the front of the lens. You can view and frame the image you're about to take on the camera's LCD, allow the autofocus capabilities to ensure a sharp image, or set the focus yourself.

More advanced digital cameras have even more sophisticated close-up capabilities, and digital SLRs are the best of all. With a dSLR you're *always* looking through the same lens used to take the picture, and with Live View options you can preview the image on the LCD on the back of the camera. Digital SLRs are designed for bright, easy viewing and focusing of your image. Unless the light is very dim indeed, you can usually see almost exactly what you're going to get as well as whether your camera's autofocus mechanism (or your own trusty fingers) can capture the exact point of focus you want. Digital SLRs can turn a fun activity into an uproariously good time.

However, as I noted, you don't need a dSLR or camera with an electronic viewfinder (EVF) to enjoy close-up photography. Most point-and-shoot cameras can do a more-than-passable job, and any intermediate digital camera has all the features that you need to take really great close-ups that will astound your family, friends, and colleagues. And although a beautiful scenic photo or an attractive portrait will elicit praise and appreciation, a well-crafted close-up photo is guaranteed to generate *oohs* and *aahs* and "How did you ever take that picture?" comments. Close-up photography takes us into fascinating new worlds without the time or expense of an exotic trip.

For example, if you collect coins or stamps, miniature teddy bears, porcelain figurines, model trains, or nearly anything smaller than a breadbox (or breadboxes themselves), you'll love the ability to document your collection. Have a garden full of prize-winning roses? Display them even in the dead of winter through digital photos. Have a thing for insects? Grab a picture of the little beasts in their natural habitat. Some of the best applications of close-up photography involve crafts and hobbies.

You don't have to be a forensic expert specializing in crime scene investigations to find interesting photos in the macro world. Just about any household object, if photographed from an inch or two away, is transformed into an abstract scene worthy of the most artsy photographic expression.

If you haven't tried close-up photography, I hope this chapter encourages you to do so. I show you here how to take close-up photos with no special accessories at all, and then later reveal how to set up a close-up studio and take macro photos with a more professional look.

Defining Macro Photography

The first thing to do as you begin your exploration of close-up photography is to get some jargon out of the way. There's nothing wrong with calling up-close-and-personal pictures *close-ups*, but within the photography realm, you commonly find some other terms in frequent use (and misuse). Here are some of them:

- **Close-up photography:** This term has been co-opted by the movie industry (as in "All right, Mr. DeMille, I'm ready for my close-up," from the film classic *Sunset Boulevard).* A *close-up* is generally considered to be a tight shot of a single person (say, only the face and shoulders) or of another object of similar size. It's okay to refer to close-up photography for what you do with your digital camera, as I've done in the chapter title. That's a term that most people, even photographic neophytes, understand.

- **Macro photography:** This is the brand of close-up that is the focus of this chapter. Generally, *macro photography* is considered any picture taken from about 12 inches or less from the subject, down to half an inch or even closer. *Macro* is derived from the Greek word *makro,* meaning *long,* but it has come to mean *large* and the exact opposite of *micro.* However, that's not exactly the case in photography. A macro photograph is not a huge picture (the opposite of a microphotograph), but rather a normal-sized photo of a tiny object that has been made to appear large, as shown in Figure 2-1. You might not even be able to recognize common objects when enlarged in a macro photograph.

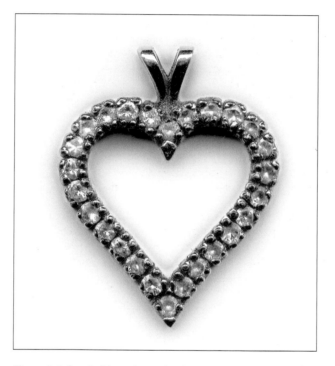

Figure 2-1: Small objects becoming large are the result of macro photographic techniques.

- ✔ **Microphotography:** *Microphotography* results in microphotographs — that is, microfilm images — (those long rolls of images used for storage of documents and other data before the days of computers). You wouldn't apply this term to pictures taken through a microscope, although it is sometimes (incorrectly) used that way.

- ✔ **Photomicrography:** This is the correct term for taking pictures through a microscope. Although photomicrography is chiefly within the purview of scientists and researchers, it can also be a fun activity for digital photographers who have the special equipment needed to connect a digital camera to a microscope. Everything from microscopic animals to human hairs can make fascinating photographs, but you generally need a higher-end digital camera and some specialized gear to capture the images. Photomicrography is beyond the scope of this book.

Why Digital Macro Photography Is Cool

Digital cameras and macro photography were made for each other. In many ways, digital cameras can be far superior to an ordinary film camera when it comes to taking close-up pictures. Consider these advantages:

- **Close-focusing lenses:** Digital camera lenses are ideal for focusing up close. Without getting too technical, macro photos are made with any camera by moving the lens farther and farther away from the film (or sensor, in the case of a digital camera). Film cameras require moving the lens quite a ways out to get a decent macro effect. For example, a 50mm lens on a 35mm single-lens reflex camera (or a digital SLR with a full-size sensor) must be moved four inches out from the film or sensor to get a life-size (1:1) image. In contrast, an 8mm lens on a digital camera with a small sensor, roughly the equivalent of the 50mm lens on an SLR, needs to move only a total of about ⅝ of an inch to provide the same magnification. Clearly, close focusing is much easier to incorporate into a digital camera.

In the macro photography arena, you'll see close-focusing capabilities described in terms of magnification rather than the distance from the subject. As a beginning macro photographer, you might be more interested in how close you can get: six inches, three inches, or whatever. However, realize that the size of the final image at any given distance varies depending on the zoom setting of your lens. That is, an image taken from six inches away at the wide-angle setting might be one-fourth the size of one taken from the same distance at the longest zoom setting. Comparing the amount of magnification is more useful. For example, a 1:1 image is exactly the same size in your camera whether taken from one inch away with the wide-angle setting or six inches away with the zoom setting. (Although the size is the same, the way the image looks is quite different, and I discuss that later in this chapter.)

- **Easy framing of your image:** Virtually every digital camera features an LCD screen, like the one shown in Figure 2-2, that shows almost exactly what you'll get in your finished photograph. (The LCD might trim a bit of the edges from the image, but getting more than you expected is far superior to getting less.) Cameras with an electronic viewfinder (EVF) are also easy to use for framing close-ups.

- **Immediate results:** Close-up photography can be tricky, and the last thing you want to do is wait for your film to come back from the photofinisher to find out whether your pictures came out. With a digital camera, you can review your results on the LCD immediately, delete bad shots, and keep taking pictures until you get exactly what you want.

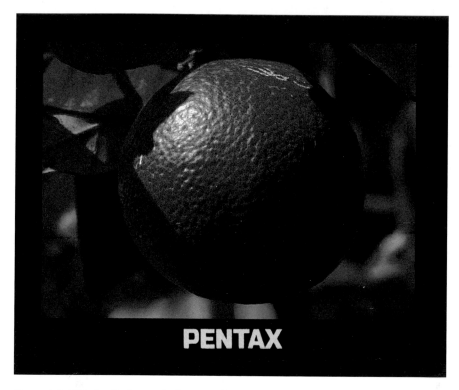

Figure 2-2: LCD viewfinders make it easy to frame your close-ups.

Picking a Place to Shoot

Where you shoot your macro photos can be as significant as what you're shooting. You might want to take your photographs in the tightly controlled environment of your kitchen, using a tabletop as your platform for your model trains or other objects. Maybe you want to venture out into the field to stalk the creatures of nature.

Sometimes you have a choice of where you shoot, and sometimes you don't. For example, if you want to photograph sea life at the beach, you pretty much have to take your pictures there. Comparatively, you can photograph a tree frog on a tree or pop him in a mayonnaise jar along with a leaf and stick to precisely re-create, as the late, great, comedian Mitch Hedberg said, his natural environment.

Table 2-1 shows some of the advantages and disadvantages of location and studio shooting.

Table 2-1	Location Shooting versus Studio Shooting	
Factor	*Location*	*Studio*
Setting	Natural environment.	Studio environment.
Transport	Equipment such as tripods and reflectors must be carried. Some items might not be available.	All equipment is right at hand.
Background	Little control over background, unless you bring some props.	Background can be chosen to complement subject.
Lighting	Realistic natural lighting, but you have less control.	Lighting might look artificial, but you have perfect control.
Environment	Bad weather can be a problem.	Weather is not a factor.
Setup	Setting up pictures can be tedious; settings might be transitory and impermanent.	Setups can be left in place as long as desired.
Consistency	Taking groups of pictures with a similar look is difficult.	Control over lighting and backgrounds means a consistent look that's useful for photographs of collections and so on.

Shooting Macros Simplified

You don't really need a lot of equipment or accessories to take close-up photos. The camera you already have, and household items that are readily available are probably all you need.

Many of the close-up photos in this book, such as Figure 2-1, were taken on impulse right here at the desk where I work. I just grab a piece of white paper from my inkjet printer, lean it against any convenient support, and drop the object I want to photograph on my miniature, seamless backdrop (the white paper). I often use the built-in flash of my digital camera with one or two other pieces of printer paper strategically located to reflect the light onto my subject. Less than a minute after I start, I plug my camera into the USB cable that rests by my keyboard and watch my photos appear on the screen.

Here's a quick checklist to work from:

- ✔ **Camera.** Any point-and-shoot digital camera of recent vintage has the close-focusing capabilities you need to take decent macro photos.

Digital SLRs are even better. Either type of camera probably has a Close-Up or Macro Scene Mode that will make the camera settings you need for this type of photography.

If you're more experienced, any of the "semi-automatic" modes, such as Program, Aperture-Priority, Shutter Priority, or even Manual modes will work, too. Most P&S cameras focus down to a few inches from your subject. If you're using a dSLR, experiment with your lenses (if you own more than one lens) and settle on the one and zoom setting that focuses the closest.

✔ **Support.** Unless you're working with very high-light levels (for example, flowers in full daylight), your camera must be "locked" into a fixed position so that sharp focus can be maintained (once achieved) and the camera won't shake during exposure.

Camera shake is accentuated by close-up photography. If you don't have a tripod (even a $9.95 tabletop tripod is better than nothing), you can often nestle your camera on a suitable support — even a bean bag — that keeps it immobile. Then, use your camera's self-timer to trigger the photo, so you won't introduce camera shake by "punching" the shutter.

✔ **Lights.** Outdoors, daylight may work fine, supplemented by a sheet of white cardboard you can use to bounce light into the shadows. The cardboard can also shield your macro subjects from gusts of wind that may throw them out of focus or out of the frame.

Indoors, high intensity desk lamps make a perfect macro light source. Use them direct for dramatic, contrasty lighting, or bounce them off pieces of white cardboard to make the light softer.

✔ **Background.** Plain backgrounds are best for many subjects.

A piece of white posterboard, a cloth, or fabric are ideal. Sometimes I pile up a stack of books on a table, and use them as a support for a piece of velour fabric I use as a macro background.

If you need a sharp, clear photo for an eBay sale or your hobby newsletter, that's probably all you need to do. If you want professional-quality results, a small investment in equipment and space can make a big difference. The rest of this chapter shows you how to select it, set it up, and use it.

**Book III
Chapter 2**

**Close-Up
Photography**

Setting Up a Macro Studio

You don't need a real studio for very high quality macro photography. That's one of the cool parts of taking close-ups. Any nook or cranny that you can spare in your home or work environment can be designated as a studio area. All you need to do is keep the area reasonably neat and free of clutter so that you can set up and take macro photos on a few minutes' notice.

You can also keep a semipermanent close-up studio, like I do, for stuff that my wife sells on eBay. I have a seamless backdrop up in a little-used corner so that an item that's destined for sale can be set up and photographed anytime. A *seamless backdrop* is simply one that doesn't have distracting lines from folding or construction of the material. A piece of paper that hasn't been folded or a solid piece of fabric — rather than two pieces of fabric sewn together — are considered seamless. A macro studio, such as the one shown in Figure 2-3, requires very little space.

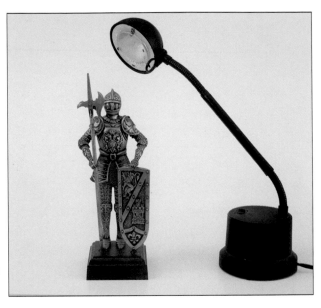

Figure 2-3: Any small corner can become a macro studio.

Background check

In many cases, you want close-up backgrounds that are plain and unobtrusive because they allow your subject to stand out without any distracting extraneous material. That generally means a light background for darker objects and a dark background for light objects. You don't need to stick with stark white or inky black backgrounds — unless your plan is to drop out the background in Photoshop or another image editor so that you can combine the subject with some other photograph. A light pastel background often works well for dark objects, and a medium-dark shade looks good with very light objects.

The amount of light that falls on the background helps determine its lightness or darkness. A soft gray background can appear to be almost white or fairly dark depending on the amount of illumination that reaches it. Don't be afraid to experiment.

So-called *seamless* backdrops are very popular. They provide a continuous (seamless) surface on which the subject can rest while blending smoothly into a vertical background. Depending on how you light the seamless backdrop, it can appear to be a single shade or can provide varying amounts of separation between the foreground and background, as shown in Figure 2-4.

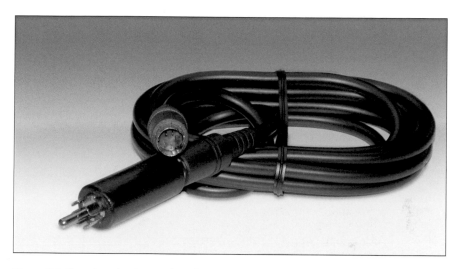

Figure 2-4: Seamless backgrounds make an attractive setting for close-up photos.

Here are the main types of backgrounds that you'll probably use for your macro photography:

✔ **A few yards of cloth:** I really like plain, solid-colored cloth as a backdrop because it's rugged and versatile. If it gets dirty, you can usually just throw it in the wash. I buy pieces about 45–54 inches wide and 8 or 9 feet long in several different colors, including pure black and pure white as well as soft pastels and bright colors. The longer lengths let me use the cloth as a portrait background if I need to.

Artificial velour is extremely useful. One side has a soft surface that really soaks up light. A black velour cloth can make a perfectly black background almost guaranteed not to show shadows. The other side of velour has a shinier texture that you can use for some types of photos. Leave the cloth smooth. Avoid fabrics with a pronounced reflective sheen, such as satin/sateen and vinyl. The simplest fabrics won't cost you more than a few dollars a yard.

✔ **A roll of seamless paper:** Rolls of true photographic seamless paper can be expensive (around $40 for a 9-x-36-foot roll) and hard to find — you need to seek out a camera store that sells to professional photographers. If you can't find such a store locally, online sources sell paper in 53-inch-wide by 12-yard rolls for about $20, although shipping can add a considerable amount to the cost. If seamless paper is what you want, however, you can take a hacksaw and cut the roll in half to make the size a little more manageable for ministudio work. Because seamless paper eventually gets torn and dirty, it's nice to be able to unroll a little more so that you always have a fresh background.

Check out craft and packaging stores for large rolls of sturdy wrapping paper as an alternate source for seamless backgrounds. Avoid the paper with mistletoe and bunnies and stick to plain colors. However, don't be afraid to experiment. A smooth section of Kraft paper (like that found on rolls of brown shipping paper) might make a handsome backdrop for some subjects.

✔ **Posterboard:** I've used a lot of posterboard as seamless backgrounds for close-up photos of smaller objects.

Use duct tape to curve posterboard into place. At a few cents a sheet, you can afford many different colors. However, watch for posterboard that has a slightly shiny surface. If you use it with soft and diffuse lighting, however, that shouldn't be a problem.

Visible means of support

You have to provide support for your background material, your lighting equipment (if you use some), and your camera. Fortunately, the same supports that work for close-ups serve admirably for other types of photography. (See Book III, Chapter 3 for a discussion of gear for people pictures.) If you plan to take a lot of studio-type photos, buying some good-quality equipment of this type can be a shrewd move. I'm still using the same tripod and light stands that I purchased while in college. A few hundred dollars for that stuff seemed like a lot of money at the time, but I haven't had to spend a penny since then even though I've gone from large professional cameras to teensy digital cameras in the interim.

You can buy tripods, light stands, and other equipment relatively inexpensively. However, I can tell you from personal experience that a $100 tripod is a lot more than twice as sturdy and twice as useful as a $50 model. If you're going to spend the money replacing a flimsy tripod or two anyway, start out with a good one.

Here are some of the supports you can find:

✔ **Background supports:** You'll find that cloth backgrounds are so lightweight that you can support them with almost anything. Duct tape can suspend a piece of cloth from any piece of furniture that happens to be around.

I tend to use 7-foot *light stands,* which are aluminum supports that telescope down to a compact size and have tripod legs at the bottom to keep them upright. Set up a pair of light stands, suspend a wooden dowel between them as a horizontal support for your cloth, and you're all set.

Light stands can also support some rolls of paper if you substitute a wooden closet pole or metal pipe for the wooden dowel. You can also build a simple background stand out of lumber. Or if you do a lot of shooting in a basement area (as I do), use metal supports fastened directly to the ceiling joists, as shown in Figure 2-5.

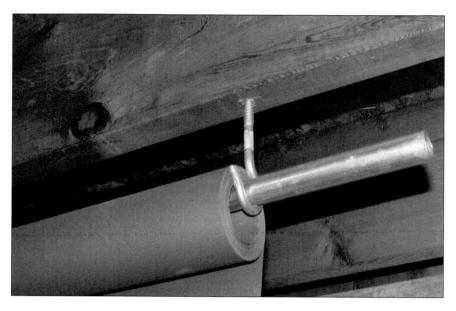

Figure 2-5: Seamless paper can be supported in a variety of ways.

✔ **Lighting supports:** Light stands are good but might be a little too large to position effectively for close-up photography. In many cases, you can skip light stands or special lights altogether and use household desk lamps that rest right on your background setup.

✔ **Camera supports:** A tripod is essential for sharp macro photography. You need to be able to fix your camera in one position and lock it down while you take your photos. That's particularly true if you use your digital camera's LCD screen to compose or focus your image. It doesn't matter whether you're relying on your camera's automatic focus or focusing manually: A tripod can give you the fixed position that you need. A tripod also allows you to photograph several subjects from the same distance and angle, thus adding an important measure of consistency.

Lighting equipment

Unless your subject is a candle or a glow-in-the-dark Halloween skeleton, you need some sort of lighting to illuminate the scene. Your choices include the existing light in the room, electronic flash, and incandescent illumination, such as desk lamps or photoflood lights. The following sections explain what you need to know about each option.

Existing light

Photographers used to refer to existing light by the term *available light* until someone pointed out that a 400-pound Klieg light is technically *available* if you happen to have one left over from the last motion picture you shot. Today, we call it *existing light* on the presumption that lighting doesn't exist if it isn't already available on-site. Here are some tips for using existing light:

- ✔ **Use with modulation:** You can *modulate* (modify) existing light, of course, if you have reflectors or other gadgets about. If existing light is too harsh, you can soften it by using a piece of white cardboard as a reflector. Foam board also works and is stiffer and easier to position than cardboard.

   Avoid reflector colors other than white unless you really, really want a color cast in your photo.

- ✔ **Foiled again:** A piece of aluminum foil can make a brighter, more contrasty reflector. Crinkle it up so that the light it reflects is more diffuse. Otherwise, foil behaves a lot like a mirror, which is something you don't want. Mylar space blankets also make lightweight, portable metallic reflectors.

- ✔ **For all in tents:** Pros often use miniature white tents when photographing a shiny object.

   You can make a simple one out of a translucent milk jug. Place your subject inside the tent, apply plenty of light from the outside of the tent, and then shoot through a hole in the top or side. You'll end up with beautiful soft lighting and no reflections of the surrounding room on the shiny subject matter.

   Make sure that the camera lens doesn't reflect on the object!

- ✔ **Block that light:** Sometimes you want to subtract light rather than add it to your subject. Put black cloth or cardboard outside the subject area to absorb light and darken shadows for a dramatic effect.

When using incandescent lights, make sure that your camera's white balance control has been set for interior illumination. Many digital cameras can be set to automatically recognize and adjust the white balance for various lighting conditions. Fluorescent lighting often requires a different setting, and some cameras will have adjustments for both warm and cool fluorescent bulbs. You can find out more about correcting colors in Book V, Chapter 1.

Incandescent lights

Incandescent lights — including gooseneck desk lamps (which I use), high-intensity lamps, or photographic floodlights — are great for lighting close-ups. Their advantages include

- **Easy preview:** You can see exactly what your lighting effect will be.

- **Flexibility:** Your options are wide open. Use one, two, three, or as many lamps as you need. Arrange them as you like. Create backlit effects or soft lighting. Use a high-intensity lamp when you want a very contrasty quality to your illumination. Turn to a soft-white desk lamp when you need diffused light.

- **Inexpensive:** I buy desk lamps for less than $10 and use them in various combinations to get well-lit close-ups. What other photographic equipment can you buy that cheap?

Their disadvantages include

- **Heat:** Don't let your high-intensity lamps burn your subject. And forget about using them to photograph ice cream sundaes.

- **Power:** You need lots of power and cords that can accommodate high amperages if you're using multiple incandescent lights.

- **Color of light:** You need to make sure that your camera's white balance is set correctly for the reddish hue of incandescent lights.

- **Burnout:** Have some extra bulbs available in case one of your lamps burns out during a shooting session.

Electronic flash

Electronic flash is often useful for quickie shots like those I take right at my desk, but flash is often not the best choice for close-ups. Here are some reasons:

- **It provides too much light.** Flash is often too powerful for close-up pictures taken inches away from the camera. Flash is intended for shooting from several feet or more.

- **You can't project the outcome.** The effect of the lighting isn't easy to visualize with electronic flash because the subject is illuminated for only a fraction of a second. After you take your photo and review it on the LCD screen, you might find that the light is too harsh, is placed incorrectly, or illuminates the wrong part of your image.

- **You don't need it for stop-action.** One of the major advantages of electronic flash, stopping the action of moving subjects, doesn't really apply to close-up pictures, which are usually taken of stationary subjects at a fixed distance.

You can use four kinds of electronic flash when taking close-up photos. You can find a more thorough discussion of these flash options in Book III, Chapter 3 (where I discuss photographing people). However, here's a quick summary of your choices.

**Book III
Chapter 2**

**Close-Up
Photography**

✔ **Your camera's built-in flash:** This is usually your worst choice for illuminating your subject. For one thing, the flash is likely to be aimed quite a distance past your area of interest — or in many cases, blocked by parts of the camera or lens. When I use my camera's built-in flash for close-ups, I always include several pieces of white reflective material outside the field of view to bounce the light back onto the subject. Your flash is likely to be too harsh, thus washing out the details of your subject.

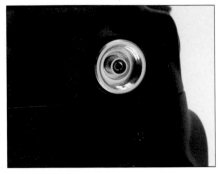

Figure 2-6: Your camera may have a connection for plugging in an external flash unit.

TIP

Light placed at an angle, rather than straight on, can often produce better close-up illumination.

✔ **External flash:** You can find a connector on many digital cameras for linking to an external flash unit, which you can buy for $50 to $400 or more (for the dedicated units built specifically for the more advanced amateur cameras). Sometimes these are located on top of the camera in the form of a shoe (a hot shoe) that can be used to mount the flash and provide an electrical connection at the same time. Or your camera might have a special connector — a PC/X connector, as shown in Figure 2-6.

TECHNICAL STUFF

PC doesn't stand for *personal computer,* but rather *Prontor-Compur,* which is the German mechanical shutter–building company that invented the connection.

✔ **Slave flash:** These are a kind of external electronic flash that includes a photocell that triggers the unit automatically when another flash unit is fired. Slaves let you use several flashes at once, if you can match the slave's operation to your camera's flash functions. (Some cameras use a pre-flash that can trigger some slaves prematurely.)

✔ **Ring lights:** These are circular flash units that can be fitted around the circumference of your camera's lens. They provide even lighting that is designed especially for close-ups. Usually, only professionals who do a great deal of macro photography can justify the price of a ring light.

Other equipment

You might find some other equipment handy when shooting macro photos. For example, *slide-copying attachments* are available for some digital cameras. These attachments let you make high-resolution digital grabs of 35mm color slides without the need for an expensive slide scanner. Even if your digital camera focuses closely, special close-up lenses let you get even closer. Here's a rundown of some of the most popular add-ons for close-up photography:

✔ **Slide copiers:** Slide copiers are great for converting your existing collection of color transparencies to digital form. All you need is a close-focusing digital camera and a copier attachment, which mainly consists of a holder for the slide and a diffusing panel that sits behind the slide to soften the light you use to illuminate it. You might be able to get good quality with such a device, and the quality is certainly better than what you get with most flatbed scanners jury-rigged to scan slides.

✔ **Single-lens reflex add-ons:** If you happen to own a digital camera with removable lenses (with basic SLR digital cameras finally dipping below the $600 price point, that's not altogether unlikely), you can use similar accessories offered for film-oriented SLRs, such as bellows, extension tubes, and reversing rings.

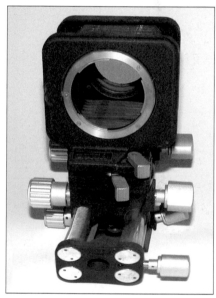

Figure 2-7: This bellows is a versatile accessory if you have a digital SLR camera.

- *Bellows:* Moves your camera's lens farther from the sensor, enlarging the image over a continuous range. (You can see this device in Figure 2-7.) The downside is that the farther the bellows is extended, the less light reaches the sensor, producing long exposures.

- *Extension tubes:* Do much the same as a bellows but over fixed distances. Make sure you buy the automatic kind to preserve your camera's automatic focusing and exposure features.

- *Reversing rings:* Let you mount your camera's lens on a bellows so that the front of the lens faces the sensor. With removable lenses that weren't designed for macro photography, reversing the lens can produce sharper results *and* increase the magnification.

- *Close-up lenses:* Even if your digital camera focuses very close, you might want to get even closer. That's where close-up lenses come in. Although they're called lenses (because they function like lenses), close-up lenses look like clear glass filters with a curved surface. These lenses fasten to the front of your digital camera's lens using a screw mount or other arrangement. Labeled with designations such as #1, #2, and #3 (referring to a measurement of magnification called *diopter strength),* you can use only one or use them in combination to produce varying amounts of magnification. For example, you can combine a #1 and a #3 for a plus-four magnification. The amount of magnification that a particular close-up lens or combination provides depends on the zoom setting of the lens and its normal close-focusing ability.

For example, if you have a lens that focuses as close as one meter, a +1 close-up lens enables you to focus down to half a meter, a +2 diopter to one-third of a meter, and a +3 diopter to one-fourth of a meter (which is a little less than ten inches, for the non-metrically inclined). As you can see, these close-up lenses can bring macro capability to optics that aren't able to focus very close (one meter is the pits, close-up-wise) and can bring super macro capability to lenses that already can focus very close to your subject.

Serious macro photographers purchase a set of several close-up lenses and use them in combination to get the magnification they want.

Shooting Tips for Macro Photography

The first part of this chapter helps outfit you for macro photography. Most of the equipment and gear discussed can be used for location shooting or in your home or office studio, although outdoor close-ups can make some of the tools, such as cardboard reflectors, tricky to use.

This next section provides you with tips for shooting good close-up photographs, using common techniques that the pros take advantage of all the time, plus a few things I learned the hard way myself.

Positioning your subject and background

You've chosen your subject to photograph, whether it's a pewter soldier from your collection or a terrified tree frog. You've selected a background to isolate and/or flatter your subject. What's next?

Set up your subject on its background so that it won't move. Although that can be tricky with the tree frog, it's less of a challenge with an inanimate object, such as the pewter soldier. I often use bits of modeling clay that can be hidden underneath an object to hold it at the correct angle. I also use pieces of wood, bent paper clips, and inexpensive clamps. One of the advantages of digital photography is that you can easily remove any supporting device in an image editor.

In the studio, positioning your subject might be all you have to do. On location, you'll likely have to remove unsightly leaves, ugly rocks, maybe some bugs that are wandering through your frame. Clean up any dirt, dying stems, or other objects that you don't want to photograph.

Setting up your camera

In the studio, it's fairly easy to set your camera on a tripod or other support and not have to worry about it shifting. On location, you might need to make sure that the ground underneath your tripod is firm and solid. Put a rock under one or more legs, if necessary. If you're shooting on a slope, you might want to lengthen one or more legs of the tripod and shorten others.

Set the tripod a little shorter than the height you actually want to use. You can use the center pole to raise or lower the camera a bit. Don't make the common mistake of setting the tripod too low because if you really crank up the center column, the tripod will become top-heavy and unstable. It some-times helps to tie a weight onto the center pole to give the tripod a bit of ground-hugging heft. I use mesh bags, like what oranges or onions are sold in, as a receptacle for rocks. Mesh bags tend to be strong but lightweight, which makes them ideal for this particular task. (Plus, if you happen to encounter an orange grove during your shooting session, you're all set to bring home some dessert.)

You can reverse the center pole of many tripods so that it extends down between the legs of the tripod, thus letting you shoot at an angle on your subject. Often that's the only way to get the viewpoint you want without having the tripod's legs interfere.

Lights, please

Use your lighting equipment or the existing light to illuminate your subject. In the studio, position two or more lights so that they light up the subject evenly. In the studio or on location, work with reflectors to fill in dark shad-ows, darken spots that are too bright, and even out your illumination.

The light that falls on the background can be just as important as the light that you use to illuminate your subject. The background light can separate your subject from the surroundings and provide a more attractive photo. See Book III, Chapter 3, for more information on lighting backgrounds.

Remember that the more light you are able to use, the smaller the lens open-ing needs to be and better the *depth of field* (how much of your image is in focus) you'll achieve. If you want a really sharp picture with lots in focus, pump up the light as much as possible — although if you're using electronic flash, not having enough light is rarely a problem. I explain more about depth of field later in this chapter.

The quality of the light is as important as the quantity. If you're using electronic flash, you want to avoid the harsh illumination that flash typically provides. I often drape a handkerchief over my camera's flash. This reduces the flash illu-mination to a more reasonable level while softening the light.

If the electronic flash is still too strong, move back a step or two and zoom in closer. Bear in mind, though, that not all digital camera lenses can focus closely at all zoom settings. Because of the perverse square law (er, I mean *inverse square* law), a light that is 12 inches from a subject generates only one-quarter as much illumination as it does from 6 inches.

You'll find a discussion about getting the correct exposure in Book II, Chapter 2.

Ready . . . aim . . .

You're all set to frame your photo and press the shutter release. But first, a few words from our sponsor. Keep these final advisories in mind as you take your best shot when shooting up close:

- **Watch proportions.** For any particular magnification, the closer you get, the more emphasis is placed on objects very close to the lens. Photograph a figure of a clown's head from two inches away, and his nose will be very large and his ears too small in proportion to the rest of his face, as shown at left in Figure 2-8. Move back a few inches and zoom in to produce the same size image, and the proportions are much more realistic, as shown at right in Figure 2-8.

- **Don't forget focus and depth-of-field considerations.** Good macro focus is no different from achieving focus with any other subject — you'll need to use your camera's autofocus tools properly, or focus manually. You should be careful that you're focusing correctly, because when shooting up close, only a small portion of your image might be in focus. Make sure that's the most important part of your subject! If your camera lets you lock in a focus setting by pressing the shutter release button part way, make sure you've focused on the right area before locking. Depth-of-field is a range, extending one-third in front of the plane of sharpest focus and two-thirds behind it, as you can see in Figure 2-9. In this figure, very little in front of the cat is in focus, but the cat's face is fairly sharp. The background, of course, is too far away to be in focus at all, which is how the picture was conceived.

- **Crop and center.** Crop (trim) extraneous material and center your subject in the frame (most of the time). Good composition, as I describe in Book III, Chapter 1, usually calls for an off-center subject, but that rule might not apply when shooting close-ups. It might be best to feature your main point of interest right in the center of the frame.

- **Use your camera's close-up features effectively.** That includes double-checking to make sure the camera is in macro mode and keeping close tabs on the in-focus indicator (usually an LED) that might appear in your viewfinder.

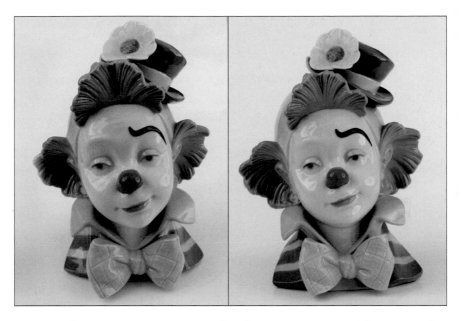

Figure 2-8: Shot close up, the clown's nose (right) appears proportionately larger than when photographed from a distance (right).

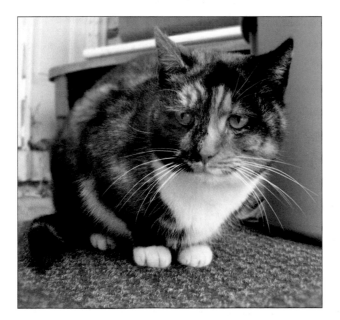

Figure 2-9: Depth of field extends one-third in front of and two-thirds behind the plane of sharpest focus (the cat's face).

✔ **Aim and frame.** Make sure that you've framed the subject correctly, without accidentally chopping anything off. You often have to use the camera's LCD screen to examine your composition because the built-in optical viewfinder doesn't show the image 100 percent accurately. You don't want to chop off the top or sides of your image by mistake. Of course, if you're using a digital SLR, you won't need to worry about this at all.

If your digital camera has a connector for linking the camera to a monitor or TV, you can often use that capability to frame your indoor close-up photos.

Fire!

When you press the shutter release button, a lot of things happen. One quite likely (and none-too-happy) event is that you press the shutter release button too hard, jar the camera during exposure, and produce a blurry picture. Another possibility is that you see something wrong with your composition in the last *ohnosecond*.

An *ohnosecond* is that interval between the time when you press the shutter release and the instant when you realize that you've made some sort of serious error. (An ohnosecond also occurs after you slam your car door and before you remember your keys are in the ignition.)

Depth of field and digital cameras

Throughout this book, I mention the copious amounts of depth of field that digital cameras offer. This is a good place to mention it again. Because of the relatively short focal length of their lenses, digital cameras help ensure that just about anything you shoot at normal distances is sharp. Even at close-focus distances, you have to work a little to throw even part of your image out of focus.

If you *want* to reduce depth-of-field a little, say to blur a background for creative purposes, you can do several things:

✔ Try using the telephoto zoom position of your camera. One of my favorite digital cameras works fine in macro mode at its 200mm (equivalent) zoom setting, which has an actual focal length of about 50mm, and it can cut down the depth-of-field a bit.

✔ Use your camera's aperture priority mode (if it has one) and set the camera for the largest lens opening (smallest f-stop number) available.

✔ If you want to throw the background out of focus, try focusing a teensy bit *in front* of your main subject, which will probably remain acceptably sharp as the background grows blurrier. Or focus *behind* the main subject (but only a little) if you need to throw the foreground out of focus.

Avoiding blur

Avoid human-caused blur by using your camera's self-timer to trip the shutter after a few seconds rather than using your big fat finger. In self-timer mode, you set up your composition, make sure everything is okay, press the shutter button, and then step back and take a few deep breaths until the camera actually takes the photo (blur free).

An alternative is to use an electronic or mechanical remote shutter-release control to trip your camera's shutter without touching it. A remote release can be a cable that attaches to your camera or an infrared remote control like the one that operates your television, VCR, and virtually everything else in your household. Unlike a self-timer, a remote release lets you take the photo at the exact instant you want — say, when the tree frog has a cute expression on his face.

Some cameras and lenses have anti-shake features that can help you avoid blur, too.

Making sure the camera is done

For heavens sake, don't do anything after you press the shutter button until you're 100 percent positive that the camera has finished taking the picture. If your camera has an optional shutter release sound, turn it on so that you know when the picture is being taken. Learn to differentiate between the sound the camera makes when the shutter opens and the sound made when it closes again.

If your camera has a flashing LED that indicates that a photo is being saved to your digital film, look for it to begin flashing as an indication that the photo has been taken. The automatic exposure mechanism of your camera just might need to use a long exposure (several seconds or more) to take the picture, and you certainly don't want any sudden movements or grabs at the camera to ruin your shot. Wait a few seconds after you hear the camera's shutter click before doing anything until you're sure that your camera isn't making a lengthy exposure or time exposure. That click might have been the shutter opening (or the digital camera's simulation of a shutter sound), and the camera might still be capturing the picture.

Reviewing your shot

After the photo has been taken, do take the time to review your picture on the LCD for defects. Look for these common problems:

**Book III
Chapter 2**

**Close-Up
Photography**

✔ **Poor focus:** The best tip I can offer for macro focusing is to use your camera's zoom-in feature during picture review to make sure your focus is correctly set. If not, correct and reshoot.

✔ **Bad exposure:** If your pictures are too dark or too light, make adjustments by using your camera's available exposure compensation modes. (Check your camera manual.)

✔ **Bad reflections:** Move your lights or move your camera until the reflections go away.

✔ **Missing tree frog that has departed the scene:** You know, they do make quite realistic-looking plastic tree frogs these days.

Digital SLRs and Close-Up Photography

As I mention at the beginning of this chapter, digital SLRs are the almost perfect choice for close-up photography because of the increased accuracy you can get with framing and focusing, as well as the greater control that most dSLRs provide over your picture taking. Here are a few things to consider when using a digital SLR for macro photography. Some of these also apply to cameras with electronic viewfinders.

✔ **Don't forget to use depth-of-field preview.** The digital SLR typically shows you a bright, clear image with the lens wide open and then closes the aperture at the moment of exposure. As you know, the depth of field at that smaller aperture is likely to be much greater than what you see with the lens wide open, so if selective focus is important to you, you'll want to use your camera's depth-of-field preview button to glimpse the true focus just before you shoot. An object that appears soft and out of focus through the viewfinder can be objectionably sharp in the final image, as you can see in Figure 2-10.

✔ **Investigate add-on focus aids.** An SLR image is usually viewed as projected onto a focusing screen underneath the pentaprism/pentamirror. High-end digital SLRs can offer removable focusing screens that can be easier to focus in dim light or in close-up mode. If you have a dSLR with that capability, investigate the focus aids available to you from the manufacturer of your camera.

✔ **Not all digital SLRs show the full image area.** When I began my photographic career, the Nikon film camera was highly prized because it was said to display 100 percent of the film image through the SLR viewfinder. Other cameras might not. Today, many digital camera viewfinders trim off some of the image, providing only 92–98 percent of the full image. You actually get *more* than what you saw through the viewfinder, but if absolute framing is important to you, be aware that what you see is only *most* of what you get.

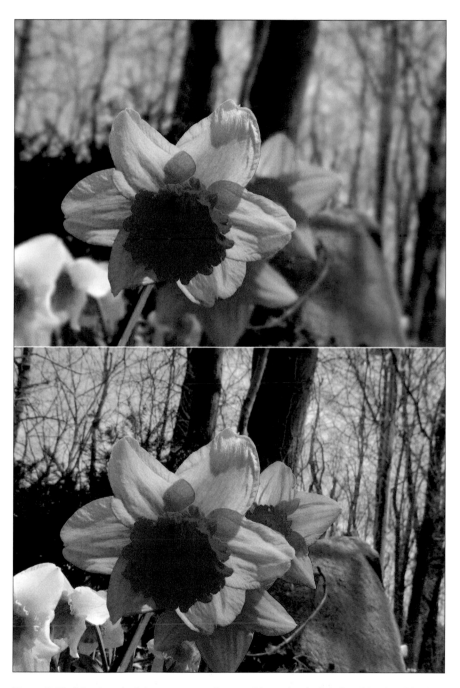

Figure 2-10: A background that appears to be out of focus (top) might be objectionably sharp at the taking aperture (bottom).

✓ **Avail yourself of the mirror lock-up feature, if provided.** Close-up pictures can be especially sensitive to vibration, such as that caused by a pivoting mirror. (The mirror reflects the lens view upward to the viewfinder, then flips up out of the way during exposure to let the light pass unimpeded to the sensor. This quick up/down flip inevitably provides a tiny amount of vibration, no matter how carefully the camera was designed.) If you're shooting very close or if your exposure is long, see whether your digital SLR has a *mirror lock-up* feature, which will let you flip the mirror up prior to the exposure. Then when vibration has been damped, take your picture with the self-timer or remote release.

✓ **Check out bellows, extension tubes, reversing rings, and special macro lenses.** These specialized devices can let you get closer, take sharper pictures, and improve your results, especially if you have a digital SLR with a full-frame sensor.

Chapter 3: Photographing People

In This Chapter

✔ Making satisfying portraits

✔ Shooting informal portraits

✔ Building an informal portrait studio

✔ Discovering the basics of lighting

✔ Arranging multiple lights

✔ Creating your first portraits

Although the first successful photograph, a scene taken from a Paris rooftop by Nicéphore Niépce in 1827, was a scenic photo unpopulated by humans (largely because the exposure took eight full hours!), the most memorable pictures since then have included people. Indeed, the desire to photograph family, friends, and colleagues is why many people own a camera.

When you think of the daguerreotype, Civil War–era portraits probably come to mind. When you imagine a prize-winning photograph, images such as Dorothea Lange's *Migrant Mother* leap into your thoughts more quickly than, say, Ansel Adams's portraits of the U.S. National Parks. And when you photographed an architectural treasure such as the Eiffel Tower, didn't you include a family member in the picture?

We're fascinated by photographs of people, so we take lots of them. However, people are the most difficult of all subjects to photograph because of the complexity of human ego, awareness, and opinion. When was the last time the Eiffel Tower complained that your picture made it look fat? Has anyone ever told you that your photo of the Grand Canyon didn't really look like the Grand Canyon? Has anyone worried that the presidents on Mount Rushmore would blink during an exposure?

Satisfying people photography is within the capabilities of every digital camera owner. You don't need an expensive camera to take portraits (although digital SLRs can have some advantages when it comes to using certain accessories, such as multiple light sources). Your basic 6- or 10-megapixel camera will do just fine. Available light or your camera's built-in flash might work for some portraits, but I show you the advantages of using off-camera flash in this chapter. The best part about taking digital pictures of people is that you can review the photos instantly, with your subjects, and retake them if the results are less than satisfactory.

This chapter is an introduction to the many facets of people photography. You find out how to take great portraits, capture vivid candid photos, and manage unruly group pictures. If you can handle those, all other forms of digital photography are a snap.

Candid People Pictures

You're at a company picnic and want to shoot some photos that will please (or embarrass) your co-workers. Your kids are dressed for Hallowe'en, or your daughter and her date are leaving the house for the prom. You don't have time to set up a complicated picture — you just want to capture a memory that will endure, in the simplest way possible. Don't panic!

Candids are unplanned pictures taken of people in the act of being themselves. Getting good candid people pictures is easier than you think:

✔ **Have your camera ready. Always.** The biggest roadblock separating you from good quickie candid photos is having your camera set for shooting fireworks, when you need to grab a pleasing snapshot.

Get in the habit of returning your camera to its default settings when you're done shooting. Then, when a photo opportunity pops up unexpectedly, you can grab you camera and shoot without having to make changes to weird color or sensitivity (ISO) settings you might have used last week.

Think like a scout: Be prepared. If you ever expect to take pictures on an impromptu basis, make sure your camera is ready to go in an instant.

✔ **Use a Scene mode.** Most digital camera have Scene modes, like Portrait, Sports, Landscape, and Close-up. Even if you prefer using one of the other, semi-automatic modes, when you want to take a candid picture of someone or a group, Scene modes may be your best friend:

• Flip to Portrait mode for indoor or outdoor portraits.

• Use Night Portrait outdoors at night, so your camera will provide extra background light even when you're using flash.

When you select a Scene mode, your camera makes all the best basic settings for you — even if you *were* shooting fireworks last night.

✔ **Flip up your flash.** Indoors, you'll usually get much better results with simpler cameras if you use electronic flash:

- For a point-and-shoot camera, select one of the "flash on" modes.

- If you have a digital SLR, some Scene modes may flip up the flash for you. In other modes, you may need to press a button or manually flip up the flash.

✔ **Use Red-Eye mode.** If your camera has a red-eye prevention mode to avoid those demon-like glowing pupils, you should have it switched on most of the time. When you take candid people pictures, most of your subjects will be looking directly at the camera. And if you're using your camera's built-in flash, it's likely to have a tendency to produce some red-eye effects.

Your camera's red-eye mode will usually trigger a pre-flash just before the actual picture is taken, so your subjects' pupils contract, reducing the effect.

✔ **Choose your background.** A plain wall or other simple background may be best, but don't line your subjects up directly in front of the background. If you do that, it's likely that shadows from your flash will be clearly visible on the background. If there's enough room to move your subjects forward three or four feet, the shadows will fall behind them, and the plain background will be just that — plain — rather than mottled with distracting shadows.

✔ **Line 'em up.** No, don't line them up in a straight line. If you're shooting more than one subject, arrange them so that individual heads are on different levels. Have some people standing, some seated on a chair, or some sitting on the floor.

Later in this chapter, I show you how to arrange people in interesting array. But you don't need to be fancy.

✔ **Watch your posture.** Look for stray hands doing weird things, wrinkled clothing, "leaners" and other people arrangements that are awkward. Creating a pleasing composition isn't complicated or time-consuming. You just need to pay attention and make adjustments.

The simplest thing you can do is to have your subjects rotate their bodies towards the center of the image. You don't want to photograph them as if they were in a firing squad.

✔ **Use props.** Hallowe'en bags and costume accessories, the volleyball your boss just used to defeat the team of guys from the loading dock (they let him win), or your future-son-in-law's gift of a corsage to your daughter can all spice up a photo.

✔ **Fire away.** Take *lots* of photos. When shooting groups, I always take at least one or two more pictures than there are in the group. For six people, I shoot a minimum of eight to ten shots. That will let you weed out the blinkers and those who manage to turn their heads at the last instant.

Book III Chapter 3

Photographing People

Capturing Satisfying Portraits

Portraits are posed photos taken in a controlled environment;

In general, portraits show people as they'd like to be seen, and candids portray them as they really are.

To make the step up from mundane isn't hard. In fact, the average novice can achieve significant improvement through better composition and lighting alone.

You don't need a lot of training to shoot informal portraits after you master the features of your digital camera and the rules of composition. You just go out and take pictures, paying special attention to how your subjects are posed and how the lighting appears. The good news is that these capabilities are within the range of the average photographer; you just need someone to fill you in on the tools and techniques that work. That's what this chapter is for.

But first, a few ground rules. Take care of these simple aspects and you can't go wrong:

✓ **Make it possible for your subjects to look their best.** If you're looking for a portrait rather than a candid photograph, you can even suggest what your subjects wear. Have them wear suitable clothes and also invite them to have a change of outfits so they can have pictures with different looks. Encourage them to use a friend or family member to help them prepare. Provide access to a good-sized mirror so that they can check their appearance. (It's smart to take one along with you if you're planning to shoot outdoors.)

A portrait subject who feels confident about his or her appearance will photograph well!

✓ **Get to know your subject's personality.** Be careful about trying to make a somber, serious individual look cheerful and gay; the picture can look forced and fake. It's easier to get a happy type to look serious. Unless it's an executive portrait (where serious is good), go for the smile. Use what you know about the subject to create a portrait that reflects his or her personality.

✓ **Provide comfortable surroundings to help people stay relaxed.** A clean, organized shooting area puts your subjects at ease, as can some soft mood music. If your subject doesn't feel like he or she is standing in front of a firing squad, your photos turn out much better.

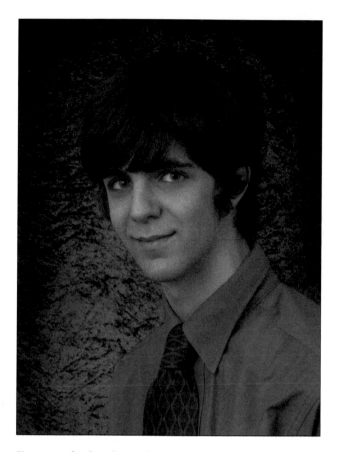

Figure 3-1: A relaxed portrait is the best kind.

Successful portraiture begins with getting your subjects into the right frame
of mind. Relaxed, confident people pose better than nervous, tense ones, so
make every effort to start things off right if you want to get a portrait like the
one shown in Figure 3-1. The picture is actually much less professional than it
appears. I asked (forced) my son to put on a nice shirt and tie, posed him in
front of a piece of fabric, and took advantage of the flattering light in our living
room to snap the portrait. No studio or fancy lighting equipment required!

Where to Shoot Informal Portraits

Because even informal portrait sittings are generally carefully arranged,
these kinds of shoots offer the photographer the advantage of being able
to exercise a great deal of control over creation of the image, both in location and lighting. You can choose to shoot indoors (which can be any room,

including your living room or garage) or on location (which can range from your backyard to a park or other site).

You don't need to have a real studio to shoot informal portraits. You might have a place that serves double-duty as an indoor shooting location as well as some other function. For example, I took some of my favorite portraits in an attic space that was little more than a large area arranged with various backgrounds. When I moved to a newer home without an attic, my favorite shooting area moved, too, to a 16-x-20-foot basement area with 10-foot ceilings directly under my home office. The backgrounds were easy to hang from the ceiling joists.

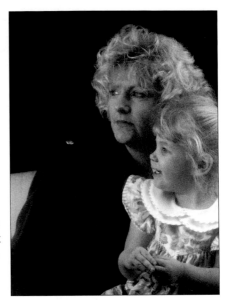

Figure 3-2: Your own living room can be the scene for your portrait photography.

For one book I wrote that called for lots of head-and-shoulders portraits, I pinned a long length of fabric to cover the drapery in front of my patio door, set up a couple of lights, and was able to snap a quick portrait on a moment's notice without the need to run down to the basement where the roomier setup was available. You can even take informal portraits in your own living room, which was the case for the mother-daughter picture shown in Figure 3-2. I've left the couch in the photo (at left) but probably would have cropped or retouched it when making a print.

And even if you don't have room to set aside for a home shooting space, you probably have an area that can be temporarily reconfigured to serve as a photographic environment. For example, back the car out of the garage and hang a background — and you have an instant portrait setting.

Deciding whether to shoot at home or on location must be based on the kind of photos you want to take. Shooting at home offers the utmost in control for a photographer, particularly when you're working in a space you've set up and become comfortable in. Your designated area can become a warm, comfortable cocoon that lets your creativity and talent grow.

Of course, sometimes, we all have to leave our comfortable surroundings and brave the outside world. Location photography may pull us out of our comfort zone, but it also gives us something hard to find in the studio — scenery.

Most of the techniques described later in this chapter apply to location photography. But when shooting at home, all you need is your camera, perhaps a fill flash for illuminating shadows, and some pieces of cardboard to use as reflectors (which are a basic tool of amateur photographers; even the least expensive flash unit has its own built-in reflector to bounce light).

The chief differences between location and home shooting are as follows:

- **Portability:** If you plan to shoot on location regularly, you need to assemble a versatile kit of equipment and props (which need be nothing more complicated than a tripod, supplementary flash, some foldable reflective material, and a few objects to hold, funny hats, or other gadgets). Find a duffle bag or two that you can pack your location equipment into quickly so that you can be ready to go at a moment's notice. I know an outdoor portrait shooter who keeps a box full of crazy hats and fabrics in her car, ready for a spur-of-the moment portrait snapshot.

- **Flexibility:** Because no two location shoots are identical, try for a portable location kit that provides the greatest flexibility for lighting both your subject and, if need be, elements of the location appearing in the shot.

- **Creativity:** Put together a portable system that lets you create different shots and moods. Consider props that are portable and versatile.

Location shoots give you the chance to provide your subjects with something different from the typical indoor portrait. Every area has a special site of some sort that can serve as a backdrop for memorable images, such as a gorgeous hotel lobby, public park, forest, or lake. One photographer I know lives on some wooded acreage complete with meadows, stands of trees, and a pond. You can bet that he uses these environmental settings as often as possible for his people pictures.

Setting Up an Informal Portrait Environment

Many photographers who pursue their art as a hobby or sideline prefer a simple, informal home studio that can be set up easily and broken down when the shoot's done. Such a studio fills their needs without taking over part of their house.

Depending on your needs, an accessory flash unit or two helps give you the balanced lighting that you need if you want to capture that natural-lighting look. You'll find that an investment in slightly better equipment can be worth it. Gear that I purchased for use with film cameras a few decades ago work just fine with my latest digital cameras, and their initial cost averages out to just a few dollars a year.

Choosing backgrounds

Sometimes you want to pose people in their natural environments. A family can be posed in their living room seated on a couch. An attorney can be pictured in front of a wall of law books. (This is almost a tradition. Don't forget to include a flag!) If you apply the same rules of posing and lighting to such a portrait as for more traditional studio portraits, the results will be quite good.

The best informal portraits call for real portrait backgrounds. For an indoor setting, you'll want something more attractive than just a bare wall for a background; fortunately a wide variety of choices is available for every budget.

I suggest having a selection of backgrounds available in a variety of colors, specifically blues, greens, and browns, as these hues seem to go best with a variety of shades of clothing. If you have several choices, you can select the color that goes best with the attire, hair coloring, and skin tone of your subject. For example, some types of skin look ghastly against a green background, but redheads may be flattered by the same kind of background. Backgrounds should not have a distracting pattern or texture.

- ✔ **Go disposable with paper.** The simplest choice is an inexpensive roll of seamless background paper ($18 and up), which, for an amateur photographer, is likely to last for years and years. These rolls are available in a wide variety of colors and are easy to use. Usually, you just suspend a roll on some kind of hanging support and then unroll as much as you need for a shoot. *(Hint:* Bring enough down to cover a couple of feet of floor and have your subject stand on it.) When a section of the backdrop paper becomes dirty or wrinkled, you just roll down some clean paper, cut off the damaged part, and throw it away. You can keep a selection of three to five different rolls and switch them as needed. Figure 3-3 was taken using a roll of blue paper as a background.

- ✔ **Upgrade to fabric.** Other background choices include painted linen backdrops that provide a more interesting texture and color gradient.

   I go to fabric stores and buy close-out bolts with only a few yards left. You can buy interesting colors and patterns and have a variety of backgrounds.

- ✔ **Use more than one backdrop.** The more backgrounds you have available, the better. Different colors work better with different clothing ensembles, and some hues may be especially compatible with certain hair colors and skin tones. If you have many background options, you can vary your looks to suit your subject.

Basic lighting options

You don't need fancy studio lighting equipment to shoot informal portraits indoors or outdoors. You can use the existing light in a room or outdoor environment or supplement that light with simple electronic flash equipment. Here are some options:

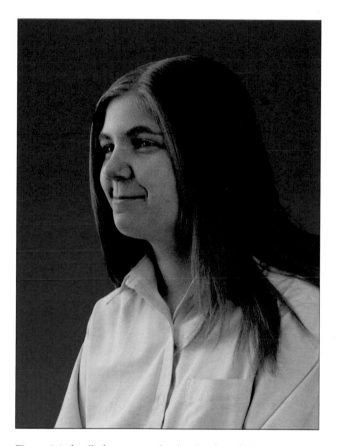

Figure 3-3: A roll of paper can be the simplest choice.

Existing light

Existing light is the light that's already there in your environment — that is, before you add flash or other extra light sources.

It's also called *available light* — or, by wags, *available darkness* — but all three terms are misnomers. After all, *all* light that you can use exists (unless you're into quantum mechanics, in which case, it only potentially exists until it's observed). *Available light* is equally murky: If you have an electronic flash or a flashlight in working order, both of those are technically available. However, I'll apply those terms to the light that's already on a site, and not the kind of illumination you'd use to photograph Shrödinger's cat.

To make the most of existing light, consider these points:

- **Reflectors:** Professional photographers use umbrellas, softboxes, and other equipment to modify and shape light. You don't need anything that sophisticated. *Reflectors* are any objects or surfaces that enable you to bounce light into areas of the scene that need it. Any material that can bounce light into areas of heavy shadow can help make existing light work in your favor. Whether your reflector is a piece of foam board held by another family member or friend or a reflective disc you tape up or prop in place, this kind of illumination can be an inexpensive and a portable way of making your lighting better. Although some pretty fancy (read *expensive)* reflectors are on the market, spending a lot isn't necessary. A simple piece of white foam board does the job beautifully.

  Use your main light source (daytime outdoors, that will be the sun) to light a three-quarter section of your subject and then position the reflective material to bounce sunlight onto the remaining quarter. This will lighten the shadows and give a greater sense of dimension to your photo. If you want a little less softness in the shadows, use a metallic reflector. You can even press a metal serving tray into use, like the one shown in Figure 3-4, if you can convince a friendly observer to hold it up for you.

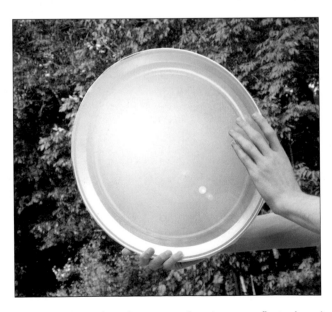

Figure 3-4: A metal serving tray can function as a reflector in a pinch.

✔ **Room lights:** Sometimes your goal is the most natural possible setting and feel to an image. If this means working without accessory lights, managing the room's lights properly can be a big help. If you can position a lamp to throw a little more light to a shadow area, you can clean up a heavy shadow. Or depending on the mood you're aiming for, you can bring your lights all to one side and have your subject emerging from the shadows.

Working with available darkness is one of photography's greatest challenges. However, if you can use it successfully, you can produce exceptionally natural-looking images. Look for ways to control the impact of the building's lights; remember, you don't have to accept what's there. Shift a lamp closer or farther from your subject. Unscrew some light bulbs while leaving others on or mask lighting fixtures with cardboard or *gaffer's tape* (a special kind of tape that won't leave a residue when pulled off the lights when you're done). The difference is worth it.

Figure 3-5 shows General Robert E. Lee (as portrayed by a Civil War re-enactor), shot by available light — but with my camera's pop-up flash used to fill in the shadows. The general's face was heavily shrouded in shadows, but a simple piece of white cardboard bounced enough light into the dark areas to produce a more balanced look.

Electronic flash

Accessory flash units are an important tool in the battle to correct undesirable lighting conditions. These small, portable light sources provide you with a lot of options and can be used to produce some amazing results. Photographers using a multiple flash setup can produce lighting results similar to those produced by pros.

✔ **Supports:** If you decide to use a couple of portable flash units, you can benefit from some sort of system for holding your flash units in position. Lightweight minitripods that can be set on tabletops or other elevated surfaces and positioned as needed work well. The marketplace has also produced a wide variety of clamps with standard ⅜-inch tripod threads that can also hold a flash and be used to position it high enough to work effectively. Some tripods also come with feet or stands that they can be mounted on so that they can be set erect on a flat surface.

✔ **Light modifiers:** After you position your flash units, make the quality of your light as pleasing as possible.

When used head-on, direct flash is harsh, showing every flaw and imperfection. Experienced photographers solve this problem in a number of different ways. One solution is *bounce flash*. Here, the flash units are pointed toward the ceiling and the light is reflected back down to the subject, thus spreading and softening the light and making it more pleasing. Other tools for improving the quality of light are devices that attach to the flash head and reflect light (such as white cards) or ones that cover the flash head and soften the light as it comes through the device (such as the Sto-Fen Omni Bounce [www.stofen.com, about $20] or a small soft box, which is basically nothing more than a piece of white cloth or other material stretched over a frame).

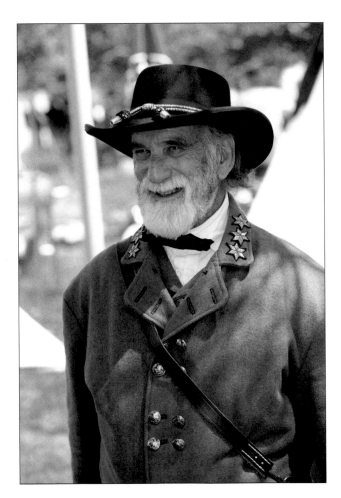

Figure 3-5: A softer snapshot using reflector illumination to fill in the shadows.

Figure 3-6 shows a typical electronic flash with its built-in reflector extended.

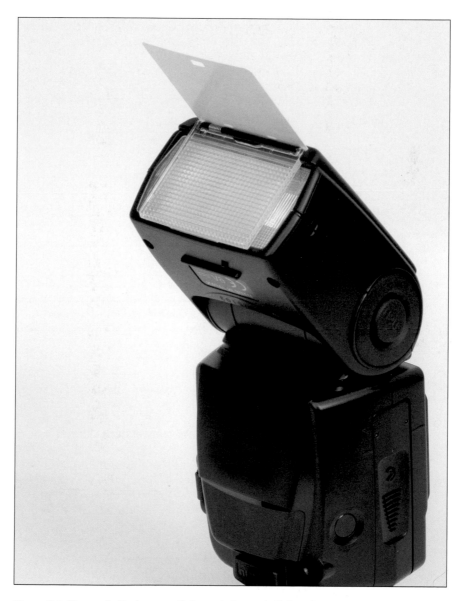

Figure 3-6: Electronic flashes usually have their own built-in reflectors to provide bounce light into the shadows.

✔ **Power:** Keeping your flashes firing during a long shoot can be a daunting task if you're relying solely on AA batteries. Devices such as Quantum rechargeable batteries (www.qtm.com, prices vary widely depending on your model) can provide enough juice for your flash units to keep pace even with your most frenetic shoots. Many of these units can provide power to a pair of flashes simultaneously

Incandescent lights

Incandescent lighting is the same lighting most of us use to light our homes. Enterprising manufacturers have created inexpensive photo lighting kits that use regular light bulbs instead of more expensive tungsten-halogen lighting setups.

You would choose one of these kits if you intended to do a lot of indoor photography (both people, or macro subjects) and wanted a kit you could transport from place to place, or set up and tear down quickly when used at home.

Lighting gadgets

A huge assortment of lighting gadgets are on the market, all promising to be easy to use and to produce a higher quality of light. For the most part, these claims are reasonably true. Here's a quick summary of what's available, ranging from useful and just about free all the way up to high-tech and pricey.

Inexpensive (or free!) gadgets

No such thing as a free lunch? Guess again! Check out these great ideas that won't blow your budget:

✔ **The White Card Trick:** If your external flash doesn't have a built-in reflector, you can make your own. Set your flash to bounce mode (point it at the ceiling) and take a 3-x-5-inch index card or other card and attach it to the flash with a rubber band. Have the card extend three or more inches beyond the flash head, like the factory-installed reflector shown in Figure 3-6. When you fire the flash, some of the light bounces off the ceiling while more light kicks off the white card to throw some light into your subject's face.

✔ **The Spoon Trick:** If your supply of index cards has been depleted, you can always give The Spoon Trick a try. Similar to the preceding method, use a cheap, white plastic spoon in much the same way as you would use an index card. Some photographers maintain that the curvature of a spoon throws the light out in a curve to provide a more pleasing effect. I've used both methods, and they both work pretty well. It's also pretty easy to carry some rubber bands, plastic spoons, and index cards in your camera bag or find the stuff at most shooting locations.

✓ **The Aluminum Trick:** A third version for those with just a hint of mechanical ability is to take a piece of aircraft aluminum (white or copper colored) and cut it in a roughly squarish or 3-x-5-inch shape. Use hook-and-loop tape on the square and the back of your flash head. Store the card by attaching it upside-down when not in use and then just pull it off, flip it, and reattach for use.

Using a copper-colored piece can warm the color of your light a little, which can be flattering for portraits.

✓ **The Alcohol Bottle Trick:** Just so it doesn't look like all I know is different versions of the White Card Trick, here's one that's a little different. Get one of those white frosted plastic bottles of rubbing alcohol (one whose waist is about the same diameter as your flash head). Remove the alcohol (this is important) and then cut the bottom of the bottle about two inches down the waist. Then snug the waist (the end with the bottom) over the flash head. You can now shoot with the flash head angled almost vertically with a much softer light. (The Alcohol Bottle Trick creates an inexpensive alternative to a product known as the Sto-Fen Omni-Bounce, described in the next group.)

✓ **The Clear 35mm Film Canister Trick:** If you have only a small, fixed flash — *fixed* as in it won't pivot or tilt, not fixed as in *repaired* (but this won't work if the flash is broken either) — here's another way to soften and spread the light from it. Take a clear 35mm film canister (see whether one of your less technologically advanced friends has one you can get from them or try a camera store) and tape it over the flash head. Variations of this trick involve placing a sheet of facial tissue inside the film canister to diffuse (soften) the light a bit or using colored tissue papers to change the color of the light the flash produces. This isn't as big a deal these days, when you can produce all sorts of similar effects in an image-editing program. Still, if you're not real comfortable trying effects in the computer, this method lets you experiment while taking the shot.

✓ **Flash brackets:** Many department stores carry cheap, L-shaped flash brackets. Your camera mounts onto the flash bracket while your flash fits into a flash mount at the top of the L. To use a setup like this, you have to have some way of triggering your flash when it is not attached to the camera. There are several ways to do this.

- If your camera has a PC/X connection (a small circular electrical linkage, as shown in the preceding chapter), you connect your flash via a PC cable.

- A second method is to use a photoelectric slave to trigger your accessory flash unit. To do this, you use your camera's built-in flash unit, perhaps blocking most of its light output with gaffer's tape or masking tape.

As you can see, you have many inexpensive ways of improving the quality of your artificial light. Even the simple White Card Trick combined with bounced flash gives you much better results than bombing away with direct flash. Keep this method in mind even when your available light is enough for a good exposure because the light kicked forward from the white card is a great way to fill in shadows from ball caps and other similarly billed haberdashery items.

Moderately priced gadgets

For just a few dollars more, you can add the following items to your lighting toolbox:

- **Omni-Bounce:** Sto-Fen (www.stofen.com) makes several inexpensive light modifier devices. Best known is the Omni-Bounce, which is a frosted plastic attachment that fits over the flash head and softens the light considerably. The device is used by setting the flash head to a 45-degree angle — unless your subject is more than 15 feet away, and then you set the flash to fire straight on. It costs about $20. The company also makes colored versions of the Omni-Bounce, which cost a few dollars more.

- **Two-Way:** Also made by Sto-Fen, the Two-Way bounce is a sturdier approach to the White Card Trick and works in a similar manner. It also costs about $20.

- **LumiQuest attachments:** LumiQuest (www.lumiquest.com) makes a whole range of flash attachments offering a bunch of different capabilities. These range from simple bounce hoods that kick the flash's output forward and spread it out to ones that perform very specialized functions. Variations of the basic bouncer include attachments to allow some light to bounce off the ceiling while the rest is kicked forward. Another version sends the light through a frosted panel to soften it even more, and a third variation permits insertion of colored panels to change the color of the light that the flash produces while bouncing it.

- **Soft boxes:** By soft box, I don't mean the large box-like attachments for studio flash units. Simple plastic attachments of the same name are available to mount on the head of the flash. They extend about six to eight inches, with a frosted white panel at the end. This attachment lets the light from the flash spread out a little bit inside the soft box, softening it as it passes through the frosted end. Lumiquest, as well as several other companies, also make soft box attachments for portable flash units.

- **Snoots:** LumiQuest also makes a snoot. (No, the company is not snooty; it makes a snoot.) A *snoot* is a tube-like (almost conical) device that focuses the flash's light to a very small area.

   Photographers often use a snoot to create a highlight on someone's hair.

- **Barn doors:** LumiQuest's barn doors attachment fits several of its bounce flash attachments. *Barn doors* are flat panels that can be swung open and closed to more finely tune light output.

- **Flash brackets:** Moderately priced flash brackets tend to be sturdier than their inexpensive counterparts. Plus, they usually tend to lift the flash higher above the camera. Otherwise, things work pretty much the same way.

A decent light modifier can be a pleasure to work with, can significantly improve your photos, and needn't cost you an arm and a leg. You'll find that many can be had for less than $50. A wide variety of choices are available, depending on your needs. For photographers who work mainly out of a camera bag, a small, collapsible light modifier is a better choice than one of the bigger, more cumbersome units. Those who work from a home studio are better off with one of the bigger soft boxes that give a nice-quality light.

Lighting Basics

The idea behind using light — both existing and artificial — is to provide enough illumination to adequately light your subject in a pleasing manner. Sometimes, the light you need is in your shooting environment, ready to use, with no modification required. Figure 3-7, for example, was taken using nothing more than the overhead fluorescent lighting at my camera club's meeting room. You'll luck into fortuitous lighting outdoors, too. But in other situations, you'll need to manipulate the available light or provide your own.

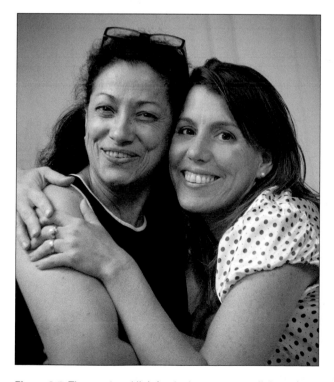

Figure 3-7: The overhead lighting in the room was all that was required for this portrait of two friends.

Using available light

Available light may actually be preferable to your camera's built-in flash for people pictures, because, unlike your camera's flash, you're not locked into straight-on direct lighting. Your camera's internal flash is predictable, always available, and provides high intensities of light, but those are its only advantages. Available light, on the other hand, gives you room to be more creative, even if you want to use nothing more than the lamps already present in the room.

There are some things to keep in mind when working strictly by available light:

✔ **Countering subject/camera motion.** The light levels when using available light are usually lower, so you must be careful to avoid getting blurry pictures caused by slower shutter speeds. Your solutions are to turn on your camera's "anti-shake" or image stabilization features, to increase your camera's sensitivity (ISO) setting to a higher value (such as ISO 800 to ISO 1600) or, (often as a last resort) use a camera support such as a tripod. But most of the time you can get by without the fuss of setting up one of those three-legged monsters.

✔ **Uneven lighting.** Indoor lighting will be very bright near the light source, and fade off rapidly as you move away. This can be good when you want to shoot a moody portrait of someone seated next to a lamp, and not such a good idea when the light is coming from directly overhead and your subject is a fellow with a bald pate. For the simplest kind of available lighting, just be aware that the light does fall off, and position your subjects so they are attractively lit. Later in this chapter I'll offer tips for supplementing indoor light with "fill-in" reflectors, which can be as simple as a piece of white cardboard — or even a white shirt worn by a cooperative by-stander.

✔ **Odd colors.** You'll find that available light comes in colors — and sometimes more than one.

All indoor lighting is likely to have warmer tones than you'll find outdoors, so set the white balance of your camera for Incandescent or Fluorescent light (as appropriate).

✔ **Mixed colors.** The trickiest aspect of shooting by available light comes when you encounter mixed light sources. You may have a subject standing next to a window, with blueish daylight streaming in from outdoors, while the side of your subject away from the window is illuminated by the warm interior lighting. The result? A subject who is blue on one side and yellow on the other.

Professional photographers sometime put up yellow filter material on windows so their light matches the interior lighting. But you don't need to go that far. When faced with window lighting situations, you can turn off the inside lights and let the window light serve as the only source of illumination. Or move your subject so that he or she is not lit by two sources at once.

Later in this chapter I present some techniques for using multiple light sources. Although the descriptions often involve using lamps and flash units designed for photography, you can apply many of the suggestions to ordinary available light people pictures. Just use various lamps that exist in the room; reflectors you create in an ad hoc way from available objects in the room. You can arrange these available light sources in ways that closely reproduce "studio" lighting, but without all the fuss.

Using a single external flash

The simplest, most basic method of providing light is to use a single external flash — preferably with some form of light modification or bouncing — with the flash unit raised higher than the camera. By a single flash, I mean an external flash, rather than the built-in flash that's part of your camera. Your camera's built-in flash doesn't offer the kind of options or the control you need to use lighting creatively. You pop up the flash and fire away. I offer tips on shooting people with the camera's built-in flash in the section "Candid People Pictures" at the beginning of this chapter.

The foremost way to maximize the effectiveness of a one-light photographic system is to get the flash higher than the camera. The closer the flash is to the lens, the greater the likelihood of *red-eye* (that nasty red glare that appears in the eyes when light bounces off the subject's retina), so extending your flash unit's height helps your photography quite a bit. Ways to do this include

**Book III
Chapter 3**

**Photographing
People**

- ✔ **The ol' Statue of Liberty play:** Use an *off-camera shoe cord* (an intelligent cord that communicates between the camera and dedicated flash unit to retain the camera's ability to meter light through the lens) or a PC cord to lift the flash high above the camera. Then either point the light directly at your subject or bounce it off the ceiling.

- ✔ **L-brackets:** Use an L-bracket — or something based on an L-bracket design, such as a Stroboframe grip — to raise the flash up above the camera.

- ✔ **A flash stand with a simple reflector:** This requires either a long PC cord or a wireless transmitter to trigger the flash unit.

One advantage of getting the flash higher than the camera is that it re-creates the single high light source that you're used to seeing naturally — the sun. A second advantage is that by getting the flash higher than the camera and at a higher angle, you reduce the likelihood of red-eye. That's because red-eye is caused by a flash reflecting straight back off the retina of the eye into the camera lens. When the light strikes the back of the eye at a higher angle, it's reflected downward and away from the lens.

Using multiple light sources

Both indoors and out, when using available light or electronic flash, you'll often find it desirable to use more than one light source.

By multiple light sources, I don't necessarily mean scads of electronic flash units and reflectors. You can get by with just one light source and either a secondary source to fill in the shadows, or a simple reflector to perform the same function. Your results are likely to be more pleasing than if you'd used just one source of lighting.

Advantages of a multiple-light-source system include

- ✓ **More control over how much illumination you provide for a scene:** Even if your lights or reflectors are more powerful than you want, you can reduce output or shift your lights farther back.

- ✓ **More control over the mood of the image:** You can control the location and intensity of shadows and highlights, which can affect the overall mood of the image, whether it's stark and full of contrast or soft and moody.

- ✓ **An adaptable lighting kit:** You can adapt your lighting kit to a wide variety of shoots and any number of subjects. Some lighting kits are even versatile enough to be brought on location.

Multiple lighting setups can mean the difference between an adequate portrait photo and a good one. Although a multilight setup doesn't guarantee better quality, getting the hang of such an arrangement will do a lot to improve your informal portrait photography.

With a multiple-light setup, each light has a different role to play. Understanding the basic arrangement helps you get started down the road to good portrait photography.

Main light

Surprise, surprise. The main light is your primary light source, whether it is an existing light source, or one that you provide. The main light provides most of the illumination for your subject. Look at Figure 3-8, in which the main light was soft overhead lighting on an overcast day. The light is coming from the left side of the young man and slightly behind him, leaving the side of his face closest to the camera in partial shadow. (For this picture, the shadows were illuminated with a piece of white foam board used as a fill reflector.)

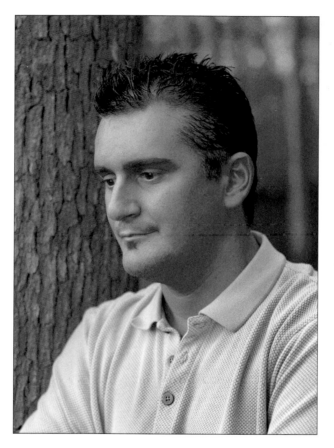

Figure 3-8: The main light is coming from the left and slightly behind the subject.

You can also provide main light (most often indoors) using an off-camera flash or a room lamp placed appropriately. The following list fills you in on some ways to maximize the effectiveness of your main light:

- ✔ **Get it up high.** Your main light should be higher than your subject. You don't have to be ridiculous here; keeping the light about a foot or so higher than your tallest subject will do the trick. Outdoors, if you use the sun as your main light, it will be automatically placed in the ideal, high position.

- ✔ **Make an effort to improve the quality of your light.** You can do this with a reflector. (Yes, reflectors can soften main lights; you aren't forced to use them to fill in shadows.)

✔ **Provide enough power to shoot at a small aperture, thus giving you greater depth of field.** Because bouncing light off a reflector costs you some light, you need a lot of power to shoot a big group at f/11 or f/16.

✔ **Recycle quickly.** If you're using electronic flash, how quickly your main light *recycles* (recharges so that it can be ready to fire again) is very important. You want your lights to keep pace with your workflow, not the other way around. During a sitting, it's important to develop a rhythm with your clients while posing and photographing them. A break in that rhythm, particularly one caused by your lights not being ready, can make your life difficult.

Fill light

The *fill light* is the light that fills in the shadow areas created by the main light, as you can see in its most basic form in Figure 3-8.

If you are using an external flash that doesn't let you reduce or increase the power, try moving it back a bit or perhaps placing a diffuser (such as a hand-kerchief) over the flash.

Thanks to your digital camera's review feature, you can quickly see whether you've reduced the amount of light enough.

Here are some tips for setting up your fill light:

✔ Your fill light or reflector should be roughly the same height as your main light, although slightly lower is okay.

✔ The fill light should also receive some kind of modification, via the soft reflective surface of your reflector or a *diffusion screen* (a thin screen-like material that diffuses or softens the light — think nylon stocking).

The fill light helps balance your portrait lighting and creates a sense of depth to your image. Used properly, it can also create a moody or romantic image through the carefully controlled play of shadows.

Hair light

Professional photographers often use a *hair light,* which is a small, carefully controlled light that puts a highlight on the subject's hair. This type of lighting can also be referred to as a kind of *rim lighting.*

You can produce the same effect without using fancy studio lighting. Figure 3-9 shows an informal portrait that features flattering hair lighting, but no flash or other artificial light was required at all. I simply positioned the model so that the sun was coming from behind her, illuminating her hair, and I used a white foam board reflector to bounce light into her face.

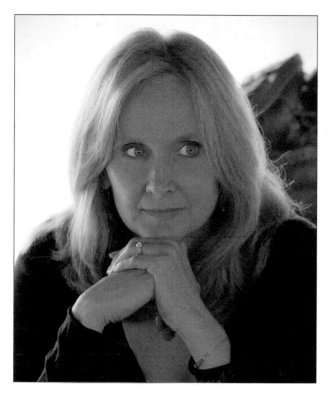

Figure 3-9: A hair light emphasizes the edge of the head.

To use a hair light, position it so that the light is directed almost straight back into the camera, raking across the top of the subject's head. The hair light is emphasized in this example for clarity, but it would be more subtle in your final portrait unless you choose to use extreme backlighting (lighting coming from behind your subject) as I did.

Background light

A *background light,* as its name suggests, lights the background and creates some separation between the subject and background by making the background lighter than the main subject. Figure 3-10 shows an informal picture I snapped of a bride, using *only* the lighting already present in the church, except for a light directed at a paneled wall in the background.

The shot might look professionally set up, but in truth, I moved myself and the bride around so that an overhead spotlight illuminated the side of her face away from the camera. There was enough light bouncing off by-standers who were clad in light colors to fill in the side of her face closest to the camera, and a helpful light in the background lit up the wall behind her.

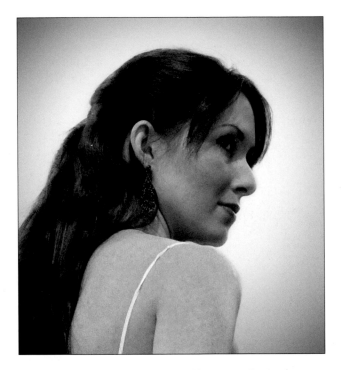

Figure 3-10: A background light provides separation.

If you are forced to provide your own background light, an incandescent lamp or flash is pointed upward at the background. Be careful to position it so that the lighting support (if required) stays hidden behind your subject.

When using the background light, keep the following tips in mind:

- Set the background light about two feet from the backdrop and about two to three feet off the ground.

- Angle the background light upward about 45 degrees so that the light spreads upward and outward from below your subject(s).

- Mount a diffusion screen (which can be as simple as a handkerchief or any other diffusing material) on the light head to soften it as it spreads up the backdrop. Using the screen helps prevent the light from creating a *hot spot* (those annoying bright areas that can crop up in a background if the light isn't spread evenly).

Adding a background light to your portrait setup makes for a cleaner, more pleasing portrait because it helps separate your subjects from the background. Although hardly the most important light in your setup, your subjects can get lost in a dark background without a background light.

Additional light sources

Using the four lights discussed in the preceding sections will take care of the majority of lighting situations, but they're certainly not the only tools to create interesting lighting. For some neat alternatives, try one (or more) of the following:

- ✔ **Reflectors:** Rather than using a fill light, a photographer sometimes bounces light from an angled main light into a reflector positioned near the model but still outside the picture area. This can be a good solution if you don't own a second electronic flash.

- ✔ **Window lighting:** Another charming source of light can be the nearest window. Window-lit portraits require a bright, sunny day with sunlight pouring through the window. Position your subject on a chair near the window. Make sure that your digital camera takes its exposure reading from the portion of his or her cheek that's illuminated by the sunlight. If done properly, your subject appears to emerge from the shadows bathed in a golden glow. A variation of this lighting technique is to use a reflector to kick some light back into the shadow area so that some detail is returned to the side that doesn't receive sunlight.

- ✔ **Sun and fill:** A typical example of this form of lighting is the swimsuit model at the beach. The model is positioned so the early morning sunlight acts as the main light, and a reflector is positioned to direct some light into the shadow areas. This is a very nice style of lighting; unfortunately, it requires you to get up early!

The latter two methods can produce some beautiful lighting but are hard to use for groups or a large number of sittings. It can be hard to schedule a sitting for this kind of lighting technique, too.

Preparing to Take Your First Portraits

Good portraiture is about making your subjects look as they would like to appear — not necessarily as they really are. When you're setting up your poses, reflect upon how to make people look their best.

A good portrait photographer inspires confidence not only in himself but also in the client. The better you can make a person who's posing for you feel about how they look, the better her pose — and the better her feeling about the whole portrait experience. This works in your favor because your subject will likely be interested in buying your photographs. This section provides the basic information you need to get started.

The diamond pose

Diamonds are a photographer's best friend. Professional portrait photographers use a diamond formation as their basic foundation for a group photo.

- Establish your anchor person (usually the mother in a family portrait) and seat him or her.

- Place the father (or second individual) behind the anchor and halfway to the side.

- Elevate the seated person so the top of his/her head is level with the nose of the standing person.

- Have the standing person place his or her hands one on top of the other, slightly angled on the seated person's shoulder. (This is the basic pose for a couple, by the way.)

- Then do the same with the third person to balance the trio. (This gives you a basic pose for three people.)

- Place the fourth person directly behind the first person and positioned so that the heads of subjects two and three come up to the nose of the fourth person. (If possible, have sturdy wooden boxes or blocks of varying sizes for people to stand on.)

- Have subjects 2–4 lean slightly forward from the waist so that their faces are as close as possible to being on the same plane as the first person.

Avoid gaps between bodies, and make sure that people are close to each other.

This basic posing system is expandable to fit 20 people or more.

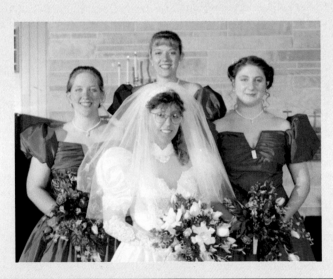

Working on a tight schedule

When you're working for free, it's common for the people you are photographing to be tight with the time they provide you to shoot their pictures.

People pose for portraits for different reasons and in different situations. If you're working on a tight schedule with a lot to do and not much time to do it (this is especially true if you're taking photos after a wedding), you don't have a lot of time. Instead, consider a routine that works something like this:

1. **Pose the family.**

2. **Shoot the family portrait.**

3. **Pull the kids from the family pose.**

4. **Keep Mom and Dad in place and photograph their portrait.**

5. **Pull Mom and Dad from the sitting and set the kids up into a new diamond pose (depending on how many kids you need to photograph).**

   Usually, it's best to pose a group of male children in a line from tallest to shortest. If there's a sister or two, seat the eldest boy and pose the eldest girl as the next diamond element with her hands on his shoulder.

6. **Ask the parents for any special poses they would like.**

   Don't be afraid to take special requests; they're usually very likely to be appreciated.

7. **Divide and conquer.**

   If you're at a wedding, get separate shots of the bride and groom, complete wedding party, bride and attendants (see Figure 3-11), in-laws, and other combinations.

   With most families, Mom is usually the decision maker when it comes to things such as family portraits. Make sure you keep her happy. Have brushes, combs, and lint brushes on hand so that everyone can make sure they look their best. It also doesn't hurt to have some conservative ties and scarves on hand just in case someone has an accident on their way over. Have a hand mirror available so subjects can check themselves out, too.

When you're doing large numbers of portraits (after word gets out about how good you are, you're bound to be the hit of the next family reunion!), strive for the most efficient posing setup and flow possible. People who are sitting around in their finery waiting to be photographed can get pretty grumpy, particularly if there's more than one group waiting.

Try to be flexible enough for a special request because sometimes these can be very profitable. I was once part of a team shooting portraits for a church directory when a husband mentioned that he and his new wife never had a wedding portrait done. We suggested that they come back after our shooting schedule was done in their best suit and wedding gown, and we'd do a series of portraits for them. The couple loved the idea, and we spent an hour creating different poses and portraits and ended up with a huge order! Most importantly, we accomplished this without inconveniencing other members of the church and gained a reputation for enthusiasm and service among that particular church's members.

When you have more time

If you're working with a more generous time schedule, take the time to make your subjects comfortable and see what they're looking for in an informal portrait.

Although you might still be looking at the basic family portrait set (family, couple, children), it's also very possible that each family member might enjoy having you take individual portraits as well.

Here are some of the kinds of groups to expect:

- **Husbands and wives:** Offer husbands and wives the basic couples pose, but also suggest a second pose that illustrates their love and commitment to each other (standing close, gazing into each other's eyes).

  Depending on their age and demeanor, a more whimsical pose, like the one I took of my brother-in-law and his wife for Figure 3-11, might also be in order. If you want a whimsical pose, having the husband get down on one knee to re-create his marriage proposal while the wife "thinks" about it can be cute.

- **Kids:** A brother and sister can be posed in a diagonal with the boy seated and the girl angled behind him with her hands folded on his shoulder. This is a basic couples pose, but the relationship issue isn't important. If you have two posing stools, you can seat them diagonally, one behind the other. A pose that works with two boys is to have them sit back to back with their heads turned toward the camera.

- **Mothers and daughters:** Seat Mom and have her daughters arranged in the appropriate number of elements for a diamond pose. Another option — if you have the posing boxes to do so — is to seat Mom on a posing stool and have a daughter or two seated at her knee. A third daughter (the eldest) would be diagonally behind Mom with her hands on Mom's shoulder. If I had them, I'd load the scene with flowers.

- **Fathers and sons:** A simple pose would be to seat Dad and build a diamond around him. A more adventurous pose would be to have Dad standing slightly sideways with his off-camera hand in his pocket looking at his son(s) posed about a foot away (one diagonally behind the other) while one tosses a ball in the air. (The sons watch the ball; Dad watches the sons.) A simpler variation would be to have the sons remove their suit jackets (if this is a dressy portrait) and sling them over their shoulders (off-camera side) while Dad regards them with arms folded across his chest (still properly attired).

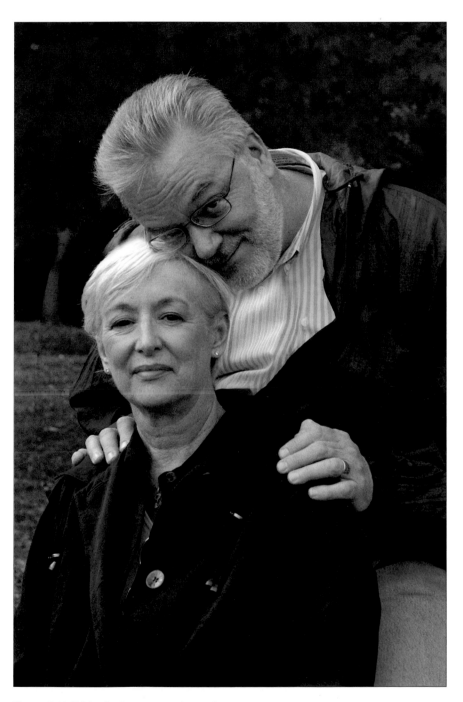

Figure 3-11: Whimsical poses are always fun.

**Book III
Chapter 3**

Photographing People

Advantages of digital cameras

Digital cameras offer you many advantages in portrait photography. Most important of all is the chance for the photographer to review the pose before the subjects leave. Because you can spot problems before your victims skedaddle, you have a chance to correct them while everyone's still there.

Another huge advantage of the digital camera is that it gives you a chance to make sales while your customers are still excited from their sitting and still in high spirits after all that positive feedback you've been giving them. (You have been giving them positive feedback, haven't you?)

Film photographers have to factor the cost of film, processing, and making proofs into their costs of doing business, thus driving up their margins. As a digital photographer, you can afford to take all the shots you want without damaging your bottom line (provided you have enough media to get you through a long shooting session, of course).

Learn to use your digital camera's review feature to its best effect. Here's a list of some of the things you should analyze as you play back your shot:

✔ **Make sure that the photo is properly focused.** Although you can't be dead sure while reading your camera's LCD screen, you can at least eliminate really poor shots. If you have a digital camera that can be hooked up to a television to play back images, by all means do so! This will help you get a better look at your images. You can also show the images to your clients while at the same time taking their orders. (If they're not satisfied, you can also offer to reshoot the sitting while they're still dressed for it.)

✔ **Check for any obvious errors.** Such errors could be gaps between people, bad expressions, or wrinkled clothes. Straighten out the clothing, and make sure the subject's hair looks good and that the image is properly exposed.

✔ **Check for any lighting errors.** These include lights that shine where you don't want them to, bad shadows, and so forth.

✔ If your subjects are wearing glasses, check for any hot spots that might be too difficult to clean up in an image-editing program. Repositioning someone's glasses is easier than heavy computer retouching, so make your job easier when you can.

✔ **Check for any blinkers.** This can be pretty tough with small LCD screens; a TV monitor makes this easier.

✔ **Infants:** For a fancy pose, look for an old-fashioned baby buggy or other such prop. A lot of choices are available, including simulated giant seashells for the baby to sit in or bearskin rugs to lie on.

Generally, how you pose an infant depends on his or her age and physical abilities, such as whether the infant can sit up unsupported. Babies younger than six weeks old usually can't focus their eyes on any specific point, so they present a special challenge. Usually, it's best to leave them in their carrier and go for a reasonably tight shot.

As a general rule, pose multiple people closer together than they would normally stand if left to personal space comfort levels. Your goal is to maximize the use of space by filling the frame as effectively as possible with people, not backdrop or props. This doesn't mean that you're doing nothing but headshots, though. If you're doing a wedding or prom shoot, people will be in their finest clothes, and showing that clothing is appropriate. Certainly, the bride in her wedding gown deserves at least one photo that shows her entire dress, including the train.

Portrait Tips

Posing your informal portrait subjects need not be tricky, even though neither you nor they may have much experience in this arcane art. The best way to start is to have your subjects focus their eyes slightly to one side of the lens. Have them bring their chins up slightly so they're looking slightly up and away from the camera.

While seating your subjects, remember the following:

- ✔ **Make sure that your subjects are sitting up straight.** Slouching just doesn't look flattering to anyone.

- ✔ **Check to make sure clothing is as wrinkle-free as possible.** Tug suit jackets to straighten out wrinkles if need be.

- ✔ **Use your camera's Live View or picture review feature to make sure you minimize the glare from eyeglasses as much as possible.** Tilting the head or angling the glasses themselves slightly downward can minimize bounce back from flash or other illumination.

- ✔ **Provide a mirror so your subjects can check themselves over just before you take the picture.** Knowing they look good helps people relax.

Use this time to get your subjects in position and into the right mood for the portrait. Remember to stay positive and encouraging. Be sure to tell them they look good. Crack a few jokes while positioning people to keep them relaxed, too.

I recommend triggering the camera via a remote so that you can maintain eye contact with your subjects. Many digital cameras (both digital SLR and point-and-shoot types) offer some method of triggering the shutter without tripping the shutter button. If yours doesn't, you can still fire the camera via the shutter button while looking over the camera at your subjects.

Before tripping the shutter, go through this very quick checklist:

1. Is everyone standing up straight?
2. Are their heads properly arranged so that their faces are directed toward the camera?
3. Is everyone looking either directly toward the camera lens or in the direction you've designated? (Some poses may look better if you have your subjects looking slightly past the lens.)
4. Is everyone smiling?

Be ready to work fast. Holding a pose is a tiring chore. People lose their patience if you take too long to trip the shutter, so be ready to run through the checklist quickly.

Don't be afraid to stop and correct someone who's relaxed his or her pose. It doesn't do you any good to trip the shutter if someone doesn't look good.

I usually hold the remote behind my back when tripping the shutter during a portrait session in order to keep people from realizing I'm about to take the picture. This is important for two reasons:

- I don't want to give people a reason to shift their eyes in the direction of my hand when I'm taking the shot.
- Many people anticipate the flash firing and blink their eyes when the lights fire.

Remember to keep watching your subjects as you trip the shutter. You can usually catch any blinkers and know that you need to take another shot.

Chapter 4: Shooting for Publication

In This Chapter

- ✓ Finding outlets for publication
- ✓ Shooting for local newspapers
- ✓ Publishing in magazines and similar markets
- ✓ Photographing for company newsletters
- ✓ Effective public relations photography

For some readers of this book, becoming a published photographer might be a lifelong goal. Many avid photographers hone their skills, trying to reach ever higher levels in a quest for a published credit line.

However, the average digital camera buff more often ends up shooting for publication for more practical reasons. Perhaps your parent-teacher association drafted you to publicize school events. Or maybe your small company doesn't have a full-time photographer, so you — with your digital camera wizardry — seem perfect to snap a portrait of the founder for the organization's newsletter. Perhaps you're a recognized expert in your hobby, customizing vintage Atari game consoles, and would like to have a few photographs published in one of the technical magazines devoted to '80s-era games.

Digital photography lends itself to all these situations because you can take a picture on a moment's notice, review your results on your camera's LCD, take *another* picture if you need to, and then produce a digital file or print that's ready for publication in a few minutes. Most professional photographers shooting for newspapers, magazines, catalogs, and other publications now use digital cameras — and you can, too.

In all these cases, your digital pictures are going to end up in print, and you need to know some things in order to shine when shooting for publication. This chapter explains the differences between taking pictures for print and for Web sites, desktop presentations, or a personal photo album. You can also find some tips on how to get published and advice on preparing your work for publication.

Finding Outlets for Print or Digital Publication

Whether you want to get published simply to satisfy yourself or you need to have your photos published to satisfy the expectations of your friends, boss, or colleagues, you can find lots of outlets for your digital work. Here are a few of the most common:

- ✓ **Local newspapers:** Although larger newspapers rarely publish photos from readers in their print editions, even the largest may have a reader photo section on its Web site. You may be able to take photos and upload them directly from your computer and then, if they are approved, they'll be displayed in a reader photo section. Smaller local papers usually welcome submissions of photos on behalf of your school, club, or even business for their print or Web editions. You can make a habit of showing up at public meetings or fast-breaking news events. If you supply enough good shots in a variety of situations the paper might take you on as a part-time *stringer* (a freelancer with an ongoing affiliation with a publication). Because digital pictures can be snapped and transmitted to a newspaper over an Internet connection just minutes after an event takes place, electronic photos are especially apt.

- ✓ **Trade magazines and Web sites:** These are the unseen publications that nobody knows about, except for the millions of people within a particular industry. Many of them have Web sites in addition to their print versions. You might never have heard of *Repro Report* magazine unless you're a member of the International Reprographics Association. I had never heard of it, either, when I started taking pictures for the magazine (way back when it was still called *Plan and Print*.) However, that publication (and many like it) are constantly looking for photos taken at member businesses, conventions, and other venues. These trade publications are good outlets for digital photography, and I've managed to have my own photographs published in hundreds of them. If you belong to any sort of club or trade organization (and don't particularly care about getting paid for your work), you'll find lots of opportunities in trade publications. Most of the pictures in many of these magazines are taken by amateur photographers just like yourself.

- ✓ **Company publications:** Companies of any size can never have enough people taking pictures. If your organization is small, management might be delighted to find a photographer who's outfitted with fast and flexible digital gear and who's also ready, willing, and able to snap photos for company newsletters, annual reports, and other official publications. Even larger organizations with a full-time photography staff might be receptive to photos that you take at events that their pros are unable to cover. And if they are unable to use them in their printed publications, you may find an outlet on the corporate Web site.

- ✓ **Special-interest publications and blogs:** Every hobby or special interest, whether it's collecting Seat Occupied signs from defunct airlines or protecting your right to arm bears, probably has a publication of some sort. If you share that interest, you can easily get your digital photos published. Bloggers may be especially open to submissions from folks with similar interests.

- ✔ **External PR and advertising:** Most organizations, clubs, and other groups can use photos for public relations or advertising purposes. Perhaps your chess club is having a membership drive and will be using news releases or small ads in your local newspaper. If you're good, your work can accompany news releases or be incorporated into less formal advertising layouts. Digital cameras are good for these applications because you can create a photo in a few minutes, ready for review and approval by the high mucky-mucks in an organization.

- ✔ **Self-publication:** The fastest route to getting your digital photos printed is to publish them yourself. Whether your interests stem from a favorite hobby or from the most arcane conspiracy theories, if you have a computer, you can create a newsletter, fanzine, or other publication and spice it up with your own photos.

The best part about self-publication is that you have absolute control over which images are used, how they are sized and cropped, and who gets to see them. And who knows? If your work is good, you might get paying subscribers to cover part of your costs. In my case, I knew that no publisher would possibly want to print my illustrated guidebook to repairing vintage video games, so I took the photos, laid out the manual, and published it myself, as you can see in Figure 4-1. I've sold thousands of copies on eBay of something that I put together just for fun.

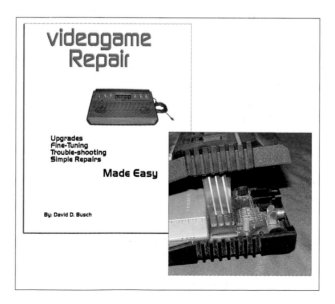

Figure 4-1: Publish your own fan magazine or other publication and put your photos to work.

✔ **Product photographs:** Your company probably needs photos of its products for use in advertising, PR, and so forth. You can take them with your digital camera.

Shooting for publication isn't as hard as many people think, provided you remember that you don't start out shooting for slick, nationally distributed magazines any more than aspiring ball players begin by playing shortstop for the New York Yankees. If *National Grocer* is your target, rather than *National Geographic,* you have a shot.

Breaking into Newspaper Photography

Your local paper is probably willing to consider your digital photos of a local event, particularly if it's a small paper, either for its daily or weekly edition or for its Web coverage. Larger newspapers prefer to use their own photographers for official photography — not because they don't think your photos are good enough but because of journalistic ethics reasons. Big papers frequently face charges of journalistic bias and must be able to vouch that a given photograph hasn't been manipulated in ways that would make it misleading. Photographs supplied by businesses can't be used unless they are clearly labeled as a photograph originating with that organization. However, bear in mind that even big cities have small, special-interest papers that can be a market for your pictures.

Newspaper photography is fun and challenging. This type of shooting isn't especially rewarding financially, but it does provide valuable experience because you learn to adapt your photographic ability to the environment. No other type of photography offers the shooter as little control over the shooting conditions as photojournalism. For some of us, that's the best thing about it.

Submitting photos to your local newspaper

The key to getting published in your local paper is understanding what it does and doesn't need from you. Newspapers have small photo staffs and can't be everywhere at once. They'll send a photographer *(shooter,* in the lingo of photo editors) to a major event or fire or accident, but if several events happen at the same time, shooters probably will have to cover one or two events and let the others slide. For example, I regularly cover events at my kids' school and submit them to the newspaper, which uses them on its Web page or in the hard copy edition. Our paper even prints the articles that accompany the photos, as you can see in Figure 4-2.

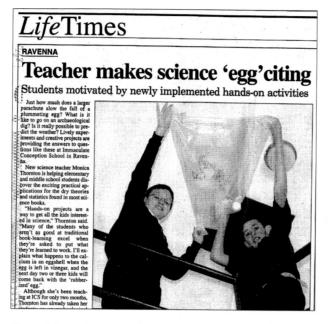

Figure 4-2: Local newspapers are welcome territory for freelancers.

Here are some of the kinds of photos that smaller newspapers would love to receive:

- **Events:** Your club or fraternity is having its annual barbecue or banquet or get-together of whatever form. It's not a big enough deal for the local paper to send someone to cover. If you can produce some usable images along with enough information to caption them properly, you can probably get at least one of them published. Newspapers are willing to run photos like these because people like to see their pictures in the paper — and that helps sell newspapers.

- **Sports:** The paper's shooters cover the big events, such as football, basketball, baseball, and so on. Your opportunity comes with the sports that don't quite get their due. For example, shoot track and field events (not necessarily the big weekend meets with 50 schools and a thousand athletes, but the local dual meet). Sports like tennis, field hockey, and lacrosse seldom get as much coverage as the big three (football, basketball, and baseball). Study your local paper to see what sports it seems to favor and then try submitting shots for the sports it doesn't seem to cover. Good action photos are particularly important. If you can regularly capture peak action well, your photos will be used. See Book III, Chapter 5, for more information on how to take good sports photos with a digital camera.

✔ **Spot news:** *Spot news* includes things such as traffic accidents, fires, and robberies. It can be tough to succeed at selling this kind of photo unless it's your main focus. If so, a police/fire scanner is a must. Remember, though, that it doesn't do you any good if you're covering the same news as the paper's staffer. Small-town papers tend to need this kind of material most and are sure to send out their own staffers at the first hint of a big story, but you might have a shot at publication if you're in the right place at the right time to take a photo of something that no one else managed to grab. (Some spot news opportunities don't last very long, which is why they're called *spot news.*) And because your digital camera film doesn't need processing, your photos are timely.

Although dramatic photos of spot news events can produce eye-catching portfolio shots, don't forget that human emotion creates the most memorable images. This is perhaps the most difficult part of photojournalism — intruding upon the tragedy of others and recording it for the world to see. Pros don't really have a choice in this matter — it's part of the job. Freelancers, however, can choose either side of the deal.

You might run across groups claiming that, as part of their membership fee, you'll receive a press pass that will get you across police lines or into events. *Be very skeptical of such claims.* Usually, an organization, such as the state police (in some states at least) or event organizers, issues a press pass. There is no universal press pass that gets you into any event. In fact, even working news photographers with state-issued press passes won't get into many events (pro sports and rock concerts for instance) unless they're specifically cleared for that event by the event organizer as well.

✔ **Hard news:** These are major news events, such as a speech by the mayor, a visit by the governor, certain press conferences, demonstrations, and political rallies. They're frequently open to the general public, although official photographers might be given a special area to shoot from.

✔ **News feature photography:** Feature photos and *news* feature photos are different. A news feature image accompanies a legitimate story with a feature edge — say an article on family TV-watching habits or a story on an upcoming play that will be performed this weekend (as shown in Figure 4-3).

✔ **Feature photography:** This part of the paper deals with the lighter side of life. You might shoot a feature package on Elvis impersonators or pictures of a local restaurant for a review. This is the one section of the paper where you'll frequently see *created images,* or what are sometimes called *photo illustrations.* You can often tie some local happening in to a historical event to give your feature photo an interesting angle. For example, on May 4 of every year, I always find a ready market for photos of the 1970 shootings of four students on the Kent State University campus.

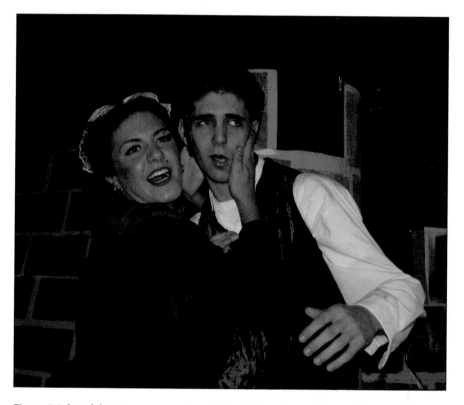

Figure 4-3: Local theater groups can be a subject of good news feature photographs.

You don't have to limit yourself to just one community newspaper. More often than not, neighboring newspapers have circulation areas that overlap. If you know your neighboring communities well, you can also market your talents to their newspapers.

Taking pictures for your local paper

Whether you submit photographs to newspapers as a representative of your organization or just for the thrill of being published, there are lots of points to consider.

Gathering publishable photographs

Never forget this omnipresent law of the photographer looking to have images published: *In focus and properly exposed.* It's amazing how often these basics aren't met when people submit photos to their local newspaper. I know from personal experience: At one newspaper I worked for, I was the one who had to weed through all those pictures trying to find something we could actually use.

Special considerations for news photography

Here are some things to think about when photographing news events:

✓ **Be aware of emotions.** Tempers can run high at both spot and hard news events. Sometimes, law enforcement personnel can overreact when things go wrong. Cameras can be broken, memory cards can get confiscated, and photographers can be threatened. More and more often these days, police (although to be fair, still not that often) try to stop photographers from working, First Amendment considerations be damned. In such situations, newspaper photographers tend to have their newspaper's resources behind them, whereas an amateur or freelancer probably doesn't. It's best to accept that you're not on a level playing field in such circumstances. In small towns, you can avoid problems by getting the police and firefighters on your side. Give them prints and work hard at getting favorable photos in the newspaper.

✓ **Be different.** Your best bet is to deliver something different from what everyone else is doing. One of the best news shots I've ever seen came from a presidential campaign several decades ago. The photo is of a president answering questions with a mountain of photographers pressed together shooting away. One enterprising shooter had enough of a sense of the moment to take a few steps back and record the insanity of the situation. In the process, he got a timeless photo that far exceeded the images his counterparts created.

✓ **Look for unusual angles.** Shoot from up high and down low. Try to get the shot with several different focal lengths, too.

✓ **Be careful not to get locked in on the main event.** Sometimes, the best shot comes because you look beyond the setting and uncover human nature at work. Young children can offer interesting opportunities because they don't hide their reactions or feelings as much as adults do. A sleeping child at a political event or wedding can show humor and make a comment about how sometimes adults take themselves too seriously.

✓ **Look at the participants who aren't center stage.** Is there a clandestine conversation going on? Do they look bored? Are they looking in the opposite direction of everyone else?

News photography strives for impact. Eye contact and emotions are key ingredients. Don't be afraid to compose your shot tightly. The image should have a single focal point, not multiple ones. Whether you're shooting for a newspaper or the World Wide Web, space is valuable, and images should be tightly cropped and easily understood.

So start by sending your best work. Publishable photographs are different from fine art. Their purpose is to communicate as simply and effectively as possible. Because you can do that, here's how to take the next step toward seeing your work in print:

✓ **Be organized.** Have a filing system that enables you to identify and locate a particular image.

✔ **Be ready to do some research.** Your local library is sure to carry references, such as the publication you're interested in selling to as well as *Photographer's Market.* Consider investing in your own copy because *Photographer's Market* provides information on a wide range of possible markets. You can easily locate publications looking for amateurs like yourself who can supply interesting pictures.

✔ **Consider ordering your own business cards and stationery in order to look professional — even if you're not.** If your personal budget allows, consider a promotional piece, such as a four-color postcard or print showing some samples of your best work. The piece will open doors for you, giving you access to more situations in which you can take photos, and help "sell" your work, even if you're giving it away for free.

Making contact with a publication or Web site

The magazine industry and typical commercial Web sites do not respond well to unsolicited photographs. Although you have a better chance of getting published with a trade journal than with most other types of publications, you improve your chances by sending the publication's editor a carefully worded missive indicating what he or she can expect.

Sometimes, a publication or Web site accepts unsolicited photos or manuscripts. You can usually find this information noted in the magazine's *masthead,* located inside the first few pages of the magazine and listing the publisher, staff, and contact information. For Web sites, check out their About page or the Contact Us forms. If a publication does accept unsolicited submissions, be selective. Don't bombard an editor with a submission per week or more. (Editors can get restraining orders, too.) Instead, send your best. Either include an SASE (self-addressed, stamped envelope) with enough postage for the editor to return the photos to you or attach a note saying they don't have to come back.

Introduce yourself in a query letter. Talk about your experience in the industry, plus your experience as a writer and photographer if it might help. Let the editors know what your photo or story idea is and how you plan on approaching it. Also indicate that you're familiar with the publication's guidelines for writers.

Writer's and photographer's guidelines are frequently available on the Web or by mail and are sometimes even noted in the publication itself. Books such as the *Writer's Market* and *Photographer's Market* appear yearly, providing useful information about many publications. Generally, this information tells you how publications want materials submitted. (Do they accept digital photos? Should you submit prints with them? How should prints be packaged? Do the publications even accept work from amateurs or freelancers?) Publications such as trade journals are more forgiving if you violate their writer's guides than other magazines are, but it's still best not to do so. (Remember, you're trying to convince them that you're a professional.)

Whatever individual guidelines a publication has, you'd be wise to keep the following in mind:

- ✔ **Be enthusiastic!** You can't expect editors to get fired up about your idea if it sounds like you find it dull. Tell them why you think their readers will want to read your story.

- ✔ **Send in your tear sheets.** If you have samples of published work (usually referred to as *tear sheets),* or a Web page where your photos can be seen, go ahead and submit the best one or two (three at the most) pieces you've done, or a URL for your own Web page. Typical tear sheets are shown in Figure 4-4. Quality is tremendously more important than quantity here.

If you don't have something good to submit, don't submit anything at all unless the editors or guidelines ask for it. Frequently, editors take on mediocre writing with good photography simply because they can improve poor writing but might have trouble finding good photography.

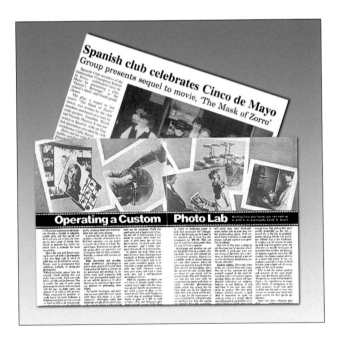

Figure 4-4: Send in some clippings or tear sheets of your published work.

Trade journals are the best place to start if you're interested in expanding beyond newspaper work. They tend to be receptive to freelancers and provide the opportunity to contribute both photos and text. If writing isn't your thing, see whether you can team up with a newspaper staffer or stringer who's also looking to expand his or her reach.

Editors and content supervisors of Web sites hate submissions and query letters that make it obvious the people contacting them haven't even looked at their magazine or site. You can study a given Web site for clues about what they'd be interested in, and if you'd like your photos in a magazine, you should study the magazine itself. Most publications offer copies at a reasonable rate for would-be contributors, or your local library may have back issues available. Get to know the magazine or site before you propose a story idea. Studying back issues or online archives tells you whether you've been beaten to the punch by another contributor — or you might find out that a publication is the wrong market for your submission.

Submitting your photos

Web sites usually welcome electronic submissions, but a dwindling number of print publications remain cautious about digital submissions for final publication (perhaps accepting CD submissions for portfolio samples) and might not even be willing to consider them. If the fact that your images are digital is the only thing preventing them from acceptance, consider converting them to analog artwork. A few publications accept prints, but these are in the minority. Generally, the favorite format for publications that do not accept electronic submissions is still transparencies, or *slides*. The good news is that you have a couple of ways to get 35mm slides made from digital files:

- Online photo labs frequently offer this service. One such lab is www.slides.com, which charges about $2.50 per slide.

- Get a 5 x 7 or 8 x 10 print made from your digital file and load your film camera with a good quality slide film. Then, either set up a *copy stand* (the camera is placed perfectly parallel to the print with two lights placed at 45-degree angles to the print) or your tripod and photograph the print.

As time goes by, more and more publications are accepting digital images. Odds are high that your local newspaper will. It's a nice feeling to discuss an image with an editor, e-mail him or her the image, and find out that it has been accepted, all in a single afternoon (particularly when you're selling a shot for the second or third or fourth time).

Getting model releases

A *model release* is written permission to use a person's likeness. These documents, available from any photo store, are popular with publishers because they help protect the publisher from nuisance lawsuits. The need for model releases depends upon how the images are to be used. Newspaper photographers, for instance, seldom bother. Editorial use is generally recognized by the courts to support the public good and provides some protections to such publications expected to meet that need. Usually newspapers, news magazines, and books are considered to meet the editorial-use standard, although most book publishers desire model releases anyway. Advertising photography, on the other hand, receives no such help. If your photo is going to help sell a product, have a model release for every *recognizable* individual in the shot.

Even as a newspaper photographer, I still try to be careful when it comes to photographing children. Usually, I look for the adult caretakers first, introduce myself to them, explain my purpose in taking pictures of the kids, and give them one of my business cards before asking their permission to shoot. Perhaps this was more than I needed to do, but parents rarely object after they know who I am and why I am taking pictures of their kids. Skip this approach, and you might end up explaining yourself to a state trooper instead. Also, a parent or guardian must sign model releases for minors if you want those releases to count.

A model release doesn't give you *carte blanche* to play with a person's image, which is something that's very easy to do with a digital photograph. Taking someone's image under innocuous circumstances and then placing it into what could be considered an embarrassing photo composite could leave you open to a lawsuit. When in doubt, be careful and consult a lawyer or discuss the potential use with your subject (making sure your model release reflects the potential use and the subject's awareness of it). Model releases are particularly important for stock photography, where the image could end up being used for just about anything.

In some cases, public figures receive less privacy protection than private citizens when it comes to editorial photography. (Think of how the paparazzi chase celebrities. If you followed your private citizen neighbor around that way, no doubt your future cellmate would probably be amused to learn how you ended up in jail.) No such leeway exists to advertising-related uses, particularly because celebrities can argue that their likeness does have a monetary value and that your image is lowering its value.

Shooting Groups for Publication

This section details the special needs of each of the most common types of group photography for publication, such as PR photos. In each section, you can find suggestions for taking great photos in a variety of situations. You'll find that these photos fit in with many different types of publications, from newspapers to trade magazines to company in-house newsletters to popular magazines. The tips in this section can be applied to many different types of print destinations.

Understanding group photography basics

Photographing groups can be an interesting challenge, one that calls for greater skill as the number of people in the shot grows. As you add more and more people to the frame, it becomes more difficult to catch a moment when everyone has a pleasant expression. As the numbers increase, faces get smaller, making it increasingly difficult just to make sure everyone is visible in the shot.

Group shots are popular — and for the photographer who can do a good job, rewarding. As souvenirs of large events, they're a well-accepted and comparatively easy way to commemorate a gathering. People have also become so trained to expect a group shot that trying to get through an event without taking one is almost a sacrilege. Thankfully, good group photos aren't impossible; they just need some planning and the right tools. They're perfect for trade publications looking to publicize member groups, or for your local newspaper.

Pose your group to conform to your camera's image area. For virtually all digital cameras, this means a horizontal rectangle that conforms to a roughly 2:3 aspect ratio.

Posing a group depends upon how many people you're working with. Book III, Chapter 3 covers this topic in more detail, but the following sections dish out some helpful information.

Book III
Chapter 4

Shooting for
Publication

Photographing groups of two to two dozen

Although 20 people might not seem like a small group, the techniques that you use to photograph collections of two dozen people or fewer are similar. Diamonds are a photographer's best friend. Professional portrait photographers use a diamond formation as their basic foundation for a group photo.

The way it works is to establish your anchor person (usually the main person in a group picture, such as the president of your club) and seat that person. Place the second individual behind the anchor person and halfway to the side. Elevate the anchor person so that the top of his or her head is level with the nose of the standing person. Have the standing person place his or her hands, one on top of the other and slightly angled, on the anchor person's shoulder. (This is the basic pose for a couple, too.) Now, on the opposite side of the anchor person, pose the third person the same way you posed the second person to balance the trio. (This gives you a basic pose for three people.)

Now place the fourth person directly behind the anchor person and positioned so that the heads of subjects two and three come up to the nose of the fourth person. (Have sturdy wooden boxes or blocks of varying sizes for people to stand on.) Have subjects two through four lean slightly forward from the waist so that their faces are as close to being on the same plane as the first person as possible. You do this so that everyone is on the same plane of focus. Make sure that people are close to each other so there aren't any gaps between bodies. Now you have a basic posing system that's expandable to fit 20 or more people.

If you can't use a diamond-shaped pose, switch to a row arrangement, with a mix of sitting, kneeling, and standing subjects. Generally, four people or fewer make your first row. If you have five people, you can shift to a two-person front row and three-person back row. Figure 4-5 shows a modified diamond arrangement. If you look carefully, you'll see that the six historical re-enactors are arranged in two half-diamonds, side by side. Their heads are each at slightly different levels, too, which makes for a more pleasing composition than if there were two rows with all the heads of the same height.

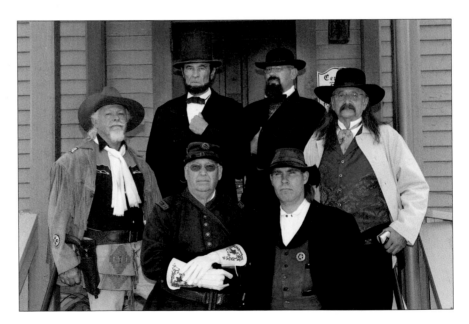

Figure 4-5: Even when you arrange your subjects in rows, an interesting pattern can be produced.

Composing effective group shots

The general rule is that people don't buy portraits because their knees look good. Compose the shot from roughly above the waist to a little bit above the tallest person's head. Of course, this rule has a couple of exceptions. Wedding pictures should include all the finery, and so should any other formal events in which people are wearing fancy dress like gowns and tuxedos. When in doubt, take two shots — one long and one tight — and let your subjects pick the ones they prefer. Here are some tips for arranging groups:

✔ **Five to 7 people:** Start with your basic four-person diamond pose (see the preceding section) and then start building a second diamond on top of the fourth person of the first diamond. Use that person as the anchor person for the second diamond.

✔ **Eight to 20 or more people:** As you add more and more people, keep joining new diamonds with existing diamonds until this system starts becoming unwieldy. Generally, this happens somewhere between 10 and 20 people, although experienced photographers can manage bigger groups.

✔ **More than 20:** At whatever point you feel uncomfortable with fitting a larger number of people into diamonds, switch to rows. Once again, remember the dimensions of your viewfinder. Keep the number of rows and columns proportioned so that you fill the frame effectively. With the rows and columns approach, divide each row in half and angle the halves into each other so that you can bring people closer together. Have your tallest rank kneel, position your shortest rank behind them, and then work your way back (tweaking if the tallest and shortest are so extreme that this alignment doesn't work). As you position each row, make sure that you can see each person's face from your camera position. When you use this technique for a large group, your first and most important goal is to make sure nobody's face is blocked.

Managing the group

People tend to get impatient in such situations, especially if they're among the first to get posed. Staying enthusiastic and cheerful buys you time and patience from your subjects. Here are some ideas that have proven to work in the past:

✔ **Don't worry, mon.** Explain to your subjects not to worry about posing until everyone is in place. Keep them relaxed as long as you can because posing is tiring and stressful for most people.

✔ **Please, stay put.** I usually stress to people that I'm going to take more than one photo and ask them not to flee like startled deer the first time my flash goes off. (Every time they laugh at one of your jokes, you've gained a couple of more minutes of patience from them.)

✔ **Avoid flashers.** If your digital camera uses a preflash or red-eye reduction of any sort, either turn it off (if possible) or alert your subjects to ignore the preflash. Otherwise, they'll release their poses just as the main flash fires. When you're ready to shoot, tell everyone to look directly into the camera lens. Look carefully through your viewfinder and quickly check each person to make sure you can see everyone's face. If you can't, stop and correct poses. If you can, start shooting.

Keep your sense of humor no matter how challenging the group shot gets. If you can keep everyone smiling and relaxed, you'll get a good shot sooner or later.

Try to have people say something that will make them smile. *Vacation!* is usually successful, as is *Hawaii. Stock options* used to work well with business types, but with the current market conditions, you might get tears these days. (Remember, you're going for smiles, not hysterical laughter here.) Having people say, "Cheese" is a no-no.

Back in my days shooting portraits, I had different phrases for families, parents, boys, and girls. *Vacation* and *Hawaii* work for just about anyone. *Yes, dear* and *honeymoon* work nicely with couples, as does *10 more kids!* (Some moms get a look of terror when they hear this one, though.) Young children generally smile for *Cowabunga, dude* (even if it is getting kind of dated), but any cartoon hero catchphrase will probably work. For teenage boys, a sequence beginning with *girls* for shot one, *lotsa girls* for shot two, and *lotsa girls in skimpy bikinis* for shot three is just about guaranteed to work. These days, a similar male-oriented sequence for teenage girls also works.

Lighting groups

See Book III, Chapter 3, for more information on lighting. Here are some general tips that you can use when lighting group photos that you hope will be publishable:

✔ **The serious amateur way:** A less professional setup that can still deliver good results is to use multiple slaved portable flashes, which are triggered by the burst from a main electronic flash unit.

✔ **The not-so-serious amateur way:** One external flash, pointed straight ahead. It's not elegant, the light's kind of harsh, and you run the risk of red-eye, especially with kids. Getting your flash up higher helps prevent red-eye and gives you a nicer light, but even one flash can do you some good because it helps clean up shadows on your subjects' faces.

✔ **The "Oh my god, what were you thinking?" way:** The camera's built-in flash. You've got to be kidding. Most built-in flash units have a range of about 8 feet. It might do some good with a small group, but it's useless with a big one.

PR Photography

Public relations (PR) photography frequently looks like photojournalism, but note an important difference: If you take photos for eventual publication in newspapers as editorial matter, you must try very hard to be balanced, objective, and unbiased. PR photography doesn't have that restriction.

The goal in this kind of shooting is to present your club, group, or organization in the best possible light. This kind of photography calls for a good sense of diplomacy — and if the organization happens to be a large business, the ability to work as a member of the team with the company's public relations personnel. Generally, the PR department has some specific ideas of what message it would like the image to convey.

PR photography can take many forms, ranging from creating executive portraits for senior company personnel to special event photography to taking photos for the company newsletter or a sales brochure. PR doesn't apply only to businesses, either. Your social organization or church might need some useful PR. Perhaps a new church has opened and the parish could use an attractive photo, like the one shown in Figure 4-6, for publicity or for the bulletin. Anything newsworthy is ripe for PR photography. The next sections cover the particular varieties of PR photography in greater detail.

Executive portraits

If you have a staff position with a company or operate your own photography business, you may be called upon to shoot pictures of the top brass of a company or organization. Executive portraits can vary and include basic head-and-shoulders portraits, commanding-executive-in-charge-at-the-helm/desk photos, and leader-with-his-or-her-troops pictures. You can find more on shooting portraits in Book III, Chapter 3, but for now, check out the basic kinds of executive portraits you might be asked to shoot.

**Book III
Chapter 4**

**Shooting for
Publication**

- ✔ **Head-and-shoulders shot:** This is a basic portrait. Take a variety of shots and poses, including smiling, visionary, and serious. Don't be surprised if an executive has some very clear ideas about how he or she wants to look. You and the PR staffer should look the execs over carefully to make sure they look their best. If they don't, offer them a mirror and a comb (if their hair is out of place) or a lint brush if their clothes need it. Also use an appropriate backdrop. The PR types in your organization might be able to suggest the best backdrop for a particular executive.

- ✔ **Desk shot:** This portrait shows the captain of industry hard at work at his or her desk. Skip the backdrop, but check the background thoroughly through your viewfinder. Some honors and photographs are fine, but if it's too cluttered, consider changing camera angles a little to clean things up. Because you're shooting the exec at his or her desk, indications that it's a working space are important. A neatly arranged pen set and a single document on the gleaming mahogany desk is plenty. Whatever you do, don't show a messy, cluttered desk.

- **Confab:** This shot's a bit trickier. The idea is to show the exec as an in-charge leader. Usually, it's done with the standing exec giving instructions to a pair of underlings. The exec is turned toward the camera (slightly angled) with the underlings posed mostly away from the camera. Underlings should be carefully selected (this is the PR department's job) because it's an opportunity for the company to show it's an equal opportunity employer, or minority employer, or whatever.

- **Setting:** The setting is usually in the nicer section of the company headquarters, but it could also be in a location shoot that showcases something about the firm. The location could be anywhere business-appropriate, such as a shipyard, an oil field, a factory assembly line, or a restaurant.

- **One of the gang:** This shot is for the charismatic executive whose rapport with the troops is legendary. Forget the suits, mahogany desk, and rich carpeting. Instead, he or she is dressed casually. In fact, it should be hard to tell the executive from the employees, except for the fact that everyone in the photo is hanging on his or her words.

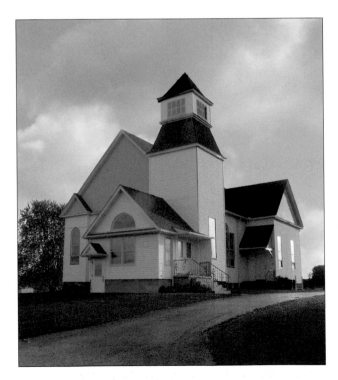

Figure 4-6: You might be the only one qualified to take an attractive shot to publicize the opening of a new building in your area.

✔ ***Really* one of the gang:** From time to time, you'll need to take a head-and-shoulders shot of someone who really is one of the gang: a non-executive, non-manager, ordinary star-of-the-warehouse type. Maybe she had a great bowling score on behalf of the company team. Or he had perfect attendance for 10 years. In such cases, a formal portrait would be inappropriate. You need to be prepared to grab a simple, flattering, head-and-shoulders shot, like the one shown in Figure 4-7.

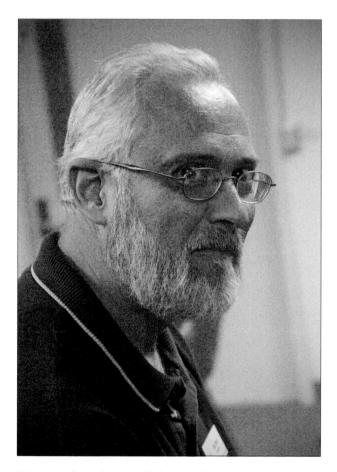

Figure 4-7: Sometimes you'll photograph non-executives for the company newsletter, too.

Being able to produce a wide range of executive photos is a good skill for a PR photographer because there's always a place for these images, whether it be the company newsletter or the latest annual report.

Company events

Shooting company events usually revolves around documenting activity for outside company publications and also for distribution among employees. Usually, this means that the photographer is expected to take a lot of pictures — and the biggest challenge is being thorough enough.

Here are the main types of company events you'll be called on to capture:

- **Company dinners:** A company holds a dinner for a lot of reasons. Plan on getting photos of the speakers, award recipients (if any), company executives, and as many attendees as possible. Special-event dinners (fund-drive events, seasonal parties, recognition of company accomplishments) should also include photos that show why the event is being held. For tips on how not to shoot presentations, see the "Avoiding the Grip 'n' Grin cliché" sidebar.

- **Company outings:** Sometimes, an organization holds a retreat or conference. These gatherings feature a variety of events — some meant for fun and others for training. Plan on lots of shots of individuals participating in these events. Start by making sure you get the bigwigs. While you're looking for good photographs, make sure that your shots are positive and also present the employees in a good light.

- **Company-sponsored sporting events:** The information in Book III, Chapter 5 applies here, with the added reminder that you're still shooting a corporate event first and an athletics meet second. Document elements that show the company relationship to the sports event (banner, logo, or whatever) and get good souvenir photos for the amateur athletes (particularly if they are company employees). Posed shots and camaraderie photos are good, too.

- **Family events:** Sometimes a company holds an open house for employee families to come see what their family members do and where they work. Get plenty of shots of employees demonstrating their jobs for their families.

- **Community relations events:** Many companies work hard to be good corporate neighbors. Employees are encouraged to volunteer as mentors or to give time to public service efforts, such as Habitat for Humanity. If you're asked to shoot a community relations event, plan on getting newspaper-type photos for use in the company newspaper or newsletter (and remember, positive images here). You should also take pictures for the company to hand out to its workers as well. (Companies motivate and reward employees for doing things like this. T-shirts, coffee mugs, and souvenir photos are the top three incentives.)

Avoiding the Grip 'n' Grin cliché

Grip 'n' Grin is the standard shot of any event. One person is giving an award, and one person is receiving it. They stand there gripping the award, each looking right at the camera and grinning. Photo editors hate these pictures. They all look alike, and the only people who are interested in looking at them are the ones receiving the award and maybe the ones giving it. Take the shot, give the awardee a print, and then get a shot that has a chance of being used.

Rather than take a Grip 'n' Grin shot, provide a sense of what the event is about. If it's a barbecue, get behind the grills and take a shot of somebody getting a hot dog through a haze of smoke with a big smile on his or her face (hopefully wearing a cap or T-shirt with the name of the organization on it). You can mention the award presented at the event in the *cutline* (caption), but there's really no need to show it. More information on preparing images for publication appears later in this chapter.

Arranging a PR event worth photographing

If you're shooting for your own company and your company is a small one, you might find yourself dubbed the in-house PR expert and be asked to help put together events covered by other photographers. You really need to understand the needs of other photographers, too! Putting together a photo-worthy event calls for an understanding of the needs of the photographers you're inviting and for optimizing your own chances to get good photos alongside them. Press photographers are paid to create strong, exciting visuals.

Here are some things you can do to make an event more likely to be a success:

- ✔ **Pick a location that provides a strong backdrop for the speaker or ceremony.**

- ✔ **Include elements that reinforce the purpose of the event.** For example, at a groundbreaking or building dedication, try to get some construction equipment in place to frame the podium or platform. Hang banners from the buckets of front-end loaders that identify your company and project.

- ✔ **Give the other photographers handouts that will make it easier to identify each person participating in the event.** This should include a photo of each person, with his or her name and title securely attached to the picture. (It can be a printed sheet with bio. It doesn't have to be an actual print.)

- ✔ **If holding an outdoor event, be prepared for bad weather by having an awning available on-site.** Try to set up things so that photographers can still get a good backdrop for their photos.

On the day of the event, check all the small details that can come back to haunt you, such as confirming the presence of equipment, banners, handouts, and so on. Next, check the weather forecast. Have some people available to help answer questions from the photographers or provide extra handouts.

Refreshments for the press and guests are a good idea, but you don't need to go to extremes. Actually, you should probably worry more about having the appropriate refreshments for the company bigwigs than for the media.

Other photo-worthy events

Sometimes, your company welcomes members of the community inside its doors. This can be a welcome opportunity for creating images that you can place in your local papers.

- ✔ **School tours:** Does your company do something that might make a good tour for the local school? If so, bringing a group of school kids in will provide tons of photo ops (opportunities). Some typical images include an employee demonstrating a piece of equipment to the kids or one of the kids learning to use a piece of gear (keeping safety in mind at all times). Be sure to have your company's name or logo on equipment so that it shows up in the photo.

- ✔ **Mentors:** Does your company have a mentors program? If so, the interaction between your employees and their protégés can also make a good image. In this case, you're shooting at the school instead of your facility, so you won't have as many ops to get your company's name in the shot — but at least make sure it's in the caption.

Producing placeable PR photos

Successfully placing images taken specifically for PR purposes for your local media (both print and Web sites) is both an art and a science. Remember that you're trying to meet your needs (placing your organization or company's photos) as well as the newspaper's (strong images).

Newspapers know what you're trying to do — namely, get your company some free publicity and credibility. They also know that they have an advertising department that exists to help pay the bills. They're not giving away free space, but if you supply a good image, it has a chance at being used.

Also, understand your markets. Many local newspapers are willing to consider photo submissions, but each paper has its own criteria for acceptance. Newspapers use PR photos for a variety of reasons, including these:

- ✔ The images are of high quality and show members of the community doing something newsworthy (building homes for Habitat for Humanity, running a dunk tank to raise money for charity, and so on).

✔ The images fill a need that the newspaper or Web site couldn't fill on its own because it was understaffed or it was a weekend and too many events were going on to cover them all.

✔ The newspaper is willing to sacrifice a couple of pages or some Web space to run photos from groups that want publicity. It's easy to tell whether your newspaper does this in its print edition; look for the section near the back that has a couple of solid pages of Grip 'n' Grins (those trite photos of two people shaking hands and grinning at the camera). On their Web page, look for a special page devoted to such photos.

Many newspapers also run a Neighborhood or Region section or Web page. (There are lots of names for this part.) Such a section is geared toward the local community. In fact, when a newspaper hits a certain size, it will probably print a different section for local communities as a special insert, which gives you even more opportunities to place photos. Even if your company isn't located in a community that the paper has a section for, some employees who work for your company probably live there.

Submitting your PR photos

Digital submissions are easy; you carefully crop your photo, and if necessary, resize it to the pixel dimensions your target publication or Web site may specify. (Of course, you've checked with them, first, haven't you?) Finish up by delivering the file format they request, which will probably be JPEG if you're uploading the image(s) or TIFF if you are submitting them on a CD or DVD. Be sure to include information about the photo, in the form of Microsoft Word or text documents accompanying the image. (See the next section for more on that topic.)

For photographs that will be submitted as prints, make the best prints possible to improve your chances of getting them used. Read Book VII, Chapter 1 to find out about printing digital images in detail, but here are some general observations.

As a bureau chief for one publication I worked for, I was frequently amazed at the number of low-resolution inkjet prints that I received from PR and marketing people. To make matters worse, they were frequently printed on cheap typing paper. Needless to say, they weren't used. (I'm not referring to proof images accompanying a digital file here either; those are okay.)

Instead, you should use one of the newer, high-resolution ink-jet printers (1400 dpi or higher) capable of producing photos that are as good as those you get from conventional film and photofinishers. If you don't have such a printer, your local drugstore or department store might have a stand-alone kiosk or an in-house digital mini-lab that can produce high-quality photos from your digital files.

Writing cutlines

Cutlines, or captions if you prefer, are vital to getting your photos used. Newspapers know nothing infuriates a reader more than seeing his or her name misspelled or being misidentified in a newspaper photo. As a result, most papers set very strict policies for their own staff on this kind of thing (usually three strikes and you're out of a job).

Good cutlines provide the basic information and get it right. Here's the kind of information to include:

✔ **Identify subjects.** Make sure that each name is identified with the proper person. Usually, it's done from left to right (or *l to r*).

Make sure that you have the correct spelling for the names of everyone appearing in the picture and triple check to make sure that no typos sneak through.

✔ **Summarize the event.** Describe what they're doing and why it's important. Make sure to also identify your company or client.

✔ **Identify yourself.** Provide your photo credit *(Photo by)*. Include contact information in case the publication needs more information about the people in the picture or the event.

Cutlines need to be accurate, concise, and informative. Plus, the cutline is your chance to mention your organization's name in the publication. Although short cutlines will do the job in most cases, longer versions can serve as mini-news releases. Here's a (slightly modified) example of a longer cutline, from a photo actually published in my local paper:

> *When faced with a barnyard full of animals who didn't want to help, "Do It Yourself" was the solution for the Little Red Hen in a production of the children's play, performed by the kindergarten class at Immaculate Conception School in Newtown. The young thespians who demonstrated the importance of cooperation included, from left, Johnny Smith, Janie Doe, William Roe, and Samantha Brown. For more information on the kindergarten or preschool classes, call the school office at (331) 555-1212.*

Preparing the cutline for submission

After you write your cutline, affix it to the print — and do it in such a way that the print and cutline won't be separated by accident. The standard method is as follows:

1. **Set your margins for the cutline so they're narrower than the print's horizontal dimension and give your cutline a top margin of about one-and-a-half inches.**

2. **Print the caption and trim the sides and bottom to about a quarter-inch from the text while leaving the top margin alone.**

3. **Turn the print face down and position the face down cutline on top of it. Align the cutline so that the top line of text is slightly below the bottom of the print and use a small piece of tape to affix the cutline to the back of the print.**

4. **Turn the print and cutline face up and fold the cutline sheet up and over so that it covers the photograph.**

   Now your picture and cutline, as shown in Figure 4-8, will fit neatly into an envelope, and with the cutline sheet offering some protection for the face of your print.

5. **Before sticking your print in the envelope, though, sandwich it between two pieces of corrugated cardboard and rubber band the sandwich together to keep it from being damaged in transit.**

Professional packaging and presentation will help you put your best foot forward and improve your chances of getting your photos accepted.

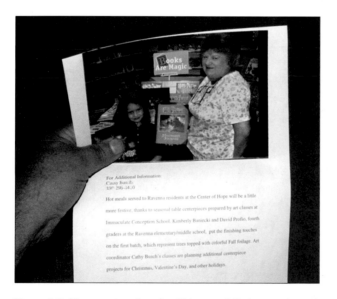

Figure 4-8: Photo and cutline should be carefully fastened together.

Submitting the photo

After you assemble a nice professional package, prepare a cover letter telling the editor why you're sending these photos.

- ✓ **Be brief.** You need only a few paragraphs to explain what the event was about, when it was held, and where.

- ✓ **Include contact info.** Make sure that the appropriate contact information is also provided in your letter.

- ✓ **Send to the photo editor.** Check the newspaper's masthead and address the envelope to the photo editor (if the paper is big enough to have one), to the Neighborhood section editor if the paper has a Neighborhood section, or just to the editor if it's a really small paper.

- ✓ **Keep a log.** Identify the image (something like 20050821.03 for "2005, August 21.third photo release of the month"), the newspaper(s) you've sent the photo to, and the date you mailed it. Make sure your cutline includes this release number. Also identify whether the photo is for immediate release or for use on a particular date.

Following up

A few days after mailing your photo submission, call the newspaper and ask to speak with the appropriate editor. Tell whomever answers the phone that you're calling to follow up on a photo submission. When you're connected, identify yourself and say you're checking to see whether the editor needed any additional information.

Also be sure to check the appropriate papers to see whether they've already run your image. If so, buy a couple of copies for tear sheets for your files. Note the log number on your file copy so that you can match it with the appropriate photo. Get in the habit of comparing your successful and unsuccessful images so that you can see what kinds of images your local paper favors.

Chapter 5: Sports and Action Photography

In This Chapter

- Choosing your equipment
- Taking outstanding sports pictures
- Choosing your spot for your sport
- Capturing your first action photo
- Shooting sequences

igital cameras offer at least one advantage and one disadvantage when used for sports and action photography. The big advantage lies in the ability to shoot an almost unlimited number of pictures in your quest to capture the peak moment of action but without burning up dozens of rolls of film. In times past, professional photographers had an edge in this department because they could justify using tons of film at a single event. Today, mistakes and bad shots can be erased from reusable digital film, so your errant photos aren't necessarily captured for eternity.

The chief disadvantage to digital cameras is that the models that are *not* digital single-lens reflexes (dSLRs) may not respond as quickly as you like when the shutter release button is pressed. Even a pause of half a second is too long when the decisive moment in a contest is framed within your viewfinder or LCD for only an instant. If you are using a dSLR, you're in good shape: Most of these cameras will snap off a picture as quickly as you can press the shutter release. If you *don't* have a digital SLR, you can work around this potential problem by using some techniques I show you later in this chapter.

Choosing Your Weapons for Sports Photography

Sports photography calls for a range of tools that can help put you in the best possible position to get the shots you need. This doesn't mean that you need to break the bank to get good images, though. Many of the current crop of digital cameras — from digital single-lens reflex cameras (dSLRs) to point-and-shoot versions — offer powerful capabilities of their own.

I cover the basics of choosing a camera, lenses, and accessories in more depth in Book I, Chapter 1. However, sports photography does have several particular needs. Here are some of the things that you should consider when assembling your sports photography arsenal. I explain these key needs in more detail later in this chapter, but this summary will get you in the proper equipment frame of mind:

- **Go long with telephotos.** To get the best sports photos, you want to get as close to the action as possible. That's enough of a challenge for pros equipped with press passes and access to areas set aside for their use. Imagine how tough it is for someone who has to get shots from the stands. If you can't get close, your digital camera's telephoto zoom setting or add-on telephoto attachment is your best friend.

  For sports photos, a camera with a 3:1 or 4:1 zoom lens is almost essential. You can find prosumer digital cameras that take you even closer with 12:1 to 18:1 zoom ratios. These long lenses provide the equivalent of a telephoto lens in the 200mm to 500mm range on a traditional full-frame (film or digital) camera. Of course, if you're using a dSLR, you can swap the lens you have on your camera right now for one that is longer, up to preposterous focal lengths. (There are lenses with 1000mm and longer focal lengths.)

- **Go wide.** Wide-angle capability also comes in handy for sports photography. Certain sports, such as skateboarding and roller blading, photograph quite well from a low position using an extreme wide-angle view. A wide-angle capability is also great for getting an overall view of a sports venue or crowd, as you can see in Figure 5-1.

- **Light up your sports life.** If you want to shoot sports at night, an accessory flash unit can greatly improve the quality of your photography because that brief flash of light can freeze action. External flash units can even be a big advantage during the day if you're photographing outdoor sports such as baseball because the flash lights up those inky shadows under the caps many athletes wear to shield their eyes. Of course, you have to be close enough for the flash to be useful.

- **Take along lots of digital film.** Sports photography can fill your digital storage media faster than most other photographic enterprises. At an exciting game or match, you might find yourself shooting more photos in two hours than you took during your entire vacation. Yet, other than timeouts or half-time, you have very little time to review your photos and erase the duds to free up storage space. The solution is to take a lot of digital film with you and use it freely.

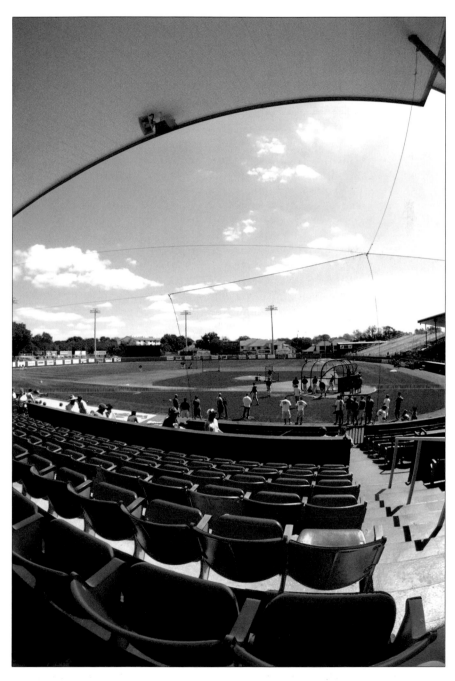

Figure 5-1: A wide-angle lens attachment for your digital camera can provide ultra-wide views of the venue.

Digital Camera Features and Action Photography

You can find information on specific digital camera types and their features in Book I, Chapter 2. The following sections review how some of those features can best be applied to action photography.

Viewfinder

Most non-SLR digital cameras have an optical viewfinder and a color LCD panel or, perhaps, an LCD alone. Others have an electronic viewfinder (EVF) and a color LCD panel on the back of the camera. And of course, dSLRs have optical viewfinders that see the same lens used to take the picture. You need to determine when to use each of them when taking sports photos. Some general rules to keep in mind are

- **Non-dSLR owners should use the optical viewfinder to follow action prior to squeezing off a shot.** You can view the subjects continually through the viewfinder under just about any lighting conditions. Although optical viewfinders can be difficult to use under very low light levels (when you need to use a flash instead of existing light to take the picture, anyway), optical viewfinders are still a better choice than the LCD panel for following fast-moving events.

- **Try keeping your other eye open while looking through the optical viewfinder.** This trick gives you some peripheral vision that will alert you when the action is about to enter the frame.

- **If your camera has an EVF, you might find it convenient for viewing fast action prior to snapping the shutter.** Note, though, that some EVFs produce a smeared image when you move the camera to follow action and may blank out a split second before the photo is taken, so you'll be shooting blind.

- **Digital SLRs are even better for sports photography.** They provide a bright, clear view (like an optical viewfinder), but you can see through the taking lens except for a tiny fraction of a second when the picture is actually being taken. You'll be "blind" for a much shorter period than with an EVF; you might barely notice the interval.

- **The LCD screen is invaluable for reviewing your images immediately after creating them.** Most cameras can be set to display an image on the LCD for a few seconds while it's being saved to your digital film. Take the opportunity to review the image. Even if it's great, you might learn something that will enable you to do better on the next shot!

Using your camera's LCD review feature

Here are some things to look for when reviewing your action shots:

✔ **Composition:** One of the most valuable things that your LCD screen can do for you is confirm that your composition is what you want it to be. With sports photography, you're dealing with athletes moving quickly and sometimes (seemingly) at random. Being sure they're where you want them to be in the frame is a good thing.

✔ **Sharpness:** LCD screens aren't necessarily an accurate way to judge image sharpness. However, some cameras offer the ability to magnify a portion of your image, which can help you see whether your camera's autofocus or your manual focusing is close. If not, you can switch autofocus modes (some cameras let you choose which area of the frame to focus on, or whether the camera locks the focus when you press lightly on the shutter release) or switch to manual focus.

✔ **Exposure:** Your camera's LCD screen can help you determine whether your exposure is on target. Some cameras let you call up a *histogram*, which is a kind of scale that shows the distribution of brightness values throughout the image. The histogram can help you judge your exposure. If your exposure isn't spot on, you can make changes immediately so that subsequent action shots are better.

Shooting outside in bright sun makes it hard to use your LCD screen effectively. The Hoodman company (www.hoodmanusa.com) makes a variety of hoods that offer some shade for the LCD screen and make it easier to read in the sun.

Electronic flash

An electronic flash unit can be a big help to your action photography whether it's day or night. You can use flash for good photos in a number of ways. Here are a few:

✔ **Let there be light.** An accessory flash unit can provide enough light for you to shoot by when it gets too dark for even your highest ISO (film speed) setting to be usable. (For more on ISO ratings, see the upcoming section, "Setting your ISO speed.")

✔ **Freeze your frame.** Accessory flash units produce an incredibly brief burst of light (somewhere on the order of up to 1/10,000 of a second). Also, because the flash unit, if it has enough power, provides the main source of light, it has the ability to stop action.

When using flash at a slow shutter speed setting, the *ambient* light (the available light other than the flash itself) can register a ghost image trailing the image captured by the flash. This can sometimes be a cool effect — but only if it's intentional.

✔ **Cleaning up the shadows.** Even when you have more than enough light for good sports photography, many times even the brightest conditions can't change the fact that athletes wear ball caps or that tree limbs cast shadows.

An accessory flash unit can help get rid of those shadows if you are close enough.

Tripods and monopods

Sports photography usually calls for such high shutter speeds to stop action that no photographer would use a tripod or monopod (the single-legged version of a tripod) to prevent blurry photos from camera shake, unless working with a high-end digital camera with a huge telephoto lens (which isn't something the average digital photographer needs to worry about). Instead, sports photographers sometimes use a tripod (or, more often, a monopod) to simply help support the camera. Here are some considerations specific to sports photography.

✔ **Great support:** A good sturdy tripod can be invaluable for holding and steadying your camera, particularly at telephoto lens settings.

- Some sports, such as football, call for too much movement on the photographer's part for tripods to be useful. (You'll constantly be running up and down the sidelines.) Monopods are more popular for those sports.

- When photographing track and field, baseball, and softball, you might find opportunities to use a tripod to support your camera.

✔ **A second camera rig:** When shooting baseball and softball games, I frequently prefocus a second, tripod-mounted camera on a key spot, such as first base, second base, or home plate. A tripod enables you to switch between two cameras easily and quickly.

✔ **Panning:** This technique involves following the action as it moves across your image frame. Panning is discussed in greater detail in the "Panning" section a bit later, but a tripod with a panning head can greatly improve your efforts at this technique because it allows free horizontal movement while keeping the camera steady vertically. Figure 5-2 shows some action stopped by panning in the direction the runner was moving.

✔ **Monopods:** For sports that call for photographers to be active, a monopod frequently works much better than a tripod because it's easier to pick up and carry around. A good monopod is fairly thick and heavy, both to be strong enough to support the weight of a big telephoto lens and also so that you can brace against it.

A lot of inexpensive units promise all sorts of capabilities; make sure you hold out for a good solid monopod and not one of the flimsy ones.

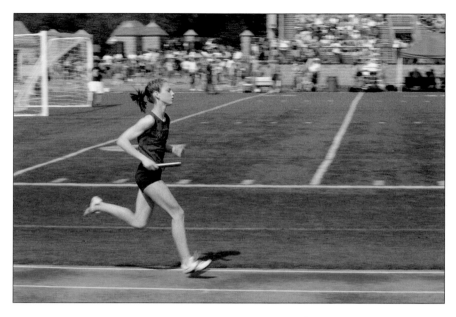

Figure 5-2: Pan the camera in the direction of movement to stop action at slow shutter speeds.

  ✔ **Shoulder stocks:** These devices are modeled after rifle stocks and work on the principle that by bracing the lens into your shoulder, you can hold it steady.

Lenses and attachments

Because sports photography requires you to cover large swatches of field and fast-moving athletes, long lenses or attachments to extend the reach of your point-and-shoot camera's built-in zooms will really help improve your results. Your choice of lens or zoom settings is in part dependent on what sports you plan on shooting.

Because the effective focal length of a digital camera lens depends on the size of the sensor, when I give focal lengths in this chapter, I use the traditional equivalent figure — the magnification you'd get if using the lens on a 35mm film camera or a full-frame digital camera.

  ✔ **Wide-angle settings:** Wide-angle settings will be a big part of your sports photography if you're shooting up close. For example, wide-angle lenses are currently in vogue for skateboarding photography. These lenses can give your sports shots a very different look, if you can get close enough to your subject to fill the frame.

✔ **Short telephoto settings:** Telephoto settings equivalent to a 35mm camera's 85mm–135mm lengths (which is how digital camera manufacturers measure their optics' magnifications) have a lot of uses in sports photography. These are great for indoor sports, such as basketball and volleyball, and can also be handy for nighttime sports under the lights.

If your digital camera has a maximum aperture of f/2.8 or larger, you can take photos in lower-light levels. Make sure that your camera doesn't use a smaller lens opening, which would defeat your ability to take indoor shots.

✔ **Medium telephoto settings:** These are usually in the 180mm–200mm range. This is a very versatile setting that can come in handy when shooting almost any type of sport.

✔ **Long telephoto settings:** Some digital cameras have long telephoto settings that are the equivalent of 300mm–400mm on a 35mm film camera. These are the lenses of choice for both football and baseball photography because they allow great reach and the ability to keep shooting even when outdoors under lights.

Be careful that your long lens doesn't reduce your shutter speed beyond the ability to capture the action.

✔ **Super telephotos:** You probably won't have access to super telephotos unless your digital camera is a dSLR with interchangeable lenses. I'm talking about the really big guns here — the 500mm and 600mm telephotos. These lenses are almost too big for many kinds of sports photography and are almost the exclusive reserve of nature and bird photographers. They can be useful when you just can't get very close to the action and have a pretty small subject. (Gymnastics events and skiing come to mind.)

✔ **Add-on lenses for point-and-shoot digital cameras:** Many point-and-shoot digital cameras can accept lens converters that attach to the front of the camera's built-in zoom lens. These converters can screw into the lens filter mount, clip onto the lens barrel, or attach via an ingenious adapter barrel and are frequently available in both wide-angle and telephoto flavors. I recommend going with the manufacturer's version, which is specifically designed for your camera, but if your camera's manufacturer doesn't offer the accessory lens you need, look at third-party options.

Be very careful if someone tries to sell you an add-on lens for a video camera. Video cameras get by with much lower resolution than digital still cameras. A lens designed for a video camera probably won't produce very good results on a digital still camera.

Latency and Shutter Lag

Before you move on to tips for taking great digital sports photos, you probably should spend a few minutes considering the deep, dark secret that digital camera manufacturers don't want you to think about: When you press that shutter release button, many cameras have a noticeable time lag before the picture is actually taken. Although this lag is but a minor inconvenience if you're taking a photo of the Eiffel Tower, that delay can be fatal (to the shot, not to you) when photographing sports. Fortunately, there are some things you can do about the phenomena known as *latency* and *shutter lag*.

Once upon a time, you pushed the shutter release button and the camera took the picture. As cameras have gotten more sophisticated, more and more things have to happen before an image is created.

Dealing with latency of your camera

Latency is the time required to write the image you've just taken to your storage media. When you take a picture with a film camera, the shutter releases, and the image is immediately registered on the film at the speed of light, so to speak. When you take a picture with a digital camera, the image has to be captured and then recorded onto your memory card. The image capture and storage process can take a second or two — or even longer. How long the process takes and whether your camera will continue taking additional photos while writing to the card are important questions.

Digital cameras use *buffers* (built-in memory) to temporarily let you keep shooting while the buffer contents write to removable memory. If you keep shooting, eventually the buffer fills, and you have to stop until it has made enough room for you to resume shooting. Other cameras might not be able to use their buffers quickly enough for their highest resolution files but will let you keep shooting if you choose a lower-resolution setting. It's a tough choice, but sometimes the ability to keep shooting overrides the desire for the highest possible resolution. Things that affect latency (that you can control) are

✔ **Media:** Some forms of media accept data faster than others. CompactFlash cards tend to write information faster than *microdrives* (tiny hard disk drives). Some CompactFlash cards write data faster than others. Look for ones rated for faster write times (frequently marked 8X, 50X, 80X, or 133X). Several photo-oriented Web sites have conducted their own tests of CompactFlash cards. Check out www.robgalbraith.com for the most highly respected card test results.

✔ **Resolution:** The more data the camera has to write to the card, the greater the latency period. Non-compressed formats like RAW and TIFF can take the longest to write. If you know that you can get by with a lower-resolution setting, you can speed up things considerably by going with the lower resolution. This can be a tough decision because after you give up quality, you can't get it back. On the other hand, missing a shot because you're waiting for your last few images to write to your memory card is one of the more frustrating experiences that a photographer can endure. Film photographers miss shots while changing rolls of film, but digital photographers miss them because of latency. It's not a perfect world, but it is a great reason to get a second camera.

If sports photography is your overriding concern, several cameras on the market are geared toward the sports shooter. Both Canon and Nikon's top-of-the-line digital SLRs are highly capable photographic tools well designed for this kind of work (but they're not cheap!). For those of us on a tighter budget, Olympus makes a lower-resolution digital camera capable of 15 fps (frames per second) bursts (for a maximum of 10 frames). It may be worth considering.

Coping with shutter lag

Latency isn't the only thing that can slow your picture taking. Many things happen when you press the shutter, including activating light-sensing features and bringing autofocus up to speed. The result is *shutter lag,* which is the delay between the moment you squeeze the shutter and the camera actually fires. In practice, most of the delay is caused by the autofocus system. Thus, you have to anticipate the decisive moment and trigger the shutter early enough to cause the image to be created at the best possible moment. This is true even if you're using a fast-responding digital SLR, and it's especially the case when using non-interchangeable lens digital cameras, such as point-and-shoot and EVF models.

Timing your shot properly

Here are some ways to time your shot so that you can take a great picture even when shutter lag delays capture of that decisive moment.

✔ **Anticipate the action.** Many sports and non-sports action activities have a particular rhythm. If you can become sensitive to that rhythm, you can anticipate that peak moment of action and learn how far in advance to trigger the shutter.

- If you're shooting a baseball or softball game, you can position yourself down the third base line and wait for a play at first. It takes a certain amount of time for a throw to make it across the field to the first baseman, so you can trip the shutter in time for the ball to reach the mitt.

- When shooting a basketball game, you can usually tell when someone is about to drive to the basket.

Anticipation can work for you in non-sports action photography, too. You can wait until just before the real action starts, as shown in Figure 5-3; which was taken just as the flume ride started down the incline.

✔ **Go with the flow.** Follow the action with your camera and gently squeeze the shutter as you keep your eye on the ball (or athlete). In sports like basketball or soccer, you can track the person bringing the ball down the field.

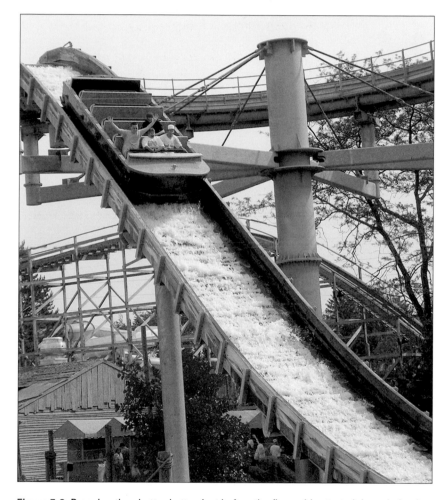

Figure 5-3: Pressing the shutter button just before the flume ride started down helped freeze the action.

✓ **Pick your spot.** Many sports direct action to a particular location. For instance, long jumpers are headed toward the landing pit, so you know within a couple of feet where the athlete will land. Be prepared to trigger the shutter as the athletes launch themselves and stay with them until landing. Some sports have goals, some bases, and some baskets; every sport has a spot that you know will see action.

✓ **Use manual focus.** Some digital cameras allow more control over their capabilities than others. If your camera lets you deactivate autofocus, for instance, you can prefocus on the expected action spot and reduce your camera's shutter lag time.

A similar technique works for cameras that let you lock focus. Lock focus on the spot you're keying on just before the play starts, and you give yourself a head start on the action.

✓ **Lock your focus.** If your digital camera requires you to press the shutter halfway to activate autofocus and autoexposure (and with cameras using mini-hard disks, to start your microdrive spinning), you can do this in advance and have everything operating at just the right time.

This technique can drain your camera's batteries in a hurry, so plan on having lots of extra juice if you want to do this.

✓ **Choose your autofocus mode.** Most digital cameras, dSLR and non-dSLR alike, have two autofocus modes:

- AF-S (autofocus single) locks focus when you press the shutter release halfway and keeps focus at that point until you release the button or take the picture.

- AF-C (autofocus continuous) also sets focus when you press the shutter release part way, but it then continues to refocus if your subject moves or you reframe the shot.

Usually, AF-C is best for sports (if you're using autofocus at all), but it rund down your battery more quickly and can be fooled if something moves between you and your primary subject, even momentarily.

✓ **Use autofocus selectively.** Does your digital camera let you pick a different button to activate autofocus instead of the shutter button? If it does, you can combine this feature with the previous technique to decrease battery drain. (Autofocus uses lots of power.) Keep the shutter pressed halfway while awaiting the next event. Then, as soon as you need to, press the second button to activate autofocus. (This takes a little practice, but it does work.) It also works well for the prefocusing suggestion made a couple of paragraphs earlier.

Some cameras have a continuous or single autofocus setting. Switching to the single setting can save power because your camera doesn't constantly refocus each time you move the camera a little.

Choosing Your Sport and Your Spot

This section deals with tips for taking great digital action photos in a variety of sports situations. That's the great part about sports photography: There are so many different sports. Just when you think you've explored everything that can be done for soccer, soccer season is over, and it's time to grab some basketball shots!

Elementary, middle, and high school sports are great training grounds for people who want to become good sports photographers, for these reasons:

- **Speed:** Because the players aren't as fast and as skilled as those at the college level (and up), the excitement generally unfolds at slower speeds, making life easier for the novice sports photographer who's trying to follow the action.

- **Access:** School athletic events are much more accessible than college or the pros. Return the favor by offering the coach or the boosters a copy of your shots for their awards dinner.

Don't be afraid to experiment, either. There are always elements of an event that provide dramatic imagery, even if it's not the typical sports action shot. Think about close-ups of equipment, low-angle shots of the playing field, and portraits or studies of spent, exhausted athletes at the end of the game. Look for shots that show the emotion and intensity that the athletes bring to the sport.

Knowing where to position yourself can be a real challenge for novice sports photographers. It's also vital to give yourself the best possible opportunities to get great shots. Your goal is to be in position to capture peak action in the right direction (getting that great catch with the athlete's back to you doesn't do you much good). Generally, this means you want to be far enough in front of the action to be effective, yet close enough to fill the frame.

Determining the right spot is largely dependent on the sport you're shooting. Your choice of available zoom settings can also play a role.

Football

If you're photographing high school or peewee football, you can often get right down on the sidelines to take photos like the one shown in Figure 5-4.

At the lowest levels of the sport, you can pretty much get whatever access you want. Even at the high school level, you can probably get on the sidelines if you explain that you're trying to build a sports portfolio. For most college and professional games, you need some form of accreditation from the team. Still, sometimes even a small, local newspaper can secure such access for its photographers, so working for such a publication could get you in.

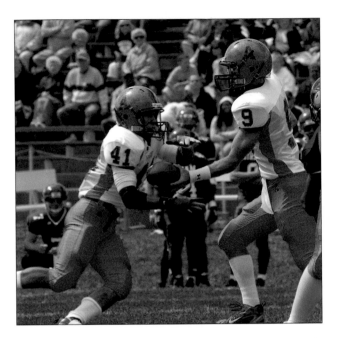

Figure 5-4: Most football action can be captured from the sidelines.

Here are some tips for photographing football:

- **Keep your distance.** Photographers generally stand about 8–15 yards up field from the line of scrimmage. Don't get much closer than this, or the line officials block your view. This puts you in place for a shot of a running play or quarterback sack in the backfield while still giving you a chance to turn and lock on to a receiver in case of a pass play to your side of the field.

- **Keep other spots in mind.** As teams approach the goal line, you can move to the area behind the end zone and shoot straight at the quarterback or running back attempting to leap over the defensive line. Because the team's players sit near the midfield, you can't shoot around this area. Also, plan on getting some shots of the coach yelling from the sidelines and players on the bench. Cheerleaders are good for a couple of shots. If it's a particularly cold day, some shots of the fans bundled up in the stands are worth taking.

- **Be patient.** Football demands patience and determination on the part of the sports photographer simply because so much of the sport takes place too far away from where you're standing for you to be able to shoot it effectively. Just stay with the game and be prepared for the action when it finally does head toward you.

✔ **Use a second camera.** A second digital camera set to its wide-angle setting can also be a good idea. This camera can be quickly grabbed and brought up to shooting position if a play comes right at you. (Be careful to avoid being run over.)

The more you know about football and the particular teams that are playing, the more effective you can be. Knowing that one team favors short, quick passes while another favors a more conservative ground game helps you predict where the next bit of action will take place.

Baseball and softball

For these sports, there are several likely places for a photographer to work from. One of my favorites is directly behind the backstop, shooting through the links to get a shot of the pitcher just as he or she releases the ball (ideally framed between the batter and umpire). I also like shooting from just behind the dugout, which is where I took the picture shown in Figure 5-5.

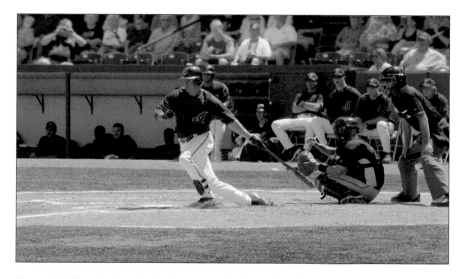

Figure 5-5: Shooting from behind or next to the dugout can give you a great perspective at baseball or softball games.

Here are some other tips for shooting ballgames:

✔ **Get behind the plate.** Many times, I start behind the plate to make sure I get a usable image as quickly as possible before moving on down either the first or third baselines. Usually, I head down until I'm about 5 or 10 feet below the base. From this spot, I can get good shots of the batter, a side view of the pitcher, and a good angle for plays at second base.

- **Move down the baseline.** After that, I continue on down the line until I'm as much as 15 or 30 feet past the base. This position gives me a shot at the runner racing to first or third.

- **Watch that runner on first.** If there's a runner on first, sometimes I pre-focus my tripod-mounted camera on second base in case there's a close play there. Here's where knowledge of the sport and the teams involved can give you a big advantage. The stolen base is one of the more exciting plays in baseball or softball. If you're ready before the play begins, you have a much better chance of getting a good shot of the action.

Much like football, baseball's lowest levels of skill are wide open to any photographer. College and the pros are much harder to gain access to — although once again, a newspaper job might give you a chance. Softball tends to be easier to gain access to. Sometimes, a one-sided game is easier to shoot than a close one. There tends to be lots of scoring, including plenty of people stealing home.

Basketball

Hanging out behind the backboard is a great place for getting good shots. I probably spend 80 percent of the game here. Rebounds, scoring, fights over the ball — it all happens under the boards. Here are some other good locations for shooting hoops:

- **Take to the bleachers.** I take some shots from up in the bleachers with a telephoto prefocused on the rim. This is a good location for getting the rebounder pulling the ball off the rim and a good look at the player's face. Try to find a spot a little higher than the rim. This generally calls for a longer zoom lens setting, about 100mm–135mm for a digital camera.

- **Head for the sidelines.** I also shoot along the sideline with a longer zoom setting to get a shot of a ball handler bringing the ball up court. From this position, I can also look for a shot of the coach yelling instructions to the players and pivot to grab some crowd intensity shots. Sometimes you can catch a tense moment as the ball is fired towards the basket, as shown in Figure 5-6.

- **Don't forget half-time.** Half-time is the time to look for shots of the coach and players talking strategy. A wide-angle gets you in close when possible (easy for high school ball and younger, but you probably won't be able to get that close for college and the pros).

Basketball is a great sport for a novice photographer to build a sports portfolio. It's possible to get good photos without breaking the bank on a camera with an ultralong telephoto lens zoom setting.

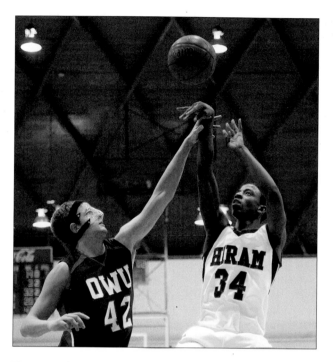

Figure 5-6: Sometimes the tension of the confrontation of two players can make a good photo.

Soccer

Soccer is a little like football in terms of the field and sidelines action, but this sport has lots of unique aspects, as well. Here are some tips:

- **Get behind the net.** Behind the net and to one side of it are good locations to catch scoring attacks, but you spend long periods of time counting blades of grass when the action moves to the other side of the field.

- **Take to the sidelines.** Positioning yourself on the sidelines puts you in place for good ball-handling shots. If you move down the sidelines closer to the net, you'll be in position to get the goalie in action.

- **Reach out and grab someone.** If you have a digital camera with a long zoom lens, you can try to reach from one end of the field to the other to get the goalie straight-on. Or you can even grab a shot from the stands.

- **Going for the wide look.** For variety's sake, try a shorter focal length while lying on the ground. This will give you a second shot, but not a main photo.

Soccer can be a difficult sport for the point-and-shoot digital camera simply because of the size of the field. The best place to work from is the spot behind the net and to one side, as in Figure 5-7. An occasional shot through the net works, too, but it becomes a cliché if this is the only image you ever capture.

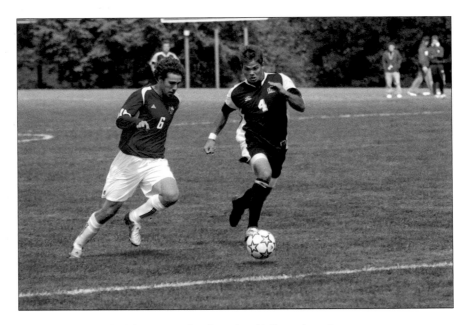

Figure 5-7: This action photo was taken from the sidelines of a college soccer game.

Other sports

Other sports have their special challenges and opportunities. Here's a brief rundown on some other popular action opportunities:

- **Hockey:** Stand behind the goalie or on the sidelines just above the goal. Players tend to make a lot of contact behind the net trying to control the puck, so there's some good action there. Another place where big hits happen is the area between the blue lines — the neutral zone. If your lens is long enough, get some shots of the face-offs. Don't forget about reaction shots either. Hockey is tough simply because your movement can be so restricted.

- **Tennis:** You can stand behind the court shooting the player on the far side of the net straight-on. Don't worry about the fence; if you're using a telephoto setting, you can shoot through the links. On the sidelines, I favor shooting when the player is running from side to side after a ball, but only when the player is moving toward me. Either a monopod or tripod will work for tennis.

✔ **Golf:** Shoot from the side when the player is teeing up (but not during their swing) or straight-on if the course conditions permit. You can also shoot straight-on from a safe distance when a player is putting.

✔ **Track:** So many events, so little time. Whenever possible, I try to shoot track events from as close to straight-on as possible, generally as runners are coming around the turn or at the start of a race when the line of runners is beginning its break.

✔ **Field events:** So many events, so many ways to shoot them. Unlike track, which tends to use the same quarter-mile track surface for its events, the field competition presents more challenges.

 • Shot put, javelin, and discus can all use the same basic philosophy: Get in front of the athlete with a little offset to the side (and far enough away to be out of range) so that you can shoot straight-on as the athlete releases whatever it is he or she is throwing.

 • Setting yourself up behind the landing area is a good strategy for both the long jump and pole vault.

 • Positioning yourself to the side and slightly behind the bar works well for high jumping.

 The hard part is racing from side to side because jumpers will come from both the left and right.

✔ **Gymnastics:** Any position that lets you shoot the athletes coming directly toward you is a good location. If circumstances allow you to get close to the action, wide-angle lenses can give your images a different look.

✔ **Adventure water sports:** I'm talking white-water rafting, kayaking, and canoeing here. Generally, you have a choice of two good locations.

 • Downstream, just below a rapid, so that you can get the boaters in action.

 • From a bridge, looking down on the river, which gives you a nice alternate shot.

Compose from the top of the boater's head down to his or her paddle in the water. It's not necessary to show the entire boat.

Book III, Chapter 6 covers special equipment for shooting in wet environments.

✔ **Rock, alpine, and speed climbing:** If possible, either get on top of the rock and shoot down on the climbers, or get on a ledge that's level with a point the climbers will reach during their ascent. If you're on the ground when they begin the climb, a wide-angle shot from the side and below gives a usable image, and you can play with silhouettes if you want to try something different. Also from ground level, you can try a telephoto shot of the climber against the wall.

For a speed climbing competition, a longer telephoto setting gets you in tight and compresses the competitors more closely together. I prefer to shoot speed climbing from the side because it emphasizes the extreme body contortions the climbers go through.

- **Extreme sports:** Both straight-on and profile shots provide good images for many of these sports:

  - For skateboarding, inline skating, and BMX bike events, shorter focal lengths work well, depending on how close to the event you can get.

  - Wakeboarding calls for very long lenses, a monopod, and a position on the riverbank that gives a good view of as many jump points as possible.

- **Motor sports:** These sports are among the fastest growing events from a fan standpoint. Auto racing is one of the toughest photographic challenges, even for modern professional camera equipment. Those cars are fast!

Try to catch them on the curve when they're moving a little bit slower. This can also give you a three-quarter view of the car. Or pick a spot where you can get the cars coming at you. This type of action is easier to capture. Fast-moving racing cars can also present a good opportunity for creative blur shots (more on this topic later). Use a modest shutter speed (say 1/125 of a second) to keep the starter sharp as he waves the flag to begin the race. If you do it right, the starter stays sharp while the cars and flags are blurred. Other good opportunities include shots at the starting line or in the pits.

For motocross events, where the motorcyclists are catching big air, you want to be some distance away from their take-off point. Side shots of the athlete and bike as they come even with your position are also good, as you can see in Figure 5-8.

- **Horse racing/dressage:** For horse racing, station yourself where the track curves so that you can shoot the animals coming straight toward you; then get three-quarter and profile shots as they round the curve. For the specialized horse maneuvers called dressage, study a book on the desired movements and looks each animal should present. Be ready to shoot them head on and in profile and three-quarter pose.

- **Swimming:** Shots from head-on and from the side are pretty much your only choices here. Start by shooting head-on and time your shot to catch the swimmer rising from the water. You might need an accessory flash unit and a butane-powered hair dryer for battling lens fogging.

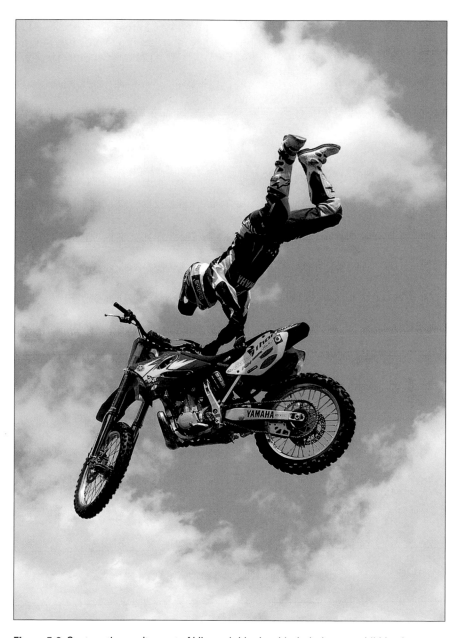

Figure 5-8: Capture the excitement of bike and rider in mid-air during an exhibition jump.

It's difficult to keep your equipment in working condition because of all the moisture and humidity in the air. Keep extra packets of *desiccant* (a powdered moisture-grabbing agent) in your camera bag and a microfiber cloth within easy reach. Try to get to the swim meet site at least a half hour early so that your equipment has a chance to come up to room temperature and humidity. Package your camera and lenses in sealable plastic bags during this warm-up period so that condensation forms on the bag, not the lenses.

Winter sports: A special case

The 2006 Winter Olympics renewed interest in shooting sports like skiing and snowboarding, so you can expect lots of action in the years leading to the next edition of these Olympics in Vancouver, British Columbia, Canada in 2010. These sports present a special challenge for the digital photographer because of the amount of contrast inherent in snowy conditions. Such lighting conditions often fool your camera's exposure system. If your digital camera lets you shoot in RAW mode (a relatively unprocessed mode that captures the image information before the camera's settings are applied — check your camera's instruction manual to see how) use that option. It gives you the maximum amount of information when you're editing the image later.

Generally, a good image occurs when the skier or snowboarder turns about 15 or 20 feet from your position. (Try to avoid the snow spray.) Another good shot is when the athlete becomes airborne. Be careful that you aren't so busy looking through the viewfinder that you lose track of the skier or boarder coming right at you. (It happens.)

Increasing dynamic range

High-contrast situations, such as ski slopes, present a special challenge for digital cameras. Because sports photography frequently revolves around frame-filling action with just one or two athletes, the easiest way to deal with high-contrast lighting is to use flash to balance the light between your subject and the background.

✔ **Metering:** Take a meter reading off a *midtone* (something equivalent to medium gray, such as the palm of your hand) and find the correct exposure for the overall scene. Then set your flash to output enough light so that your subjects' illumination matches

the background. (This tip probably applies only to those with higher-end cameras and very powerful flash units.)

✔ **Filtration:** Special low-contrast filters have appeared on the market in the past few years. Although sticking another piece of glass in front of your high-quality lens risks degrading image quality, a well-made filter can be worth the investment. Photographs made with low-contrast filters generally require a little extra tweaking in an image-editing program (nothing extreme), but the results can be well worth it.

I usually rely on medium to longer zoom lenses plus an accessory flash. Because these sports are done on snow-covered mountains, I try to travel light and with my equipment balanced in waist pouches or equipment belts rather than a camera bag. A camera backpack works well, too, but makes your equipment harder to get at in a hurry. Having a flash available is very important because, otherwise, you have to choose between overexposed snow and an underexposed subject.

Exploring Action Photo Techniques

As a would-be sports photographer, one of the most important things you can do is become knowledgeable about the sports you want to shoot. The most successful sports photographers are the ones who can anticipate the next play or event and put themselves in position to trip the shutter in time to record the moment.

Accessibility

Most events are accessible at all but the highest levels of play. Even high school and junior college sports cut serious amateurs some slack if they want to get closer to the action (on the sidelines or behind the baseline).

When you get to the point at which the athletes are making their living playing the sport — or for the highest levels of NCAA play — that starts to change. Even minor league ball has restrictions on what you can do and what kind equipment you can use. Pro-level events are even more restrictive. Plus, most professional organizations grant access based on your agreement to use your images only for editorial purposes. High-profile sports organizations like Major League Baseball, the National Football League, and the National Basketball Association guard the marketing potential of their sport and athletes very closely.

At least one type of competition, extreme (or *action)* sports, provides unparalleled access for the average enthusiast. Many times, while shooting events at the X-Games, I've been on one side of a fence chatting with spectators a foot or two away on the other side, who were in position to get the exact same shot I want.

Extreme sports tend to be very photogenic, too. Plus, the athletes tend to be fan-oriented, which can lead to good fan-athlete interaction shots. Because the financial rewards for many of these sports come more from endorsements than from prize money, the athletes actually try to cultivate their fans — a lesson that some professional sports seem to have forgotten. Extreme sports fans tend to be almost as flamboyant and colorful as the athletes, too. Look for mohawks, spiked hair, body piercings, and tattoos. Most fans don't mind if you want to get a shot of their particular fashion statement; they're usually pretty proud of it. Just ask whether it's okay first.

Many times, you have decisions to make long before the action starts. Is this a situation in which you'll use the zoom on the camera and try to react to what happens? Or are you picking a spot, prefocusing, and waiting for action to reach that location? Both are valid methods, and most photographers alternate between them as the game goes on.

Whenever possible, sports shooters try to analyze the situation to see whether they can understand what will happen next. Third and long yardage or first and ten in football are good examples. In the former, a pass is likely; in the latter, a running play. You can follow the receiver on your side of the field if you think a pass play is likely or key in on the quarterback to get a shot of the pass or the pass rush. For the running play, you can key in on the backfield and be ready to catch the hand-off and ensuing running play.

Setting your ISO speed

Being able to change the film speed or ISO (International Organization for Standarization) rating of your camera on the fly is one of the great benefits of owning a digital camera. Be sure to check your camera's instructions to see how to change the ISO setting.

When conditions permit, I always try to work at 100 or 200 ISO to get the highest quality images. Most digital cameras are optimized to provide their best quality at those settings. If I'm shooting outdoors under most daylight conditions, an ISO setting at 100 to 200 usually allows an action-stopping shutter speed of 1/2000 of a second or higher, which is good for most sports. If I have to move indoors or if the sun is getting lower in the sky, I increase the speed to 400 ISO and use a flash unit if circumstances permit. In uneven lighting situations, being able to change ISOs whenever you want is a great help.

Although my digital camera allows ISO settings as high as 800 and 1600, I try to avoid these settings unless it's the only way to keep shooting. Images shot at this ISO tend to need a little more tweaking in an image editor than lower ISO shots and also offer less margin for error when it comes to exposure. Cameras vary, and so do photographic tastes. Test your camera out before taking your first action shots so that you can determine whether your ISO choices produce results that meet your standards.

High ISO settings let you use faster shutter speeds, which means sharper images, but higher ISO settings also produce noisier images: *Noise* is the digital film version of conventional film's grain. Still, a sharp, noisy image is preferable to a noise-free, fuzzy one.

Freezing action with fast shutter speeds or an accessory flash

Today's athletes are well trained, well conditioned, and well prepared. As a result, they're faster than ever. To freeze their movements, you need to use either a fast shutter speed or an accessory flash unit. Another consideration is the relationship between the direction in which your subject is moving and your camera's orientation. Here are some tips to keep in mind:

✓ **Fast shutter speed:** If your subject is moving toward you or away from you, you can get by with a slower shutter speed than if your subject is moving across your field of view.

The shutter speed needed to stop action varies from sport to sport, but faster is always better. Figure 5-9 shows a speedboat and water skier headed away from the camera. The action was stopped at a relatively slow 1/125 of a second.

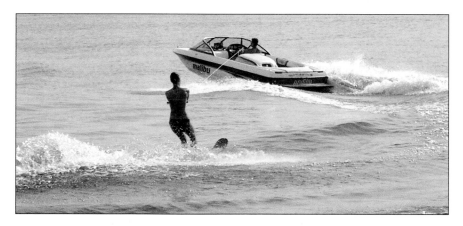

Figure 5-9: Action headed toward or away from the camera can be stopped at a relatively slow shutter speed.

✓ **Accessory flash:** As light levels drop, an accessory flash's quick burst of light can freeze action that a slow shutter speed might not. Whether you can use flash tends to depend on the particular sport you're shooting. I've never had any problems shooting football or basketball with a flash unit. Athletes such as tennis players tend to be more sensitive to flash photography, so I plan accordingly. When in doubt, check with the event organizer to see whether they have a specific policy or watch what other photographers are doing. Many times, if you're setting your flash for fill lighting rather than as your main light source, the burst of light is brief enough and low enough in intensity that the light won't be a problem. Keep in mind that you have to be within the effective range of your flash's output capability for it to do any good.

Short-duration shutter speeds can often be the key to stopping action. The brief time that the shutter is open registers only an instant of motion. Longer shutter speeds give your subject time to move farther or make more movements while the image is being recorded, which results in blurred photographs.

Generally, your choice is to use the fastest shutter speed possible. For many digital cameras, this frequently means 1/1000 of a second. This speed is fast enough to stop any human motion and will freeze many other elements of most sports. Digital SLRs usually have shutter speeds up to 1/4000 or 1/8000 of a second or faster.

Stopping action with slow shutter speeds

You can often stop action by using a slower shutter speed, too. Indeed, the effects might be more realistic than the frozen-statue look that you get when sports participants are stopped dead in their tracks. Here are some tips for stopping action at slower shutter speeds:

- **Look for momentary pauses.** Many times, a sport has a moment of peak action where the action hesitates before movement returns. Think of a jumper on the ascent. At the top of the leap is a moment of stasis — hanging in space before dropping back down. Or in the case of the pole vaulter shown in Figure 5-10, there was a moment when the vaulter planted his pole and flexed it mightily for an instant before it straightened out and launched him skyward. If you're forced to shoot at too low of a shutter speed, try to time your shot for that moment. Another example is a tennis player, just after tossing the ball to serve. If the server uses a high toss, he or she has to wait for the ball to drop before hitting it. The tennis player up at the net is another example. Although the racket and ball might be moving very quickly, the athlete's body usually isn't traveling very far or fast.

- **Try to shoot the action moving directly toward the camera.** Athletes and machines moving toward the camera require a slower shutter speed and faster autofocus to freeze motion than those moving laterally across the camera's field of view.

- **Concentrate.** The most dramatic image can be the concentration of the athlete the moment before he or she begins play. Think of the pitcher looking to the catcher for a sign, or a tennis player just before serving the ball. Another example is the linebacker poised for the snap of the ball before rushing the quarterback. There's also the free-throw shooter pausing a moment before shooting.

- ✔ **Find action in nonaction moments.** Another shot to look for is one that shows the price the athlete pays for his or her sport. This can be football players on the bench with steam rising off their heads or a spent distance runner leaning on a teammate at the end of a race.

A shot of a distraught athlete being consoled by a fellow athlete is a classic sports photograph.

Also watch for the emotions of the fans or cheerleaders.

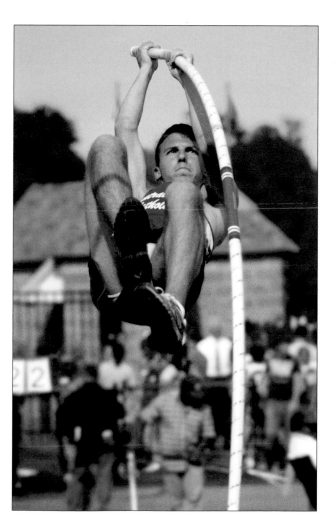

Figure 5-10: Catch the action at its peak.

Controlling shutter speed

How do you get your camera to use a short shutter speed to stop action? You might have to check your camera's instruction manual to find the exact controls, but here are the options you should look for:

✔ **Shutter priority mode:** In shutter priority mode, you can choose the exact shutter speed you want to use (such as 1/500 or 1/1000 of a second), and the camera's automatic exposure control will choose the f-stop lens setting appropriate for that shutter speed.

Depending on the lighting conditions, you might not be able to use the very shortest shutter speeds at all. In dim light, for example, your camera might not be able to take a photo at any shutter speed shorter than 1/250 or 1/125 of a second because there simply isn't enough light.

✔ **Manual shutter speed/exposure settings:** On some cameras, you can set both shutter speed and f-stop manually. If you can do that, it's up to you to interpret your camera's light meter to provide the correct combination of shutter speed and f-stop for a proper exposure.

Panning

Panning (moving the camera horizontally in the same direction of motion as your subject) is a technique that should be part of every serious sports photographer's repertoire. This procedure gives you the best of both worlds: freezing the important part of the scene while blurring the background to show the furious motion of the moment.

The idea behind the technique is to use a slower shutter speed while following an athlete or an object laterally with the camera. The result is a subject in relatively sharp focus while the background is blurred.

Here's how to put panning to use:

1. **Select a moderately slow shutter speed to give yourself a long enough stretch of time for the lateral movement of the camera to register — but not so long as to create overall blurriness from camera shake.**

    Don't you just love precise directions like this? But seriously, if I could give you exact numbers, your camera would already be programmed to do it for you. There's no exact recommendation; you have to experiment to see what works best for you. The speed will vary from sport to sport as well. Start out by trying something in the 1/45–1/60 of a second range for running humans. Work your way to around 1/350 of a second for motor sports and see how this works for you.

2. **Begin following your subject with the camera before tripping the shutter.**

   You want a smooth lateral motion here, so beginning the move first and then shooting helps you do that. Your panning movement is steadier if you limit your movement to your waist and hips while keeping your feet planted and your knees together. This will also help reduce camera shake.

   Keep your elbows braced against your body to help turn yourself into a *human monopod.* Most people find that using an actual monopod generally doesn't work very well, but for a few, it works. If circumstances permit, a tripod with a tripod *panning head* (one that allows the tilt and yaw controls to be locked while the panning direction swings free) can make for a smoother pan. Certainly, a photographer who's just starting to experiment with the panning technique might find that a tripod makes things easier.

3. **Trip the shutter as gently as possible.**

   You're trying to avoid a downward snap in your movement.

   The cliché is to squeeze the shutter — not press it.

4. **Continue your lateral panning movement for a second or so after the shutter has closed.**

   This is a case where proper follow-through is just as important for the photographer as it is for the athlete.

5. **Repeat this process at least a half dozen times or more.**

   It seldom works perfectly the first time. (It's okay; you're not paying for film here.) Good panning is something you have to work at. Don't give up on the technique if your first few attempts (or more) don't *pan out.* (Sorry, just couldn't resist the pun!)

This technique gives you dramatic images that accurately convey the sense of motion the sport involves. Sometimes, the photograph of the athlete flying through the air or running down the baseline with the background blurred (see Figure 5-11) does a better job of conveying the speed of the event than a moment of frozen action.

**Book III
Chapter 5**

Sports and Action Photography

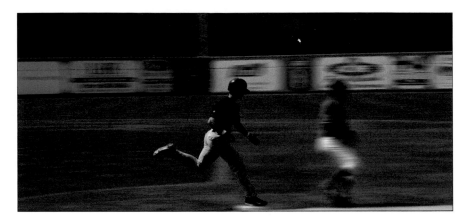

Figure 5-11: Panning freezes action at a slower shutter speed.

Capturing action approaching the camera

Action approaching the camera is also more dramatic because the camera can maintain eye contact with the athlete or create a sense of power from the approaching machine coming right at the viewer.

Because these images produce such drama, work on capturing them well. Mastering this aspect of sports shooting will improve your sports photography. Help your camera's autofocus system work its best by prefocusing on a spot a few feet ahead of where you hope to take the picture. Lock on to the approaching athlete and give your camera a chance to acquire the athlete and bring its autofocus up to speed. If you're working with a digital SLR with a zoom lens, you can give yourself more time and distance for the shot by acquiring your subject at the extreme telephoto end of its range and continuing to shoot while racking the zoom through its full range to its widest setting.

Circumstances don't always permit you to get this shot. Still, photography is about putting yourself in a position for the best possible chance to catch the action. If you couple that with shooting a large number of images, you can increase the likelihood of success.

Using blur creatively

In some circumstances, you just don't have enough light or a fast enough lens to set the shutter speed as high as you would like. Stopping action can be a good photographic technique when you're covering sports, but it's certainly not the only one. When circumstances don't allow you to freeze motion or when you want to create something that looks different from what everyone else is doing, deliberately trying to blur your image can create something special. Blur works for non-sports action, too. Figure 5-12 shows a picture in which the blurring creates a photo that says "action!" more clearly than any frozen-in-time photo.

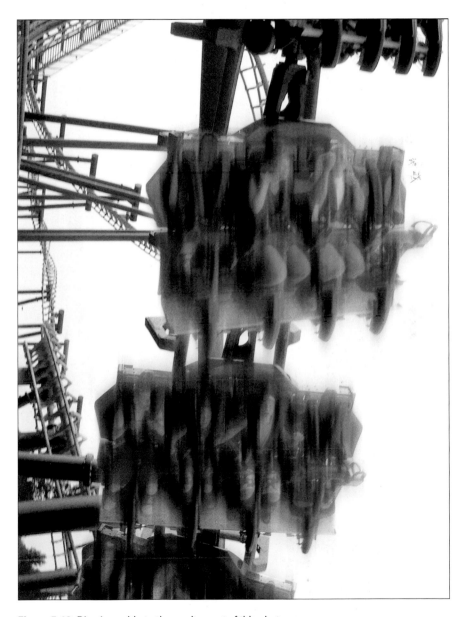

Figure 5-12: Blurring adds to the excitement of this photo.

To create a successful photograph, the key elements of the image — not necessarily every single part of it — need to be in focus. Your subject's eyes and face need to be in focus. Blurred body, hands, or feet show just how fast they're actually moving. Some sports, such as tennis, are easy. There's a pretty forgiving difference between the shutter speed you need to freeze the athlete's body and the speed necessary to freeze the moving tennis racket or ball. The same goes for hockey because the player's stick and the puck blur quite easily at shutter speeds that comfortably freeze the player.

When successful, this kind of image can actually be more dramatic than freezing action. Here's how to try this technique:

1. **Figure out what shutter speed is slow enough to blur the faster moving parts of the body while fast enough to freeze the face.**

    This varies from sport to sport, so be prepared to experiment.

2. **Time your shot to coincide with a moment of peak action, such as the athlete at the top of his or her leap.**

    Many sports call for the athlete's head to stay still while the rest of the body explodes in action. (Think of a golf swing where the player's head stays down through the entire stroke.) Other sports require the head to travel through a range of movement as they stroke through the ball. (You know, *keep your eye on the ball.*) For these sports, the head eventually stops as the athlete follows through to complete the stroke. The end of this follow-through determines where the athlete's body movement is frozen, although the ball or puck and stick or racket might still be moving.

After you get the hang of using blur creatively, you've added a powerful tool to your photographic arsenal. The essence of many sports is the athlete's ability to move as fast as possible. Blurred hands, feet, limbs, and wheels convey the speed of modern athletes and machines in a way that frozen figures can't. Try to experiment with creative uses of blur each time you're on a shoot. Just manage it the way most photographers do: We start out working for an image that we know gets the job done. After we get our money shot, we can start looking for something a little more creative. This is the time to try the panning or creative blur photos.

Taking the Picture

After you choose your shutter speed, take a strategic position, know what kinds of opportunities might be coming your way (literally!), and take the picture. Watch the action closely, frame the image in your viewfinder, and snap away.

Capturing great sports moments

As you shoot, keep some simple concepts in mind. For example, here are some things to look for in a great sports image:

- ✔ **Full extension:** The athlete at the top of a leap or in full stride is one example of the decisive moment in sports photography.

- ✔ **The coiled spring:** The moment before release when muscles are tense and the body is coiled is another key moment in sports. This image shows the athlete just before he or she explodes into action.

  Think of the shot put thrower just before release, the shot still pressed into the chin; or think of the baseball pitcher, arm reared back, ready to reverse direction and fire the ball at the batter.

- ✔ **Emotion:** A great sports image doesn't even need to be a good action shot. Catch the athlete or fan in a moment of extreme emotion, and you've gotten a memorable image. Watch the fans, watch the coaches, and watch the athletes watching other athletes.

Most sporting events are carnivals of colors, patterns, and personalities. They provide a wealth of photographic opportunities not limited to just the playing field. Enthusiastic photographers, curious about the world around them and with an eye to more than just the game, can produce great sports photos no matter what camera they're using.

Setting up for predictable action

Having an understanding of the sport you're photographing can put you in a position to take advantage of your ability to predict impending action. Here are a couple of ways to use that ability.

- ✔ **Prefocusing:** Sometimes an athlete needs to reach a specific location as part of a play. If I'm photographing a baseball or softball game and a runner makes it to third, I swing my tripod-mounted camera to cover home and prefocus on home plate. I still follow the action with my hand-held camera, but I also position myself so that I can quickly fire the second camera for a shot of a runner sliding home. Prefocusing on the forward end of the basketball rim is another example. You're now ready to get a shot of the center leaping for a rebound.

- ✔ **Zone focusing:** This technique takes advantage of the depth of field that comes with using a smaller lens opening. (Depth of field is covered in greater depth in Book IV, Chapter 2. In simple terms, the smaller the lens opening, the greater the range of sharp focus from one point to another on a line from the lens.) The idea here is to choose a lens opening that's small enough to create a zone of sharp focus. The zone should be deep enough to give you about a 5-foot range in which everything is in focus.

Zone focusing works well for a sport like basketball, where you know you can expect action to take place in a location about 5 to 10 feet from the basket. Using an external flash unit (which many point-and-shoot digital cameras can do) should enable you to shoot at f/5.6 or f/8, which gives you that 5-foot range or greater. In Figure 5-13, the focus was set ahead of time for the ramp, so when the athlete spun around, the camera was already set for the picture.

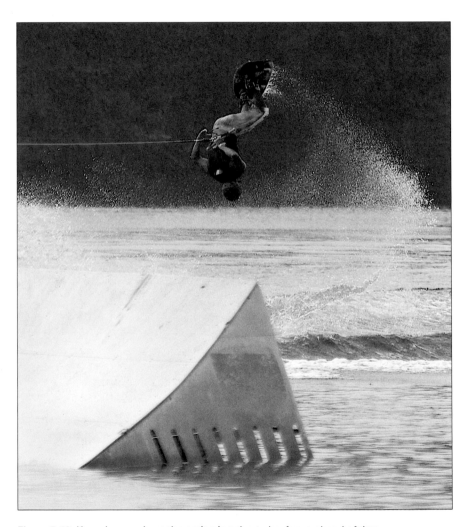

Figure 5-13: If you know where the action is going to be, focus ahead of time.

Photographing action sequences

Sometimes, you need to do more than just capture one good shot of sports action. You need to get the sequence of movements that make up an entire run or the execution of a particular move or trick.

Pros get these sequences by using cameras that can capture as many as eight pictures per second (usually expressed in fps — frames per second). Although one or two non-dSLR digital cameras are capable of high-speed, motor-driven photography, most are good for only about 2 or 3 fps at best. Usually, you must work with a digital SLR to get 3 to 5 fps and have one of the high-end pro models to get as many as 8 fps.

Even with a limited burst mode capability, a photographer can still create effective photo sequences. Once again, a little planning and foresight can help you get the best possible results. If you can predict the path the athlete is going to take, you can better follow that path with your camera. Another thing that you can do is back out your composition a little to give you some margin for error. You don't want to have a great sequence of shots with your subject ruining it by drifting in and out of the frame.

Here are some tips for getting good action sequences:

- ✔ Visualize the path that you expect your subject to travel.
- ✔ Prefocus on the point where you expect to start shooting.
- ✔ Set the fastest shutter speed you can to give your motor drive the best possible chance of advancing at its best speed.
- ✔ Compose your shot to give your subject some room to move within the frame.
- ✔ Shoot several sequences to make sure you get at least one usable sequence. Remember that you're trying to get four or five good shots in a row, not just one, so it becomes that much harder to be sure that they're all in focus and well composed. Take lots of shots.

Don't expect to get a good sequence on your first attempt. This is another one of those techniques that you need to practice beforehand. You're trying to understand how your camera works in this kind of situation and determine whether you can tweak your gear to perform better. Some cameras require you to drop down to a lower resolution in order to shoot fast enough to get a good sequence of images. Because you're trying to get multiple images, the loss of resolution might not be as bad as you think. After all, you'll have the group of images to take the place of one shot.

Some digital cameras don't offer a continuous shooting capability. Others offer it only at a lower resolution setting than you're really comfortable using. Just because you can't blaze away like the pros doesn't mean you can't tell a multiple-picture story of a sports event.

A good sequence of photographs tells a story. If you're shooting an event in which an athlete makes more than one run or attempt (long jumpers get six tries, for instance), work on getting the sequence you want by shooting a different aspect of each attempt. Be careful how you identify the finished result, though. There's nothing wrong with showing how each element of the jump works through a sequence of images, but representing it as the individual elements of one jump is the kind of thing that gets photographers in trouble.

Chapter 6: Travel Photography

In This Chapter

- ✔ Choosing the right equipment
- ✔ Getting ready to go on the road
- ✔ Mastering the best travel photography techniques

Taking pictures while traveling can be the most rewarding long-term benefit of a trip. Although memories of a particular location fade as the years go by, the images that you create will still be there to remind you of a special time in your life. Plus, face it: Photography is fun! Knowing that you've taken a good picture of that special location gives you a particularly satisfying feeling. Lasting friendships can be made during a trip, and being able to send your new friends pictures of the time you shared together can help cement your friendship.

If you've traveled with a film camera in the past, you'll find that vacationing with a digital camera offers some terrific advantages over traditional picture-taking tools. Digital cameras can be smaller and lighter than their film counterparts, so they take up a lot less space in your luggage. They have no film that airport security X-ray cameras can damage. And as you take photos, you can check them using your digital camera's built-in LCD screen.

This chapter offers advice for aspiring photographers who are intimidated by the idea of trying to take good pictures in unfamiliar surroundings. If you want to know more, I recommend *Digital Travel Photography Field Guide*, also from Wiley Publishing and written by yours truly.

Getting the Right Gear

A photographer on the road needs a selection of gear that's versatile enough to handle the unexpected without burdening the photographer like a Sherpa on a Mount Everest expedition. Carefully considering which key pieces of equipment to take — and which to leave behind — can make the trip less stressful and more productive.

Selecting a camera for your needs

Choosing a camera to use while traveling is an important decision, one that you might have already made long before your trip. After all, most of us are unable to buy a camera specifically for a vacation. You'll want to keep a camera's travel photography capabilities in mind whenever you purchase a digital model. Key decisions revolve around lens versatility (for more options while taking pictures), file size (more megapixels equal bigger pictures), and how much control the camera gives you over shooting decisions.

When purchasing a camera, most of your decisions revolve around what kind of photographer you are and what kind of travel pictures you expect to take, as the following sections make clear. No matter which category you fall into, your digital camera should have the basic features that you need to make a broad range of travel photography easy and carefree.

Vacationers who simply want to take good photos

You know who you are: You want pictures that are sharp and clear, colorful, and good enough to make a batch of 4-x-6-inch snaps of your best shots. You like digital photography and want to capture some travel memories, but you can't spend a huge amount for your equipment. These photographers need

- Low- to medium-resolution (8- to 10-megapixel) cameras (especially pocketable compact models) with the ability to accept interchangeable memory cards.
- A versatile zoom lens, at least a 5X zoom, preferably an 8X or longer zoom.

Enthusiastic amateurs

Amateur photo enthusiasts love photography but have other interests — such as travel! With more limitations on their budgets, they need top-quality *prosumer* cameras. These cameras are aimed at consumers but have features that will please advanced photographers. These include the following:

- Medium- to high-resolution (10- to 14-megapixel) camera with decent capacity memory (with the ability to accept interchangeable memory cards). These cameras enable you to print vacation snapshots in sizes as large as 5 x 7 to 11 x 14 inches.
- Versatile zoom lens (between 5X and 10X — up to the equivalent of a 300mm to 400mm lens on a full-frame camera) for taking close-up shots of distant scenic features or for capturing locals being themselves. Figure 6-1 shows the reach of various typical zoom ratios.
- Add-on accessory lenses to extend range even farther or to widen the view to take in monuments, castles, or cathedrals penned in by their surroundings.

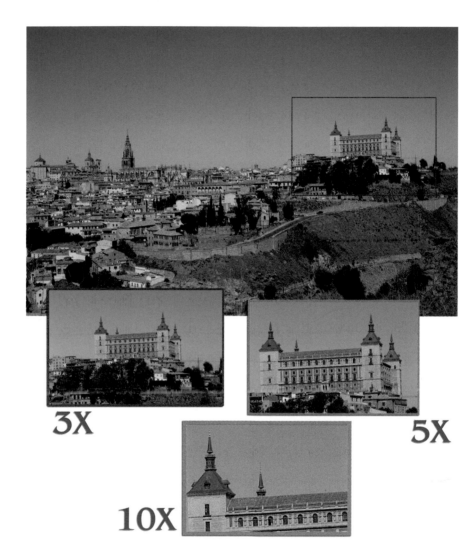

Book III
Chapter 6

Travel Photography

Figure 6-1: Zoom lenses let you reach out and capture distant details.

Serious amateurs

The best serious amateur photographers are often professionals in every aspect except monetary reward. They frequently spend a lot on their hobby and might even be looking at the same systems desired by pros. Their needs will certainly include the following:

✓ A high-resolution (10- to12-megapixel) camera with large-capacity memory (with the ability to accept interchangeable memory cards). These features enable you to grab travel photos suitable for printing at large sizes, which you can then display on the wall.

✓ Extreme zoom lens capabilities, preferably with a 10X range or the equivalent of 300mm to 400mm on a full-frame camera. This range is ideal for reaching out and grabbing a small detail from a panoramic scene.

✓ Add-on accessory lenses (called *teleconverters*) to extend a zoom's capability even farther.

✓ Rapid shooting capability to allow taking pictures quickly at festivals or other fast-moving travel experiences. (The running of the bulls at Pamplona comes to mind!)

Choosing key features for travel photography

Here are some key features to look for in a camera, no matter what kind of travel photographer you are.

✓ **Optical zoom range:** A powerful zoom enables you to compose your image carefully and cover a lot of photographic territory on your travel treks. With a good zoom, you can also take advantage of lens effects, such as selective focus.

✓ **Interchangeable memory cards:** Most camera vendors expect you to buy your own memory cards sized to fit your needs. Be sure to take more than one card! When your memory card is full, you either stop shooting or delete images, neither of which is a happy option during a once-in-a-lifetime vacation. The ability to change cards enables you to just keep shooting.

✓ **Sufficient megapixels:** The more megapixels, the better. This is true for several reasons. First, higher resolution (more megapixels) allows for larger prints of your prized vacation shots. Second, higher resolution lets you crop to a smaller view of that monument you just couldn't get close enough to and still get a good-quality print.

✓ **Interchangeable lenses:** These days, an increasing number of affordable digital cameras use interchangeable lenses. These give a photographer a wide range of choices for high-quality travel photography. Being able to select from a range of different focal lengths — plus being able to control depth of field (the range of image sharpness as it appears throughout the photograph) — gives the photographer tremendous power over the photographic image. Sometimes manufacturers offer add-on lenses for non-interchangeable-lens cameras, too.

Think about taking a second camera along, too, particularly if this is more than just a run-of-the-mill vacation. A small digital camera might not cost much. If your primary camera fails, your backup camera could be worth its weight in gold photographically. Shop for or borrow one that uses the same type of batteries and storage media as your primary camera, if possible. The extra camera can also entice a spouse or child into sharing your love of photography. Encourage them to shoot their own photos on the trip.

Selecting lenses for travel

Look at your camera's built-in capabilities, including the range of magnifications available from your zoom, as well as the ability to add supplementary telephoto, wide-angle, or close-up lenses. You can find more about lenses in Book I, Chapter 2.

Travel photographers need three basic capabilities:

- **Wide-angle:** Being able to fit more into a picture comes in handy when you're shooting scenics and architecture, like the image shown in Figure 6-2.

- **Telephoto:** Capturing native wildlife or sports shots without getting dangerously close is an invaluable capability.

- **Macro:** These lenses are essential for getting close-ups of native insects, signs, or documents.

Book III
Chapter 6

Travel Photography

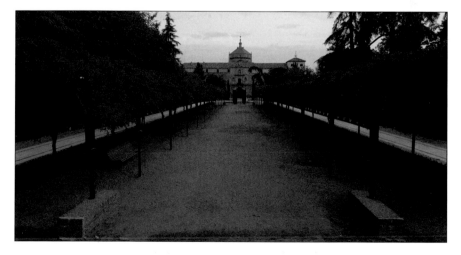

Figure 6-2: Wide-angle lenses, like the one used to take this shot, can be useful in tight quarters.

With at least some capabilities in each of these ranges, you can shoot a broad selection of travel photos without necessarily having to physically move closer or farther away from your subject.

Considering a tripod

A *tripod* is a three-legged stand designed to hold your camera steady. You can find more detailed coverage of tripods in Book I, Chapter 2.

Although a tripod can be a little cumbersome to carry along on a trip, this camera support can do several things for you. A tripod is great for holding the camera steady if you are using longer shutter speeds in dim light or using a telephoto lens. If your camera has a timer feature, you can use a tripod to get yourself in the picture.

A tripod definitely leads to better pictures, but only if you use it. If you find the idea of lugging one around too much of a bother during your vacation, plan on a different tool, such as a monopod, beanbag, or one of the other options discussed later in this chapter. It's okay — you're on vacation!

Investing in an accessory flash

Although most digital cameras have some sort of built-in flash capability, these are usually only good for a range of about eight feet or so, which isn't always enough. Because available light (more commonly known as *available darkness*) is undependable, the traveling photographer should consider carrying an accessory flash unit.

Accessory flash units do more than just provide extra light when it's too dark to shoot without it. The reasons an extra flash can be particularly helpful for travel photography include the following:

✔ **Using fill flash:** If you're planning to shoot a companion who is in partial shade or wearing a ball cap, an accessory flash can help you clean up the shadows. Because the supplemental light isn't trying to light the whole scene, filling can be accomplished by smaller, less powerful flash units (such as the camera's built-in flash) or even by a reflective surface. A 3-x-3-foot piece of folding Mylar or a silver-coated auto sunshield held by a helper to reflect the sunlight into the area where the sunlight can't reach provides a nicely lit photo, as shown in Figure 6-3.

✔ **Painting with light:** If part of your trip takes you into a dark place, such as a thirteenth-century church that doesn't have spotlights shining on it, an accessory flash might help. You can use the *painting with light* photo technique, covered later in this chapter, with a tripod or firm support.

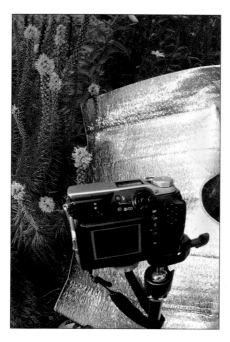

Figure 6-3: Keep a compact reflector in your travel bag to fill in shadows.

✔ **Macro/close-up photography:** If you want to take close-up shots of typical local jewelry, markers, or insects, you need to provide a lot of light in order to get enough image sharpness to create a good-looking image.

Many higher-end digital cameras offer some method of triggering an accessory flash unit, either by a cable connection or via *hot shoe* (the connection found on the top of many digital cameras that holds the flash and provides electrical contact with the camera). Figure 6-4 shows the hot shoe found on one digital camera model. Many consumer-priced digital cameras, however, offer no such provision. If your camera doesn't have the means for adding an additional flash, a slaved flash specifically designed for digital cameras might be your answer. (A *slaved* flash has a built-in light sensor that triggers the slaved flash when your camera's flash fires.)

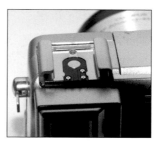

Figure 6-4: A hot shoe lets you attach an external flash.

Selecting a camera bag

Depending on the size of a digital camera and the accessories accompanying it, a camera bag or pouch could be a necessity. For just the basics — a small camera, extra batteries and memory cards, and a lens cleaning cloth — a simple fanny pack will do the job and leave room for hotel keys, money, and identification. If you're a more serious photographer who's carrying a larger digital camera or an interchangeable-lens digital SLR, you need more space. Although a larger camera bag could be the answer, the active traveler should consider these factors:

- **Size:** Your camera bag should be roomy enough to hold your basic camera setup and also leave some room for an extra piece of gear or two, such as filters or extra batteries that you'll be glad you have when you're hundreds or thousands of miles from home.

- **Flexibility:** An ideal bag includes multiple compartments that can be reconfigured (with hook-and-loop tape) so that you can adapt the bag to the different configurations of camera outfit that you might need. You'll often find that your equipment needs vary from place to place on vacation. At one destination, you might need easy access to your extra flash unit. At another, you'll want to grab your add-on wide-angle lens quickly.

- **Sturdy strap:** Much travel is done on the run. A travel-friendly bag has a main strap that runs around the sides and bottom of the bag — that's securely stitched, not grommetted into the fabric. (Don't underestimate the importance of this one, folks!)

- **Toughness:** To stand up to the rigors of travel, a bag should be made of rip-stop nylon or canvas. If you're really into leather, though, you don't have to rule this material out, either — if the bag is well constructed.

- **Security and convenience:** The bag should offer multiple methods of closing. Usually a good bag offers a fast method of closing (frequently with hook-and-loop tape or clasps) and a more secure method of closure (zippers or clips) that takes more effort to open and close but makes accidental opening less likely. Figure 6-5 shows such a bag.

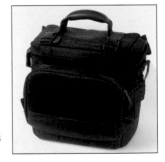

Figure 6-5: A sturdy bag with multiple ways of closure offers the most flexibility.

- **Protection from the elements:** The bag needs a top flap that closes over the main compartment in such a way that if it's hit by rain, the water is channeled down the bag sides. Water shouldn't be able to seep through a zipper channel or closure point. Although the zippered closure on this bag looks secure, it does little to protect the sensitive digital camera equipment inside from rain.

At some point, you can cross over the line that divides vacation photographer from pack mule. Do a dry run with all your gear before leaving. Now ask yourself whether you're comfortable with the idea of lugging that stuff around with you on your vacation. The only right answer to the question is the one that satisfies you.

Keeping your camera powered

Modern cameras use batteries like there's no tomorrow, particularly digital cameras with their power-draining LCD screens and built-in flashes. That's not much of a burden when you're shooting close to home. But if you're traveling — far from AC power or a ready source for batteries — power is a prime consideration. If you plan to shoot pictures for more than a couple of hours, take along spare batteries to use until you get back to civilization.

Predicting battery life is a bigger challenge than taking good pictures simply because the figure varies depending upon your particular camera, how much you review your shots on the LCD finder, how many pictures you take, what kind of media you're using, how often you use your internal flash, what type of batteries you're using, and what the temperature is. (Batteries drain faster in the cold.) If you're careful with the LCD screen and flash and keep the camera warm, four AA batteries could last for several hundred to 1,000 or more shots, depending on the camera.

Here's how to maximize your battery life when on vacation:

- ✓ **Short reviews:** Most digital cameras let you set how long the LCD stays on for review after a shot is taken. Choose the briefest setting. You can always review an individual shot for a longer period if need be.

- ✓ **Flash with care:** Built-in flash units reduce battery life by half. Use an accessory flash if possible.

- ✓ **Battery choices:** AA lithium batteries tend to last longer than other battery types, so if you use these, you can extend the active life of your shooting session before replacements are necessary. They also handle cold weather better. You should always carry at least one set of extra AA batteries (more if you shoot a lot).

If you're traveling in your home country, chances are you already know how easy or difficult it is to feed your camera, but even here in the United States, not every type of battery can be found in every area. If your camera requires one of the less common types, your digital camera can become a paperweight before your trip is half over.

Camera bag alternatives

If a traditional camera bag doesn't do everything you need, consider some alternatives. Here are some of the most popular:

✔ **Backpacks:** An alternative to the camera bag is the camera backpack. These range in size from small — big enough for just the camera, a couple of lenses, and some accessories — to massive carry-alls. One drawback is that you have to take the pack off and put it down every time you need to retrieve something.

✔ **Modular belt systems:** I use one of these myself, and it's great if you don't plan on sitting down very often. It puts the weight on your hips and leaves multiple lenses and accessories within easy reach even when wearing a backpack. The modularity of the system means that it can be configured for almost any sort of shoot.

Several manufacturers make modular belt systems, including Tamrac (www.tamrac.com), Lowepro (www.lowepro.com), and Kinesis (www.kinesisgear.com). These belts are festooned with loops, and separate pouches are mated to the belt with hook-and-loop tape. The advantage to this system is that the belt can be configured for different needs and matched to each day's shoot. Pouches are also available to hold cell phones, water bottles, and other nonphotographic items.

✔ **Chest bags:** A chest bag enables you to carry your camera harnessed to your chest, where you can get to it quickly and easily. Most of these style of bags can also be switched to a belt and positioned to ride on the hip as well.

If your camera uses AA or AAA batteries, rechargeable batteries are the best answer (with an extra set of backups, or two or three sets) for each device you bring that needs them. Choose nickel metal-hydride (NiMH) rechargeable batteries if you can because they have more power, are safer for the environment, and have several technical advantages over other types. If your camera doesn't use a common battery type, bring lots more than you think you'll need. Remember, if you have to buy batteries at a popular tourist destination, you'll probably pay a lot more than you normally would at home. If you're lucky, you'll have a camera that can accept a rechargeable battery pack and use regular AA batteries as well. Some packs, like the one shown in Figure 6-6, are the same form factor as a pair of AA cells.

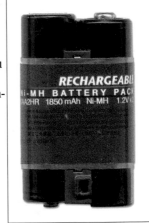

Figure 6-6: Some rechargeable packs can be replaced with conventional AA cells.

Of course, rechargeable batteries need to be recharged. If you're going overseas, make sure that you have the proper adaptors for whichever country you're visiting. Don't automatically assume there will be plenty of outlets, either. I recently went on a Bahamas cruise and found that our stateroom had only one outlet. Because I'd come prepared with a power strip, we could still plug in my laptop, battery chargers, fan, and my wife's hair dryer and curling iron. Without such foresight . . . well, my wife and I would surely have ended up fighting over a single outlet.

Another option, especially for those headed for a week or two in the backcountry, is a solar-powered battery charger from ICP Global Technologies (www.icpglobal.com/html/pp.htm). This unit can charge four AA batteries in four hours or so, depending on how bright a day it is. (Good luck if you're hiking in the Pacific Northwest.) The hard part might be finding a way to keep the device pointed toward the sun while you're backpacking through the forest. You may also want to consider whether carrying the unit's weight (1.3 pounds) in extra batteries would be more efficient.

Many of today's camera makers have resorted to marking the battery compartment orientation markings through indentations (+ or –) in the molds used to make the compartments, rather than painting the markings on with white paint. If your camera is one of those, consider finding a way to mark it yourself with something more visible, such as nail polish.

Picking up other useful devices

Gizmos. Gadgets. Thingamajigs. Many of these items don't fall into any particular category except that they do something useful. Here are some of the most popular photo widgets:

- **Cleaning kit:** A cleaning kit includes these items:

  - *Microfiber cleaning cloth:* These are useful for keeping lenses and bodies clean.

  - *Blower brush:* Use this first and blow off any dust or small particles.

  - *Silica packets:* These absorb any moisture that gets in your camera bag. Keep them in a plastic freezer bag that can double as a camera raincoat in bad weather.

- **Rain poncho:** I always keep a cheap plastic rain poncho in my camera bag, along with a better rain poncho in my car. Add to that a supply of plastic bags of various sizes and some artist's tape that's easy to apply and remove from the camera.

Make a raincoat for your camera from a plastic freezer bag. Draw the end of the bag over the camera's lens barrel and cut a hole large enough for it to shoot through. Wrap the artist's tape around the end of the barrel and bag to hold the bag in place, and you've got a low-cost rain poncho for the camera. Thread the camera strap through the end of the bag that opens and press as much of the seal together as possible. If it's hard to see through the viewfinder, turn the LCD display on and use that to compose the photo. Figure 6-7 shows you what this camera raincoat looks like. Put a clear or ultraviolet filter over the front of your lens to provide even more protection from the moisture.

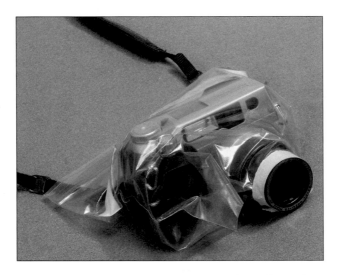

Figure 6-7: A zip-closure bag and tape can make a raincoat for your camera.

- **Towel:** Carry some paper towels so that you can towel off any moisture that gets inside the freezer bag. Toss a silica packet or two in with the camera before closing the bag to help keep the inside dry. It's also a good idea to have something to dry your hands so you're not touching the camera with wet hands. A good choice for this kind of thing is a Pack Towel, which is a lightweight towel that dries quickly and is sold in many department stores' camping sections.

- **A pencil eraser:** Sometimes a thin film of corrosion builds up on the battery and terminal contacts. The cure for this one is to gently rub both the battery and terminal contacts with a pencil eraser and reinsert the batteries, making sure that they're right-side-up.

- **Polypro gloves:** Several outdoor clothing companies make lightweight gloves out of polypropylene or some brand-name version, such as Capilene or Thermax. Outdoor enthusiasts prize these synthetic materials because they *wick* (transfer) moisture away from the skin to the outside of the material, making them seem warmer because the skin stays dry. Wearing a pair of these in damp conditions will help keep your hands dry. When you need to touch the camera, pull a glove off, and you have a dry hand to work with.

✓ **Artist's or masking tape:** If the conditions are both dusty and windy, protecting the camera can be vital and difficult. Fine-grit sand or dust can blow inside the camera's seals and mess up internal mechanisms. The same plastic bag technique described in a preceding bullet is good, but consider taping as much of the bag end shut as possible to get the best possible seal.

If you're traveling abroad and want to be sure you won't be hassled on your return, visit a U.S. Customs and Border Protection Office and ask for a Certificate of Registration (form CF4457). You have to bring your gear to the customs office where they will confirm your gear and stamp the form. This will guarantee you won't be asked to pay a duty on your gear. Find the location of the nearest customs office at `www.customs.ustreas.gov`. Most travelers skip this step and do just fine, but if you have new gear and are going somewhere known for electronics, filling out the form can be a good idea.

Getting Ready to Go on the Road

You won't like surprises after you leave home and begin taking pictures. One key to successful travel photography is making as many preparations as you can ahead of time so you'll be organized and confident when you begin capturing memories. Here is a checklist of things to do before you leave:

✓ **Create a packing list:** As you prepare for the trip, put together a packing list for the photographic gear. Plan a dry run to make sure everything fits in whatever camera bag or case you're using.

✓ **Carry it on:** All but the cheapest camera equipment should be included with carry-on luggage. If you're taking more than just a basic digital camera and memory cards, make sure that the camera bag is small enough to meet carry-on space limits. Airlines are getting more restrictive and may limit you to one carry-on item plus a personal item, such as a laptop, purse, or — with luck — a camera bag. Record serial numbers for pieces of equipment that have them and have a packing list in a separate bag in case the camera bag gets lost or stolen. Check with your insurance company to see whether camera equipment is covered under your policy. If it isn't, see whether you can add a *rider* (a special add-on to your policy) for the trip.

✓ **Have some in-flight reading:** How familiar are you with your camera and accessories? Maybe it would be a good idea to dig out the instruction manuals and pack them in your carry-on so that you can reacquaint yourself with some of the camera's more esoteric features. The book you're reading right now also makes for some good travel reading. I also recommend *Digital Travel Photography Field Guide*, also from Wiley and yours truly.

Meeting Your Storage Requirements

Just like going on vacation with a film camera, the digital camera needs a steady supply of (digital) film. Because of the newness of the technology (particularly overseas and in developing nations), photographers need to ensure that they have enough memory capacity for the trip.

Here are some considerations when bulking up your storage for a trip:

- ✔ **Have enough memory.** Will you be able to get an entire vacation's worth of pictures with your current supply of memory cards? Remember that you tend to shoot a lot more while traveling. If you don't think you're going to have enough capacity, consider buying more. Alternatively, you can carry a laptop computer (if you have one) so that you can transfer images and free up memory each night. (Test this process before you go to make sure you have what you need to transfer images.)

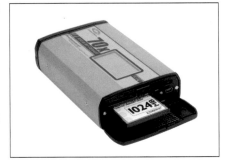

- ✔ **Try a portable hard drive or CD/ DVD burner.** In between a pocketful of memory cards and a notebook computer are portable hard drives and CD/DVD burners. These drives can accept CompactFlash cards and other types of removable storage with the proper adapter. For about $200–$300, far less than a laptop, you can get a portable hard drive (like the one shown in Figure 6-8) with 40–60GB

Figure 6-8: A portable hard drive will let you copy your photos and free up your memory cards.

of storage space for fewer dollars per byte than a memory card. The portable CD/DVD burners, although a bit larger, can copy your photos to durable CDs and DVDs, which can hold gigabytes of information at a very low cost. If you go this route, try to acquire the device a couple of weeks before the trip so you have time to make sure you can work it properly.

Even with all the extra memory cards or a portable hard drive, you're still carrying less weight than the equivalent in number of shots worth of film.

Tried-and-True Travel Photography Techniques

If you've prepared well, you'll be ready to take great pictures when you reach your destination. This section tells you a little about some of the most popular types of travel photography and provides tips on getting the best shots.

In all cases, keep local, regional, and national sensitivities in mind when choosing your subjects. Some buildings, installations, and people shouldn't be photographed because of security, personal, or religious concerns. When in doubt, ask for permission.

Shooting scenics

Scenic photos are high on the list of pictures people try to bring back from their travels. After all, you have to prove you went someplace nice, don't you? Here are some tips for shooting great scenics:

- **Don't hurry.** The effort to record a site's beauty all too often results in quick snapshots hurriedly snatched while with a tour group or during a sightseeing drive. Some places are spectacular enough that this approach actually works; most of the time, it's hit or miss.

- **Not all light is created equal.** The best light of the day occurs when the sun is low in the sky. Early morning and late evening sunlight produce dramatic shadows and rich, warm colors, when the sun's light is more red/orange than any other time during the day. If a site on your trip is particularly important, plan on being there during the *golden hours* (early morning and late evening). Try to do a reconnaissance of the location a day or two beforehand so that you can see whether the sun rises or sets behind what you're shooting.

When the sun is rising or setting behind the scene, it creates the opportunity for a dramatic backlight silhouette. This is a difficult exposure situation because the camera is pointing directly into the sun. Don't underestimate the additional risk for the photographer, who must be careful not to stare directly into the sun.

- **Create silhouettes.** For a good, solid black silhouette of a building, structure, landscape feature, or person, the camera should be set about two full f-stops smaller than what the light meter indicates for the main scene. Your goal here is a bright, orange-red sun (the most dramatic kind). Depending on your camera, you can either change aperture settings directly, or you can use the exposure compensation dial to get the exposure you need. Take several shots at one f-stop increment to make sure there's a good exposure, like the one shown in Figure 6-9.

✔ **Keep it steady.** Have your camera mounted on a tripod while doing scenics. The added stability reduces the effects of camera shake and allows for a slower shutter speed. Reducing the shutter speed enables you to use a smaller aperture (larger f-stop number), which creates greater overall depth of field for the sharpest possible picture. If a tripod isn't available, try to find something sturdy to brace the camera on or against. Walls, car roofs, wooden chairs, and countertops can all make excellent emergency tripods. Bracing the camera vertically against a post or column will also keep it steady enough to help compensate for too slow a shutter speed for hand holding.

✔ **That cloud looks like a. . . .** Take advantage of cloudy skies, which provide more visual interest than a plain, washed-out blue sky, as you can see in Figure 6-10. When the clouds are in hiding, compose the image so that it has minimal empty sky at the top of the frame.

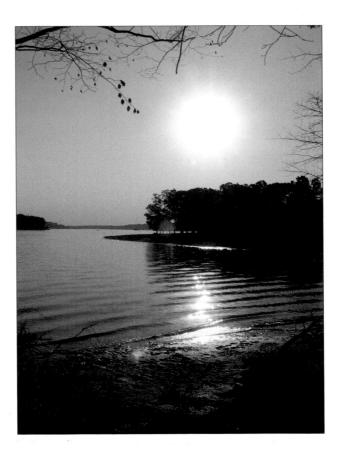

Figure 6-9: A sunset offers the opportunity to create dramatic silhouette photos.

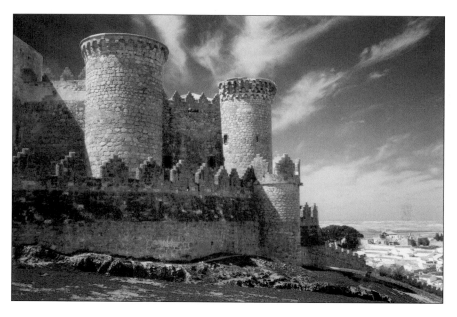

Figure 6-10: Clouds can add a dramatic element to travel photos.

Capturing monuments and architecture

The Arc de Triomphe, the Empire State Building, the Golden Gate Bridge. Monuments, architecture, and engineering marvels can provide stunning images and a record of your journey. You can take your photography to a whole new level by following some simple techniques.

Many of the techniques described earlier for scenics also apply to photographing these man-made wonders. Some special techniques, however, apply only to man-made objects.

Taking a shot in the dark

Don't put your camera away when the sun sets. Buildings, monuments, and bridges take on an entirely different look at night when they're all lit up. Here are some of the things to keep in mind when taking pictures of monuments after dusk:

- **Support your camera.** Once again, use your tripod or some other camera support. Many cameras suggest using flash at this point; don't. Some cameras automatically set the flash under such conditions; override it if you can. You don't want to overpower the existing illumination with flat, bright, electronic flash. Most of the time, flash used in nighttime scenes spoils any existing mood or ambience.

✔ **Go long.** The idea here is to get a long enough exposure to turn the headlights from cars and trucks into long ribbons of color wrapping around the base of the structure, while its own lights help give a sense of its form.

✔ **Shoot by the sea, by the sea, by the beautiful sea.** Finally, if you're photographing in a river or ocean town, a boat can make a fine shooting platform. Just keep in mind that motor vessels' powerful engines cause the decks to vibrate, and a tripod isn't much help in such circumstances.

When the sun goes down, check out the nearest amusement park. Set your camera on a tripod or something solid and do a long exposure of the Ferris wheel or roller coaster or any of the other rides with bright lights and fast motion.

Painting with light

Sometimes, a building is too big and too dark for normal photographic measures to do the trick. For these situations, the pros paint with light. This technique calls for using a long exposure and firing off multiple flash bursts to illuminate the object in sections. Here's how to do it:

1. **Set your camera on a steady surface.**

   A tripod is good, but so is a short wall or the ground. Keep your camera steady because if the camera moves, the illuminated areas move, too, putting them out of alignment.

2. **Adjust the camera for a time exposure.**

   Check your camera manual to learn how to set your camera for a time exposure.

3. **Decide what areas of your subjects need painting.**

4. **Trigger a time exposure (or have a helper do it) using your digital camera's particular time exposure controls.**

   Experiment with different times, from ten seconds to a minute or longer.

5. **Paint by triggering your external flash multiple times.**

   Move the flash around to illuminate the subject in sections. As you move, keep your body between your light source and camera if you don't want the light source to appear in the photo.

Photographers use another technique called *writing with light,* which can be lots of fun. It's an especially apt technique for travel photography because it can be used to photograph buildings, monuments, and other scenes that would otherwise be difficult to capture at night. This is another trick that takes advantage of a long exposure and a solid shooting platform, such as a tripod, a wall, or the ground. The idea is to take a pencil torch (penlight) and point it toward the camera lens while the shutter is open. You can either swirl it around or try to write a specific message. Here's how to do it:

1. **Plan what you want to do. It's good to rehearse a couple of times with someone watching through the viewfinder.**

   This way, you know if the camera's positioned properly to get everything. Besides, you have to write backward — don't you think that takes some practice?

2. **Set the camera to shutter priority and give it a long time (long enough for you to do what you want, probably several seconds or more).**

3. **Write with light by pointing the light at the camera lens from your subject position.**

4. **Review the image with the camera's LCD screen.**

5. **If necessary, make some adjustments to your shutter speed based on what you see in the LCD, using a longer or shorter speed as required.**

6. **If you want to get really fancy, have a friend or spouse fire off a small flash after you're done writing but before the shutter closes.**

   This helps illuminate you while still allowing your writing to show.

Book III
Chapter 6

Travel Photography

Keystoning

Keystoning, also known as *perspective distortion,* happens when the photographer tries to fit an entire building in a photo by tilting the camera up. The problem with this approach is that when the camera is no longer perfectly parallel with the building, any straight lines on the long axis of the image converge until they meet at the top. The photographer ends up with a photo of a building with a wide base and a pinpoint top that appears to be falling away.

How to avoid it? Because the problem comes from the lens and the building not being perfectly parallel, the easiest way to correct that problem is to bring them into line. You might be able to do this by finding a way to gain some elevation. Sometimes, a nearby hill can provide a distant vantage point. Sometimes, another building with an accessible roof is available. Unfortunately, all too often, neither solution is available, and the only option is to point the camera up and take the picture.

Don't forget that fireworks, like those shown in Figure 6-11, are a kind of writing with light. You can use the same techniques that I just described except that you let the aerial display create your image for you. Use a tripod and set your camera for exposures of a second or two. Set the camera for about ISO 100 and start your exposure just before the fireworks reach the top of their arc. Try leaving your shutter open for several sets of displays, covering the lens with your hand between displays to capture several in one exposure. Take along a penlight so you can adjust your camera's settings in the dark! Time exposures of moving lights and traffic (think the Strip in Las Vegas) are also great ways to paint with light.

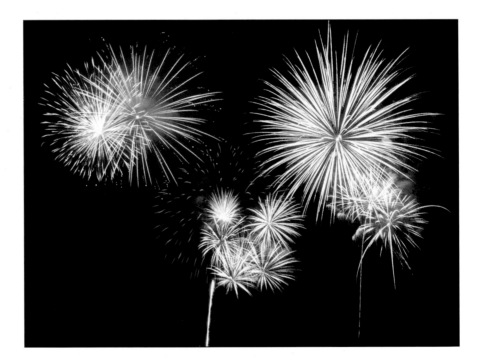

Figure 6-11: Fireworks are a kind of writing with light.

Shooting panoramas

One of the most frustrating moments of travel photography comes when you find yourself literally surrounded by the beauty of nature and have no way to capture all that surrounds you in a single photo. A digital camera, tripod, and the right image-editing software, however, make capturing a 360-degree panorama possible. Basically, you take a series of shots for your panorama and then stitch the shots together (line up the images into one image) on your computer. Although you can stitch images together in any image editor, specialized stitching applications are easy to use. Follow these steps to shoot a panoramic shot:

1. **Mount your camera on a tripod and set the camera's appropriate zoom setting.**

   You don't have to set the zoom lens to its widest setting. Zooming in a little closer means that you'll capture more detail per photo. If your main subject is distant, zooming in lets you capture more of the important part of the scene without wasting space on unnecessary foreground details.

   The more shots you take, the more you'll have to stitch together, and the greater the chance the software might have trouble creating a seamless panorama. Generally speaking, three to six images are most manageable.

2. **Level the camera.**

   The closer you can come to a perfectly level camera, the better job your software can do with the final image. Buying an inexpensive level (as small a unit as possible) at the local hardware store is highly recommended. Set the level on top of the camera and adjust the tripod until the camera is level.

3. **When you take the first picture, waste a shot by photographing your fingers in front of the lens. Don't worry about focusing or exposure.**

   This makes it easy to see where you began the sequence. Do the same when you've completed each sequence.

4. **Make your first shot of the scene at either the left or right end of the panoramic swing that you intend to make.**

   If your camera is capable of manual exposure, take several readings throughout the scene and try to come up with an average setting for the entire range.

5. **Take subsequent pictures.**

   Make sure each shot overlaps the previous one by 20–30 percent.

6. **If possible, do a second sequence of images, particularly if lighting was erratic.**

7. **Stitch them all together back home, using an image editor or stitching software.**

   Packages such as PhotoStitch (furnished free with Canon cameras for Windows and the Macintosh) or Photoshop and Photoshop Elements' built-in PhotoMerge panorama capabilities (see Figure 6-12) are easy to use and a lot of fun. Your digital camera may come with similar applications.

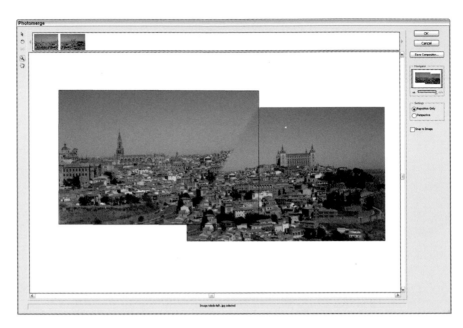

Figure 6-12: Stitch images together in Photoshop or Photoshop Elements.

Photographers who are really serious about getting good 360-degree panoramas can try a special tripod head made by Kaidan (www.kaidan.com). The Kaidan head enables you to mount the optical center (or *nodal point)* of the camera lens directly over the tripod's pivot point for the most accurate positioning possible. These heads range from a little over $140 to several hundred dollars or more. Unless you're a perfectionist, though, you can get satisfactory results without one.

Equipment for shooting adventure sports

I cover sports photography in detail in Book III, Chapter V. All the tips listed there apply equally well to travel/adventure sports. The big difference, however, is the equipment you need for this type of action photography. Adventure sports, such as white-water rafting, rock climbing, scuba diving, and similar activities, entail different risks and require different precautions and tools to protect your precious equipment:

- **Dry boxes:** Climbers and hikers need to keep their gear dry by using waterproof camera bags or other equipment. Sports like white-water rafting and kayaking call for even greater protection. Usually, these boaters protect their gear in a dry box setup. The best known manufacturer of these is Pelican (www.casesbypelican.com), which makes cases with foam insides that can be cut to fit specific camera gear. If using one of these, take very good care of the O-rings that provide the watertight seal for the box. Veteran river runners sometimes rely on Army surplus ammo or rocket boxes, which also provide a watertight container for gear, but without the form-fitting foam. If you use one of these, make sure that the camera is properly cushioned from the bumps and jolts that white-water rafting entails.

If you protect your camera from water, you can easily take photos like the one shown in Figure 6-13.

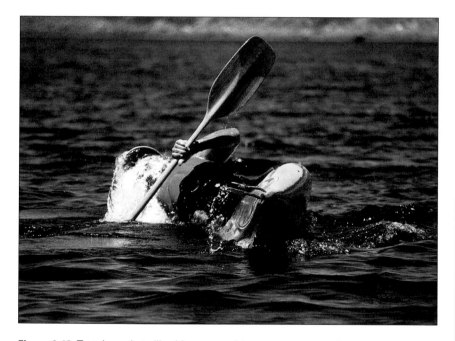

Figure 6-13: To take a photo like this, you need to protect your gear from water.

- ↙ **Carabineers:** These are the oval clips that climbers use to secure themselves to safety ropes; you can use them to clip the dry box to your off-road vehicle. If you're immersed in a water activity, the clips can also secure your dry box to the raft or inside the kayak. The boaters will run the rapid, catch an eddy at the end of it, unpack the camera, and start shooting. Once again, placing a silica packet or two in one of these cases will help keep dampness from damaging equipment.

- ↙ **Underwater digital cameras:** Another option for those who want to shoot a lot in wet conditions is a new underwater digital camera. I've used underwater cameras even when I wasn't *planning* to go in the water. (You never can tell where a hike will end up.) The SeaLife ReefMaster underwater digital camera comes in a waterproof housing and works both on land

and underwater. The camera, which retails for under $400, produces only a 3.3- to 5.0-megapixel image but saves you the trouble of trying to find a housing to fit an existing digital camera. The camera also has an LCD screen that works underwater and a fast delete function, both of which make it easier to operate underwater. Check out the manufacturer's Web site at `www.sealife-cameras.com` for more information.

- ✔ **Waterproof casings:** More extreme conditions call for better protection. Waterproof casings that allow photography are available from several companies, including ewa-marine (`www.ewa-marine.de`). These are useful for both underwater photography (careful on the depth, though) and above the water if sailing or boating.

Keep in mind that salt spray is very possibly the worst threat to camera electronics there is. A camera's housing provides good protection against wind and salt spray.

- ✔ **Deep-diving housings:** For serious underwater enthusiasts, heavy-duty Plexiglas camera housings now exist for small digital cameras. These housings are available for a wide range of digital cameras and can be found for as little as $200.

Photographing people

There are lots of reasons to photograph people while traveling, and also some reasons not to. Photographing law enforcement or military personnel without getting their permission first can be a bad idea.

With the heightened concern about terrorism these days, many security forces, including our own, have become much more sensitive about people photographing and videotaping government facilities and employees. While traveling in Israel and South America, it wasn't unusual to see armed military personnel walking the streets. Even a decade ago, it wasn't a good idea to grab a snapshot of them, and I wouldn't even consider it these days unless I'd gotten their permission first.

When photographing people in other areas of the country or in foreign lands, remember that effective travel photography needs to create a sense of place. Any time the photographer can use lifestyle, surroundings, work, or clothing to show the region or culture involved, he or she has achieved at least one measure of success. Certain elements can help your photos convey your location:

- ✔ **Clothing:** Different cultures have different tastes in clothing and jewelry, as you can see in Figure 6-14.

- ✔ **Design:** Advertisements, homes, and buildings will look different whether you're overseas or in the United States.

✔ **Products:** Soda cans, candy bars, and other packaging is different in other countries, and sometimes even in the United States.

✔ **The natural world:** Plants and wildlife might be noticeably different in other locations.

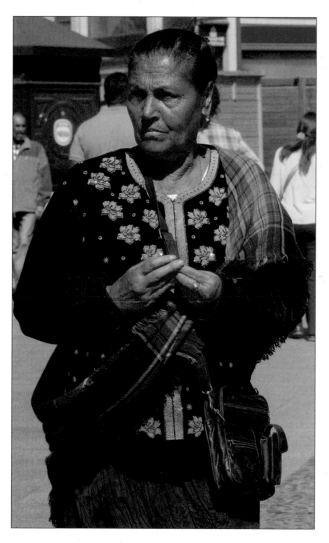

Figure 6-14: The everyday clothing in foreign lands can provide a fascinating glimpse at a culture.

In addition to creating a sense of place, these tips can help you effectively photograph people while traveling:

- ✔ **Be aware of cultural sensitivities.** Some cultures frown upon photographic images of other human beings (that includes cultures in the United States, as well). In many Middle Eastern and developing nations, women wear clothing designed to hide their appearance. In some of these countries, photographing them can be a serious taboo (as can a man speaking to one of them to even ask permission to take their photo).

- ✔ **Check out the local customs.** Although taboos that have their origins in religious beliefs can stay constant for millennia, official taboos can shift frequently. Check with the U.S. consular office for the country that you're visiting to learn what's okay and what isn't. The Web site `http://travel.state.gov/travel/warnings.html` also has information on individual countries and policies.

- ✔ **Ask first.** As a newspaper reporter and photographer, my philosophy was to shoot first and ask questions later. (You can always talk to people after an event's over, but you can't re-create photos.) Photojournalists working in a news-gathering capacity are afforded some liberties that are considered out of line for tourists, though. (And that's in this country; the rules vary from country to country.) In the case of a traveler photographing others without their permission, it's a behavior that many would at least consider rude.

- ✔ **Pretend I'm not here.** One of the reasons pros prefer to shoot first and then ask is because people appear more natural when they don't know that they're being photographed. A common way of dealing with this problem is to ask permission and then explain you'd like the picture to look natural and could they please go back to what they were doing and forget you're there.

- ✔ **Be forgettable.** Although your subjects likely start out self-conscious, after a few minutes, they tend to become involved in their activity and forget you're there.

- ✔ **Give them feedback.** Be aware of human psychology. People who are posing tend to wait for some feedback at first — namely the click of the camera that tells them you're satisfied. If they don't hear it because you're waiting for them to forget you're there, they tend to become concerned that you're not happy with what they're doing. Use your digital advantage (being able to delete bad shots) and take a photo or two at the start. Your subject will relax a little and begin to forget you're there.

Another technique works well if you have a camera with a fairly wide-angle lens. Set the zoom to the widest possible focal length and hold the camera at waist level and as perpendicular to the ground as you can. I usually try to do this one-handed with the camera strap helping me keep the camera under control. Most people relax even more at this point because they don't expect you to shoot now. At this point, when I see the shot I want, I trip the shutter. This technique works better if you're familiar enough with your camera to have a good idea of what its wide angle covers from a certain distance.

This shooting from the hip can be a tricky proposition ethically. At least one journalism professor I know feels that it's a violation of trust between a photographer and the subject.

As a photographer, I believe it's important to be sensitive to your subject's feelings on the matter. Because I'm shooting digitally, I take the shot and then explain that I've taken a shot and show it to the person I've photographed. I then let him or her decide whether the photo should be deleted. Most people don't mind at all, but I've slept better at night by immediately deleting the shot if the person is unhappy with it. This all gets a lot harder if you and your subject don't speak the same language. Sometimes, the combination of pantomime and the preview capability of the digital camera can be enough for you to get by.

Capturing people and their environments

After the issue of getting permission from your subjects is out of the way, consider how to photograph them. Being able to capture people in their environment is where you can really feel the advantages of your digital camera. It's lightweight and versatile and can take plenty of photos. Here are some ways to make the most of its advantages:

- **Shoot as much as it takes.** If what you want can be achieved in just one shot, so much the better. Still, there's nothing wrong with multiple shots to achieve the same thing, provided the images build upon one another.

- **Capture the environment.** At least one shot should show the individual within his or her cultural environment. After that image is out of the way, focus on smaller details. Look for things that would be unusual back in your own home.

- **Move in close.** Medium shots and close-ups provide greater intimacy than full-body or head-and-shoulder shots. A well-focused, tight composition of a person's face (cropped in to just eyes, nose, mouth, and not much more), packs a lot of intimacy. Whatever you do, don't make the mistake shown in Figure 6-15, in which the subject is so far away that you can barely tell who he is.

- **Hands can speak volumes.** Sometimes a person's hands can reveal his or her work history. Work roughened hands can speak of years of manual labor and toil. Or a close-up of hands holding small tools or repairing a watch, for instance, can show great dexterity.

Book III
Chapter 6

Travel Photography

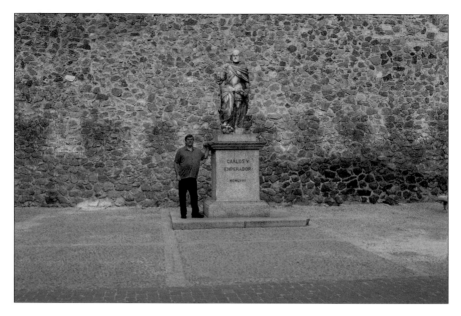

Figure 6-15: Don't make this mistake! Get in closer!

- ✓ **Capture the essentials.** Who is this person? What shows your subject's identity? A new mom cradling her baby, a farmer on his tractor, and a cyclist on her bike are just a few possibilities.

- ✓ **Use lighting.** Don't forget to consider lighting. Unless your subject's in direct sunlight, some sort of fill flash is necessary. (The term *fill* flash comes from its use not as a main light source, but as an additional light to fill in areas that are hidden from the main light.)

- ✓ **Go for variety.** Make sure to take a mix of horizontal and vertical photos. For people shots, take lots of verticals because the human body breaks down to a series of elements that are taller than they are wide.

- ✓ **Show people working, playing, and relaxing.** Even on a mountain climb, like the one shown in Figure 6-16, quiet moments reveal another side of your subjects. Social gatherings and religious meetings are also prime opportunities for good photographs. Look for community festivals, too, where you can get lots of people, costumes, and events going on. In such freewheeling settings, people are less concerned about being photographed, and you can probably get away with taking wider shots without having to check with every individual for their permission. Performers, in particular, are quite used to being photographed.

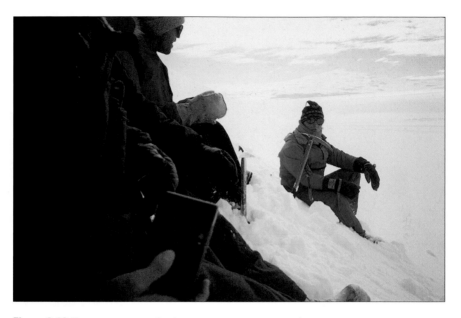

Figure 6-16: Even on a mountain slope, you can capture a quiet moment.

Documenting Your Trip

Pull together everything from the earlier sections in this chapter to create memorable photos of your trip. Documenting a vacation is more than grabbing some pretty pictures of your travels; it's creating a visual narrative that re-creates the magic of your trip all over again. This section wraps up travel photography with some final tips for getting great vacation pictures.

Varying your shots

Try for a mix of shots and camera angles. Shoot some close-ups, and shoot from far away. You can do a lot of things to avoid having all your photos look alike:

- **Put the camera on the ground for a worm's-eye view.** Makes that church look even more imposing.

- **Get a bird's-eye view.** Renting helicopters gets expensive, but there are other ways of getting up high and shooting down. You were going to climb that monument anyway, right? Take advantage of the elevation. Take advantage of cable cars. Take advantage of a hot-air balloon ride for some once-in-a-lifetime scenic photos. Even simpler, climb a staircase and shoot straight down, as shown in Figure 6-17.

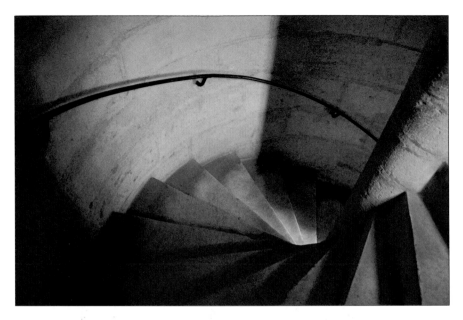

Figure 6-17: A bird's-eye view can provide an unusual vantage point for travel photos.

✓ **Turn the camera vertically when appropriate.** Many scenes lend themselves to vertical images, yet most people still grip the camera horizontally. Monuments, people, and buildings are all taller than they are wide. Turn the camera on its side.

✓ **Shoot from more than one vantage point.** Do like the pros do. Shoot it high, shoot it low, shoot it horizontally, vertically, get closer, move back, walk around it. While doing this, remember to consider what's in the background.

Composing your shots

How you arrange the elements within your photo has a lot to do with how much impact they convey. I talk about composition in more detail in Book III, Chapter 1, but here are some things that can help improve your photographic composition:

✓ **Leading lines:** Strong linear elements can pull the eye into an image. Straight lines, diagonal lines, and S-curves all show movement and can depict strength, direction, or grace. For example, a U.S. flag rippling in the wind combines an S-curve with the strong lines of the stripes.

✓ **Framing:** Use natural elements, such as window frames or tree branches, to form a natural border along a corner or around the image. Figure 6-18 is an example of this concept.

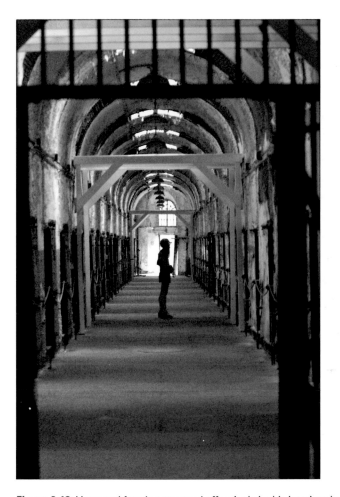

Figure 6-18: Lines and framing are used effectively in this interior photo.

✔ **Rule of thirds:** Divide the frame in thirds horizontally and vertically. Where the thirds intersect is a good place to position your subject. You can also use this to show a course of movement. For example, putting an airplane coming into the frame into the top-right third conveys a sense of moving downward through the frame.

✔ **Balance:** Ever see a picture of someone sitting on a park bench with one end of the bench missing? Without the missing support, it seems like the person is going to drop like a rock off the unbalanced bench. You can find examples of photos using balance and these other prime rules of composition in Book III, Chapter 1.

Getting organized

Close focusing (or macro capability) is another one of the digital camera's best features. By introducing details of the location you're visiting, you can trigger memories of your experience years after the trip has ended.

On that cruise I mention earlier in this chapter (in which the stateroom had only one electrical outlet), my wife and I were fortunate to stay in an owner's suite, one of the nicest cabins on the ship. Each afternoon, we received a treat of some sort from one of the ship's staff along with a card announcing whom it was from. Before enjoying our delicacies, we made sure to photograph the dish and card together, as shown in Figure 6-19, and kept the card for a scrapbook as well. The photo album from this trip includes many such details and provides a much fuller and richer representation of our trip.

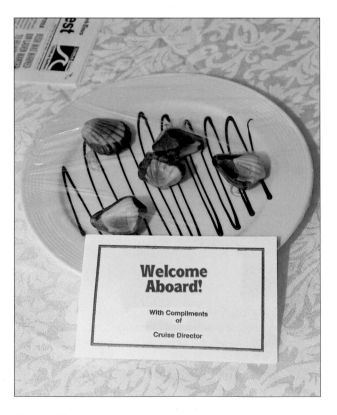

Figure 6-19: Photograph keepsakes and other unusual bits of your environment as you travel.

Now take it a step further. Think of your photographic coverage as a series of still images that tell a story rather than a group of individual pictures that stand on their own (even though they should).

✔ **Signs, signs, everywhere there's signs:** Use street and highway signs, or even the one and only South Pole (shown in Figure 6-20), to show where you are or where you're going. Photograph maps and brochures, too. Don't just settle for snapshots of these images; try to use lighting and depth of field to turn them into interesting images in their own right.

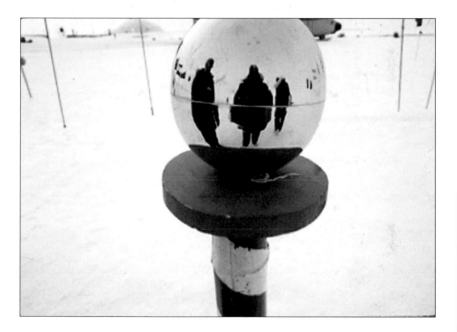

Figure 6-20: The South Pole is one sign that you've traveled far and wide.

✔ **Cultural and language differences:** Signs differ from country to country. In the United States, signs read *End of Construction.* Years ago, on a trip through New Zealand, I photographed a sign, shown in Figure 6-21, that proclaimed, *Works End,* with a cemetery in the background.

✔ **More signs:** Street and road crew signs are only one type of photographic target, though. Distinctive shop, restaurant, and tavern signs also provide reminders of where you've been.

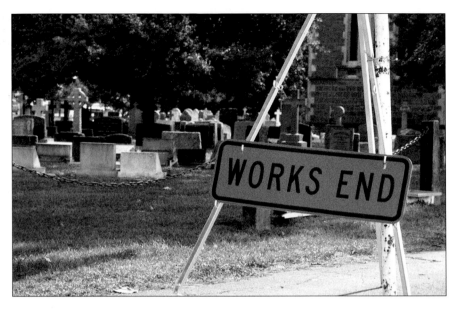

Figure 6-21: A sure sign that your travel work is never really at an end.

- **Newspapers/newsstands:** Check the local newsstands. In at least some countries, newsstands say something about where you're visiting. For that matter, a close-up of the day's headline during your visit can make a good introductory graphic if you're giving a presentation.

- **Trailheads:** On a wilderness trip, most trailheads are well marked. Photograph the signs. Shoot the trail maps, too. Your packs, supplies, and other gear should also be documented. Follow the same approach if you're on a white-water, skydiving, or ski trip.

- **White water:** For white water, shoot as many rapids as possible. (Only my fellow paddlers will get that pun.) Photograph the rapids from the side because that field of view gives a better sense of scale than a head-on shot. If you can, get a raft or kayak in the photo because that will help show the rapid's size.

- **River scenes:** Wilderness rafting trips include many other photo opportunities as well. Photos of *swimmers* (the white-water euphemism for someone who's inadvertently become one with the river) and their rescue provide dramatic images. The lunch buffet (if on a commercial trip) provides an opportunity for humor if you get shots of some of the sandwiches the guides make. (Guides traditionally eat after the paying guests have gone through the buffet. As a result, some of the sandwich ingredients get pretty creative. Mine usually included cold cuts, veggies, chunky peanut butter, and thick slices of onion.)

✔ **River scenes (part 2):** Don't forget that white-water rivers generally offer spectacular scenery, too. Plus, you can take shots of all the preliminaries — inflating the rafts, getting gear together, and putting on wet suits and life jackets.

✔ **Rock climbing:** Scenery, gear, climbers. Oh yeah, don't forget the rocks. Seriously, mix close-ups, wide-angle shots, and action images of the climbers. Take advantage of the bright colors and patterns of the clothing that rock climbers wear; and the chocks, friends, and *nuts* (protective equipment climbers use to anchor into the rock, for all you nonclimbers) are great subjects for close-up shots. So are chalk-covered fingers. Also, get lots of angles: Shoot from below, above, and alongside the climbers.

✔ **Moods:** Everything doesn't have to be bright and sunny in your travel photos. Don't be afraid to shoot moody, misty, rainy days, like the one shown in Figure 6-22, to show yet another side of your journey.

✔ **Papers, please:** Don't forget close-ups of your travel documents. They're also part of the story you're telling.

You'll soon discover that good photography is all in the details. Visiting foreign cultures provides a wealth of these details that help show how different or similar we are. Close-ups of jewelry, magazines, and candy and food packaging help emphasize that you've gone somewhere different.

**Book III
Chapter 6**

Travel Photography

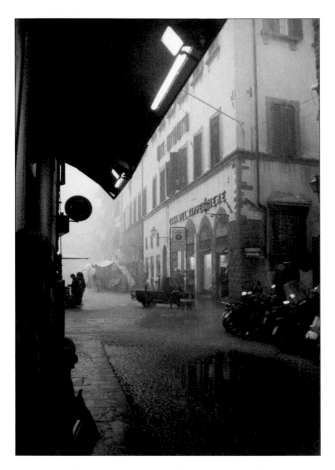

Figure 6-22: Even moody scenes can tell part of your travel story.

Book IV
Basics of Image Editing

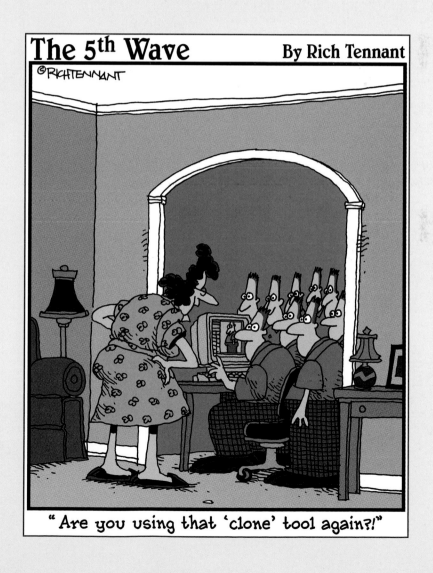

The 5th Wave   By Rich Tennant

"Are you using that 'clone' tool again?!"

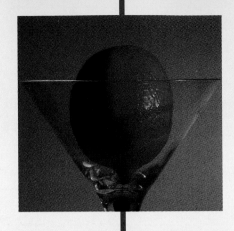

*E*very journey begins with a first step, and if you still haven't taken the plunge into image editing, this book helps make that step a gentle immersion rather than a plummet from the high-dive platform. I show you exactly what you can and can't expect to do with image editors such as Corel Paint Shop Pro, Corel PhotoPaint, Ulead PhotoImpact, and Adobe Photoshop and Photoshop Elements. You'll see the capabilities of each of these applications and discover the full range of tools each puts at your disposal.

I close out this book with a chapter that compares and contrasts the most popular image editors so you can choose which one (or perhaps two!) of these image editing programs you really need to make your digital photos look their best.

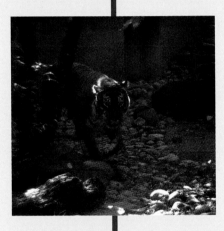

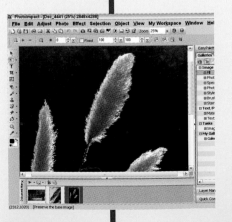

Chapter 1: What You Can and Can't Do with Image-Editing Tools

In This Chapter

- ✓ Fixing faded and distorted color photos
- ✓ Adjusting lights and darks
- ✓ Fine-tuning sharpness and contrast
- ✓ Eliminating dust, blemishes, and other artifacts
- ✓ Rearranging, removing, and adding content
- ✓ Merging images

*W*ith all the seemingly miraculous things that you *can* accomplish with image-editing tools, it would be easy to assume that there's nothing you *can't* do. You'd think that you could take any image, in any condition, and make it beautiful — but is that really the case? Not always. Although you can do a great deal to repair serious tears, rips, stains, and scratches, as well as the effects of aging and improper photographic technique, you can't solve every problem every time — at least not easily.

You can't, for example, take a photo in which everything is out of focus and make it as crisp and clear as the photographer probably intended. If, however, one part of the photo is in focus and the other parts are a blurry distraction, you can blur them out even further so that they're just a pleasant backdrop to the properly focused portion. Or, you can remove them altogether, eliminating the unpleasant aspects of the image. You'll find that in some extreme cases, your images might require some compromise when editing them, giving up one thing to gain another. Or success might require a willingness to work with only the parts of the photo that are salvageable, discarding the rest. This chapter provides a quick introduction to the kinds of fixes you can expect to make with image-editing tools.

Correcting Colors

As you probably know, digital camera images are made up of the red, green, and blue primary colors of light. These three colors can be combined to produce the colors you see on a video monitor: that is, within the limitations of the monitor's color reproduction capabilities. When your digital pictures are printed, these colors are expressed as combinations of their complementary colors, which are the primaries of pigments. The complement of red is cyan, and it's printed by combining yellow and magenta; the complement of blue is yellow, and it's printed by combining magenta and cyan; and the complement of green is magenta, and it's printed by combining yellow and cyan. Everyone has seen a color wheel, like the one shown in Figure 1-1, that shows these relationships.

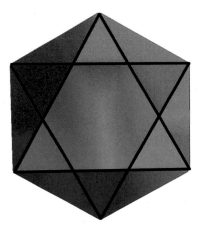

Figure 1-1: The relationships between the primary colors of light and their complements can be represented by a color wheel.

Knowing these relationships can be useful when it comes time to correct colors. For example, as you'll find out later in this chapter, you fix a photo that appears to be too red by removing some red or by "adding" its complement, cyan. (You'll see why "adding" is in quotes in the next subsection.) Similarly, you can remove green or "add" magenta; or, remove blue or "add" yellow.

We've all seen photos with a strange green, yellow, or red tinge, where skin looks weird, hair colors aren't anything close to what appears in nature, leaves are blue, grass is yellow, and basically everything looks alien. The color problem can happen either when the photo was taken or during development. Sometimes photos that looked okay in the beginning change color over time. Regardless of the cause, you can fix most color problems — with some exceptions, of course.

Most image-editing applications provide tools for adjusting a photo's color levels. Depending on the features of your favorite application, you might or might not be able to add color or change color effectively, and this is perhaps one of the most important tests for evaluating multiple image-editing applications. If you can't get rid of a ruddy, sunburned look in a photo or eliminate the nausea-green tinge in a picture, consider looking to another application for serious photo editing.

You can't add color that isn't there

Typically, adjusting image color involves changing existing color levels. If the photo is a color image, you can adjust the levels of whatever color is in unwanted abundance so that the tones are more natural. However, color correction can't add color that isn't there in the first place. For example, in an overpoweringly red image, removing the red cast might not leave enough green and blue colors to produce a realistic image. One of the things that you can't do with an image editor is to fix the color of images that are too far off the deep end in terms of color balance.

Similarly, if the image is in black and white or has faded so much that it's hard to tell whether it was ever in color, adding that touch of color to a photo might not be so easy. You can't simply increase or decrease one or more colors if the colors aren't there in the first place.

 You can add layers to your image and color them in by using your editing software's fill color and painting tools. In doing so, you create a *color wash* on top of a faded or black-and-white photo. Think of it as the clear plastic overlays in the old anatomy books, in which each successive layer added some content (the respiratory system, the digestive system, and so on) until the body was complete. You can add layers of color on top of the faded image, achieving the look of rich color that's missing.

Do keep in mind, however, that when you add color layers to a very faded or black-and-white photo, the results often look fake, sort of like how colorized black-and-white movies look a little funky. To put it bluntly, people's teeth look blue instead of white, and natural things (grass, trees, flowers, and so on) never look quite natural. If you want to brighten a faded color, you can probably use an editing tool or two to bring back a bright blue dress or some lush green lawn — provided that there's enough color to work with in the original.

Fixing color casts

A *color cast* is a tinge — a shade of red or maybe yellow — that discolors your image in whole or in part. Casts occur for a variety of reasons, including the age of the photo, the quality of your scanner (if you scanned a printed original), the print from which you scanned the image, or the film used to take the picture.

If a cast appears in an image captured with a digital camera, you might need to adjust the white balance of your camera to compensate for the different colors offered by various types of illumination. (See your camera's instructions to learn how.)

Most digital-editing applications offer tools for getting rid of a cast, like the greenish tinge in Figure 1-2, usually with a name like Color Balance or Color Cast.

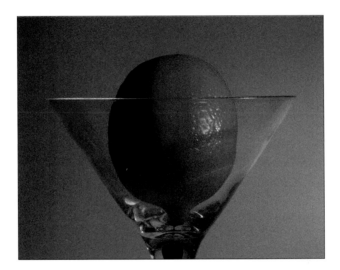

Figure 1-2: The greenish tinge makes this lemon resemble a jaundiced lime.

Here's a general description of the steps for eliminating a color cast:

1. **Open the image with the unwanted color cast.**

2. **Choose your image editor's Color Balance, Color Cast, or similar command.**

   The dialog box opens with an array of tools, similar to what you see in Figure 1-3, which is the version found in Photoshop CS4. Other editors have a similar tool.

3. **Choose whether you want to apply the change to the Shadows, Midtones, or Highlights.**

4. **Move the Cyan/Red, Magenta/Green, or Yellow/Blue slider away from the color of the unwanted hue.**

   For example, if your picture is too blue, move the Yellow/Blue slider toward Yellow.

5. **Click OK to apply the change when you're satisfied.**

Color Balance

Color Balance

Color Levels: 0   0   0

OK

Cancel

☑ Preview

Cyan ━━━━━━━▲━━━━━ Red

Magenta ━━━━━━━▲━━━━━ Green

Yellow ━━━━━━━▲━━━━━ Blue

Tone Balance

○ Shadows   ⦿ Midtones   ○ Highlights

☑ Preserve Luminosity

Figure 1-3: Use your image editor's Color Balance to help rebalance colors.

Applications such as Corel Paint Shop Pro, Photoshop, and others have a Preview option. Make sure that you leave the Preview option selected in the dialog box. Leaving it checked means that you don't have to apply the changes just to see them in your image. If you do apply them and then decide you don't like the change, choose Edit⇨Undo (or your image editor's equivalent) to go back.

If your application doesn't refer directly to a color cast, you can use any tool that adjusts tone, including dialog boxes and toolbar settings that allow you to adjust the levels of color in the image, one color at a time. This enables you to increase the level of blue, red, green, or yellow (or perhaps cyan or magenta), and you can tweak one or more of them until the photo looks more natural and normal.

In Photoshop CS4 and Photoshop Elements 7 (as well as earlier versions), the Variation tool gives you several different versions of an image to choose from, enabling you to add more red, green, or blue. You can adjust color intensity for any one of these colors in your image and view Before and After versions of the image.

✔ **In Photoshop,** choose Image⇨Adjustments⇨Variations.

✔ **If you're using the lower-priced and nearly as powerful Photoshop Elements,** choose Enhance⇨Adjust Color⇨Color Variations.

Figure 1-4 shows the Elements Color Variations dialog box with a portrait portrayed in a variety of tones.

Book IV Chapter 1

What You Can and Can't Do with Image-Editing Tools

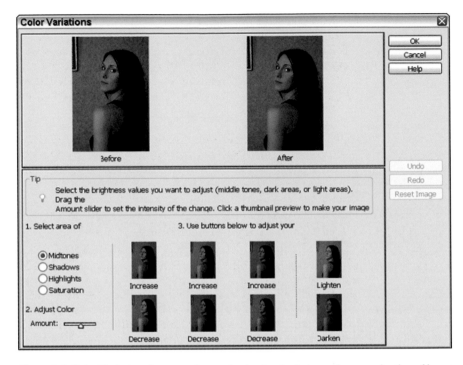

Figure 1-4: Color Variations lets you choose the best color balance from a selection of images.

What do you do if none of the color correction tools in your image-editing software does the trick? You can try a different application, or you can appreciate the photo for what it is. If it's an old photo, the color problems can add charm. If it's a new image and there's no excuse other than film or technique, just chalk it up to experience. You can also try rescanning a print on a different scanner or after recalibrating your scanner (follow the manufacturer's instructions). You can find out more about scanners in Book VI, Chapter 1.

Causes of color catastrophe

Where does bad color come from? Generally it comes from a digital camera that has been adjusted to the wrong *white balance* setting (say, set to indoor light when you're shooting outdoors); environmental color casts (such as sunsets or bright snowy conditions); or, in the case of film images, age of the film, bad film, bad development technique, poor print quality, or a bad or poorly adjusted scanner. These factors apply to most color problems in a poorly colored photo — unnatural tones; or images that are too bright, too dark, faded, and so on.

Of course, if you have nondigital photography experience, none of this is news, and you probably know what to do to make sure that the images you take, develop, and print are not color-challenged. However, if you're a fledgling photographer or simply enjoy taking photos of family, friends, and vacation spots (and have no idea what you're doing beyond focusing and shooting), you might not know how to prevent problems in the future. Some things to consider include

✔ **Use appropriate film and/or white balance settings.** When shooting with a traditional (not a digital) camera, use film intended for the types of shots you'll be taking. Some films are balanced for indoor use; some are better for outdoor use. Digital cameras, too, need to be balanced for the light source, so you'll want to make sure that your camera is set for Automatic White Balance (AWB) or adjusted manually for the type of lighting you'll be shooting under, such as Daylight, Shady, Incandescent, or Fluorescent.

✔ **Check printer settings.** If you're printing a digitally captured image, the color could go wrong entirely because of the printer's color settings, eliminating the need to edit the image. Use your image editor's calibration tools to correct for the vagaries of your particular printer. Try printing the image on someone else's printer to determine the common denominator.

✔ **Calibrate your monitor.** Use your software or monitor's instructions to calibrate your monitor to help ensure that what you see is what you can expect to get.

✔ **Fix problems by using scanner software.** If you're scanning from a print, you get whatever sins were committed when that photo was taken, developed, and printed. Take note of any problems and be ready to accommodate them by using your scanner software — if color correction tools are included in its toolbox — or by using your image-editing software. Better to have noticed the problem before you scan, print, and/or share the image online!

✔ **Store images properly.** Because aging causes many color problems when the dyes in the three color layers of prints fade at different rates, store your images in a cool, dark place and make sure that they contact only acid-free paper. Acids in some papers damage photos, and you can avoid it by using photo albums and storage boxes that were made in the last 10–20 years. Don't reuse the old photo albums that came over with your family on the Mayflower; the paper could contribute to the aging process.

If you have a precious image that you display in a frame, don't expose it to direct sunlight. Hang or stand any framed images in a place that gets only reduced ambient sunlight or low-level incandescent or fluorescent light from bulbs. Direct, bright sunlight fades images the worst. And because the colors in photos don't fade at the same rate, your previously natural-toned image can turn yellowish, reddish, greenish, or some combination thereof.

Adjusting Brightness and Contrast

Other components that you'll want to fix with your image-editing software include brightness and contrast. Detail can be lost when an image is overexposed, faded, or just too bright. Detail can also be lost when an image is too dark because of a failed flash or simply a very dark subject. A day that looks perfect for picture taking to you can result in washed-out faces, shiny foreheads, light-eating shadows, and an overall lack of definition.

You can eliminate many of these problems by adding and removing light in your image with the help of the brightness and contrast controls found in just about any worthy image-editing package. Figure 1-5 shows a photo that has been improved simply by adjusting the brightness and contrast. The brightest highlights are gone forever, but many of the middle and shadow tones have been salvaged.

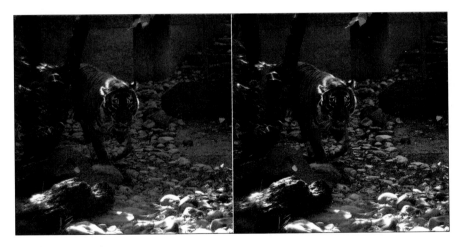

Figure 1-5: Sometimes photos need adjustments to brightness and contrast.

Most image editors have several choices for fixing these problems:

- **Quick Fix:** Many image editors have a *quick fix* command with a variety of tools for tweaking just about any aspect of an image. You can adjust brightness, color, focus, contrast, flash, and backlighting. You can also rotate the image. Like with the Variations feature (which I discuss in the earlier "Fixing color casts" section), you can also preview a Before and an After version of your image, as shown in Figure 1-6. Previewing versions enables you to see whether the adjustments are having the desired effect before committing them to the image.

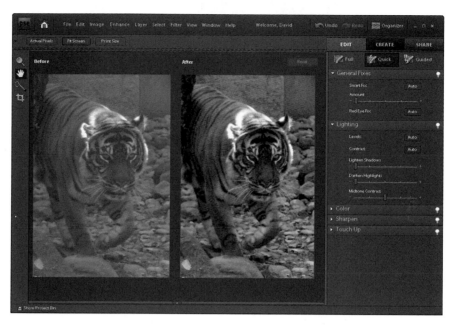

Figure 1-6: Photoshop Elements' Quick Fix feature helps tweak your images.

✔ **Auto Contrast:** This is an easy one. Many image editors, including Paint Shop Pro and the Adobe products, have an Auto Contrast or Automatic Contrast Enhancement command. Choose this command, and *voilà!* Your image is adjusted, using existing color and brightness levels to determine a happy medium.

✔ **Auto Levels:** This automatically adjusts the relationship of the tones.

✔ **Adjust Lighting:** You can also find special commands to adjust for *backlighting* (images that are illuminated primarily from behind) or *fill flash* (to provide additional front illumination).

✔ **Adjust Brightness and Contrast:** Use your image editor's manual Brightness/Contrast dialog box, like the one shown in Figure 1-7. You can enter values or move sliders or other controls to change these two integral levels in the image. Some image editors, such as Photoshop and Elements, show you the original image at all times

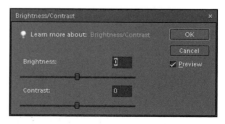

Figure 1-7: Change values to modify the brightness and contrast of your image.

so you can preview the effect. Other image editors might have a Preview option that you must use to see your changes before committing to them by clicking OK.

Murky shadows and washed-out highlights

Most of the tools described earlier in this chapter adjust the entire image, making the whole photo brighter, better, more natural-looking, and so on. If you want to tinker with specific areas of the image — an unwanted shadow in the corner, for example, or a single beacon-like forehead — you can use your image-editing software's selection tools before issuing the commands, or you can use various *brush-based tools* to apply more or less light in specific areas.

Huh? Brush-based? That means painting — painting more light here, more dark there; using a big brush here to add a lot of light to a big area; and using a small brush there to add just a little dark or light where it's needed. Most (if not all) image-editing packages offer corrective tools for adding and removing light and dark. Figure 1-8 shows a toolbox with typical color saturation tools: Dodge (lighten), Burn (darken), and Sponge (remove).

Some image editors use the regular brush to perform these tasks. For example, Paint Shop Pro has Dodge and Burn modes for its brush, turning the Brush temporarily into Dodge and Burn tools. Corel PhotoPaint tucks its Dodge and Burn tools into the Effect tool. All work in a similar manner.

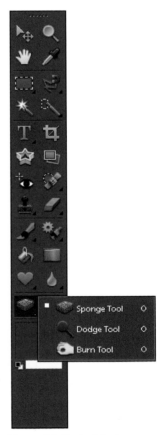

Go into the light with the Dodge tool

Use a *Dodge tool* to add light to an image by applying it with a brush that you customize in terms of the size, shape, and even texture. Most applications offer a similar tool, if not the ability to completely customize the brush. You can find more information about the Dodge tool in Book V, Chapter 2 (along with extra info on the Burn and Sponge tools, too). To use the Dodge tool, follow these steps:

1. **Click the Dodge tool in the toolbox.**

   Choose the appropriate options on the Options bar that appears above the workspace, as shown in Figure 1-9.

Figure 1-8: Typical Dodge, Burn, and Sponge tools.

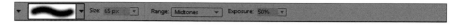

Figure 1-9: Set the options for the Dodge tool here.

2. **Set the size of your brush so that you don't apply a large light area to the image if you don't want one.**

3. **Adjust the *intensity* or *exposure* of the brush (how much light each click or stroke of the brush applies).**

4. **If you really want to control the effect, use the Range option to choose what is lightened — Shadows, Midtones, or Highlights.**

   - *Shadows:* Use this if your image has very dark corners where details are lost.

   - *Highlights:* Use this if you have a bright spot that needs to be brighter.

   - *Midtones:* Use this default if you want to brighten an area that's not in sun or shadow.

5. **Begin lightening by either clicking a single spot or by dragging the mouse over an area.**

   The more passes you make over one spot, the lighter it becomes.

Need to brighten a single object, such as a face or a flower? Size your brush to the face or flower in question (so that the brush is the same diameter as the object) and then click the object with the Dodge tool. You can click multiple times, if needed, to achieve the desired level of lightness.

Keep away from the light with the Burn tool

Opposite of the Dodge tool, which adds lightness, the *Burn tool* adds darkness.

You can revive lost facial features or other details where the sun, too much flash, or age-induced fading have washed them out, and you can add depth by simply darkening areas in the image for aesthetic reasons.

Using the Burn tool is much like using the Dodge tool except that wherever you click or drag, darkness is added, and lightness is taken away.

Living up to its name, the Burn tool can give you a singed, brown tone if you overuse it. If you click or drag repeatedly in an area with the Burn tool, instead of a simple darkening effect, the spot will look as though a flame came dangerously close to it and the area began to char. Easy does it! Figure 1-10 shows an image that has been both dodged and burned.

Book IV Chapter 1

What You Can and Can't Do with Image-Editing Tools

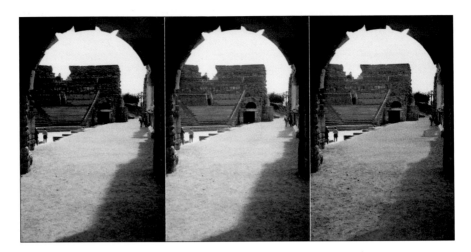

Figure 1-10: The original photo is dodged to lighten some shadow tones and then burned to darken some light tones.

Maintaining consistency

Consistency is a lot like conformity: Too much is not good, and too little can cause problems. The world would be pretty dull if everyone were the same, but some degree of conformity and consistency usually makes things run more smoothly. The same can be said for photos. No interesting photo has the same levels of light and dark throughout it; only a picture of a white wall or a black, starless sky has no need for defined depth, implied dimension, or just plain old variety.

When you're adjusting the lights and darks in your image, keep this delicate balance in mind. You don't want to make the lights and darks uniform over the whole image, yet you don't want to have very dark darks in one spot and very light lights in another. Artistic images that are meant to convey a message, and in which you want people to see that you've tinkered with reality, are another story — there are no limits or boundaries there. But for photos of people, places, and things that are meant to be realistic and clear, you want to keep the signs of your tinkering to a minimum, and you want to achieve the right levels of consistency.

How is that done? By using the right tools the right way. If you're dodging or burning an image, use brush sizes that allow gentle effects. Very small brushes over a large area will show the strokes or clicks. Using the tools too much causes some areas to be much lighter or darker than others, probably giving you unnatural results that look like you went overboard.

Of course, using the tools that apply to the entire image also gives you consistency. Any Auto command makes universal adjustments based on what's in the image to start with, and your results will be pretty tame and consistent. Using tools that allow you to drag sliders or enter new levels and have the settings affect a selected area only or the entire image if nothing is selected also creates consistency because your mouse skills and brush-based tool settings are not part of the equation. This gives you less control over the degree of lightening or darkening but can provide gentler, subtler results.

Reviving lost detail

Perhaps your photo has too much contrast, and the details of the items caught in the brightest spots are unrecognizable. Or maybe your photo has faded with time, and fine details are lost. Are the details lost forever? Probably not, assuming that you have time, patience, and the right tools to bring them back to life.

Choosing the revival method

The method used to bring back lost details varies by the situation and the situation's cause. For example, if the details were lost to too much brightness, using the Burn tool darkens the light areas and brings out the missing features, textures, or whatever has been blighted by the light. If the details are hidden in shadow, using the Dodge tool can reveal these details once again. Adjusting contrast and brightness levels can revive details lost to too much or too little of those levels, and you can even use color to bring things out. How do you choose? If parts of your image are too dark, use the Dodge tool. If they are too light, use the Burn tool.

Re-creating lost detail

If you're skilled and patient and have good eyesight, you might be able to zoom in extremely close to the details of your image that need fixing and use painting and drawing tools to re-create details that are irretrievably lost.

- You can often re-create textures (such as a brick wall or a stubbly patch of cement) and industrial or man-made items (such as the edge of a car bumper or the handle on an umbrella). The results can be surprisingly good, even for someone who might be a bit shaky with the mouse. You can use your image editor's Paint Brush and Pencil or similar tools to draw missing items.

- Avoid painting and drawing in faces and natural things (such as flowers and plants). Pulling it off is nearly impossible. Things usually look drawn and end up drawing attention to the problem.

**Book IV
Chapter 1**

What You Can and Can't Do with Image-Editing Tools

Does what's missing appear elsewhere? If so, steal a copy and replace the missing detail. I've successfully replaced lost content with faces, furniture, grass, trees, walls, cars, and sleeping dogs. You can, too, by using the tools that I discuss in the section, "Removing Unwanted Image Content," later in this chapter.

Not to be negative (pardon the photographic pun), but sometimes lost detail is simply lost. If an overzealous flash completely washed out someone's face, short of drawing in his or her features by hand, you might not be able to bring back eyelids, a nose, cheekbones, and the contour of lips. Not every photo can end up framed and admired or viewed by adoring millions online. If you've used every brightness, lighting, and contrast tool that your software offers, you can try a different or more powerful package, or do your best and hope nobody notices that Aunt Mary doesn't have a nose.

Using Blurring and Sharpening Tools

Another way to revive lost details is to apply a filter that sharpens the image by heightening the difference between adjacent pixels. This increased intensity of color and brightness makes everything stand out, as shown in Figure 1-11, where the top portion of the image has been sharpened, and the rest was left as it was. You can use the Sharpen filters that come with all image-editing applications or use the Sharpen tool found in the toolbox of just about any image-editing program. Using the filter requires selecting the area to be sharpened and then applying the filter, whereas the tool requires the standard brush-related adjustments (such as the size of the brush and the degree of sharpening it applies).

Sharpening here and there

If you want to sharpen the entire image, use a filter to do the sharpening. If your software doesn't have filters, check for a Sharpen command or reasonable facsimile thereof — any command that performs an automatic, all-over sharpening will do. The other benefit of this process is that it's a simple one in most image editors. Corel PhotoPaint, Paint Shop Pro, and Adobe's image editors, for example, all have a simple Sharpen command that you can apply directly, along with more sophisticated versions if you need more control.

If you want to sharpen an area, you can also use the filter or automatic sharpening command, but you have to make a selection first, directing the software to the spot you want to sharpen. You can repeat the process to sharpen two or more noncontiguous areas. Or if your software supports selections that are not touching, select all the areas that are to be sharpened and then apply the filter or related command.

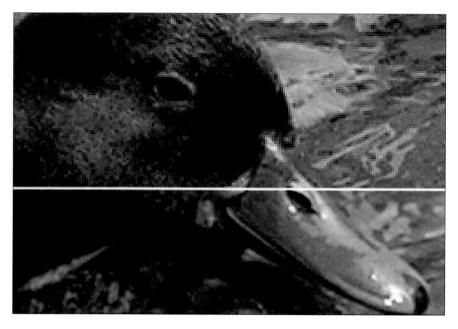

Figure 1-11: Sharpening enhances the contrast between adjacent pixels.

When I need to sharpen a little here, a little there, a bit more here, and a whole lot there, I use the Sharpen tool that some image editors provide for "painting" sharpness. It works like a painting tool in that you click and/or drag your mouse over the image to apply the sharpening effect, and you can repeat your mouse movements in the same spot if you want more of a sharpening effect in one place than in another. You can dictate the size of the sharpened area by adjusting your brush size, and you can control the intensity of the sharpening by adjusting the strength setting.

To use a Sharpen tool, follow these steps:

1. **Turn on the Sharpen tool by selecting it from your image editor's toolbox or menu.**

2. **Set your brush size so that you can control how big an area is sharpened with each click or drag of the mouse.**

3. **Set the strength for your sharpening effect.**

   A good default value is 50%, but you can raise or lower that level as needed by dragging the slider or other control.

4. **Begin sharpening by clicking or dragging over the area to be sharpened.**

Clicking sharpens an area the size of your brush tip; and dragging allows you to sharpen in a freeform area, following an edge or working within a desired region of the image.

Be careful not to sharpen too much. Too much sharpening results in bizarre-looking bright pixels that end up hiding details because the individual pixels stand out too much. Figure 1-12 shows an image in which the sharpening went a little overboard. Sharpening can also increase your file size.

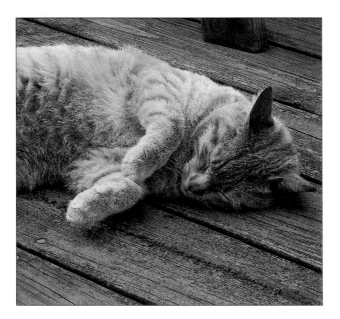

Figure 1-12: Too much sharpening is not a good thing!

To keep the sharpening results as subtle as possible, avoid using a very small brush size (10 pixels or fewer in width) if you're sharpening an area that's more than 20 pixels wide and/or tall. Why? Because you'll be able to see your brush strokes as you apply the sharpening. An exception would be the sharpening of a very small spot, which would obviously call for a very small brush, and you can select the area first, which helps control your effects by restricting them to the selected area.

Blurring for effect

Sometimes the best way to draw attention to something is to draw attention away from something else. The bride doesn't *have* to wear the biggest, most ostentatious dress to stand out against her bridesmaids; she can instead dress them in colors that blend in with the flowers — and by contrast, she stands out. The same is true for photos, especially those with a lot of content that you need to keep but want to keep people from noticing too much.

Figure 1-13 shows a photo of a dandelion against a leafy background. The outdoorsy setting is important to give the image context, but the dandelion is the real focus. To make it stand out, the background has been blurred, diminishing its details. Other than being able to tell that the background consists of foliage, there isn't much about it that you would notice or be drawn to visually.

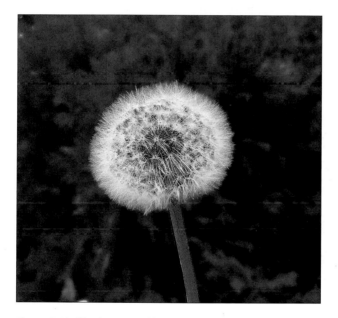

Figure 1-13: Blurring everything else makes your main subject stand out.

Blurring is the exact opposite of sharpening in that instead of heightening the contrast between adjoining pixels, the color and brightness differences are reduced so that pixels are much closer to each other in terms of their color levels, brightness, and contrast. You can go too far with blurring and end up with something that isn't even recognizable; conversely, you can blur not enough, leaving the content as distracting as ever. The key is to find a happy medium where objects are still recognizable, but nobody will spend much time looking at them.

Like sharpening, you have choices as to how to apply blurring. You can use your image editor's Blur tool (which works just like the Sharpen tool, except for its results), or you can use the Blur filters. Many image editors offer specialized Blur filters that do cool things, such as making an image look like it's whipping past the camera (the Motion Blur) or like it's spinning in place (Radial Blur). The plain old Blur filter simply blurs the entire image or a selection therein — it's as simple as that. In Figure 1-14, Motion Blur has been applied to the entire image.

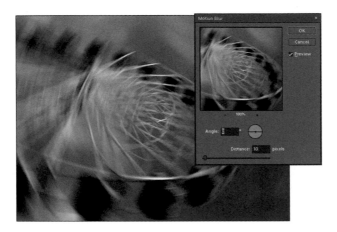

Figure 1-14: Motion Blur adds the appearance of movement to an image.

To apply a blur to everything but the focus of the image, follow these steps:

1. **Select the object or area that should not be blurred.**

   This can be done on an image that's all on one layer. Or, if your software supports layers, you can select the object or area and then cut it to its own layer to keep it separate from the rest of the image during the blurring process.

2. **If you're working all on one layer, invert the selection so that everything but the selection can be blurred.**

   Most image editors, including Corel PhotoPaint, Paint Shop Pro, and the Adobe Photoshop products, let you invert a selection by pressing Ctrl+Shift+I (⌘+Shift+I for Mac).

   With the not-to-be-blurred section protected, you can begin blurring the rest of the picture.

3. **Click your image editor's Blur tool to activate it and then set how the tool should work by choosing the brush size and strength, just as I describe for the Sharpen tool.**

4. **Begin dragging the mouse in the area to be blurred. You can go over some areas more than once, increasing the blurring effect in those spots.**

   Unlike many other types of retouching, blurring is very subtle and is hard to overdo.

5. **When you finish blurring the area, turn off the selection and view your results.**

If you chose to use the Blur filter, after making the selection and inverting it so that everything but the selected area can be blurred, you can choose your image editor's Blur filter. The blurring effect is uniform throughout the selection, and you can intensify it only by repeating the command.

Unlike the regular Blur command, the special blur filters found in most image editors have dialog boxes that allow you to set how much blurring will occur and exactly what special effect will be achieved.

When blurring your photos, keep the following points in mind:

✔ Try combining Blur effects. For example, blur by hand and then apply one of the special Blur filters, or combine more than one special blur filter for a completely unique effect. If your software doesn't offer special blurs, you might consider one that does, such as Photoshop Elements, which I used for all the figures in this chapter.

✔ If your editing software supports layers, you can do a very cool thing with the Motion blur (or a manually created motion effect, created by horizontal or vertical strokes with the Blur tool). Duplicate the object that should be in motion and put it on its own layer. Then blur that duplicate, and place it behind the static version on the original layer. *Voilà!* Your object is sitting still after rocketing into position via the Motion blur.

✔ If you're a Photoshop or Photoshop Elements user, don't confuse the Smudge and Blur tools. The *Smudge tool* literally smears adjoining pixels, as though you've run a greasy paw across a chalk drawing. You can use the Smudge tool to blend two contiguous areas of color or texture, but the effect is much more dramatic than blurring.

Removing Artifacts (Tiny Blemishes)

**Book IV
Chapter 1**

Damage comes in all shapes and sizes — little specks of dust; scratches thin and wide, short and long; water marks or discoloration from tape; missing corners. In this section, I explain how to remove artifacts from your photos. No, I'm not talking about ancient clay pots unearthed by archaeologists. *Artifacts* are the little stray marks, blips, and other tiny blemishes that appear on images when they're captured and manipulated electronically — the kinds of blemishes you can see in Figure 1-15.

**What You Can
and Can't Do with
Image-Editing Tools**

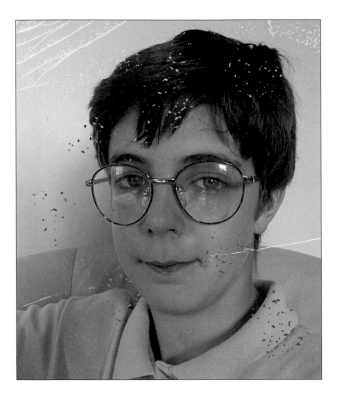

Figure 1-15: Dust and scratches inevitably show up on scanned photos.

The term *artifact* is also sometimes applied to the dust and scratches that accumulate on printed photos and that end up in the digital version of the photo after it's scanned. Unlike an ancient clay pot that you'd probably want to keep, artifacts in your images are usually not desirable, and you'll want to get rid of them. Although few photos are as damaged as the example shown in Figure 1-15, most scanned images will have at least a few dings.

Finding an artifact's source

When dealing with artifacts, it's useful to note how they got there.

- ✔ If the artifacts appeared after you resized an image or a portion thereof (stretching it with your mouse to increase its width, height, or both), the solution might be to undo the resizing and then save the file in a format that's more supportive of the resizing process.

- ✔ If the artifacts were there from the time the image was scanned, you can try brushing off the original to make sure none of the spots are from dust that can be removed (as opposed to the nastiest kind of dust, which becomes embedded in the photograph itself) and then rescanning it. In lieu of that, remove the marks with your software's various painting and cleaning tools.

So what file formats support the resizing process? JPG is a good choice as a final destination because it supports more colors than GIF (assuming that your image is bound for the Web or that you're trying to keep the file size small to facilitate sharing online). TIFF is another good choice if your image file size doesn't matter and you plan to print the image rather than display it on the Web.

Sweeping away dust

Dusting off your originals before scanning them is an obvious preventive measure, but it rarely removes the ground-in dust or the scratches and scuffs that appear over time, even on relatively new photos. If you store your pictures in a box or desk drawer and they rub up against each other, damage is bound to occur. For very old photos, the porous papers used back then absorb moisture and dirt, so stains and dust attack them much more easily than newer, coated photographic papers. Obviously, storing your images in a safe, protective environment (remember to use only acid-free paper!) is best, but if you haven't done that, all might not be lost.

You have several choices for removing dust and scratches. In most cases, personal preference, skill, and the degree of damage will dictate which tool you choose. For example, you can use any of the following tools found in editors such as Photoshop, Photoshop Elements, and others to get rid of small spots, scratches, and other tiny blemishes:

- **The Brush tool:** The Brush tool can be used to paint out the spots.

- **The Pencil tool:** For tiny, tiny spots, you may like the precision of the Pencil tool, which works much the same as the Brush tool except that the dots or lines drawn are sharp-edged.

- **The Smudge tool:** The Smudge tool found in some image editors is a favorite of mine if I just need to smear a little of the surrounding color onto the spot, much as I'd do if I had a painting with an unwanted dot of color on a field of another color.

- **The Clone tool.** This is used to paint over spots with tones that match a similarly textured portion of the image used as the source.

When you paint, pencil, or smudge out a dot or small scratch, you can't duplicate any pattern that's in place. For example, if the spot is on a piece of fabric, such as a coat or dress, the fabric's texture will be lost on that tiny spot even if the color is restored and the spot is no longer visible. For the kind of tiny spots and marks I'm talking about here, this is rarely a problem. For larger areas, however, the lack of texture stands out as clearly as the original mark did, so use the Clone tool (in both Photoshop and Photoshop

Elements, as well as other editing programs) to copy sections of the pristine textured area onto the damaged area. I discuss using this type of tool in the section, "Removing Unwanted Image Content," later in this chapter.

Painting over the dirt

Because your image contains only little marks on a plain background that you can easily remove with the Brush or Pencil, you decide that painting or drawing out the spot is the answer. You're ready to make the artifacts go away. With the photo in question opened and on-screen in your favorite editing program, follow these steps:

1. **Click the tool that you want to use.**

   - *Brush:* Use this tool if you're painting out a small dot or a tiny scratch.

   - *Pencil:* Choose this tool if you need a thin, precise line to get rid of the artifact in question.

2. **Set the size of the brush or pencil, choosing one that's roughly the same size as the dot or scratch that you want to eliminate.**

   If you're dealing with a scratch, draw or paint a line that's only a tiny bit wider than the scratch itself.

3. **Use the color-sampling tool — the Eyedropper — to sip up the color from the surrounding unmarred pixels.**

   With Photoshop or Photoshop Elements, hold down the Alt/Option key to convert the Pencil or Brush tools temporarily into an Eyedropper.

   This sets the painting/drawing color so that it matches when you brush or pencil the marks out. Figure 1-16 shows sampling in progress.

4. **With the proper color selected, go back to the desired tool (the Brush or Pencil) and paint or draw out the unwanted artifacts.**

   You can click to get rid of a small dot or drag to get rid of a scratch.

Smudging or blurring out the paint lines

If you painted out a mark but feel that your retouching is too visible, you can use Undo (usually Ctrl+Z, or ⌘+Z on a Mac) and start over, or you can use the Blur or Smudge tools (set to an extremely tiny brush size) to make the edges of the painted dot or line just a bit fuzzy. This action removes any visible edge to the color that you apply to the image. Figure 1-17 shows a painted-out scratch being repaired by blurring the edges of the scratch with the Blur tool.

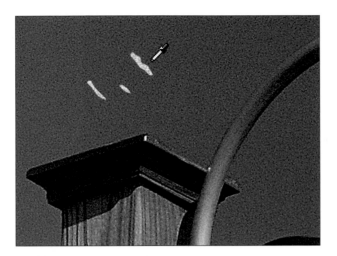

Figure 1-16: The Eyedropper samples a selected color so you can paint with that color.

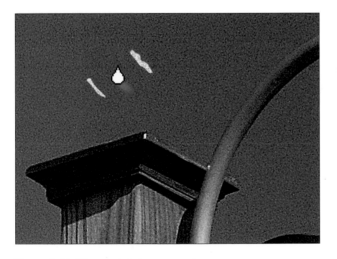

Figure 1-17: Blur a painted-out scratch.

To address any concerns about dust and scratches that can't be repaired, let me say this: Every image-editing application that I know of offers the ability to select a color from within the image and then use that color for painting or drawing so that you can brush- or pencil-out tiny blemishes. The tools involved are simple to use, and this sort of repair is easily within the grasp of beginning users.

Spackling over More Serious Damage

More extreme than scratches and scuffs, missing content is the kind of serious damage that might make you think a photo is unsalvageable.

Not all image-editing packages are capable of fixing dramatic problems, but many are:

- ✔ If your software has cloning, patching, or similar tools, you could be in luck.
- ✔ If all you have are paint brushes and the ability to copy and paste selections, you might not be so lucky.

Figure 1-18 shows a seriously damaged photo with a corner missing. Painting, drawing, and pasting are clearly not going to work in a situation like this! But given the right tools, you can restore the missing corner by filling it with the remaining image content and thus creating a nearly seamless repair.

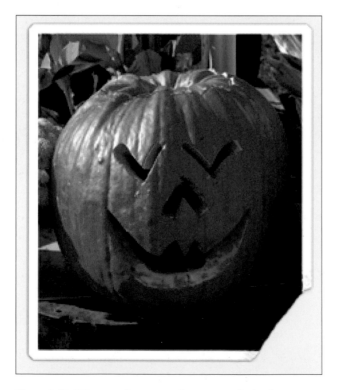

Figure 1-18: When you have an entire corner missing from your photo, serious repairs are needed.

Fixing more serious damage requires *digital spackle,* which works a lot like the gloppy white spackle that you apply to your walls to fill in holes from where pictures were hung or where someone gouged the plaster while moving furniture. Photos can also suffer from the same sort of dents and dings, and you need to fill in the holes and gashes with something, right? You can use content from within the image (or from another image), or you can create new content from scratch.

Preparing your digital spackle

Unfortunately, image editors don't come with a spackle tool, but you can create your own spackle by using the various tools at your disposal. The most common tool for this application is the Clone tool or Clone brush, depending on your image editor. The spackle that you create depends on what kind of damage you're repairing:

✔ Fill in small areas with solid colors, applied with a Brush tool.

✔ Clone existing content from nearby and place it over the damage.

Your choices are virtually unlimited, and the success that you see is based only on your mousing skills (for those tight corners and tiny repairs), patience, and how much time you can devote to the task.

Replacing content that's ripped or torn away

Although you might not be able to put the corner back exactly as it was, you can make it look as if there were never a missing corner. If that sounds like a contradiction, consider that what was in the corner might be unknown. What if the corner were missing before you even got the photo? If you don't know what used to be in that corner, you can't put it back. What you can do, however, is create a new corner from existing content and make it look like it was always there. To get started, follow these steps:

1. **Think about what you could use to replace what's missing.**

   If you know what's missing, this isn't difficult, but if the missing or damaged portion doesn't tell you about its original state, you might have to decide what remaining content can be used to rebuild the corner.

2. **Click the Clone tool.**

3. **Choose a brush size and set the Opacity to 100%.**

4. **Zoom in to the area you want to work with.**

5. **Choose the source area for cloning, as shown in Figure 1-19.**

   Some image editors require right-clicking to select a source area. Others ask you to hold down the Alt key (if you're a Windows user) or the

Option key (if you're on a Mac) as you click the area that you want to clone.

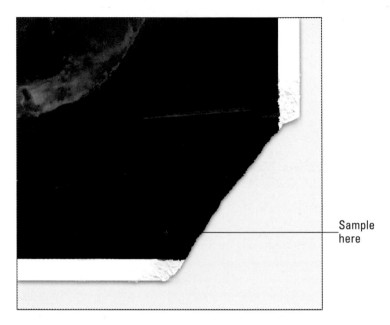

Figure 1-19: Sample the area you want to clone.

6. **Click and/or drag over the damage, watching as the sampled content covers it.**

Figure 1-20 shows cloned content filling in the missing corner.

If you want to be able to apply the same exact cloned spot to the entire damaged area, be sure to select the Aligned option on the Options bar (or the Cumulative option with some image editors) before you start painting the cloned content onto the damage. With Aligned marked, the tool clones from a position relative to where you first started cloning. When unmarked, the Clone tool always starts cloning from the same point.

Your filling needn't come from the same image! You can use the Clone tool to sample content from another image and then apply it to the damaged photo. Just open up the new image, sample the content (press the Alt or Option key as you click the content to be cloned), and then switch back to the damaged photo. With the Clone tool still selected, click and/or drag to place the cloned content in the image.

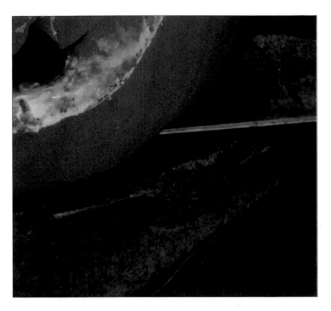

Figure 1-20: Paint over the damaged area with the cloned texture.

Removing Unwanted Image Content

Signs of wear and other types of physical damage aren't the only things you might want to get rid of when editing your images. A person, car, garbage can, building, plant, tree, or just about anything can become objectionable if you didn't want it to be in the picture in the first place. Rather than tearing all your wedding photos in half, consider replacing the unwanted spouse with more of the background or a large potted plant. Someone forget to move the car before taking a picture of your house for the real estate brochures? Get rid of the car, replacing it with curb and grass as though the car had been in the garage all along.

It might seem like some sort of complicated sleight of hand, but replacing one piece of content with another is really rather simple. If you've already tried repairing scratches, stains, and tears, you're more than ready to tackle the process of removing unwanted people, places, and things. You need software that has Clone and/or Patch tools (or reasonable facsimiles), and you need to understand how the Clipboard works (so you can copy and paste content in big chunks). Sound like too big a job? Never fear — it becomes clear in the next few paragraphs!

For example, no matter how much we love them, we sometimes wish family members would make themselves scarce, if only for a little while. But what if your ex–family member — someone you thought you'd never have to see again — is still haunting your family photos? Starting with a group photo, follow these steps:

1. **Identify the unwanted person and use a selection tool — preferably a freeform or magnetic selection tool — to select him or her.**

   Book IV, Chapter 2 has descriptions of the generic selection tools found in most image editors.

   You don't have to worry about getting a little of the surrounding image as long as it doesn't remove someone else's arm or the side of a face.

2. **Press Delete to get rid of the selected person.**

   The background layer or any other underlying layer's content now shows through the hole.

3. **Fill the hole with other content — more of the photo's background content if you were all standing in front of one of those lovely painted backdrops, or use the sky or extend a nearby wall or stand of trees.**

   Whatever's behind the rest of the group can be extended to fill in where the now-missing person once stood. Your choices for filling in are

   • Copy content from elsewhere and paste it onto the hole.

   • Use the Clone tool to fill in the hole with sampled content from else-where in the image.

   Which method you choose depends on three things:

   • How big a hole the deleted person left behind

   If the hole is huge or there's no background to use, you might need to copy content and paste it into the hole, perhaps even going to another image to get the filler.

   Smaller holes can usually be covered using cloning techniques.

   • Whether you have a lot of alternate content to use as fill

   If the hole is huge or there's no background to use as alternate con-tent, you might need to copy content and paste it into the hole, per-haps even going to another image to get the filler.

   • Whether there are lighting issues

   Perhaps everything but the deleted person is in shadow, and you can't seamlessly apply that dark content in his or her place. If light-ing is the problem — and you have Photoshop — you'll want to use the *Patch tool* (a kind of super-Clone tool that adjusts for texture and lighting) so that the lighting of the destination is preserved when you patch the hole.

Figure 1-21 shows a Before and an After of the same image. In the After version, the unwanted element (in this case, a goose in the background) has been replaced by more of the surrounding pond.

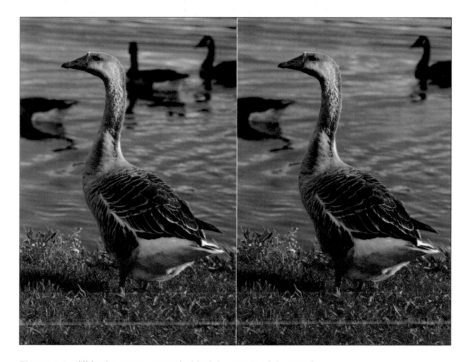

Figure 1-21: Hide the extra goose behind the water of the pond.

What if the unwanted person isn't against a background or is sitting in front of someone else and deleting him or her will leave you with half of a person? Consider bringing someone in from another picture and putting him or her in place of the person you're deleting. You can always resize a new person from a smaller or larger image, and you can use your image editor's Burn or Dodge tools to adjust lighting if the substitute person comes from a darker or lighter image. Use the Blur or Smudge tools to make the stand-in blend in so that none of the edges are obvious.

Combining Pictures

Throughout this chapter, most of what I discuss is repairing and improving individual photos by fixing spots, scratches, and tears, replacing missing content, and moving stuff around to make things better. This isn't the end of even a low-end image-editing application's capabilities, however. You can do a lot with multiple images, combining them into a single image and using special effects for a really creative result.

When combining images, there really aren't any rules. You can combine black-and-white photos with color images, professional portraits or photographic artwork with amateur or family photos, pictures of people with pictures of places — anything that makes sense to you. You can create a collage, assembling parts of various photos into a *composite image* like the one shown in Figure 1-22, or you can mix content from two or more photos and retouch the combined result to make it look like the combined content had been together from the start.

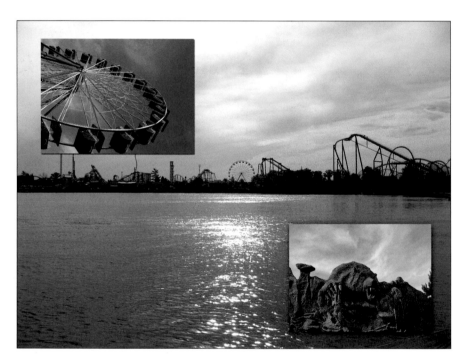

Figure 1-22: You can combine several photos into one.

Is there anything along these lines that image-editing software *can't* do? With the midrange to top-level packages, the limitations are, well, limited. You might run into limitations in special effects and retouching capabilities, which can hamper the success of the creative side of your combinations, but those are software-specific limitations, such as not being able to adjust the *opacity* (see-through quality) of content within a photo, or not being able to place different parts of a composite image on separate layers.

Pasting content from other images

Whether you're using a Windows-based PC or a Mac, you can cut, copy, and paste content from one file to another or share and duplicate content within the same file. These capabilities make it easy to take content from one photo and add it to another, either by removing content from its original location or by making a copy that appears in both photos.

To copy content from one photo and paste it into another, follow these steps, which work in virtually any image-editing package:

1. **Open both the *source image* (the one where the content you want resides) and the *target image* (the one that will receive the copied content).**

2. **In the source image, use a selection tool to select the content that you want to copy.**

   You can use either a freeform or geometric-shaped selection tool. Your choice depends on the shape of the object that you want to copy.

3. **Choose Edit➪Copy.**

   This places a duplicate of the selection in your computer's memory, where it will wait for you to paste it.

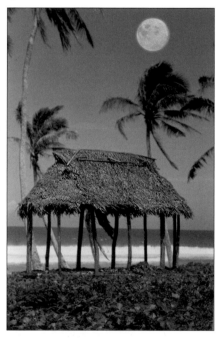

Figure 1-23: This moon has been copied from one photo and pasted here.

4. **Go to the target image and choose Edit➪Paste.**

   In Figure 1-23, a moon that was cut from an image is now pasted into a different photo.

5. **When the pasted content appears in the target image, activate the Move tool and then drag the content into the desired position within the photo.**

   If you're using software that allows you to put different parts of an image on separate layers, the pasted content is probably on its own layer — a layer created automatically through the pasting process. You can leave the content on this separate layer or use your software's layer-handling commands to merge the paste layer with the rest of the photo (sometimes called *flattening*). Of course, you'd do this only after your pasted content was placed in the desired spot and you're sure you don't want to move it again.

You can activate the Copy and Paste commands via your keyboard as well as through the Edit menu. To copy, press Ctrl+C, and to paste, press Ctrl+V. If you're on a Mac, the shortcuts are ⌘+C and ⌘+V, respectively.

Using layers to create overlapping images

Assuming that your software supports layers, your pasted content will be on separate layers — one new layer per paste. This is good in that it makes it easy to move things around, repositioning pasted stuff so that it's in just the right spot. Separate layers also enable you to hide pasted content if you're not sure you really want to use it. Rather than deleting the pasted content (which you might regret if you change your mind), you can simply hide the layer that it's on, and then you won't see it until and unless you choose to display that layer again.

Keeping things on separate layers has another benefit. By having different elements of your image on individual layers, you can overlap the layers and rearrange the layers to restack the overlapping content. As shown in Figure 1-24, the same image was copied, overlapped, and stacked in several layers. Images can be restacked in as many configurations as you can imagine but only because each individual part has its own layer.

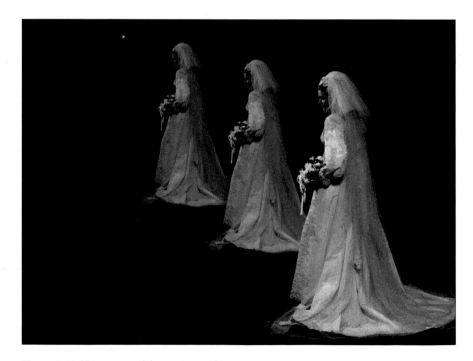

Figure 1-24: You can stack layers to overlap content.

Hiding layers

After something is pasted into your image, the pasted content is on its own layer. If you no longer want to see that layer's content, just hide the layer by clicking the icon next to the layer number. The icon varies from image editor to image editor. In Paint Shop Pro, the icon is a pair of spectacles; in Photoshop Elements, it's an eyeball.

In any case, after the layer is hidden, its content doesn't display on-screen, nor will it print. If you want to bring it back, simply click the box where the icon was, and the icon reappears, as does the layer's content.

Rearranging layers to change object stacking order

To change the stacking order of two or more overlapping elements in a photo, simply drag the layers up or down in the Layers palette. The top-most layers represent the content that's on the top of any overlapping stack, and the lower layers are underneath. Dragging a layer up moves it up in the stack, and dragging a layer down puts it beneath the other layers.

Deleting layers

If you just don't want a layer anymore and hiding it isn't the answer, delete the layer. To do this, just drag the unwanted layer to the trash can icon, located at the bottom of the palette in some image editors (Photoshop) or at the top in others (Photoshop Elements and Paint Shop Pro, for example).

Adjusting opacity for interesting effects

When layers overlap, you can achieve very cool results by making one or more of the layers less opaque (more see-through) so that underlying layers can be seen. Reducing the opacity of the elements on top of a background makes it possible to see that background image and recognize its content. Or, you can use transparency to de-emphasize some parts of an image and emphasize others. The elements on top of the background remain visible, but their slightly see-through nature integrates them more fully with the image as a whole.

Figure 1-25 shows a picture used in an eBay auction: Only the widget in the center is for sale. The semi-transparent objects at the left and right are shown to illustrate how the widget works.

Book IV
Chapter 1

What You Can
and Can't Do with
Image-Editing Tools

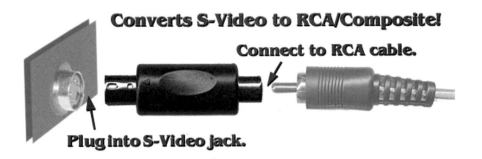

Converts S-Video to RCA/Composite!

Connect to RCA cable.

Plug into S-Video jack.

Figure 1-25: You can make some layers semi-transparent.

For applications that support layers, the opacity controls are in the Layers palette, and you adjust the opacity of an entire layer, not just portions thereof, although some editing applications allow you to select content on a single layer and reduce or increase its opacity independently. Using the Photoshop Elements program as an example, follow these steps to adjust a layer's opacity, making the objects on underlying layers more visible:

1. **Open the image containing the layer that you want to adjust.**

2. **Access your image editor's Layers palette or dialog box.**

3. **Within the Layers palette, click the layer you want to make more or less opaque.**

4. **Choose your image editor's layer opacity control and use the slider to adjust the opacity level.**

   Opacity is set at 100% (not see-through at all) by default.

   As you adjust the opacity, the results appear immediately within your image. You can undo your result if you don't like it, or simply go back to the Layers palette and readjust.

An opacity of 0% renders the active layer completely invisible, and you can use this to your advantage, making a layer disappear and then slowly increasing its opacity until you achieve the very level of visibility you want. You can also back down from 100%, but starting at 0% can make it much easier to find the right setting for a layer that you want to be very, very faint.

Chapter 2: Common Editing Options

In This Chapter

✔ Touring typical image-editing tools

✔ Creating original content with painting tools

✔ Focusing your efforts with selection tools

✔ Smoothing the rough spots with blending tools

✔ Fixing photographic errors with correction tools

The main editing tools found in virtually all image-editing applications fall into four categories: painting, selecting, blending, and correction. There are no hard and fast rules, however, as to when to use these tools, and you'll find yourself using painting tools to make corrections, blending tools to create original painted effects, and any other variety of mixing and matching of tools and tasks that your editing jobs require.

This chapter provides an overview of the editing tools common to most image-editing programs. I use Adobe Photoshop Elements 7.0 and Corel Paint Shop Pro Photo X2 as the primary examples, but most of these tools are available in other image editors, such as Adobe Photoshop, Corel PhotoPaint (part of the CorelDRAW Graphics Suite), Corel Painter, and others. Whatever application you're using now or will use, the basic concepts are the same for these four tool categories and the tasks you perform with them. Don't worry about not being able to apply instructions or examples from one application to another!

This chapter is intended to be an introduction to the tools that you'll find in virtually all image editors. I show you how to use some of these functions in more detail using Photoshop and Photoshop Elements in Book V.

Checking Out Your Editing Toolkit

As shown in Figures 2-1 and 2-2, your tools in both Photoshop Elements and Paint Shop Pro are very similar. You might even notice that some of the tools' buttons are nearly identical. These similarities exist for a very simple and logical reason: The things people need to do to photographs — reversing the signs of aging, wear and tear, mending photographic errors, or applying aesthetic preferences — are universal. Nobody has thought of something that the other guy hasn't added to his software. Other than some of the very low-end packages with extremely limited toolsets, a full set of tools for performing these tasks is found in pretty much the same arrangement, and the tools are used in pretty much the same way. So, the information you pick up in this chapter can be applied across the board.

In both Elements and Paint Shop Pro, you can choose where toolbars are displayed. They can be docked along an edge of the main window or pulled loose as free-floating strips of tools, as in Figure 2-1. Paint Shop Pro lets you resize the floating toolbar into a rectangle with several columns, as you can see in Figure 2-2. Elements allows you to arrange the toolbox in two columns, or stretch it out into one long toolbox.

If you don't see your application's tool kit, you can usually redisplay it by choosing it from the Window or View menu. The preferences settings that control features of the image editor are normally found in the Edit menu, as illustrated in Figure 2-3, which shows the Photoshop Elements Edit menu and Preferences submenu. As you can see from this list, you can control just about every aspect of the image editor's functions as well as some general settings for the application as a whole.

As you take the time to visually check out your tools, you can identify them quickly by placing your cursor over a tool to display a *ToolTip*, which shows the names and sometimes the purpose of the individual tools. As you mouse over a tool, its name appears in a small box.

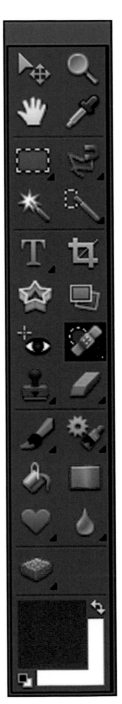

Figure 2-1: The tools in Photoshop Elements 7.0.

Just a key or click away if you're a Windows user, Help can be found by pressing the F1 key at any time. Most applications support *context-sensitive help*, which means that if you're using a particular tool or have a particular dialog box open and press the F1 key, information pertaining to that tool or dialog box appears when the Help window opens. The Mac OS also offers a Help menu, and the same Help articles appear when you search by topic.

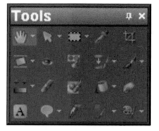

Figure 2-2: The tools in Paint Shop Pro Photo X2.

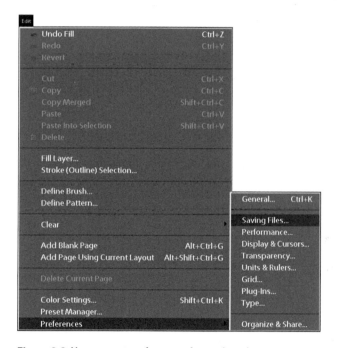

Figure 2-3: You can set preferences for each tool.

Painting Tools

Spotting the painting and drawing tools in any image-editing package isn't difficult. They look like paint brushes and pencils, and there are often airbrush and spray-can alternatives as well. When you use a painting tool, you can customize several options in just about any application. Although some applications definitely offer more options than others, any program worth its salt lets you set the following paint brush options:

- ✔ Brush size and type
- ✔ The shape of the brush bristles
- ✔ The strength of the flow of paint coming out of the brush
- ✔ The opacity of the paint applied by the brush

Figure 2-4 shows brush options in Photoshop Elements, and Figure 2-5 shows the brush options that Paint Shop Pro offers.

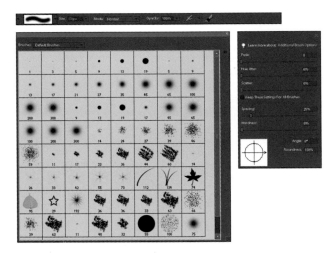

Figure 2-4: You can choose a Brush style or type before painting.

Pencil tools offer many of the same options that you can find for a Paint Brush tool — size, shape, intensity, and color. The color setting is usually established in a color selector tool unrelated to the Paint Brush or Pencil, but the foreground color chosen is the color that the painting or drawing tool applies. I talk about setting your painting color later in this chapter.

Customizing your Brush and Pencil tools

To customize your Brush or Pencil tool, you can use the options presented when the tool is activated. As shown in Figures 2-6 and 2-7, the options for painting and drawing are quite similar in Photoshop Elements and Paint Shop Pro.

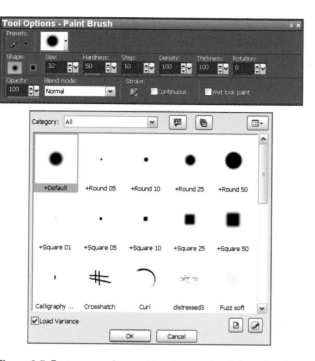

Figure 2-5: Features such as setting the opacity of the paint offer extra flexibility.

To apply customizations to a tool, click the tool to activate it and then use the available drop-down lists, radio buttons, check boxes, sliders, and menus. Sometimes, the options appear on a toolbar; other times, they appear in a palette. It all depends on the software you're using.

You can often save your settings for a particular tool as a group of *presets*. You can set up collections of options for each tool and have more than one setting for a tool, which enables you to have different paint brushes for different tasks. Select your application's preset manager, and choose Save to store your current tool parameters as a preset.

Choosing a paint color

Most applications offer a single color-selection tool that applies to any of the tools that apply color to the image. For example, in Paint Shop Pro, the color-selection tools are in a palette labeled Materials (shown in Figure 2-8), which has Frame, Rainbow, and Swatch modes you can use to choose a color with an eyedropper. Whatever color you choose for the foreground color applies to the Paint Brush, Pencil, and other painting or filling tools. Photoshop Elements uses palettes like the one shown in Figure 2-9.

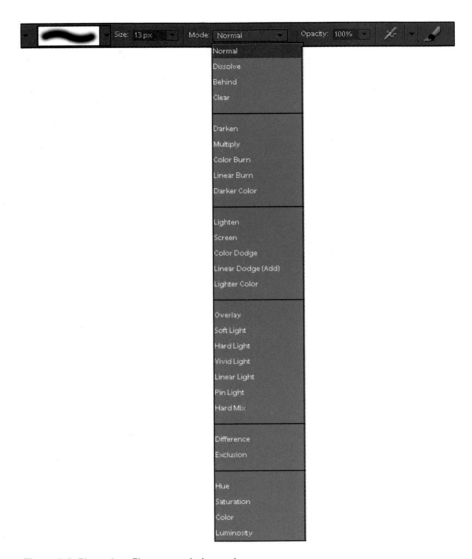

Figure 2-6: Photoshop Elements painting options.

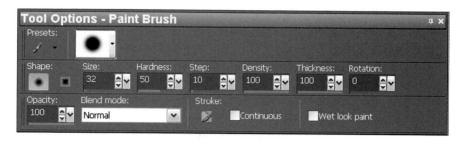

Figure 2-7: Paint Shop Pro painting options.

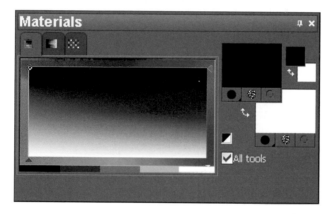

Figure 2-8: Paint Shop Pro has its own color chooser palettes.

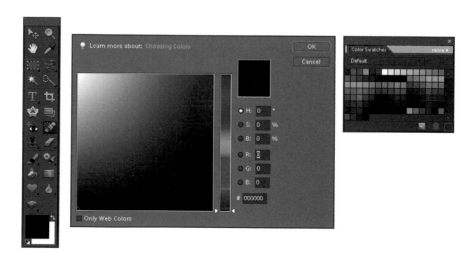

Figure 2-9: Choose colors from the Color Picker dialog box or the Color Swatches palette in Photoshop Elements.

Selecting foreground and background colors

The steps for selecting these colors depend on your application.

Paint Shop Pro

If you're using Paint Shop Pro, clicking the Foreground Color or Background Color panels at the right side of the Materials palette opens a Material Properties dialog box's Color tab (as shown in Figure 2-10), which offers several ways of choosing a color:

- ✔ **Click in the color wheel** to select a range of colors and then zero in on the precise hue you want in the box in the center of the wheel.
- ✔ **Choose a color from the swatches underneath the color wheel.**
- ✔ **Enter an exact color** using RGB (red, green, blue) or HSL (hue, saturation, lightness) values (if you happen to know them).

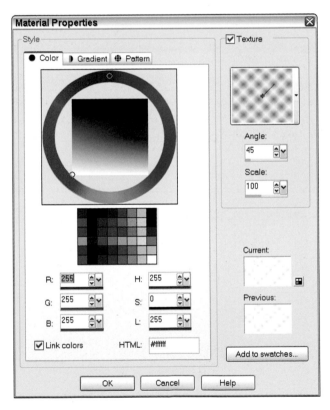

Figure 2-10: Paint Shop Pro puts the key color selection tools in this chooser palette.

Photoshop Elements

Clicking in the Foreground or Background patches at the bottom of the Photoshop Elements Tool palette (at left in Figure 2-9) produces a Color Picker dialog box with options similar to those in the Paint Shop Pro Materials palette. However, in this case, the "color wheel" is a strip located to the right of the sample color box. There is also a set of HSB (equivalent to HSL; the *B* stands for *brightness*), RGB, and HTML entry boxes to the right of the color strip. The Elements Color Swatches palette is separate and shown at the right in Figure 2-9.

After your color is set, you can use any painting, drawing, or filling tool available to you, and then that color is applied to the image.

Sampling colors from the image

If a color already appears in your image (or anywhere on the workspace or your Windows or Mac desktop), you can *sample* it, which means sipping up the color with a sampling tool, such as the Eyedropper tool or variation found in all image editors. When you sip up a sample of the color, the color information is stored, and the color that you sampled becomes the new foreground color. Figure 2-11 shows sampling in progress.

 Sampling colors makes it easy to find compatible colors and to keep your colors consistent throughout a single image or in related images that need the look of a running theme. If, for example, you retouch a photo by adding brighter colors to clothes, cars, flowers, and other objects, you can sample those colors afterward, which will allow you to use those same shades in other places.

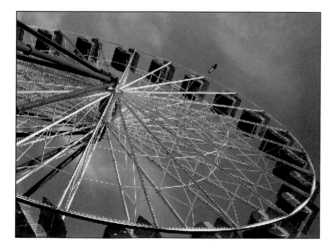

Figure 2-11: You can sample existing colors to duplicate any particular hue.

To sample a color, click the sampling tool, and your cursor changes to an eyedropper. Then click the image at the spot where the desired color is currently in use. The color you clicked then becomes the foreground color.

Remember that you can also click title bars, buttons, backgrounds, or images on your desktop — anything that's visible while the sampling tool is active can be sampled and turned into a paintable color in your editing software.

Applying the paint

After you customize your painting tool by choosing the size, style, opacity, strength, and color for the brush, pencil, or other painting device, you're ready to get painting! The technique for painting doesn't vary much from application to application. With your mouse or other pointing device in hand, you're ready to go. Just click and drag and watch the paint flow onto the image.

Painting and drawing freeform lines

When you're painting by hand and applying freeform lines, there are no real rules. You can set the line to just about any width, shape, style, and color you desire, which you see as you paint. If you set the line to a particular level of opacity, you see that, too. The only control that's not easily established is your mouse ability. If your hand is shaky, you're working too quickly, or you're not paying attention, you might not like your results.

Take your time, go slowly, and don't do the entire job in one stroke. Why? If you make a mistake at the very end, using Undo from the Edit menu will undo the entire job. Instead, paint in shorter strokes. You can see from the Undo History palette found in Paint Shop Pro, Adobe Photoshop, and Photoshop Elements, as well as other image editors (see Figure 2-12) that the Brush tool has been used several times in succession to form the apparently continuous line in the image. Every time you release the mouse button, you create an individual stroke, even if the pause doesn't show on the line itself.

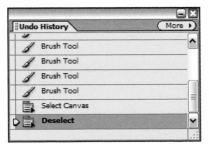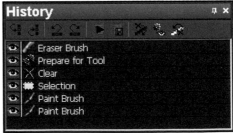

Figure 2-12: Photoshop Elements Undo History palette (left) and the Paint Shop Pro equivalent (right.)

Filling a shape with the Brush tool

Remember coloring books? You scrubbed away with your crayons, filling in shapes, trying to stay within the lines. Or, if you were like me, you went outside the lines and created new shapes altogether! In any case, you can use your editing software's painting tools to fill in shapes and areas simply by applying paint the same way you'd apply crayon to a shape on a coloring book page.

Figure 2-13 shows a border shape being filled in with the Brush tool, set to a large size and a soft style so that no obvious scribbles are visible.

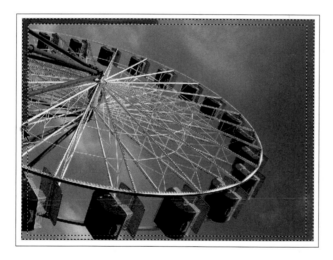

Figure 2-13: You can fill a shape with color as easily as with a coloring book.

If you want a nice, uniform fill for a shape or an area, consider using the Fill tool that comes with your software. The *Fill tool* applies a solid color with no visible brush strokes. On the other hand, if you want a brushed look or want to vary the intensity by painting over certain spots more than others, you can use the Brush tool. Don't use the Pencil tool, though, or the result will look too sketchy.

Painting and drawing straight lines

With all image-editing packages, holding down a key (the Shift key in Photoshop Elements and Paint Shop Pro) while you use the Brush and the Pencil tools constrains the drawing to a single direction. This trick is helpful when you need to draw straight lines.

To use this feature, follow these steps:

1. **Click the painting or drawing tool you'd like to use (Brush or Pencil) to activate it.**

2. **Click the image at the spot where the straight line should start.**

3. **Press and hold the Shift key.**

4. **Click where the line should end.**

   A straight line connecting the beginning and ending points will be painted/drawn automatically, with the visual characteristics of the Brush or Pencil settings you established. Figure 2-14 shows a box that was painted with a textured Brush tool.

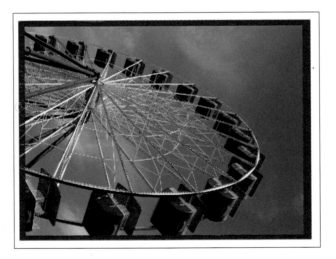

Figure 2-14: This border was painted with a textured brush.

Because the Pencil tool provides a sharp-edged, crisp line, it's a good tool to use if you need to create a very clean line or lines. It's also great if you need to draw very fine lines that measure as small as one pixel.

Using specialty painting tools

Specialty painting tools refer to any painting or drawing tools that aren't your basic Brush or Pencil. These tools often work like the basic ones, at least in terms of how you apply them. Just drag and/or click your mouse and the paint is applied. The look achieved is where these tools deviate from the basic painting and drawing tools.

With some image editors, the specialty tools are actually variations on the basic tools. For example, in Photoshop Elements (and other Adobe products), you can turn on the Airbrush option when you're setting up the Brush tool to give the lines and strokes an airbrushed look. In Paint Shop Pro, the airbrush is a separate tool; it has its own settings for size and intensity of the lines drawn, as shown in Figure 2-15. When you paint with this tool, your results really look like paint that was sprayed on.

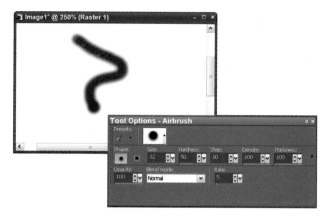

Figure 2-15: Paint Shop Pro includes a separate Airbrush tool.

Paint Shop Pro also has a Picture Tube tool that, by default, applies color as if you were squeezing thick paint out of a tube. Its results are shown in Figure 2-16, where you can see the 3-D look of the lines drawn. Not all applications have a tool like this, but many do. In Photoshop or Photoshop Elements, you could apply drop shadow and beveling options to the lines after drawing them, ending up with a 3-D-looking result.

Another cool thing that the Picture Tube tool does is allow you to paint pre-designed shapes, such as garden vegetables, blades of grass, musical notes, flowers, and stars. Figure 2-17 shows an assortment of lines drawn with the Picture Tube tool, and perhaps you can think of some ways to use them in your photos. For example, you could use the Garden Veggies option to paint a bowl of produce on a tabletop that was bare or had something unappealing on it to begin with.

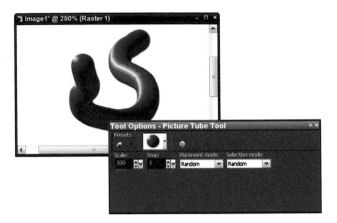

Figure 2-16: The Picture Tube lines look like you squeezed thick paint from a tube.

To choose one of these picture options with Paint Shop Pro, follow these steps:

1. **Click the Picture Tube tool to activate it.**

2. **From the Tool Options palette, click the arrow next to the large picture box.**

   An array of alternative pictures is displayed, as shown in Figure 2-18.

3. **Click the picture that you want to apply.**

4. **Go back to your image and click and drag your mouse or other pointing device on the image to dispense the picture, which is dropped on the image.**

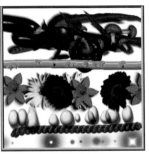

Figure 2-17: You can get these lines with the Picture Tube tool.

By setting the size of the brush, you can control the size of the pictures you apply with the Picture Tube tool. If you want tiny veggies or very short grass, you can use a small brush size to apply them.

If you're a Photoshop or an Elements user and feeling dejected because this cool tool isn't available in your application, take heart. You can apply leaves and grass with the Natural Brushes brush set, and you can download third-party brush sets off the Internet. You can also search the Internet at www. google.com for tons of brush sets that you can download for a reasonable price. Just enter **Photoshop Brushes** in the search box.

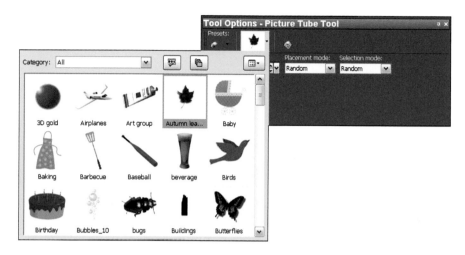

Figure 2-18: Choose the image you want to apply from the list.

Selection Tools

For many edits, you need to focus the software's attention on a particular part of the image, thus controlling where and how the edits take effect. For example, if you want to increase or decrease the contrast in a certain area of the image and nowhere else, you want to select that area before invoking the contrast-adjustment tool so that you don't end up changing the contrast in an area that's fine as-is.

All image-editing programs provide selection tools. Some provide more than others, and some provide more options for using them than others do. A variety of selection tools and options is one of the marks of a flexible and powerful application.

All good image editors offer the following tools for selecting content. The names of the following tools might change from application to application, but the jobs these tools perform remain the same:

✔ **Marquee:** This type of selection tool allows you to select geometric shapes — rectangles, ovals, and in some cases, vertical rows or horizontal columns that are a single pixel wide.

✔ **Lasso:** This freeform selection tool often comes in three varieties:

- A basic lasso

- A magnetic lasso that adheres to certain colored pixels

- A polygonal lasso that allows you to select areas with multiple straight-lined sides

✔ **Magic Wand:** This type of selection tool selects by color, based on a starting pixel or group of pixels. Need to make everything that's blue turn green? The Magic Wand is the selector tool for you.

✔ **Paintbrush or Mask Select:** Some applications offer a paintbrush-like tool that allows you to make a selection by painting. Others allow you to enter a Mask mode, where your standard Brush tool acts as a selector to create a mask of what you want to include in the selection. And when you switch back to the normal mode, your mask has turned to a selection. Alternatively, you can specify that what you don't paint turns into a selection instead.

Making geometric selections

Geometric selections — rectangular and oval-shaped regions — are good if you're preparing to make an adjustment or to apply a fill to a large area and don't mind if the area doesn't follow the shapes within your image.

As shown in Figure 2-19, you can select a rectangular area and apply paint to it to create a frame around the central images in a figure.

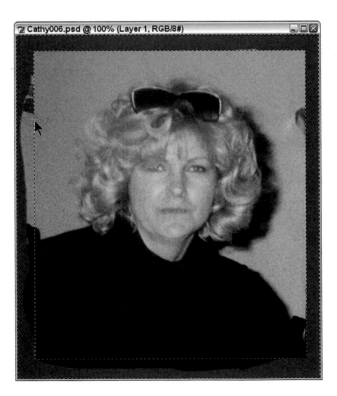

Figure 2-19: Paint around the edges of a selection to create a natural-looking frame.

Before shape tools were added to most image-editing applications, using the Marquee selection tools was the only way to map out an area and fill it with color — creating solid-filled squares, rectangles, circles, and ovals. Most applications come with shape-drawing tools now, enabling you to draw just about any geometric shape or symbol (hearts, arrows, and so on) and then fill it with color. This strips the Marquee tool of one of its original jobs, but it remains an important weapon in your image-editing arsenal.

Using the Marquee selection tools

To use the Marquee or geometric selection tools, simply click the tool and drag from the upper or lower corner of the desired selected area and diagonally away from that starting point. The farther away you drag, the bigger the selection becomes, as shown in Figure 2-20. Here, a rectangular area is being selected, and the distance and angle from the starting point dictates the selection's size and proportions.

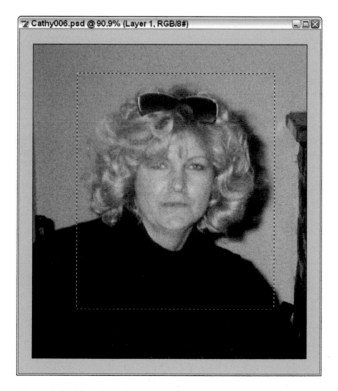

Figure 2-20: The size of the selection determines the shape of the frame.

Selecting perfect squares and circles

If you want to select a square or circle instead of a rectangle or oval (often called an *ellipse*), you can add keystrokes to the process. In most image editors, holding down the Shift key while you drag the Marquee or other geometric selection tool creates a perfect square — if you're using the Rectangular Marquee tool. If you're using the Elliptical Marquee, holding down the Shift key creates a perfect circle. Paint Shop Pro offers a set of selection options, as shown in Figure 2-21, in which the Freehand Selection tool is chosen. You can use the drop-down list within the Tool palette to select a square or a circle rather than a rectangle or an ellipse. You can also select rounded-corner rectangles in Photoshop, Elements, and Paint Shop Pro.

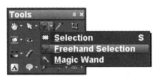

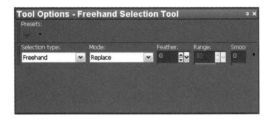

Figure 2-21: Paint Shop Pro includes a variety of selection tools.

Changing and resizing selections

If you already selected a geometrically shaped area on your image and realize that you want a different area or a larger or smaller area, you can always deselect and start over. If the area you selected is fine but you want to add to or take away from it, however, you needn't restart from scratch. You can simply augment or reduce your selection by using keyboard shortcuts or tool options that are provided while the selection tool is active.

If you're using Paint Shop Pro or any of the other higher-end applications, you can use the Shift key to add to a selection or the Ctrl key (⌘ on a Mac) to reduce a selection. Make your selection first. Then hold down the Shift key or Ctrl/⌘ key and create an additional selection. The new selection is added to or subtracted from the first selection you made. You see a plus or minus sign, respectively, appear with your selection cursor.

With most image editors, you can choose from several alternative selection modes on the Options bar. In Figures 2-22 through 2-25, I use the *Magic Wand tool,* which selects contiguous pixels based on their color, to add or subtract from the main selection. (I could have used one of the other selection tools instead, however.)

Here are the most common selection options:

- **Selection:** Figure 2-22 shows a rectangular selection made from an over-lapping rectangle and circle. The dotted lines represent the limits of the selection.

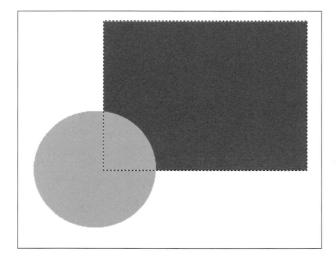

Figure 2-22: A standard selection created with the rectangular marquee.

- **Subtract from Selection:** In Figure 2-23, I held down the Alt key (Option key on the Mac) and used the Magic Wand to click in the circle area, subtracting the circle from the selection and leaving a corner cut out of the rectangular selection.

- **Add to Selection:** In Figure 2-24, I went back to the original rectangular selection and held down the Shift key while clicking in the circle with the Magic Wand. This added the circle's area to the selection.

- **Intersect with Selection:** In Figure 2-25, I used the Intersect option, which produces a selection that results where two selections overlap — in this case, creating a quarter-circle.

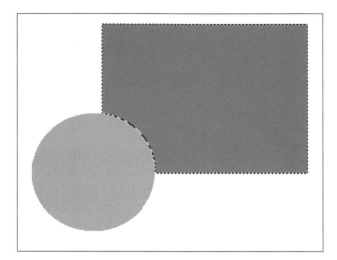

Figure 2-23: The area of the circle is subtracted from the selection.

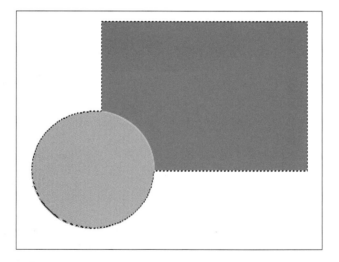

Figure 2-24: The area of the circle is added to the selection.

Want to make a selection that looks like a frame? Use your application's tool for reducing a selection to select a rectangle or square within a larger rectangle or square selection. The smaller selection cuts the center out of the first selection, leaving a frame-like selection that you can fill with a solid color or pattern. This can also be done with concentric circular or elliptical selections.

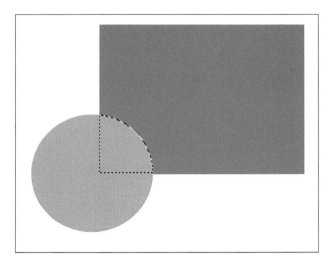

Figure 2-25: This selection results from the area in which separate circle and rectangle selections overlap, using the Intersect option.

You can move your selection without moving the selected content within the image if you point to the very edge of the selection (the dashed line) and drag *after* drawing the selection. This allows you to reposition the selection before you fill it with paint, delete its contents, or apply a filter or special effect to the selected area.

Drawing freeform selections

The ability to draw the borders of a freeform selection is what really enables you to do fine editing in a photo. Without the freeform selection tools in your application, you can't select a person's face, a scratched area, a shadowy area that needs to be lightened, or any other nongeometric region within an image. Most applications offer alternatives for the Lasso or Freeform selection tools — the ability to have the selection follow along like-colored pixels or to draw a polygon (an irregular, straight-sided shape) with the selection tool. With these alternatives, there isn't anything too large, small, or oddly shaped to be selected.

Using the Lasso or Freehand selection tool

Using the Lasso (in Photoshop and Elements) or the Freehand selection tool (in Paint Shop Pro) is really easy if you follow these steps:

**Book IV
Chapter 2**

**Common Editing
Options**

1. **Click to activate the tool.**

2. **Move your mouse onto the image and find the spot where you'd like to begin your selection.**

3. **Click to begin the selection and then drag, drawing the shape selection you want.**

4. **Come back to the beginning of the selection.**

   When you meet or pass the starting point, release the mouse button to complete the selection. If you release the mouse button anywhere else, the program will draw a straight line from that point to the original starting point, closing the selection.

Selecting polygonal areas

When you click the Lasso or Freehand selection tools, options become available. In Photoshop and Elements, the Options bar displays different Lasso modes, as shown in Figure 2-26. Similar options are available for the Freehand tool in Paint Shop Pro through the Tool Options palette.

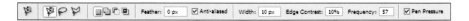

Figure 2-26: The Lasso tool Options bar in Photoshop Elements.

With the Polygonal Lasso (Photoshop Elements) or the Point-to-Point Freehand tool (Paint Shop Pro), you can make your selection by following these steps:

1. **Click to activate the selection tool.**

2. **Use the tool's options to set it to Polygonal or Point-to-Point mode.**

3. **Click your starting point on the image.**

4. **Rather than dragging, move the mouse to the next point in your polygon — where you want to make a corner and start another side — and click.**

5. **Continue clicking and moving, each time drawing a new side for your selection, until you come back to your starting point.**

6. **When you're back to the beginning of the selection, click the starting point to close the shape.**

   If you can't find the exact pixel where your selection began, just double-click when you get close. The software closes the shape for you, forcing the endpoint to meet the starting point that you couldn't see or find manually.

Your freeform selections needn't be a single closed shape. You can draw figure eights or any kind of freeform looped shape, using either the freehand or polygonal modes. Go crazy!

Using magnetic selection tools

Magnetic selection tools create a selection that "clings" to the outline of an object as you drag, according to pixel colors that define the object's edge. These tools are very handy because they enable you to follow the edge of an object or objects, restricting your selection to very finite areas of the image.

Nearly every editing package has a tool like this. In Photoshop and Elements, it's the Magnetic Lasso; in Paint Shop Pro, you select the Smart Edge option for the Freehand tool.

To use the magnetic selection tools, follow these steps:

1. **Click the Lasso or Freehand tool (or other similarly named tool in your application) to activate it.**

2. **From the tool's options, choose Magnetic (Photoshop or Elements) or Smart Edge (Paint Shop Pro).**

3. **Click the spot where you want to begin your selection.**

4. **Continue making the selection by dragging along the edge of the object or area you want to select.**

   The tool adheres to the edges of that object or area, following the like-colored pixels, as shown in Figure 2-27.

5. **If you see an area coming up where the tool might fail because the pixels aren't diverse, click again to reroute the selection process, and then continue dragging.**

   You can click as often as you like along the way, controlling the direction that the selection takes.

   The same process in Paint Shop Pro uses the Smart Edge tool, from which a rectangle follows you while you drag. While you click to continue in a new direction, the previously dragged selection adheres to the shape.

6. **Come back to your starting point and click (or double-click if you're not sure you're at the exact starting point) to end and close the selection.**

Selecting with the Quick Mask mode

Photoshop offers a Quick Mask mode, in which you can use the Brush and the Pencil tools (as well as the Fill tool) to paint a protective mask over parts of the image. This makes it as easy as painting to make a selection because when you return to standard working mode, the mask turns into a selection. Alternatively, everything *not* painted can become a selection.

**Book IV
Chapter 2**

**Common Editing
Options**

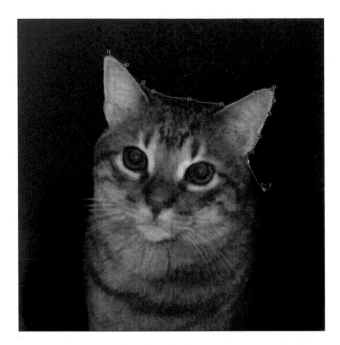

Figure 2-27: The Magnetic Lasso in Photoshop and Elements sticks to the edges of objects.

To work in and make a selection with Quick Mask mode, follow these steps:

1. **Click the Quick Mask Mode button in the bottom section of the Photoshop toolbox.**

2. **Click the Brush or the Pencil tool, adjusting its settings just as you would if you were painting or drawing color onto an image.**

   You want to increase or decrease the size of the tool's tip to accommodate the level of detail that you want to achieve in your selection.

3. **Begin outlining the area you want to select, and note that a see-through red mask appears wherever you paint, as shown in Figure 2-28.**

4. **After you outline the shape or area, use the Fill tool (which looks like a paint bucket) to fill in the shape that you want to turn into a selection.**

   This makes a solid mask that will translate into a selection of the entire area.

5. **When you finish masking the area you want, switch back to Standard mode.**

   When you leave Quick Mask mode, your mask turns into a selection. You can now work with the selection as you would one that you created directly with any of the other selection tools or methods.

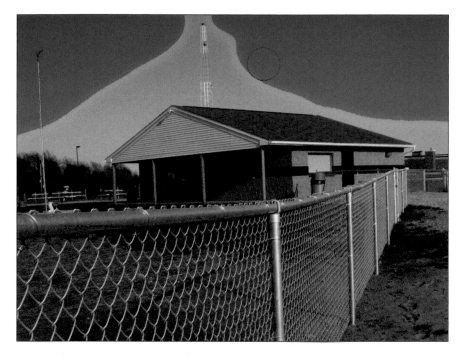

Figure 2-28: The selection you're painting appears as a semi-transparent red mask.

If you want to select everything but a particular object or area, first mask that area. Then, when you get back into Standard mode, choose Select⇨Inverse from the main menu.

Selecting with the Paintbrush Selection tool

Photoshop Elements has a Paintbrush Selection tool that you can use to paint a selection. The tool gives you the flexibility and familiarity of a Paint Brush tool and also allows you to select snaking paths or to select a freeform shape by filling in an area with the Brush tool.

Selecting pixels by color with the Magic Wand

The selections that you can make with the Magic Wand often resemble those you'd make with the Lasso or Freehand selection tools. They're freeform shapes and — like selections made with the Add to Selection option turned on — they can encompass multiple noncontiguous areas. The difference between those selection tools and the Magic Wand, however, is that the Magic Wand makes selections based on an initial pixel sample. For example, this enables you to select all the blue areas, all the white areas, or all the areas that are the same as or quite close to any color or shade within your image.

Abracadabra! Using the Magic Wand

The Magic Wand selects pixels within your image based on the color of a pixel you click. It's a simple process, but one that you can master and use to your advantage if you know exactly how it works.

To use the Magic Wand tool, follow these simple steps:

1. **Click the Magic Wand tool to activate it.**

2. **Click a pixel that's the color of the pixels that you want to select in your image.**

   Figure 2-29 shows the sampling in progress.

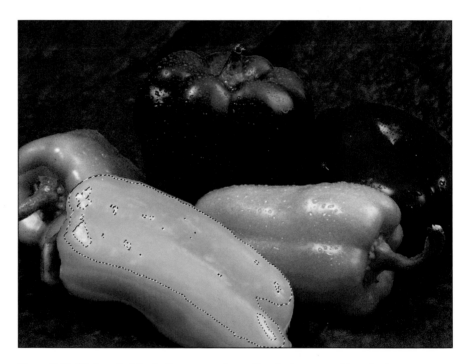

Figure 2-29: Click a pixel that's the same color as the pixels you want to select.

3. **If you don't get all the pixels you wanted, press and hold the Shift key while you continue to click pixels around in the image, adding to the Magic Wand selection.**

   Figure 2-30 shows a selection in progress.

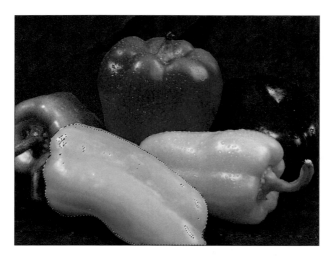

Figure 2-30: Add pixels to your selection by holding the Shift key and clicking another area.

If you get more pixels in the selection than you want, reduce your selection by switching to Subtract from Selection mode (Photoshop or Elements) or by holding down the Ctrl key (⌘ for Mac) to take away from the existing selection. When you click an unwanted area within the selection, those pixels are no longer selected.

If you didn't get as much of the image as you wanted, tweak the tool's options settings, such as Tolerance, to include more pixels. You can tweak the number of selected pixels by expanding the tolerance, or press the Shift key and click in the additional area you hoped to select in order to add to the selection.

Controlling the wand's magic

Any wand settings that you could possibly tweak are located on the tool's Options bar in Photoshop and Elements or in the palette or Tool options bar of other image editors. The settings work differently, depending on the application you're using.

In any case, you will see a Tolerance setting, which is a threshold for the sensitivity of the wand. The higher the number you set for the Tolerance setting, the more pixels that the software sees as selectable — a risky approach if you're working with a black-and-white photo or a color photo without a lot of color diversity throughout. You can make other application-specific adjustments that, when used in conjunction with the Tolerance setting, can assure you of the exact selection you wanted. These adjustments include the following:

✔ **Match Mode** (Paint Shop Pro) allows you to choose what pixel attribute is compared to the surrounding pixels. You can choose from RGB Value, Hue, Brightness, All Opaque, or Opacity. If you choose RGB Value (the default), the surrounding pixels are compared in terms of their levels of red, green, and blue. And, if they're close enough to the sampled pixel (based on the Tolerance you set), they are selected.

✔ **Contiguous** (Photoshop/Elements) is a check box that allows you to choose whether the selection includes pixels that aren't touching the sampled pixel or any of the pixels that were selected on the first click with the wand. If you turn on the option (it's off by default), you get a smaller selection, which might be just what you want. If you turn it off, any pixels meeting your Tolerance setting are selected, no matter where in the image they're found.

✔ The **Use All Layers** option (Photoshop/Elements/Paint Shop Pro) allows you to select pixels on (who'd have guessed it) all the layers of the image. If you turn this on (it's off by default), you can select all the pixels that meet your tolerance requirements, no matter which layer they're on. If you want to restrict your edits to a particular layer, however, make sure this option is off.

You might find it easier to set your Tolerance setting low so that you don't get more of a selection than you wanted and then use the Add to Selection option or the Shift key to augment the selection by clicking again on a new spot, which resamples the image and compares surrounding pixels against a different sample pixel. Like most things in life, it's easier to start small and add what you need than to grab too much and then have to give some of it back or start all over again.

Blending Tools

Blending is another word for mixing — combining separate things to make a new thing. When it comes to photos that you're retouching or editing for content, use blending to make new content seem as though it has always been in what's really a new environment. Blending is for retouching — applying strokes of paint that cover a stain or pasted areas that fill in a hole and then disappear into the neighboring content.

Any good image-editing application offers at least one or two blending tools, and again using Photoshop, Photoshop Elements, and Paint Shop Pro as examples, you'll find no lack of blending tools available, including

✔ The Smudge tool (Photoshop/Elements)

✔ The Blur tool (Photoshop/Elements and Paint Shop Pro)

✔ The Scratch Remover tool (Paint Shop Pro)

You can use other tools to blend one thing into another, but they're not necessarily tools that are classified as blending tools per se. For example, you can use the Clone Stamp tool to eliminate the signs of an obvious patch job, to add consistency to an area with spotty colors or textures, or to heal a damaged area that stands out like a sore thumb. Sometimes, the Clone Stamp's results need a little blending of their own, though, and that's when the actual blending tools come into play.

Smudging and smearing your colors

The *Smudge tool* smears color from one area of the image onto another area, much like how you blend dry pastels with your fingertip or how children finger-paint. You can use this tool to blend hard edges, to soften blemishes (when actually patching them would rob the image of too much texture), and to smear away small spots or scratches. You can use the tool in black-and-white or color images.

Using and controlling the Smudge tool

To use the Smudge tool (nested with the Sharpen and Blur tools in Photoshop Elements), just click it and start smudging. The default settings are appropriate for most uses, but you can adjust them. The most effective setting to adjust is Strength, which controls the degree of smearing that the Smudge tool achieves. A low strength creates very subtle results, and a high strength achieves dramatic results. A setting in the middle (50%) gives you an effective smudge without making a mess.

Other adjustments are available on the Mode drop-down menu, from which you can control which aspect of the smudged pixels is affected by the smudging process. You can choose to Darken or Lighten the pixels or to affect their hue, saturation, color, or luminosity (brightness). Not sure which one to choose? Tinker a bit and undo your handiwork by pressing Ctrl+Z (⌘+Z) if you don't like the results.

Smearing with the Finger Painting option

The Finger Painting option — available with the Photoshop and Photoshop Elements Smudge tool — allows you to smear the current foreground color into the area you're smudging. (A somewhat similar effect can be obtained in Paint Shop Pro using the Paint Brush's Wet Look Paint option.) You can use this tool to incorporate new colors or brighter, more vibrant versions of existing colors by virtual finger-painting.

Don't forget the role that the brush size can play in the Smudge tool's effectiveness. Too big of a brush can smear more of the image than you want it to, whereas too small of a brush can result in obvious, sketchy-looking smudges. It's a real Goldilocks situation: You want the one that's just right, and sometimes only experimentation helps you find the right size.

Blurring the edges

The Blur tool found in most image editors works by eliminating a little — or a lot — of the contrast between adjacent pixels, thereby making parts of your image blurred or out of focus. You control how much of an effect the tool has by adjusting its settings — Strength and Brush Size being the most dynamic. You also control where it works by where you place your mouse as you scrub over unwanted edges and distinctions. You can use it to draw attention to part of the photo by blurring nonessential content. Or, in the blending context, you can use it to make hard lines, the edges of pasted content, and other unwanted edges disappear into the surrounding image.

Figure 2-31 shows an image that's ripe for blurring; you can see the hard edges where the white flowers were pasted into the image. Figure 2-32 shows the blurred result. The hard edge is gone, and you can hardly tell that the new content was pasted into place.

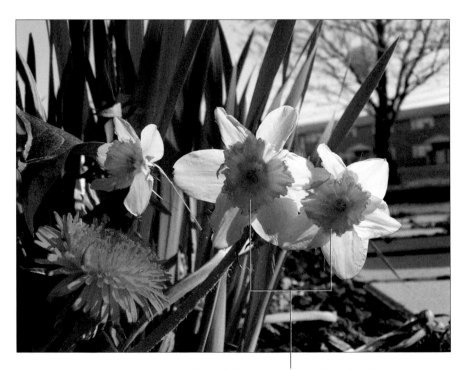

These flowers were pasted into the photo

Figure 2-31: The edges around the pasted-in flowers are too harsh.

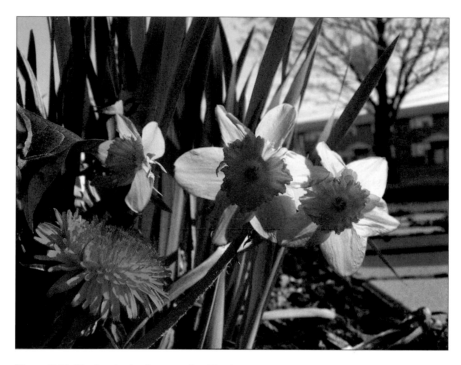

Figure 2-32: The hard edge is gone after blurring.

How do you know when to blur and when to smudge, when to clone and when to paint? There are no hard and fast rules, although I wish there were. We all spend time trying one technique and then undoing it in favor of another. A good guideline to keep in mind, though, is that *less is more.* A small problem (such as tiny scratches or minor stains or spots) should require a small solution, and that usually calls for a subtle tool. If you have a large-scale problem — such as major amounts of unwanted content, big tears, or missing portions of the photo — a larger-scale solution is probably required.

Using the Scratch Remover

Paint Shop Pro offers a very cool tool — the Scratch Remover. Unlike Photoshop's multistep Healing Brush and Patch tools, this tool works a bit more quickly and easily. (If you want to remove spots in an image in one step using Elements, try the Spot Healing Brush instead. You can find more on removing scratches with Adobe healing tools in Book V, Chapter 4.)

1. **Click the Scratch Remover (as shown in Figure 2-33) to activate it.**

    The Tool Options palette appears.

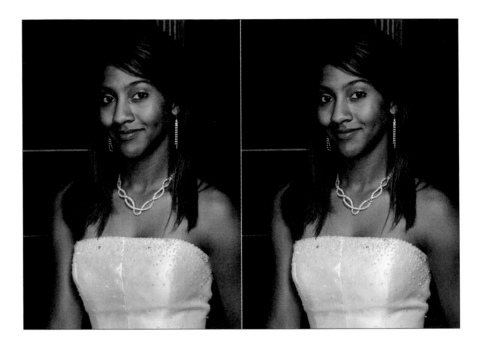

Figure 2-34: Using the Sponge tool removes most of the magenta cast seen at left, producing the image shown at right.

Why would you want to take color away? Perhaps you added too much color in a previous editing session, and the edit can't be undone. Or maybe you simply want a subtler, more faded look to your image. New photos are often faded for a more vintage look or to prepare for the use of an artistic filter that makes the photo look like a drawing or painting.

Adjusting lights and darks

Although you can use dialog boxes galore to adjust the light levels in your photos, the tools on the toolbox/toolbar that allow you to paint light and shadows where they're needed are always a real timesaver. It's also much easier to control the amount of light or shadow you're applying and to control where you're applying it if you use a brush-based tool to apply it. You can set the brush to as large or small a size as you want, and you can zoom in and adjust single pixels or very small groups thereof as needed. You can also apply light and shadow to very large areas; by going over the same spot more than once, you can easily intensify the effect.

Dodging to add light

Photoshop and Photoshop Elements offer a Dodge tool (described briefly in Book IV, Chapter 1) that enables you to add more light to any image simply by clicking and dragging the tool over the area needing more light, as shown in Figure 2-35. Many other image-editing applications have the same tool. In the case of Paint Shop Pro, for example, the application offers a retouching tool that has dodging capability.

The term *dodge* is not specific to any software product; it's a photographic term for holding back the light that forms part of an image as a print is exposed onto photographic paper by an enlarger, lightening part of the image.

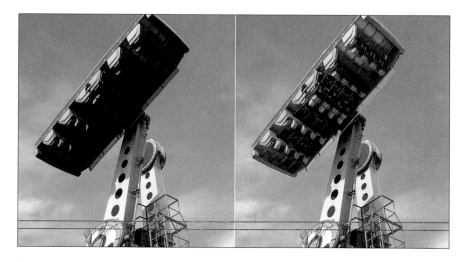

Figure 2-35: Use the Dodge tool to lighten areas, such as the shadows under this scary ride.

To use the Dodge tool, follow these steps:

1. **Click the tool to activate it.**

2. **Check the tool's Options bar and make any desired adjustments.**

   Your options are

   - *Size:* The size of the brush that you use to dodge the image. Use a size that won't show the individual strokes but that isn't so large that it dodges an area larger than you intended.

   - *Range:* Choose which tones the dodge will affect in the image — the Highlights, Midtones, or Shadows.

- *Exposure:* This percentage is set to 50% by default and allows you to control the intensity of the dodge effect. Lower numbers result in a subtler effect than higher numbers.

3. **Click and drag over the area to be dodged.**

   If you feel that you need to confine the dodge effect to a very specific area, you can select that area first, using a freeform selection tool, such as the Brush selector or the Lasso. That way, you don't end up with obvious blocks or circles of lightened image content.

   You can go over areas more than once. Each pass heightens the dodge effect, so don't go overboard!

Burning to add depth and shadow

Burning is another photographic term, and its definition is the opposite of *dodging.* It involves adding extra exposure to part of an image while a print is exposed by an enlarger.

That sounds contradictory, doesn't it? Adding more exposure time darkens the image? Note that image-forming light is held back — that's the key. The Burn tool reduces the amount of light, which deepens shadows and reduces the detail-killing light that can wash out parts of your image. Figure 2-36 shows an image in dire need of the Burn tool — if only to even out the very stark effects of the sun on specific parts of the road image.

Using the Burn tool in most image editors is very much like using the Dodge tool. Even though their effects are opposite, their functioning is nearly identical:

1. **Click the tool to activate it.**

2. **Adjust any desired settings on the tool's Options bar, including Size, Range, and Exposure.**

   These options have the same meanings as they do for the Dodge tool except that increasing exposure here increases the darkening effect. Your software might have different terms for these settings, but they do the same things.

3. **Click or drag over the area of the image to be darkened, being careful not to lose more detail by creating shadows that are too dark or too obvious.**

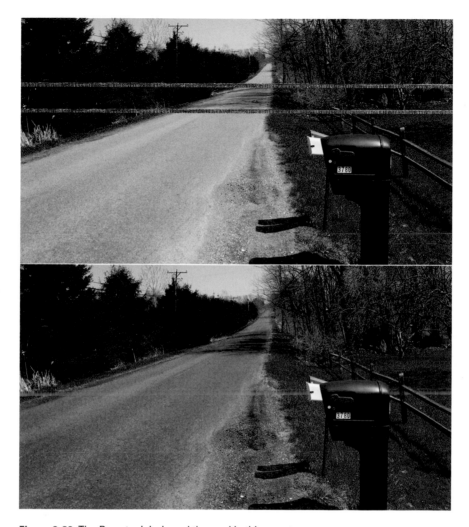

Figure 2-36: The Burn tool darkened the road in this country scene.

Living up to its name, overuse of the Burn tool can make your image look singed. If yours is a color photo or a black-and-white photo in RGB mode (which has more color information beyond simple shades of gray), the Burn tool can add a brownish tone, making the photo look as though it were exposed to high heat or flame. Unless you *want* your photo to look toasted, take it easy with the Burn tool.

Book V
Editing with Adobe Photoshop and Photoshop Elements

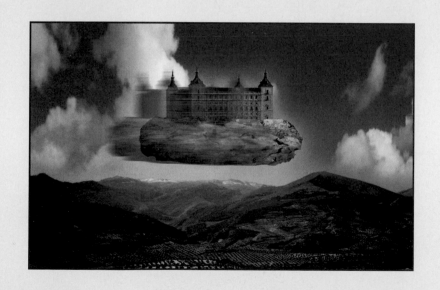

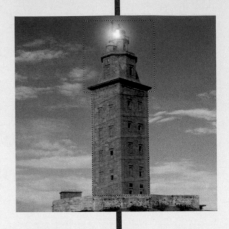

*N*ow that you've gotten your image-editing feet wet, I show you more of what you need to know with two of the most popular image editing programs, Adobe Photoshop CS4 and Adobe Photoshop Elements. As I demonstrate, Photoshop isn't just for professionals anymore, and Elements now has enough tools to appeal to dedicated photography enthusiasts. In the six chapters of this book, I reveal the power of selections, the best ways to brush away problems, techniques for correcting faded or weird colors, and how to achieve special looks using the Adobe editors' built-in filters.

If you want to want to enhance your photos, I show you how to "heal" photographic wounds, replace unwanted content with other images, and adjust light and shadows to give your pictures extra snap.

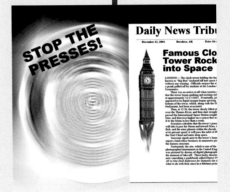

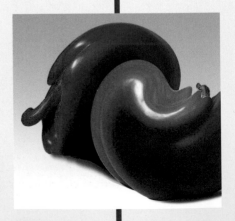

Chapter 1: Introduction to Photoshop CS4 and Photoshop Elements 7

In This Chapter

✓ Photoshop and Photoshop Elements together

✓ New features in Photoshop CS4

✓ New features in Elements 7

*W*hen I wrote the first edition of this book, the state of the art in high-end image editors was Adobe Photoshop 7. For powerful but easy-to-use entry-level image editors, Photoshop Elements 2.0 was the way to go. Within an impressively short period, however, both were replaced (several times) with newer, better, and more powerful editions with lots of extra features and improvements. For this book's fourth edition, the amazing advancements in digital camera technology have been only half the battle in updating this text. I have also had to take into account the changes made for Photoshop CS4 and Photoshop Elements 7.

Fortunately, because both applications will be introduced in about the same timeframe as this book, it's likely that no new versions will be available until late in the life of this book. I expect that it will be digital camera technology that leads the bleeding edge for a while.

The Relationship between Photoshop and Photoshop Elements

As most Photoshopoholics know, Photoshop and Elements have long shared many of the same underpinnings and programming code. Indeed, in some respects, Elements can be considered a version of Photoshop with some capabilities that Adobe has wisely left out or disabled because most users of Elements don't need them and might even be confused by the most advanced features. You don't want to learn how to pilot an airplane when you can buy a ticket and enjoy an easier and more automated way of getting to the same destination. But if you *must* go somewhere that Elements won't take you, it's comforting to know that you can learn how to pilot Adobe's flagship image editor and get there on your own.

If you have access to both programs, you'll find that their interfaces, dialog boxes, and many of their features are virtually the same. They use the same filters and also have tool palettes that are, on the surface, quite similar.

But despite the similarities, Photoshop includes some features that will *never* show up in Elements, and vice versa. Users of Elements probably don't need the ability to work with 16-bit channels or CMYK (cyan, magenta, yellow, black) files, and Photoshop workers wouldn't deign to use some of the quick fixes found in Elements. But those who need such features *really* need them. Elements, in particular, caters to those who are beginning to learn image editing, and the program's automated fixing tools allow fixing up digital images quickly while it paves the way toward more individualized image editing once you learn the ropes.

You can expect Photoshop and Elements to continue to converge and diverge, as appropriate, with features crossing from one application to the other during their overlapping development cycles.

Adobe Photoshop CS4: Alone at the Top

Adobe Photoshop, as shown in Figure 1-1, is the big kahuna of image-editing programs. Available for both Windows and Mac OS, it is the industry standard by which all the other image-editing programs are measured. You may need it (someday), but if you're just starting out in image editing, you probably don't.

Over the years, Photoshop has earned a place in nearly every digital imaging professional's toolbox. The latest version only cemented that position. In fact, for many graphics professionals, Photoshop is the primary tool for everything from resampling image files and changing the file format to photographic retouching and image enhancement to creating original illustrations and artwork.

Photoshop is a professional-level tool, but you don't have to work at a major advertising agency, photography studio, or printing plant to use it. Even though buying a copy of Photoshop requires a significant investment of money and time spent learning to use it, it's not beyond the reach of small businesses, serious digital photography hobbyists, artists, and others who need access to its powerful tools and advanced features. You'll need a computer powerful enough to run it, of course. You can find attractive upgrade offers from time

**Book V
Chapter 1**

Introduction to
Photoshop CS4
and Photoshop
Elements 7

to time that let you purchase a full copy of Photoshop for a fraction of its regular list price. When you own Photoshop, additional upgrades (as Adobe releases new versions) are relatively economical.

What's good about Photoshop

Photoshop didn't attain its stature as the leading high-end, image-editing program by accident. It has a well-deserved reputation for delivering a complete feature set. In short, this is one powerful program. No matter what you want to do with an image, Photoshop probably has the tools for it.

Photoshop can read, write, and manipulate all the industry-standard file formats, such as TIFF, JPEG, and through its Adobe Camera Raw plug-in, the RAW formats that more advanced digital cameras produce. It also supports many not-so-standard formats as well. You can resample images to change the image size, resolution, and color depth. Photoshop excels at providing images that are optimized for specialized uses, such as commercial printing and Web graphics. Photoshop also enjoys close ties with several leading page-layout programs and Web-development programs.

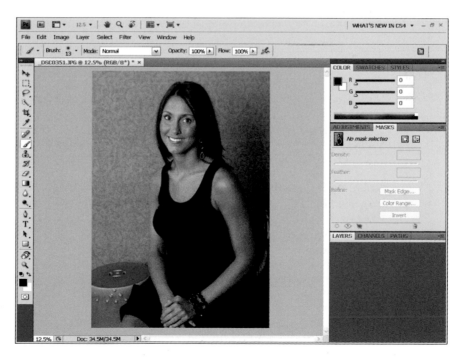

Figure 1-1: An image being edited in Photoshop CS4.

Photoshop provides a rich set of tools for everything from simple image manipulation (cropping and color balance adjustments, to name two) to selecting complex shapes from an image and applying sophisticated filters and effects to the selected area. Photoshop also includes a full set of painting tools that you can use to retouch your images or create original artwork.

As if Photoshop's built-in features weren't complete enough, Adobe designed Photoshop to accept filters and other program extensions provided by third-party suppliers. As a result, a robust aftermarket has evolved to supply a wide assortment of plug-ins that make it quick and easy to apply all manner of textures, edge treatments, special effects, and other image manipulations to the images that you edit in Photoshop.

What's not so good about Photoshop

Photoshop is undeniably a powerful program, but you do pay a price for all that power: Photoshop is expensive. The price of admission for accessing Photoshop's power is a significant investment in money and learning time.

At a little over $600, Photoshop is expensive to purchase initially. (Later upgrades won't cost you as much.) But the cost of the program doesn't stop there. If you're a serious Photoshop user, you probably want to add one or more third-party plug-in packages, which each cost as much as a typical mid-level image editor. And then there are the inevitable upgrade costs when Adobe releases the next version of Photoshop with all of its cool new features. The upgrade price for a new version of Photoshop is more than the full purchase price of most other image editors, but the cost is still reasonable when you consider what you're getting.

In addition to its monetary cost, Photoshop is also expensive in terms of the time that you need to invest in order to use it. The demands of learning to use this program are probably the most significant barrier for the casual user. Photoshop's power and versatility make it a complex program, and that complexity creates a steep learning curve. Getting started working with the program right out of the box can be challenging. Even after you learn the ropes, performing some simple tasks can sometimes be cumbersome in Photoshop. The program's breadth and depth make it difficult to master. Often, even the graphics pros who use Photoshop on a daily basis haven't explored all its many capabilities.

Photoshop is an ongoing commitment, too. It's not the sort of program that you can use once a month and pick up where you left off. It works best when used daily so that the commands and shortcuts become second nature. Attempt to use a special feature after not working with Photoshop for a month, and you'll probably find yourself diving into the (excellent) built-in Help system.

**Book V
Chapter 1**

Introduction to
Photoshop CS4
and Photoshop
Elements 7

What you can do with Photoshop

What can you do with Photoshop? The short answer is, "Almost anything!"

In fact, it's difficult to come up with anything that you'd want to do to a digital image that can't be done in Photoshop unless it's outright impossible in the first place (such as transforming a total train wreck of a photo into a work of art). Oh sure, a few tasks are faster or easier to perform in some other programs. However, it's hard to find a visual effect that can't be duplicated in Photoshop if you're willing to invest the time and effort to get acquainted with the program's tools and use those tools in innovative ways. Best of all, Photoshop has many features that are useful to those using digital cameras, including the ability to work with *RAW camera files* (the basic, unprocessed camera file with all the original information captured by the camera) for many popular models, facilities for matching colors between images taken under different lighting conditions, and a new feature for stitching panorama photos seamlessly.

The Photoshop and Elements chapters in this book are not intended to teach you how to use either program from scratch. You'd need an entire book for that. Surprise! Such books are available from the same folks (Wiley Publishing) who brought you this one. Check out *Adobe Photoshop CS4 All-in-One Desk Reference For Dummies,* by Barbara Obermeier, and *Adobe Photoshop Elements 7 For Dummies* by Barbara Obermeier and Ted Padova.

What's New in Photoshop CS4

Photoshop CS4 has some new features that weren't available in its predecessors. Amateur photographers will find that the changes will generally benefit advanced workers the most. There are no major new tools in the Toolbox, for example, other than the nifty Rotate View tool that's nestled in with the Hand tool. (It lets you spin your canvas around to view it at different angles.) Other tools, such as the Quick Selection Tool, have been enhanced, however. But here are some of the most notable changes and a brief explanation of what they do:

- ✔ **Interface changes:** The new Photoshop CS4 looks a lot like the old CS3 on your screen, but there are some interesting changes. The Title bar at the top of the Photoshop window has been put to work with new buttons and pull-down menus. You can go directly to Adobe Bridge (Photoshop's image organizer) by clicking an icon. Buttons for zoom level, arranging documents on the screen, and changing screen viewing mode also reside there. Individual documents (your photos) can be layered on top of each other and accessed by clicking on tabs — much as you switch between tabbed dialog boxes. The brightness of the interface can be dialed up or down, and buttons and dialog boxes have been improved for easier viewing.

✔ **Masking revamped:** Masks can be thought of as overlays that protect portions of your image while leaving other parts exposed to various editing functions. Photoshop CS4 supercharges the use of masks, including a new Mask palette that allows you to create masks using both traditional pixel drawing as well as line-oriented (vector) drawing. The Layer Mask Density option lets you fade away the effects of a mask, reducing the masking effect. You have to work extensively with Photoshop to see why all these changes are cool, but some folks already are ecstatic over them.

✔ **Improved Dodge and Burn tools:** It's always been easy to mess up a photo by over-using the Dodge and Burn tools (which I explained in Book IV, Chapter 1). Adobe has improved these tools to give you results that are more natural looking and less likely to create heavy-handed effects. You can still revert to the "old" versions if you prefer.

✔ **Faster filters:** The special effects tools we call *filters* (discussed in Book V, Chapter 5) now operate in real time and can be used with image files having greater than 8-bit color depth per color channel (images with more than 16.8 million colors, to we mere humans). Adobe has incorporated a new technology that off-loads the number crunching required for applying filters from your computer's main CPU (brain) to the brains found on compatible video cards.

✔ **Improved panoramas:** Photomerge, the Photoshop tool that lets you stitch photographs together to make composites and panoramas, has been given new capabilities, including a new Collage mode. (See Figure 1-2.)

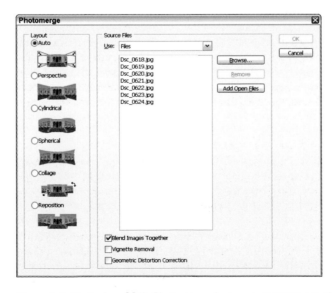

Figure 1-2: Photoshop CS4's Photomerge feature automates creating panoramas.

Book V
Chapter 1

Introduction to
Photoshop CS4
and Photoshop
Elements 7

✔ **Better High Dynamic Range (HDR) support:** HDR merging is an advanced tool that lets you take several photos of the same subject at different exposures (say, one that's too dark, one that's too light, and one that's in between) and combine them to produce a single picture with an amazing amount of shadow and highlight detail, which is extremely difficult to achieve in one photo. Photoshop CS3 had HDR merging, but this latest edition has improved options and capabilities.

✔ **Best of the rest:** Look for the new Vibrance capability in Image Adjustments to give your colors an instant saturation boost. Refine Edge improvements make it easier to select parts of your image for editing. You'll also find automatic features for aligning and blending layers, improved management of color profiles, and small but welcome touches like faster loading time for the Photoshop application.

Adobe Photoshop Elements 7

Photoshop Elements 7 is the little brother of the full Photoshop program and available as I write this only for Microsoft Windows. Adobe's custom in recent years has been to offer a Windows version of Elements first and then follow with a Mac OS edition some months later. It's a more accessible version of Photoshop for the numerous people who want to use Photoshop but don't need some of its more advanced features.

Photoshop Elements, as shown in Figure 1-3, shares much of the same user interface with its big brother, Photoshop, although in a revamped form. Compared with the full version of Photoshop, Elements has an abbreviated feature set, in one sense, but is, in another way, more advanced because of its large array of quick fixes and automated tools. It includes nearly all of the basic image-editing tools that the typical digital photographer needs on a regular basis. That includes image selection, retouching, and painting tools; a generous assortment of filters; and the ability to expand those filters by accepting the same Photoshop plug-ins as its sibling program.

What's good about Elements

Photoshop Elements is competitively priced at about $100. Elements is considerably less powerful than its big brother, but by sacrificing some of the immense power of Photoshop, Adobe created a program that is significantly less complex and is therefore easier to use than Photoshop.

In general, Adobe did a pretty good job of selecting which Photoshop features to include in Elements. The program's feature set is a reasonably good match for the needs of the typical digital photographer. Most of Photoshop's standard selection, retouching, and painting tools are available in Elements. If your image-editing needs revolve around retouching and manipulating individual pictures one at a time, you'll probably never notice the more advanced Photoshop features that are missing from Elements.

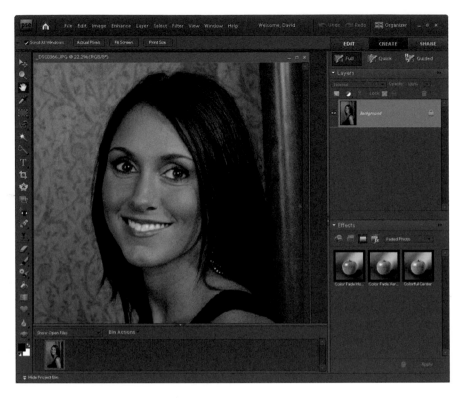

Figure 1-3: Photoshop Elements 7 at work.

Rest assured, though, that Elements isn't just a slimmed-down version of Photoshop. The program includes a few interesting features that Photoshop lacks. For example, the automated commands on the Enhance menu make quick work of common image-editing tasks, such as adjusting backlighting or color cast. As a result, an occasional user working with Elements can sometimes complete those tasks faster than a seasoned graphics pro working with Photoshop.

If you plan to eventually move up to Photoshop, Elements makes a good set of training wheels. After you master this program, you can use Photoshop much more easily than if you started with Photoshop from scratch.

What's not so good about Elements

The similarity of the Elements *user interface* (the arrangement of menus and floating palettes superimposed on the workspace containing multiple document windows) is a boon to Photoshop users and wannabes who might need to switch back and forth between the two programs. However, the

**Book V
Chapter 1**

Introduction to
Photoshop CS4
and Photoshop
Elements 7

Photoshop interface (and thus, to a certain extent, the Elements interface) isn't known for its ease of use. Many newcomers to the program don't find the menu arrangements and other details to be very intuitive.

What you can do with Elements

One very nice feature of Elements is the broad array of automatic fixer commands, which can adjust color, contrast, lighting, or even all of these at once via the Smart Fix feature. (Elements also has an Auto Smart Fix command that does all these things automatically.)

What's New in Elements 7

The biggest news about Photoshop Elements 7 is that it's moving online in a big way. If you've watched the development of Adobe's online image-editing and sharing service, called Photoshop Express, you'll easily see how Elements 7 provides an excellent complement for its Web-based sibling.

Photoshop Express allows you to upload images to a Web site, where you can do some simple editing, using tools that are much like the more advanced tools found in Photoshop Elements. You can then organize those images into online albums and share them with the world — or just your family, friends, and colleagues.

Now Elements 7 takes the concept to the next level, providing online sharing of images, online albums, backup and synchronization of albums stored on your hard disk with those stored online, and other features that can be used in conjunction with Photoshop Express and your free Photoshop.com account.

Other new features to know about include the following:

- ✔ **Improved support for audio and video files in the Organizer:** You can now include with these multimedia files fields of data, called *metadata,* including the name of the file, type, date created, date modified, and file size.

- ✔ **Smart Brush:** This new tool (and its more precise cousin, the Detail Smart Brush) lets you apply effects to specific areas of your image, with the painting strokes snapping to the edges of the objects in the image. The Smart Brush has plus/minus options so you can remove or re-paint over sections. The tool lets you paint around an object to select it and remove it from its background.

- ✔ **Touch Up in Quick Fix:** The popular Quick Fix mode now includes a Touch Up pane that has tools for fixing red-eye defects, a toothbrush tool for creating pearly white teeth in portraits, a blue skies tool to brighten dull skies, and a black-and-white high-contrast filter.

✔ **Tourist Remover:** Now renamed to Photomerge Scene Cleaner, this automated tool helps you remove passing cars, innocent bystanders (or otherwise), and other undesired elements. It works with Photomerge and your set of photos (some with, some without, the unwanted elements) and combines them to produce a clean version.

What else you got?

Of course, Photoshop and Photoshop Elements aren't the only image-editing options available. No single image editor is right for every digital photographer. There are four other editing applications you might be interested in. They've all been gobbled up over the years by graphics powerhouse Corel Corporation, which continues to offer them because of their respective unique capabilities.

Corel PhotoPaint. This is the image-editing program available only in the popular CorelDRAW Graphics suite for Windows XP and Windows Vista. It is a full-featured photo-retouching and image-editing program. It offers a full set of selection, retouching, and painting tools for manual image manipulations. It also includes convenient automated commands for a few common tasks, such as red-eye removal. PhotoPaint also accepts Photoshop plug-ins to expand its assortment of filters and special effects.

It includes the PhotoPaint Image Adjustment Lab, a one-click facility that lets you correct the color and tone of photos quickly and easily. By using the automatic correction control, you can fix most color and contrast problems. You can also manually remove color casts and adjust the brightness, contrast, highlights, shadows, and midtones of a photo. To help you choose the best photo-editing results, you can compare snapshots of a photo with different settings applied.

The Cutout Lab simplifies making selections, making it easier to isolate parts of your images.

You can touch up your cutouts by adding and removing detail, and you can redo and undo actions if necessary. In addition, you can choose to keep both the cutout and the original image or create a clip mask from the cutout.

Corel Paint Shop Pro. I describe this program in Book IV. It is a general-purpose image editor for Windows only that has gained a reputation as the "poor man's Photoshop" for providing a substantial portion of Photoshop's capabilities at a fraction of the cost. In recent years, however, Corel has stuffed in the features, going beyond achieving feature parity with Photoshop in many areas and exceeding Adobe's flagship product with specialized tools and effects. Indeed, the program has more than 500 special effects (counterparts to Photoshop's filters) that can add an amazing number of interesting looks to your photos, from the fading of an aged newspaper clipping to *faux* infrared transformations.

You need to evaluate the program carefully to determine whether its particular strengths and weaknesses are a good match for the mix of work you need to do.

Corel Painter. If PhotoPaint and Paint Shop Pro don't suit you, Corel has a third image-editing program for you to consider. Painter, available for Windows and Mac computers, is a unique image-editing program. It's more of a program for creating original images than it is an editor for images from your digital camera. Painter specializes in re-creating in digital form a wide range of traditional artist media, such as

Book V
Chapter 1

Introduction to
Photoshop CS4
and Photoshop
Elements 7

charcoal, pastels, and various kinds of paint. Painter includes a basic assortment of tools that you can use to edit existing images, but the program is really designed for artists to use to create original illustrations. It works especially well with a pressure-sensitive tablet, which lets you draw naturally.

Painter's natural media effects are really impressive. Although other programs allow you to select different paintbrush tools and adjust their color, size, edge softness, and a few other attributes, Painter takes the concept of brush effects to a whole new level.

In Painter, you can define not only the characteristics of the brush but also the texture of the paper or canvas; the thickness of the paint on the brush; and how the paint, brush, and paper interact. As a result, the program can realistically simulate the very different effects of a watercolor wash on hot-press paper, oil on canvas, pastels on a sanded board, or any of a huge assortment of other media/material combinations. Painter comes with a large inventory of predefined brushes and art materials that you can use or modify to suit your artistic impulse.

With the right settings, you can even watch the digital paint drip and run.

Corel PhotoImpact. This is a general-purpose, Windows-only photo-editing program with a particularly robust feature set. In addition to the usual selection, cropping, and fill tools, PhotoImpact features a rich assortment of brushes for painting, retouching, and cloning. You'll also find tools for text and vector shapes as well as tools for creating slices and image maps for use on the Web. PhotoImpact supports layers and includes a generous collection of effects filters, which you can expand with Photoshop plug-ins. Auto-process commands are available to automate many of the most common image correction and enhancement tasks.

If you frequently find yourself performing the same image manipulations on a number of files, you'll appreciate PhotoImpact's batch operations. With this feature, you can select multiple image files and then apply any one of a long list of filters, enhancements, or auto-process commands to all the selected files. What a timesaver!

Chapter 2: Making Selections

In This Chapter

✓ Making rectangular and elliptical selections

✓ Selecting single-pixel columns and rows

✓ Creating freeform selections

✓ Making polygonal selections

✓ Selecting image content based on colors in the image

A wag once noted that "Time is what keeps everything from happening at once." In a similar vein, *selections* are what let you modify only part of an image without your changes slopping over into parts of a picture that you *don't* want to manipulate. Selections let you fine-tune your photos a little at a time, making it easier to get the effects that you want.

Creating selections of the parts of the image that you intend to modify is the key to successful image manipulation. Indeed, the first step in many editing procedures is to focus the software's attention on the stuff you want to edit — an area that needs to be lighter, darker, a different color, or removed altogether. For this purpose, Photoshop and Photoshop Elements both offer a series of specialized tools that let you select geometric shapes, rows and columns of pixels, freeform shapes, and polygons. You can also find tools for making selections based on colors and pixel comparisons. The selection tool that you choose is based on the kind of area you want to select and the nature of the image. There are no hard and fast rules for when to use a particular tool over another; experience and experimentation show you which ones work best for different situations.

Making Simple Selections with the Marquee Tools

Photoshop has four tools that all go by the moniker *Marquee:* the Rectangular Marquee tool (for rectangles and squares), the Elliptical Marquee tool (for ovals and circles), the Single Row Marquee tool (to choose only one line of pixels), and the Single Column Marquee tool (to select a column that's one pixel wide).

The Marquee tools in Photoshop and Photoshop Elements are very simple to use. For example, you can drag the Rectangular or Elliptical Marquee tool to select a rectangle or oval. Hold down the Shift key to select perfect squares and circles. Photoshop's Marquee tools are shown in Figure 2-1. You can select the Marquee tools by clicking the triangle in the lower-right corner of the Tool palette or by pressing Shift+M repeatedly until the Rectangular or Elliptical Marquee tool is highlighted in the Tool palette.

Photoshop Elements offers the same two basic shape selection tools as Photoshop — the Rectangular and Elliptical Marquees — but does not offer the Single Row or Single Column

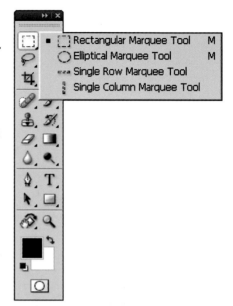

Figure 2-1: Click the shape you want to select and then drag to make the selection.

options. Figure 2-2 shows a rectangular selection in progress in Photoshop Elements.

Selecting geometric shapes

When you're ready to make your geometric selection, the procedure is quite simple. It requires only that you first select the layer that contains the area you want to edit (if your image has more than one layer). Then, you're ready to make the selection by following these steps:

1. **Click the Marquee selection tool in the Tool palette and choose the shape (Rectangular or Oval) that you want to use.**

2. **Move your mouse onto the image and click where you want the selection to begin.**

3. **Drag away from the starting point until the marquee outlines the selection you want to make.**

   If you want a perfect square or circle, press and hold the Shift key while you drag; release the mouse and then the Shift key when the selection is complete.

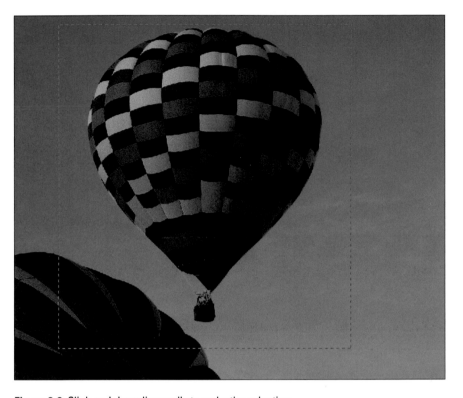

Figure 2-2: Click and drag diagonally to make the selection.

When you use the Shift key to make a perfectly square or circular selection (equal in width and height), be sure to release the mouse before releasing the Shift key when your selection is complete. If you release the key first, the selection will snap to the size and shape it would have been had you not used the Shift key at all.

Both the Rectangular and Elliptical Marquee tools allow you to choose from different Style settings. Your choices are Normal, Fixed Aspect Ratio (Constrained Aspect Ratio on the Mac), and Fixed Size. If you choose either of the latter two, additional options appear on the tool's Options bar, through which you can enter the ratio or dimensions, respectively. If you use the Normal style, these options are dimmed.

Selecting single-pixel rows and columns

Photoshop's Single Row Marquee and Single Column Marquee tools allow you to select a row or column that's one pixel wide simply by clicking the image to make the selection.

After you make the selection, you can delete it, paint it, fill it, cut it, or copy it. You can use these Marquee tools to draw lines or grids on the image, as shown in Figure 2-3, by filling selections with a solid color. These tools are also useful for creating a perfectly straight line anywhere on the image, going either up and down or left to right. If you want a soft edge to the selection, you can use the Options bar to set a Feather (fading) amount in excess of the default 0 pixels.

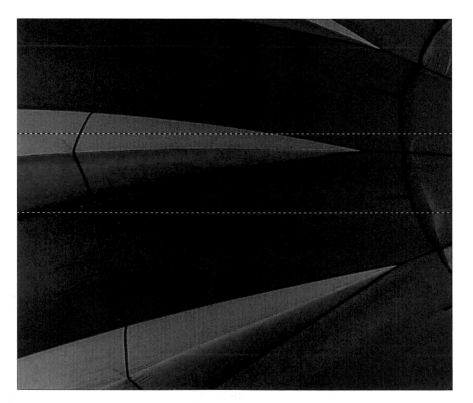

Figure 2-3: Use the single-pixel Marquees to draw lines or grids on your image.

Adding to, reducing, and combining selections

The Marquee tools' Options bar (the Photoshop version is shown in Figure 2-4) offers four icons that you can click to customize your selections. You can find these same tools, with the same powers, in the Options bars for the Lasso and the Magic Wand tools, as well. The buttons are descriptively named, and it's quite clear what they do:

- ✔ **New Selection:** Creates an entirely new selection.

- ✔ **Add to Selection:** Adds more area to an existing selection.

- ✔ **Subtract from Selection:** Removes part of a selection.

- ✔ **Intersect with Selection:** Creates a selection from only the overlapping area of two selections.

New selection

Add to selection

Subtract from selection

Intersect with selection

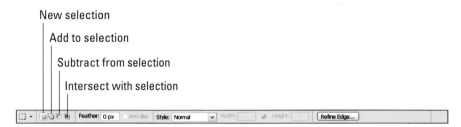

Figure 2-4: Choose one of the icons to create a new selection, or to add, subtract, or intersect with that selection.

Each button represents a selection mode and controls whether you can add to, take away from, or create a new selection based on the overlapping areas within two concurrent selections. If you're in New Selection mode, each time you click and drag the mouse, a new Marquee selection is created, replacing any other selections currently in place. If you switch to Add to Selection mode, you can select noncontiguous areas on the image, or you can make your current selection larger. Figure 2-5 shows both a set of noncontiguous selections (right), and a selection that was created by selecting three overlapping rectangles (upper left).

The Subtract from Selection mode lets you cut away from an existing selection or deselect noncontiguous parts of an initial selection. For Figure 2-6, I originally created a rectangular selection that went all around the tower; I tightened the selection by subtracting rectangular sections from the lower half of the original selection.

Using the Intersect with Selection mode allows you to create new selection shapes, such as the semicircular selection shown on the far right of Figure 2-7. This semicircle selection was formed from the overlapping areas of a circle and a rectangle. You can also move from one mode to another as you build or tear down selections.

Selection created from overlapping selections   Two contiguous selections

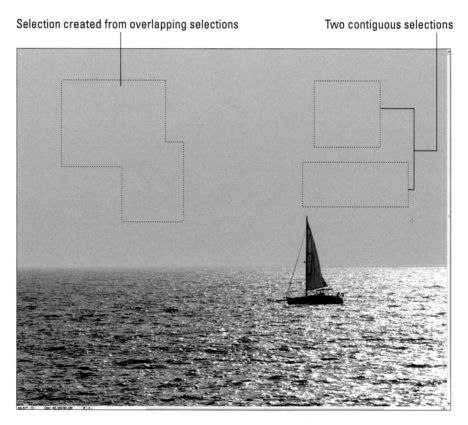

Figure 2-5: Use Add to Selection to create multiple selections or to extend a selection.

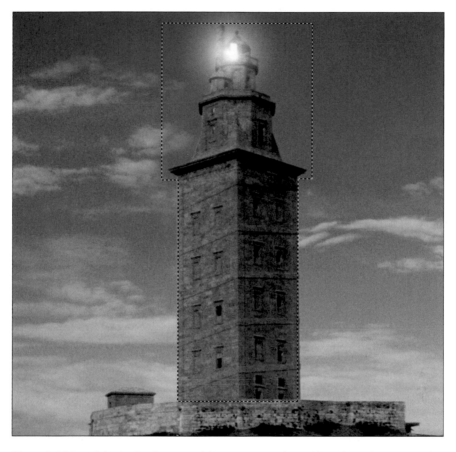

Figure 2-6: The original selection around the tower was trimmed by subtracting rectangular sections from it.

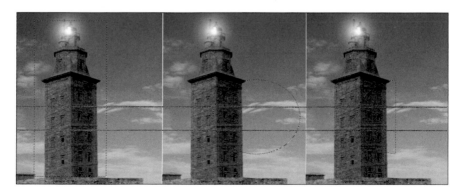

Figure 2-7: The left and middle selections produce the selection shown on the right when intersected.

Snagging Irregular Shapes with the Lasso Tools

The Lasso tool, available in both Photoshop and Photoshop Elements, is a freehand selection tool. You can use the regular Lasso tool to draw freeform shapes that become selections, or use the Polygonal Lasso tool to select polygons by dragging around an object with straight lines. You can also select by drawing with the Magnetic Lasso tool. In this case, you guide the cursor around an object, and the software selects pixels by comparing them with adjoining pixels and then chooses the ones that are different on the basis of color and light. In all its incarnations, the Lasso is a powerful selection tool — probably the one I use most when retouching photos.

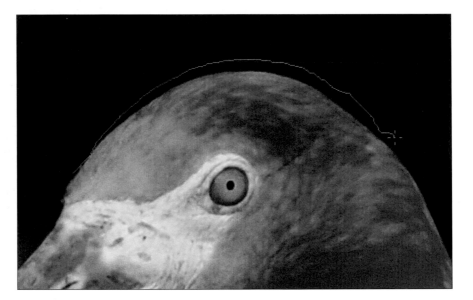

Figure 2-8: The Lasso can select irregularly shaped objects.

Selecting freeform shapes

The main Lasso tool is extremely easy to use. Just click and drag, drawing a loop around the section of your image you want to select. You can keep the selection border close to the edge of the object or grab a little more of the object to allow precise editing later on, as shown in Figure 2-8.

The other important thing to remember is to *close* your selection by coming back to the starting point. This prevents the software from guessing how you'd like the shape to finish, which usually results in some of the intended selection (the flamingo's head) being omitted, as shown in Figure 2-9. If you don't close the shape, Photoshop and Elements do it for you by connecting the start and endpoints with a straight line.

In addition to the regular Lasso, there are the Magnetic Lasso, which "sticks" to edges in your image as you drag it, and the Polygonal Lasso, which allows drawing outlines using mouse clicks to define straight lines.

Figure 2-9: Don't let Photoshop or Elements close the selection for you.

The Lasso Options bar offers a Feather setting, which allows you to add a number of fuzzy pixels to the selection's edges. This gives any fills applied to the selection a softer edge. Obviously, the higher the Feather setting, the softer the edge. A higher Feather setting also extends your fill or other edits, such as filter effects, farther beyond the actual selection.

You might remember from geometry class that a *polygon* is any shape made up of three or more straight sides. Triangles are polygons, as are squares, rectangles, and octagons. The Marquee tool takes care of rectangles and squares, but what if you want to select a triangular shape, or a shape that looks like a big sunburst, or an irregular shape? You use the Polygonal Lasso tool, shown in Figure 2-10. From simple shapes to complex, many-sided stars, the Polygonal Lasso tool gives you freeform selections with the precision of straight sides and sharp corners.

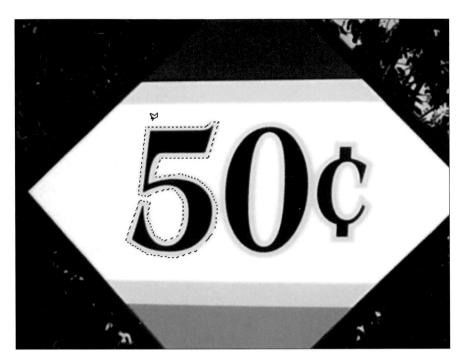

Figure 2-10: Using the Polygonal Lasso tool.

The tool works easily enough, and you can make it select just about any size or shape on your image by following these steps:

1. **Make sure that the layer you want to edit is the active layer; use the Layers palette to choose the layer.**

2. **Click the Polygonal Lasso tool in the Tool palette to activate it.**

3. **Click the point in your image where you want to begin making the selection.**

4. **Click the point where you want to create the first corner.**

    This creates the first side, and you can now draw the next side.

     Don't drag the mouse; just click where you want the corners to appear.

5. **Continue clicking until you've drawn all the sides that your selection needs.**

6. **Come back to the starting point and click (double-click if you're using a Mac) to close the shape and create the selection, which appears as a dotted line.**

You can make your sides as small as you want (just a few pixels long) or as long as you want. You can select the edges of complex shapes by drawing many short sides. You might find this handy when there isn't enough color difference between pixels to use the Magnetic Lasso tool effectively.

Selecting magnetically

If you want to select a particular object and that object is a different color or shade than the objects touching it, use the Magnetic Lasso tool to select it. The Magnetic Lasso tool works by following the edges of content in your image, comparing pixels while you drag your mouse, and automatically snapping to the edges where pixel values vary enough, based on your settings for the tool's options. Use the Magnetic Lasso's Options bar to control the Magnetic Lasso tool's sensitivity, detail, and the number of pixels it compares while you move along your desired path. Pen Pressure (or Stylus Pressure in some versions of Photoshop) might be dimmed unless you are using an accessory drawing device.

Before using the Magnetic Lasso tool, you can adjust the following settings in the Options bar:

- **Width:** Sets how far from the mouse path (as you drag) the pixel comparisons will be made.

- **Edge Contrast:** Sets the sensitivity anywhere from 1% to 100%. The higher the percentage you set, the higher the contrast must be between compared pixels before the Magnetic Lasso tool snaps to pixels to build the selection.

- **Frequency:** Changes the number of fastening points (or nodes) that you see along the line, as shown in Figure 2-11.

To use the Magnetic Lasso tool, you follow a procedure that's similar to the one you use for the Lasso and the Polygonal Lasso tools, with minor variations:

1. **Make sure that the right layer is selected so that your selection applies to the right content.**

2. **Click the Magnetic Lasso tool in the Tool palette to select it.**

3. **Make any necessary changes to the tool's settings so that it will work to the best of its ability within the photo at hand.**

    You can adjust the width of the Magnetic Lasso tool's attraction, how many points it lays down, and the amount of contrast that must be present for the attraction to take hold. The default values work best in most situations.

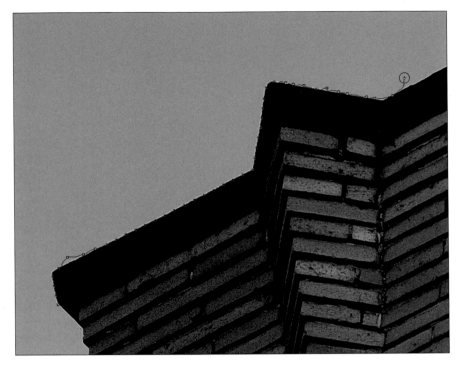

Figure 2-11: The more fastening points you specify, the closer the selection will adhere to the object you're selecting.

4. **Click the image to begin your selection.**

5. **Move the cursor and click along the edge of the desired object.**

   A click redirects the line whenever it begins to veer off the path you'd like it to follow.

6. **When your moving and clicking takes you back to the starting point, click (or double-click) the starting point to finish the selection.**

Clicking to redirect the Magnetic Lasso's path is especially helpful if you get to a section of the photo where there isn't very much difference between the color and brightness of the pixels and the object you're trying to select. Sometimes, the Edge Contrast setting won't help you, and you have to redirect the selection yourself or use the other Lasso tools to augment or reduce the selection after using the Magnetic Lasso tool to make the main selection.

Has your Magnetic Lasso gone crazy, and you can't bring it back into line by clicking and moving? Press the Esc (Escape) key to abandon the current selection and start over.

The Magic Wand Tool's Digital Prestidigitation

The Magic Wand tool selects based on color. If you want to select all the flesh tones on a face or all the green leaves on a tree, you need only turn on this tool and click somewhere on the face or on a particular leaf, and the rest of the face or tree that matches the brightness level and color of that original pixel is selected. You can adjust how the tool works by increasing or decreasing the Tolerance level required for a match, which increases or decreases the number of pixels that are selected when you click the mouse in the image. The higher the Tolerance level you set, the wider the range of pixels included in the selection.

Making and adjusting selections based on color

You can augment your selection (without changing selection modes) by holding down the Shift key while you click the image. For example, as shown in Figure 2-12, more of the picture is selected by Shift-clicking a slightly different shade of the color originally selected with the first click of the Magic Wand tool.

To reduce the amount of the image that's selected, press the Alt key (Option if you're on a Mac) and click an area that's selected. The pixels in that area are removed from the selection, and you can continue adding to the selection elsewhere or simply perform whatever edit you'd planned for the color-based selection.

Controlling the magic

To increase or decrease the threshold for the tool's selections, adjust the Tolerance setting on the Options bar (as shown in Figure 2-13). The higher the Tolerance you set, the more pixels that Photoshop or Photoshop Elements sees as a close match of the original pixel that you clicked. If you set the Tolerance to a very low number (15 or less), you'll find that very few pixels meet the selection criteria.

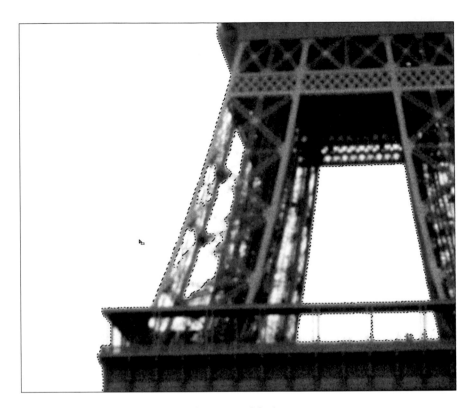

Figure 2-12: Keep Shift-clicking to select more of the image.

Another setting that's useful for controlling the Magic Wand tool's selection is the Contiguous option. This option, when selected, limits the selection to those pixels touching the original pixel you clicked and to the pixels contiguous with those pixels, and so on. If you want to select pixels that aren't touching the original pixel and the first batch that was selected, clear this option or use the Shift key and click elsewhere in the image.

If you don't get the edges of your selection exactly right, you can click the Refine Edge button in the Options tool bar to produce the dialog box shown in Figure 2-14. It lets you expand or contract the selection edge, feather it (so it fades out gradually), or smooth the rough edges of the selection edge (to make it conform more closely to the edge of your object). The Refine Edge option is available with other selection tools, too, such as the Marquees and Lassos.

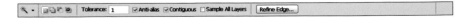

Figure 2-13: Setting the Tolerance level.

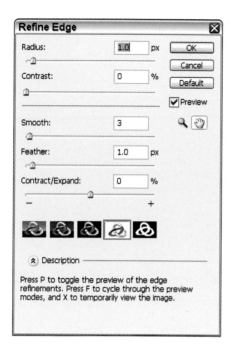

Figure 2-14: Refine Edge lets you adjust the borders of your selection.

Specialized Selection Tools

Both Photoshop and Photoshop Elements offer tools that go beyond the normal selection tools that you find in just about any image-editing application. By giving you the ability to paint your selections with a familiar tool — the Brush tool — you can make very fine or very large selections quickly and easily.

In addition, both applications offer a Select menu, which you can use to control the existing selection, no matter which selection tool you used to make it.

Working with the Quick Select/Selection Brush tools

Both Photoshop and Elements offer a Quick Select tool (nested with the Magic Wand in Photoshop, and a stand-alone tool in Elements' toolbox), which allows you to drag selections within your image. The image editor will try to find the edges of objects as you drag, and create a selection, as shown in Figure 2-15. Photoshop Elements offers an additional selection tool called the Selection Brush tool, which allows you to select a snaking, freeform line by dragging your mouse in any design you desire.

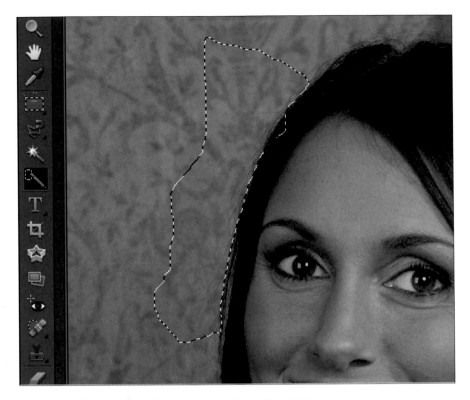

Figure 2-15: Photoshop and Elements have a handy Quick Select tool.

With the Selection Brush, you can set the size and style of the brush, and you can also set the brush to Selection or Mask mode.

- ✔ **Selection mode** simply creates a freeform, snaking selection that follows the path of your mouse while you drag. You can paint over and over in an area to select a shape rather than a snaking line, or you can use a very big brush to select a large area with a single stroke.

- ✔ **Mask mode** places a light-red wash over the whole image, except for the places where you dragged the Selection Brush tool. If you made no selection prior to entering Mask mode, your strokes with the Selection Brush tool create the masked areas. Masked areas are excluded from your selection. If you revert to Selection mode, your masked areas are not affected by any subsequent editing in the form of painting, filling, deleting, cutting, copying, or pasting.

Selecting in Quick Mask mode

Much like Element's Selection Brush in Mask mode, Photoshop allows you to place your image in Quick Mask mode and then use the Brush, Pencil, and Fill tools to make a selection or to paint the area that you *don't* want selected (whichever is easier for you). To enter Quick Mask mode, click the Quick Mask button in the Tool palette and then begin painting or drawing the outline of the area to be masked, as shown in Figure 2-16. If you want to fill a shape and make that a mask, use the Fill tool to mask the area inside the outline.

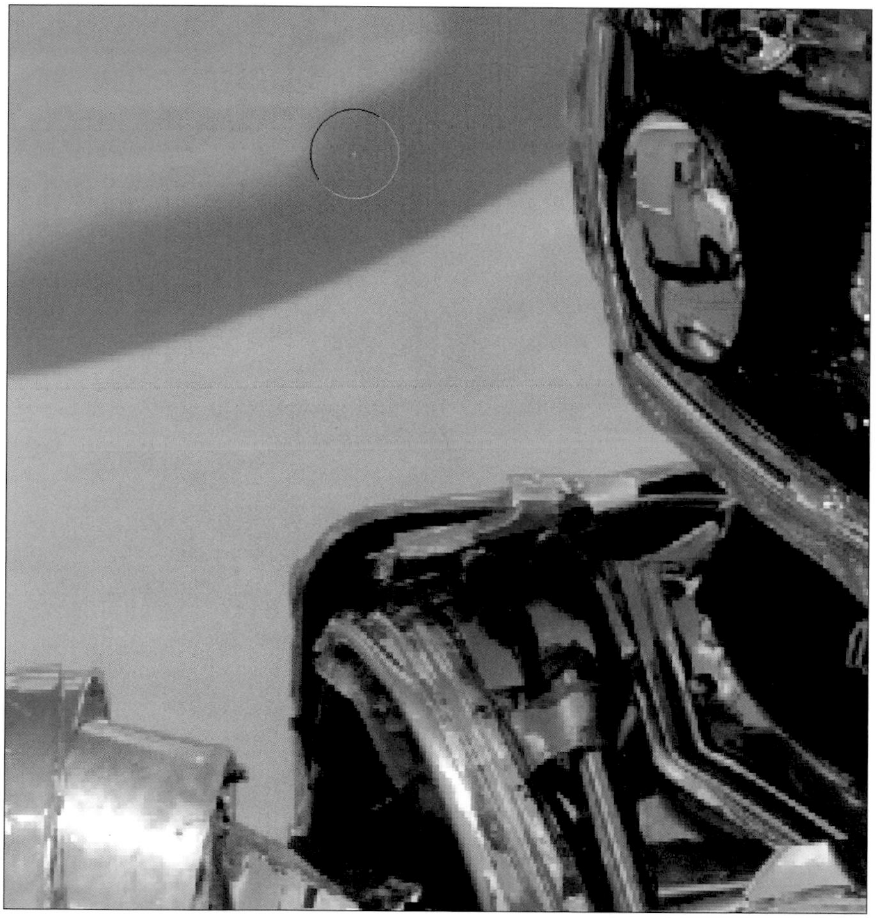

Figure 2-16: Quick Mask mode lets you paint selections.

If, instead, you want to paint the area that is not selected, double-click the Quick Mask icon on the Tool palette before entering Quick Mask mode and choose Color Indicates Mask Area (instead of Color Indicates Selected Area) in the dialog box that pops up. When you return to standard editing mode, your mask becomes a selection that excludes the areas you painted, drew, and/or filled. If you want them to become the selected areas, choose Select⇨Inverse from the main menu.

Not sure when you'd use Quick Mask mode? Imagine a selection that's so small or fine that you can't make it with anything but the Brush or Pencil tool set to 1 pixel. Or if you simply feel more comfortable with the painting and drawing tools, you might do better making your selection by using familiar features.

Using the Select Menu

You use the Select menu to control and manipulate your existing selections, to create selections, and to deselect areas that are currently selected. In Figure 2-17, which shows Photoshop's Select menu at left and Elements' version at right, many of the menu commands also have keyboard shortcuts.

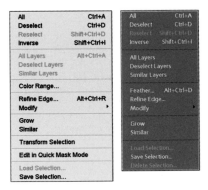

Both versions have the capability of saving a current selection under a name you choose, and loading a saved selection for re-use later. Both have a Modify option to expand, contract, and perform other transformations on a selection. In Elements, the Feather (fade out) option is

Figure 2-17: The Select menu lets you modify, load, and save selections.

in the main Select menu; in Photoshop, it's tucked away in the Modify menu. You can Grow selections into contiguous pixels, or you can choose Similar to select additional pixels of a similar color and brightness to those already selected. You can see that the Refine Edges command, which I mentioned earlier in this chapter, is also available.

One of the most convenient commands on the Select menu is the Inverse command, which you can use to turn a mask into a selection or a selection into a mask. If you selected an area with one of the selection tools, you can invert that selection so that everything but that area is selected and editable. Conversely, if you use Quick Mask mode (Photoshop) or the Selection Brush in

Mask mode (Photoshop Elements) to make a mask, you can invert that mask so that the previously masked and uneditable area becomes the selected, editable area.

Another very useful command on Photoshop's version of the Select menu (but not found in Elements) is the Transform Selection command. With it, you can reshape an existing selection, as shown in Figure 2-18. Here, I start with a rectangular selection, created with the Rectangular Marquee tool, and I reshape the box by dragging the box handles that appear on the perimeter of the selection when I issue the Transform Selection command.

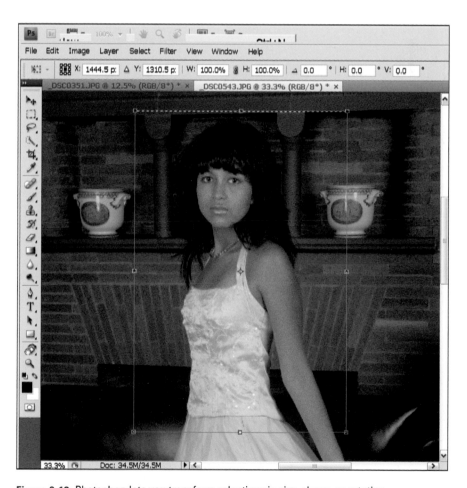

Figure 2-18: Photoshop lets you transform selections in size, shape, or rotation.

While transforming your shape, you can rotate it (point to the corner handles; when your mouse turns to a bent arrow, drag clockwise or counter-clockwise) and make the shape wider, narrower, taller, or shorter. You can also resize it from the corner handles to make it bigger or smaller while retaining the current width-height ratio. The Transform Selection command also invokes a new set of options on the Options bar. You can enter a degree of rotation, new width and height dimensions, and new position *(x* and *y)* coordinates.

When you finish making your selection transformations, press Enter to formally apply them. If you want to skip the transformations in progress and return to the selection as it was, press the Esc (Escape) key.

Chapter 3: Brushing Away Problems with Digital Photos

In This Chapter

✔ **Identifying painting and drawing tools**

✔ **Mastering brushes and pencils**

✔ **Customizing Brush and Pencil tools for specific jobs**

✔ **Finding third-party brush sets online**

*O*bviously, Photoshop CS4 and Photoshop Elements 7's painting tools have many uses when it comes to creating original artwork. You can paint pictures from scratch, starting with a white or transparent background, and paint or draw anything from the realistic to the abstract. These original works of art can end up in print, on the Web, or both. Because this is a book about working with digital images, however, I focus on using these tools for retouching and editing photographs.

Photoshop and Photoshop Elements' Painting and Drawing Tools

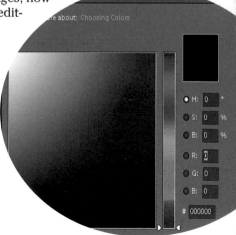

The two applications' painting and drawing tools are basically the same, but you can find a few in Photoshop that you won't find in Elements, and vice versa. Table 3-1 lists all the painting and drawing tools, identifying which of the two applications contains them.

Table 3-1	Painting Tools by Application	
Tool	**Photoshop CS4**	**Photoshop Elements 7**
Brush tool	✓	✓
Impressionist Brush tool		✓
History Brush tool	✓	
Art History Brush tool	✓	
Pencil tool	✓	✓
Airbrush tool (Option for Brush tool)	✓	✓
Color Replacement tool	✓	✓
Smart Brush tool		✓
Detail Smart Brush tool		✓

You can find more tools for customizing your brushes in Photoshop than in Elements, and more third-party brushes have been created for Photoshop and are available online. You won't feel terribly limited or bored by Elements' brush customization tools, however, and the core settings for size, shape, color, and so on are in both applications.

This chapter concentrates on the use of the Brush and the Pencil tools. The History Brush tool (which restores parts of an image from a saved version) and the Art History Brush tool (which does the same thing but adds a brush-stroke effect) are beyond the scope of this book. You can find an entire chapter on using these two tools and related implements in *Photoshop CS4 All-in-One Desk Reference For Dummies,* by Barbara Obermeier and Ted Padova (Wiley). You can find more about the Impressionist Brush tool (which paints using artsy brush strokes) in *Photoshop Elements 7 For Dummies,* by Barbara Obermeier (Wiley).

However, all the controls for setting the size, fuzziness, and other parameters of the Brush tool *do* apply to other brush-like tools, such as the Art History Brush tool, the Blur/Sharpen tools, the Toning tools (Dodge/Burn/Sponge), and the Clone Stamp. Thus, what you read in this chapter can be applied to those tools as well.

Some people consider the Smudge tool as a painting tool because it can be set to apply the foreground color if you put it in Finger Painting mode and also because it does manipulate colors in the same way a brush or your fingertip would if you were working with real paints or pastels. On the other hand, I think it's more of a retouching and special effects tool.

Working with Brushes and Pencils

Photoshop's and Photoshop Elements' brushes and pencils are easy to use and customize and can apply a wide variety of colors, textures, and special effects. Painting and drawing with Photoshop or Elements mostly requires a steady hand and the proper view so that you're zoomed in close enough to see what you're doing. Figure 3-1 shows an extremely magnified view of a portion of an image, with the Brush tool at work filling in some rough spots in an old photo.

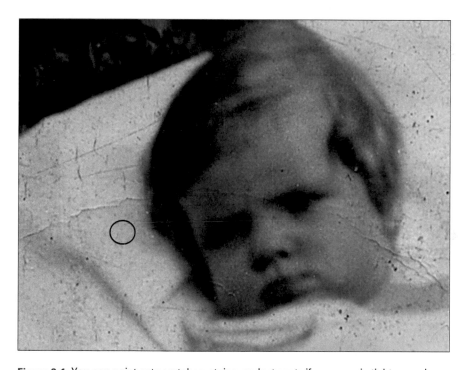

Figure 3-1: You can paint out scratches, stains, or dust spots if you zoom in tight enough.

You can also paint larger areas, filling in space lost to a tear or to add a colored frame around an image. You can even create new content: Just paint lines or shapes or simply apply a wash of color to a black-and-white or faded color photo for an interesting effect. Whatever your painting or drawing goal, these two applications offer the right tools for the job.

Painting with the Brush tool

The Brush tool, found in both Photoshop and Photoshop Elements, can paint tiny dots, short strokes, or longer lines as small as a single pixel in width or as large as several hundred pixels. Using the tool is easy. Just click it on the Tool palette (or press B on the keyboard) to activate it, and drag or click (or both) the image. You want to make sure that you're painting on the appropriate layer first, of course.

If you want to control how the brush applies paint, you can change the following settings before you start painting:

- ✔ **Color:** The color or tone painted by the brush.

- ✔ **Size:** The size of the brush. Note that in Photoshop and Elements, you can set the size directly from a slider in the Options bar.

- ✔ **Mode:** How the pixels painted by the brush blend with existing pixels.

- ✔ **Opacity:** The transparency of the pixels.

- ✔ **Flow:** How quickly the pixels are applied while you stroke.

- ✔ **Airbrush:** Changes any brush tool to a fuzzy airbrush effect.

With the exception of color, you can adjust all these settings from the tool's Options bar, shown in Figure 3-2. If you're using Photoshop, you can tinker with several more settings (and a few more for Elements users, too), but I get to those in the upcoming section, "Customizing Your Brushes and Pencils." The settings listed here are those that you'd want to adjust whenever you're painting. More elaborate changes would be needed in fewer, more specific cases.

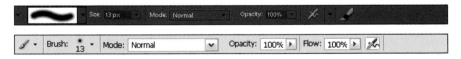

Figure 3-2: The Brush Options bars for Elements 7 (top) and Photoshop CS4 (bottom).

One setting — Color — can't be set from the Options bar but can be set through the Color Picker. You open the Color Picker by clicking the toolbar's Set Foreground Color button, shown at left in Figure 3-3. From within the Color Picker (shown at right in Figure 3-3), you can choose a color in three ways:

- ✔ **By eye:** Click in an area that contains the color you want to choose.

- ✔ **By setting color levels:** Type values in the H, S, and B (hue, saturation, and brightness) or the R, G, and B (red, green, blue) boxes.

- ✔ **By using a hexadecimal number:** Enter this number in the # field to create colors in the language of your Web browser.

Select the Only Web Colors check box if you want the Color Picker to show only the 240 colors considered completely Web safe. (With virtually all users having monitors that can show more than 256 colors, Web-safe colors are not the concern they once were.)

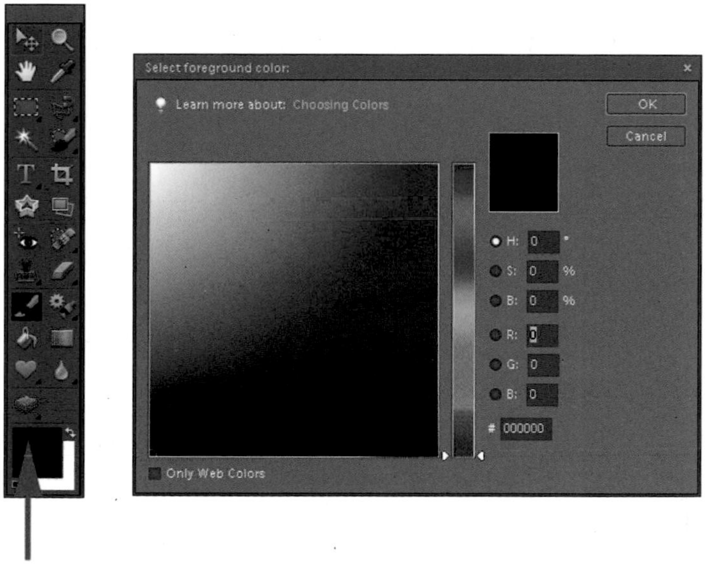

Figure 3-3: Click the Foreground Color button (bottom left) to access the Color Picker (right).

If you want to paint with a color currently in use elsewhere in the image or in another open image, click the toolbar's Eyedropper tool and sample (click) the color that you want to use. This makes that color the new foreground color.

Working with the Pencil tool

The Pencil tool is also found in both applications and works much like the Brush tool. The only real difference is the nature of the line drawn. Just like you'd expect a paintbrush to apply a relatively soft line, you'd expect a pencil to draw a sharper line, depending on the hardness of the lead. The Pencil tool offers its own set of adjustments through the Options bar in Elements, as shown in Figure 3-4. (The Photoshop CS4 version is similar.) From the Options bar, you can control the Pencil's size and density so that you can make whatever large or small edits are required.

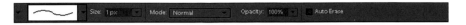

Figure 3-4: The Pencil Options bar in Elements 7.

Use the Pencil tool's settings to control the size, mode, and opacity of the line you draw. You can also choose from a smaller set of styles, most of which are solid, fine lines. The Options bar also has an Auto Erase option, which allows you to draw the background color over any pixels currently colored in the foreground color as well as apply the foreground color only where no color is currently applied. Auto Erase is sort of a confusing name because no real erasing occurs — but you get the idea.

Customizing Your Brushes and Pencils

Beyond the basic adjustments that you can make with the Brush and the Pencil tools' Options bars, you can work with an additional set of options in Photoshop Elements (see Figure 3-5) or with a set of Brush Presets (shown in the Photoshop interface in Figure 3-6).

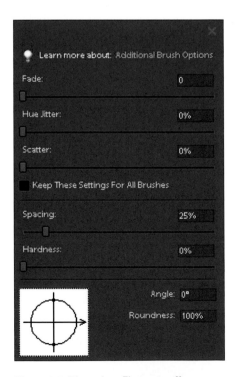

Figure 3-5: Photoshop Elements offers some extensive brush controls.

The Photoshop CS4 Brushes palette consists of 11 different options, each of which has its own dialog box. As you pass the mouse over each of the brush tips, a ToolTip pops up with information about that brush, as shown in Figure 3-6. To view each of the 11 sets of options, make sure Expanded View is selected in the Brushes palette's fly-out menu (that right-pointing triangle at the upper right of the palette). Then, selecting any of the 11 sets of options causes that option's dialog box to appear. Make the changes you want in each option's dialog box. You can activate or deactivate any particular option by marking the check box to the left of the option name. Figure 3-7 shows the settings for the Texture option.

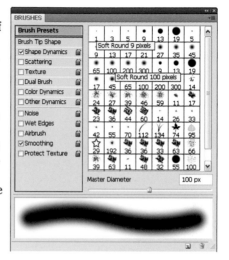

Figure 3-6: Photoshop has an entire palette devoted solely to brushes.

 Refer to the preview area at the foot of the Brushes palette to see how your new settings affect the brush size and shape that you select. The sample stroke provided shows you what effect the brush will have when you apply it to your photo.

 If your Brushes palette is missing, simply choose Window⇨Brushes from the main menu to bring it back. You can also place it on the docking well (next to the File Browser) or drag it to the workspace to move it freely like the rest of the palettes.

Choosing the right size and shape

Whether you're working in Photoshop or Elements, the success of your brush with a given image depends on setting the right size and shape for it.

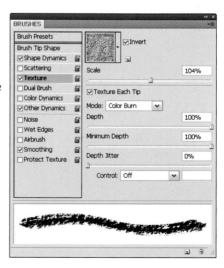

Figure 3-7: Need to clean up a vintage photo's matte finish? Use a textured brush and customize the texture here.

Photoshop Elements brush settings

Photoshop Elements offers a list of Brush Presets in the form of a drop-down dialog box, as shown in Figure 3-8, accompanied by a separate Size setting. You can change the brush tip display from Stroke (shown in the figure) to thumbnails, or text only, using the drop-down list that appears when you click the double right-pointing triangles at the upper right of the dialog box.

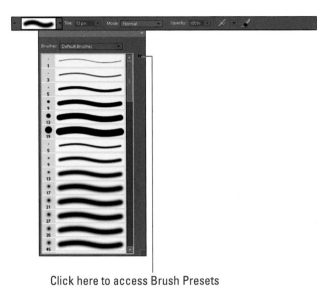

Click here to access Brush Presets

Figure 3-8: Photoshop Elements' Brush presets provide an extensive set of styles and shapes.

To change the shape of your brush in Photoshop Elements, follow these steps:

1. **Click the Brush tool on the Tool palette to activate it.**

2. **From the Options bar, set the style and size of the brush by using the drop-down list and slider, respectively.**

3. **Click the brush icon at the right side of the Options bar.**

4. **In the resulting dialog box, adjust the angle by entering a number for the angle you want to use or by dragging the arrow clockwise or counterclockwise, as shown in Figure 3-9.**

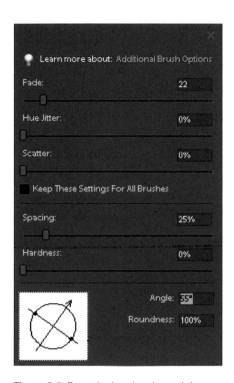

Figure 3-9: Drag the brush schematic's arrow to change the angle of the brush tip.

You might find that a specific angle is more desirable for painting the kind of strokes you want, and you can use this setting to set that angle.

5. **Adjust the Roundness setting the same way — by entering a number or by dragging the big black dots closer to or farther away from the center of the sample brush shape, as shown in Figure 3-10.**

Dragging inward makes for a horizontally flatter brush; dragging outward makes the brush vertically flatter.

6. **Tinker, as desired, with other sliders — Spacing, Hue Jitter, Hardness, and Scatter.**

7. **Click your image to begin painting or click somewhere on the workspace to close the More Options box.**

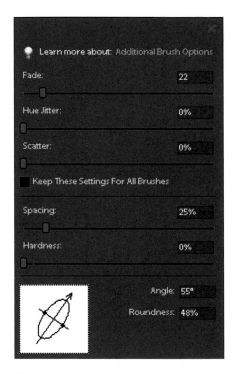

Figure 3-10: Make a soft, round, fat brush or a lean, mean, flat brush.

Photoshop brush settings

If you're using Photoshop, you can change your brush shape by using the Brush Tip Shape option of the Brushes palette, as shown in Figure 3-11. The resulting settings look much like Elements' settings. You can drag a brush tip schematic to change the angle and roundness of the tip, and you can also adjust the size (diameter) of the tip itself.

Here's a quick summary of all the customization changes you can make to Photoshop's brushes:

- ✓ **Brush tip shape:** Here, you can select the size and shape of the brush tip, including its diameter, angle, roundness, hardness, and spacing.

- ✓ **Shape dynamics:** Make your brush strokes appear to be more natural and less machine-like (especially if you're using a digital tablet) with these adjustments. They modify the degree of randomness or variation produced when a stroke is drawn, including the amount of fade, size, jitter angle, roundness, and other options. The higher the value, the greater the amount of variance produced for each option. Note that some of these options apply only when you are using a pressure-sensitive digital tablet.

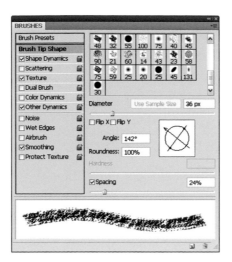

Figure 3-11: Control your Photoshop CS4 brush and its shape, size, and roundness setting.

✓ **Scattering:** Use this control to vary the amount and position of individual brush marks in a stroke. The higher the value, the larger the number of brush marks and the farther apart they are. When Both Axes is selected, the brush marks are distributed radially, as if on a curve. The Count controls the number of brush marks at each spacing point. The higher the value, the greater the number of marks.

✓ **Texture:** The Texture control lets you add a preset or custom pattern to a brush stroke. It includes these options:

- *Invert:* Mark the Invert check box to reverse the light and dark pixels in the pattern.

- *Scale:* The Scale control adjusts the size of the pattern in each stroke.

- *Texture Each Tip:* Texture Each Tip applies each tip as it is stroked, giving a more saturated effect.

- *Depth:* The Depth control sets how prominently the pattern appears against the brush stroke.

- *Minimum Depth:* Minimum Depth specifies the minimum depth that the paint of each stroke shows through the pattern.

- *Mode:* Mode lets you choose one of Photoshop's blending modes.

✓ **Dual Brush:** Yes! You can have a brush with two tips. The second tip can have attributes of its own, which you can set here. You can also specify a blending mode between the two tips so that the strokes they draw merge together in a predetermined way.

✔ **Color Dynamics:** You can also create a multicolored brush with this control. It uses your foreground and background colors to generate variations that give the stroke a more natural, organic look. You can introduce jitter to the hue, saturation, brightness, and purity of the colors as well as some randomness between the foreground and background colors as a stroke is drawn.

✔ **Other Dynamics:** These controls add some natural-looking randomness to the opacity and flow factors of a brush, again making the brush stroke look more natural and less machine-like.

Here are some tip characteristics that you can modify:

✔ **Noise:** This adds random pixels to your brush tips, giving them texture, which works especially well with feathered brushes that fade out at the edges.

✔ **Wet Edges:** This option creates a stroke that looks like watercolor, with color that builds up along the edges.

✔ **Airbrush:** This option gives the brush tip a fuzzy, airbrushed look.

✔ **Smoothing:** Use this control to help smooth out curves when drawing arcs with the brush, which is especially helpful with a pressure-sensitive tablet.

✔ **Protect Texture:** If you want all of your textured brush tips to use a uniform texture, apply this option.

Obtaining third-party brush sets

The brush sets that come with Photoshop and Photoshop Elements are fairly extensive (see Photoshop's in the Brush drop-down list options menu, shown in Figure 3-12), but you might pine for more of them.

A quick online search will net you several sites where third-party brush sets are available, usually for a small fee. Some sites probably offer brushes for free, but these are not in abundance. One site to check out is www.graphic xtras.com/products/psbrush.htm. This particular site is chock-full of interesting new brushes, which you can order for about $30 (U.S.). The site, which is based out of Great Britain, charges in pounds sterling, so the day's exchange rate dictates what you pay. Brushes are offered for both Windows and Mac computers.

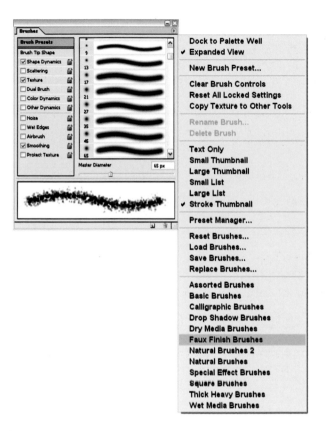

Figure 3-12: Lots of brushes come with Photoshop CS4, but you might want more, more, more!

Chapter 4: Restoring Images

In This Chapter

✓ **Shedding light and casting shadows**

✓ **Blending and bringing focus to your images**

✓ **Healing wounded photos**

*A*dobe's image-editing applications do a great job of fixing problem images. Some of the most common problems that you'll encounter with your photos (both old and new) relate to lighting, clarity, detail, and damage caused by poor storage methods. Even a vintage black-and-white or sepia photo, if properly stored, won't show unacceptable signs of age. Any photo, however, that is tossed in a drawer or put in a frame and exposed to direct sunlight for years will start to look a bit shabby and will probably lose much of its detail and depth. A color photo will lose some color due to fading. It might also have scratches and scuffs, as shown in Figure 4-1, which displays a photo with several problems that require Photoshop's or Elements' restorative tools. I show you how to repair this photo in this chapter.

Because digital images saved on a hard drive or removable media don't suffer from the same ailments as photographic prints, negatives, and slides, your restoration work will invariably involve scanned versions of these originals. This chapter focuses primarily on repairing scratches, stains, dust, and lightness/darkness problems in old monochrome images, but the techniques apply equally well to color photos with the same problems. It's just a little easier to concentrate on lightening, darkening, and repairing photos when color isn't a major concern. I show you how to work with color photo restorations in Book V, Chapter 5.

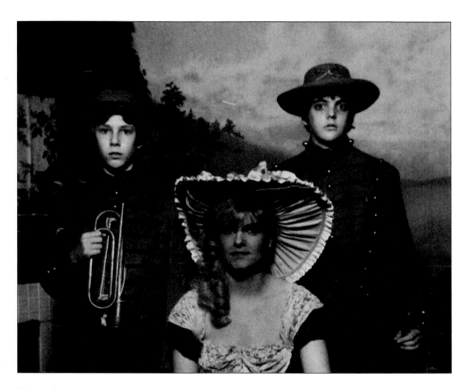

Figure 4-1: You can paint out scratches, stains, or dust spots if you zoom in tight enough.

Adding Light and Shadows

Whether because of fading with time or from poor original photographic technique, many of your photos might need more light or more shadows — or more of both — in different areas of the same photo. What to do? Photoshop and Photoshop Elements' Dodge and Burn tools rush to the rescue!

Using the Dodge tool to lighten tones

The Dodge tool lightens portions of your image. The process is simple:

1. **Click the Dodge tool in the Tool palette to activate it.**

   You might need to switch to the Dodge tool if the Burn or Sponge tool is currently displayed on that button in the Tool palette. Hold down the Shift key and press O until the tool that you want is active. (In Elements, you don't have to hold down the Shift key.)

Multiple tools that are nested under a single icon are indicated by a triangle in the lower-right corner of the icon on the Tool palette. Click this icon to select nested tools directly.

2. **Check out the Options bar, shown in Figure 4-2, and decide whether you need to make changes to the range of tones that will be affected or to the exposure (degree of intensity) that the tool will apply.**

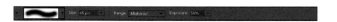

Figure 4-2: The Dodge tool's Options bar in Elements; Photoshop's Options bar is similar.

The Range drop-down menu determines which tones the Dodge tool affects: Shadows (the dark areas), Highlights (the light areas), or Midtones (everything in between). Most of the time, you want to stick to Midtones, but if you want to open up some inky shadows or darken areas that are a little washed out, you can do that, too.

The Exposure menu determines how rapidly the lightening process occurs. Avoid lightening too much, too quickly. A value between 15 and 35 percent enables you to lighten slowly. You can always return to an area and lighten it some more if you haven't applied enough dodging.

3. **Using the Options bar, set the size of the brush that you'll use to apply the light. You can set the brush size to match the size of the object you want to lighten.**

You can choose the kind of brush you use just as you would the ordinary Brush tool. Both use the exact same Brush palette. You can find more on setting brush sizes in Book V, Chapter 3.

4. **Drag over the area to be lightened or click a single spot, such as a face or some other distinct area that's suffering from too much shadow.**

Figure 4-3 shows the woman's face before and after dodging.

If your image isn't very crisp or detailed and you have no desire to make it that way, use one of the textured brush settings for the Dodge tool. This can apply light in a dappled or mottled way, matching the image's overall look — perhaps a desirable one, in the case of vintage photos.

Burning your image to darken areas

The opposite of the Dodge tool, the Burn tool darkens areas. This can bring out facial features lost to a sunny day or faded details in clothing or a garden, or it can add depth lost to a photo that has faded with time or exposure to sunlight.

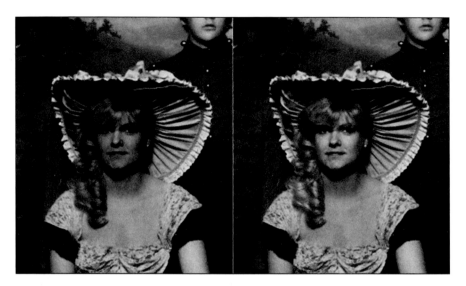

Figure 4-3: Use the Dodge tool to lighten shadows in faces.

To use the Burn tool in either Photoshop or Elements, follow these steps:

1. **Click the Burn tool in the Tool palette to activate it.**

   The Burn tool might be hidden under the Sponge or Dodge tool; they all share the same position on the toolbox. Hold down the Shift key and press O until the Burn tool is active. (You don't need to hold down the Shift key in Elements.)

2. **Check the Options bar (as shown in Figure 4-4) for any adjustments you'd like to make.**

   You can adjust the range and exposure, which respectively control which elements of the image (Shadows, Midtones, or Highlights) are affected by the Burning process and how quickly the darkening process takes place.

3. **Choose a Brush size in the Brush palette.**

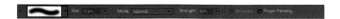

Figure 4-4: The Burn tool's Options bar.

4. **Begin darkening your image by dragging over the areas to be made more shadowy or by clicking a single spot.**

   Figure 4-5 shows a face being darkened by a single click with a brush that's set to the same diameter as the face.

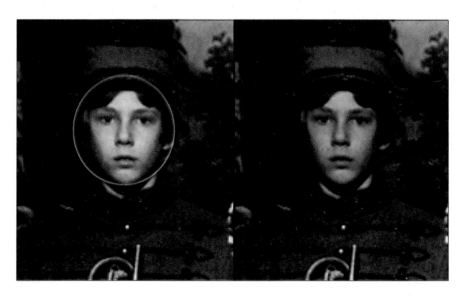

Figure 4-5: Paint with the Burn tool to darken an area.

Don't go too far with the Burn tool. If your image is in color, excessive use of the tool creates a brownish, singed look that makes the image appear literally burned. If your image is in black-and-white or grayscale, this won't happen; the worst that can occur is that your burned areas look so dark that details are obliterated.

Using Smudging, Sharpening, and Blurring Tools

When it comes to retouching photos with Photoshop and Photoshop Elements, you'll probably use the Sharpen and Blur tools quite frequently. These tools are good for heightening or diffusing details in some of an image, an entire image, or along the edges of content that's been pasted into the picture from elsewhere. The Smudge tool is also a powerful ally, but you might find that good mouse skills are required before you can make

really successful use of it. Figure 4-6
shows these three tools in Photoshop
Elements. As in Photoshop, the tools
share one button, and you must switch
between them by holding down the
Shift key and pressing R until the icon
for the tool that you want appears.
This isn't an operational hardship, but
it makes identifying them in one image
here rather difficult!

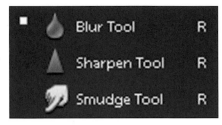

Figure 4-6: The Blur, Sharpen, and Smudge
tools in Photoshop Elements.

Although the Sharpen tool's name
clearly indicates what it does, the Blur and Smudge tool names might lead
you to believe that the tools essentially do the same thing. In reality, however, the Blur tool is a more finely grained tool than the Smudge tool is in
terms of its results. Whether applied to a small area or painted over a large
field, the Blur tool's effects are uniform: It makes the affected area fuzzy
and less distinct. (Technically speaking, the Blur tool reduces the contrast
between the pixels, and our eyes see this reduced contrast as blur.) The
Smudge tool smears the pixels into each other, and its effects are entirely
dependent on the length and direction of your mouse or pen strokes.

What the three tools do have in common is how highly dependent they are
upon their Options bar settings — or rather, how much *you* are dependent on
the settings. Without controlling how drastic or subtle an effect these tools
have, you might end up with very little blurring or too much sharpening — or
perhaps some smudging that makes it look like you were drunk when you
tried to retouch the photo. Figure 4-7 shows an image in which the Sharpen
tool was taken a bit too far; instead of adding contrast between pixels (to
make them all stand out just a bit), the result is a very unpleasant effect —
definitely not what you want.

Finger painting to blend colors and textures

You use the Smudge tool to drag tone from one spot to another spot right
next to it. Think of it like blending pastels or chalk on paper with your finger.
The smudging process can smooth an edge, blend two adjoining colors, or
smoosh out a background, as shown in Figure 4-8. You can also turn on a
Finger Painting option and bring the current foreground color into the mix,
smearing it into the image at whatever point you're dragging the mouse.

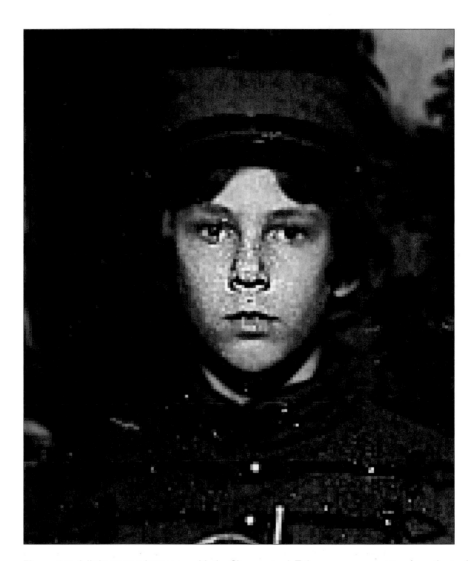

Figure 4-7: A little goes a long way with the Sharpen tool. Take care as you set up how the tool works.

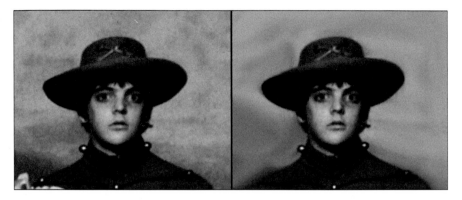

Figure 4-8: Blend a background or soften sharp edges with the Smudge tool.

To use the Smudge tool, follow these steps:

1. **Click the Smudge tool in the Tool palette to activate it.**

   This displays the Options bar, shown in Figure 4-9.

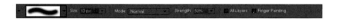

Figure 4-9: Control the effects of the Smudge tool.

2. **Using the Options bar, change the setting in the Strength drop-down menu to make the smudging more dramatic (a high percentage) or subtle (a low percentage).**

3. **If you'd also like the Smudge tool to adjust the lights, darks, tones, and colors of the area that's smudged, choose an appropriate setting in the Mode drop-down menu.**

   The Mode setting controls how the original pixels and smudged pixels are blended together. Your options are as follows:

   - *Normal:* No change to the quality of the colors or tones where you smudge. They just get smudged.

   - *Darken:* In addition to smudging, a Burn tool effect is applied.

   - *Lighten:* In addition to smudging, a Dodge tool effect is applied.

   - *Hue:* Smudges only the hue or color of one area onto another, dragging the tone from your starting point onto another adjoining area of the image.

- *Saturation:* By smudging with this setting in place, you're smudging the color intensity instead of the image content.

- *Color:* Smudge color (both hue and saturation) from one area to another without distorting the physical content.

- *Luminosity:* This mode smudges the brightness of your starting point onto the adjoining areas through which you drag the Smudge tool.

The last four mode options allow you to adjust the color and quality of the color as you smudge. I recommend that you tinker with the area using other color- and hue-adjustment tools first and then smudge in Normal mode.

4. **Set the Brush size by using the Brush palette, just like you set all other Photoshop brush-like tools.**

5. **Click and drag to smudge the image.**

   You pull color from the starting point onto the ending point.

Don't use the Smudge tool to smudge large areas of your image unless you're going for a really smudgy background, as in the case of Figure 4-8. In most other instances, although you can use a large brush size and make a big smudge, you'll regret it because you'll end up distorting the image instead of blending areas within it. For the best results with most images, use a small brush and use it in small areas.

Using the Sharpen tool to add detail

The Sharpen tool heightens the contrast between adjacent pixels so that each of the pixels stands out more. This can help you improve the apparent detail in a blurry or faded photo. Small features and textures can be brought out by making the pixels in and around them more diverse.

In versions 1.0 and 2.0 of Elements, the Sharpen tool lived all by itself on its own button on the Tool palette, but from version 3.0 to the latest version 7, it shares a button with the Blur and Smudge tools just like in Photoshop. In either case, the tool has the same options (see Figure 4-10) and works the same way.

To sharpen some of or the entire image, follow these steps:

1. **To control the area in which the sharpening will take place, use a selection tool — Marquee, Lasso, or Magic Wand — from the Tool palette to select an area within the photo.**

2. **Click the Sharpen tool to activate it.**

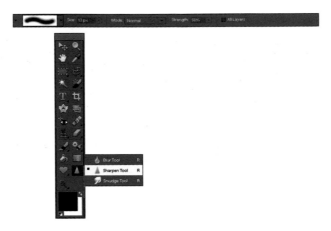
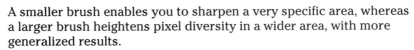

Figure 4-10: Using the Sharpen tool in Elements.

3. **Use the Brush palette to adjust the brush size and whether you want a hard-edged or soft-edged brush.**

   A smaller brush enables you to sharpen a very specific area, whereas a larger brush heightens pixel diversity in a wider area, with more generalized results.

4. **Reduce or increase the intensity of the sharpening effect by adjusting the Strength setting from its default of 50%.**

   Be careful not to sharpen too much, or you'll end up with pixels that are so bright and diverse that detail can actually be lost.

5. **From the Mode drop-down menu, choose the mode setting that you want for the Sharpen tool.**

   The mode setting controls how the pixels are blended. The modes are the same as those for the Smudge tool — described in the preceding section's step list — and include Color, Hue, Saturation, or Luminosity. Normal mode is good for most jobs.

6. **Click and/or drag over the area to be sharpened.**

   You can go over the same spot more than once, but again, don't go too far. Figure 4-11 shows both effective (left side of face) and ineffective sharpening (right side of face). Subtle effects are usually preferable.

Sharpen and Blur filters are available through the Filter menu in both Photoshop and Photoshop Elements, and you can achieve more uniform results with them than with the brush-applied Sharpen and Blur tools because the mouse is removed from the equation. However, you use the control that a brush application can supply. The filter is applied evenly over the selected area or the entire active layer of the image. You can read more about filters in Book V, Chapter 6.

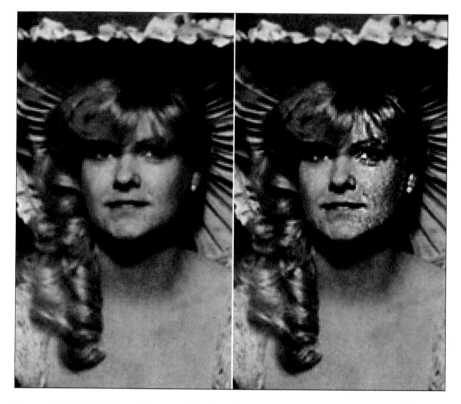

Figure 4-11: At left, the unsharpened version. At right, the left side of the face has been sharpened effectively, but the right side of the face has been sharpened too much.

Blurring some or all of your image

The Blur tool is the Sharpen tool's opposite. Instead of increasing the diversity between adjoining pixels, the pixels are made more similar (reducing the contrast), with their color and light levels adjusted so that no individual pixels stand out too much. Obviously, you can blur a lot or blur a little: The degree to which the tool is applied determines how much contrast is removed from the pixels that you brush over with the Blur tool.

Blurring can be used as a quick-and-dirty substitute for cloning over unwanted pixels. Figure 4-12 shows at left a scan of an old photograph that was folded and wrinkled along the bottom edges. I could have used the Clone Stamp to copy pixels over the wrinkles, but because this area of the subject would look better if de-emphasized anyway, blurring the lower-left and lower-right corners was faster.

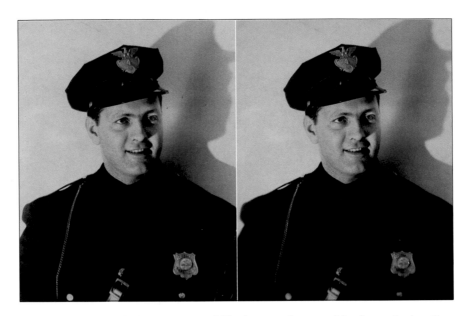

Figure 4-12: Blurring the lower corners of this photo, as shown at right, de-emphasizes the wrinkles that are clearly visible at left.

To use the Blur tool, follow these steps:

1. **Check to see that the layer you want to work with is selected in the Layers palette.**

   If the Layers palette isn't visible, choose it from the Window menu.

2. **If you want to restrict the blurring to a particular area of the image, use the appropriate selection tool (Marquee, Lasso, Magic Wand) on the Tool palette to select that area.**

3. **Click the Blur tool to activate it.**

   The tool shares a spot with the Sharpen and Smudge tools.

   Check out the tool's options on the Options bar, shown in Figure 4-13.

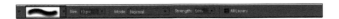

Figure 4-13: The Blur tool's Options bar.

4. **Adjust the setting in the Strength drop-down menu (set to 50% by default) to increase or decrease the amount of blurring that each click or stroke applies to the image.**

   Obviously, a low setting results in very subtle effects.

5. **Set the brush size and type (such as hard- or soft-edged) for the area you'll be blurring by using the Brush palette.**

   Use the smallest brush you can if you need to blur a very small or detailed area. If you want to blur a large area, use a large brush so that you can avoid the obvious signs of retracing your steps with the tool.

6. **Click or drag over the area to be blurred.**

   Some scrubbing with the mouse might be required if you want to get rid of a very sharp edge between two parts of the image. Figure 4-14 shows the edge of content that was pasted into a photo, and the Blur tool is making the edge disappear so that the pasted content looks like it was always there.

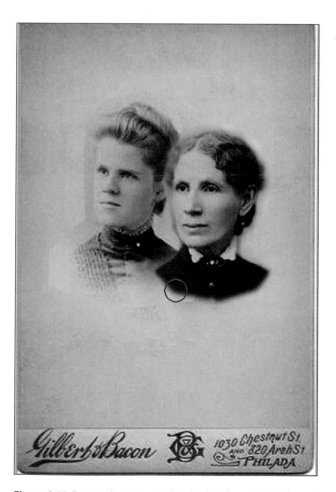

Figure 4-14: For maximum control and subtle (yet effective) results, scrub along the unwanted hard edge with a low-strength Blur tool.

Sometimes you can use the Blur tool to make another part of the image seem sharper in comparison. For example, if the Sharpen tool is having undesirable effects on your image, use the Blur tool to soften or remove the details surrounding the parts of the image to which you want to draw attention.

Finding Relief with the Healing Tools

Both Photoshop and Photoshop Elements have tools that are considered purely restorative. They're intended for removing the signs of age, wear and tear, and outright damage in the form of tears, rips, scratches, and missing content.

In Photoshop CS4, you can find two tools nested with the Red Eye tool designed specifically with healing in mind:

- ✔ The **Healing Brush,** which copies pixels from one place to another while modifying the copied pixels so that they take into account the texture and brightness of the underlying image.

- ✔ The **Spot Healing Brush,** which performs its healing magic only on specific areas you click, such as dust spots, taking its samples from the surrounding pixels automatically.

Photoshop CS4 has a fourth tool not found in Elements 7:

- ✔ The **Patch Tool,** which overlays a portion you want to repair with a patch taken from another area, but modified so that the patch takes into account the texture and brightness of the image underneath.

You can also find a Clone Stamp tool in both applications, which copies undamaged content and allows you to paint it over damaged areas. You can do this to replace missing content, cover damaged content, or simply edit the content of the image by painting over things you don't want. Unlike the Healing Brush and the Patch tools, the Clone Stamp obscures any detail being copied over.

The Clone Stamp isn't purely a restorative tool. It has many uses in the creation of original artwork and in images that aren't photographic in nature, because you can use it to create textures from any area of an image you select. Its restorative uses are extensive, however, so I've grouped it here with the healing tools.

Using the Healing Brush

The Healing Brush is so named because it repairs or heals the current image being painted over — using it doesn't replace it completely. The Clone Stamp (to be discussed shortly) replaces content in one place with selected content from another spot in the image. The color and lighting in the source spot are cloned and placed in the target location as well, which might not be what you want if you'd like to preserve a realistic look.

The Healing Brush is a bit more intelligent and a bit less heavy-handed than the Clone Stamp. As shown in Figure 4-15, this view of a single image shows the Healing Brush effects. The tear on the right side of the photograph is partially healed, and the healed portion matches the surrounding content even though the healing content was derived from a spot on the other side of the image (marked by the cross hairs to the left of the woman's face).

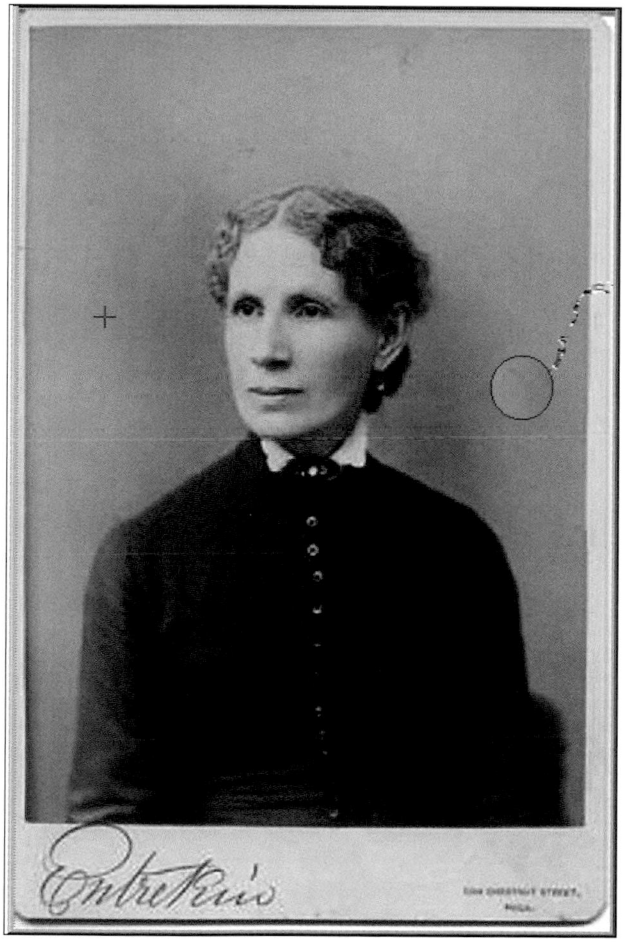

Figure 4-15: Select the healing content (at the cross hairs) and then paint over the "wound" on the right side of the image.

Photoshop's Clone palette can be used to modify the behavior of the Healing brush. You can choose multiple sources, scale or rotate the destination pixels, and use an overlay. This capability reveals that the Healing Brush is actually just a very smart version of the Clone Stamp. It copies pixels in the same way as the Clone Stamp, but it also uses its built-in programming to blend the cloned areas more smoothly with the destination pixels.

To use the Healing Brush, follow these steps:

1. **Identify the area to be healed and pick content from elsewhere in the image that you can use to heal the wound.**

2. **Click the Healing Brush in the Tool palette to activate it.**

   A set of options appears in the Options bar, as shown in Figure 4-16.

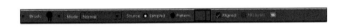

Figure 4-16: The Healing Brush's Options bar.

3. **Using the Options bar, establish the following settings. You can leave them at their default settings if you want, but you might want to make adjustments:**

   - *Brush:* The Brush setting allows you to choose the size of the brush you'll use and whether it is hard- or soft-edged.

     This is the same setting that you use to control the way any content is applied with a brush-based tool.

   - *Mode:* Choose how the pixels will blend. Normal is the default setting and is probably your best choice because it lets the tool work as it's intended. With the Normal setting, the Healing Brush takes the healing content and applies it to the damage and then lets the "bandage" content blend in with the surrounding area. You can also use the modes described in Book VI, Chapter 3.

   - *Source:* If the Sampled option is selected, the Healing Brush copies pixels from a place that you select in the image.

     This is the default because it assumes you're going to choose a spot on the image — somewhere where there is no damage — and use that as the bandage for the damaged area.

If the Pattern option is selected, you can paint a pattern over the area to be healed instead of pixels from another part of the image. If you select this option, the pattern that you apply takes on the color and lighting of the surrounding pixels. This is useful if you're replacing missing content and have to invent the fill entirely. Figure 4-17 shows a pattern applied to an area and the interesting effect that it creates to cover a stain on the carpet. The content within the circular cursor has not yet changed to match the surrounding pixels, but you can see the previous clicks that place a pattern in context.

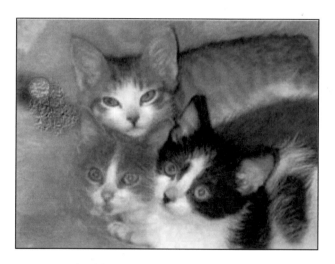

Figure 4-17: Applying a pattern.

- *Aligned:* When you select your source area (where the healing content is taken from), you can select this option so that the distance and direction between the source and target remains the same as you paint over larger damaged areas.

This option is unchecked by default, which means that the tool copies from the original source spot each time you click the mouse to paint over the damaged area with the Healing Brush. If you enable this option, new source areas are selected each time that you apply the Healing Brush.

4. **After you adjust all the settings you want or need to, begin using the Healing Brush. First, sample the spot that's used to heal the damage by Alt-clicking (Option-clicking on the Mac) the healing content that you want to use.**

5. **With your healing content chosen, go ahead and click or drag over the damaged area.**

   The content you sampled (with the Alt or Option key and your mouse) covers the damage.

You might have to wait a few moments for the healing effect to finish. A lot of calculating goes on as Photoshop matches the copied pixels to the new location's darkness and texture. At first, it might look like the exact color and lighting from the source area are being duplicated on the damaged (target) area. If you wait a second, however, you'll see the Healing effect occur — the content you applied with the Healing Brush automatically blends into its surroundings, like a chameleon blending into the leaf or twig on which it sits.

The Spot Healing Brush in both Photoshop and Photoshop Elements works the same as the Healing Brush, but it doesn't require clicking within your image to select an area to be used as a sample. Just select the tool and click over the area you want to heal. The pixels surrounding the damaged area will be examined and used to construct the new pixels painted over it during the healing process.

Working with the Patch tool

Unlike the Healing Brush and Spot Healing Brush, which allow you to paint content from one place to another, the Patch tool works by applying a selected shape from one spot on the image to a damaged spot somewhere else in the image. You can use this tool to cover damage (such as scratches, spots, and stains), or you can use it to replace unwanted content with something more visually appealing.

Photoshop Elements doesn't offer the Patch tool; only Photoshop does (starting with version 7). It's similar to copying and pasting content from one place to another, which is a procedure supported by both applications. The difference between using the Patch tool and doing a simple copy and paste to cover up unwanted content or damage is simple: The Patch tool is a little more intuitive and a little more chameleon-like in that when you place the patch over the unwanted content, the lighting and shading in the target area is applied to the patch.

To use this really helpful tool, follow these steps:

1. **Check the Layers palette to make sure the right layer is active.**

   If the Layers palette isn't visible, you can activate it from the Window menu. Using the correct layer prevents you from patching the wrong layer's content onto another part of your image.

2. **Decide which part of the image you want to use to cover the unwanted or damaged area.**

3. **Click the Patch Tool to activate it.**

   You might have to switch to it from the Healing Brush because these tools share a spot on the toolbox.

4. **Using the Options bar (shown in Figure 4-18), choose either Source or Destination for the patch.**

   If you didn't select the patch area before turning on the tool (and I haven't had you do that in these steps), select Destination.

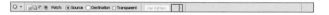

Figure 4-18: Source or Destination? Choose which direction your patch will follow.

5. **Using the mouse, drag a line around the area that you want to use as the patch.**

   It's a lot like using the Lasso tool, as shown in Figure 4-19.

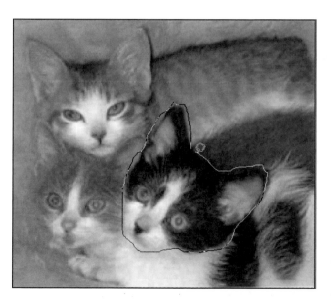

Figure 4-19: Select the Destination patch to place on top of the damaged areas or unwanted content.

6. **Drag the selected patch area onto the damaged/unwanted spot.**

   Wait a second and see the lighting and shading change to make the patch match the surrounding pixels so the patched content blends in.

7. **If you have a large area to patch, you can do it in small pieces, repeating Steps 5 and 6 for each piece.**

Figure 4-20 shows an extra kitten's face added to a former pile of three kittens. The shading and lighting of the new face match its location among the existing kittens.

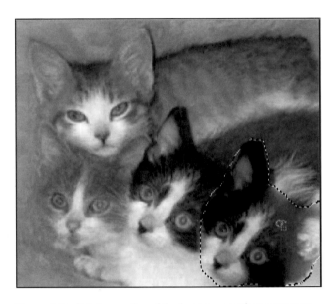

Figure 4-20: Patch a portion of the image over other content to make more of a good thing.

When your entire damaged or unwanted area is patched, you can use the Blur or Smudge tool as needed on any visible edges. If you placed one large patch over a large trouble spot, you might have to blend it with any drastically different adjacent pixels. Sometimes, if the damaged area is a very light color and a dark area is right next to it, the patch-matching won't be as smooth as you'd have hoped.

Cloning content to cover damage and unwanted content

The addition of the Patch tool, Healing Brush, and Spot Healing Brush to Photoshop might have eliminated more than half the uses for the Clone Stamp for many users, but you'll find the Clone Stamp to be a helpful tool in many applications.

The Clone Stamp duplicates content from one place and lets you click to place it one or more times in the image, covering existing content (thus the term *stamp* in the tool's name). Figure 4-21 shows a good candidate for Clone Stamp fixing. Unlike the Patch tool, there is no matching of the stamped content to the surrounding pixels in the target area. If you stamp green grass on a blue couch, you get green grass on a blue couch — you don't get a blue, grassy texture on a blue couch.

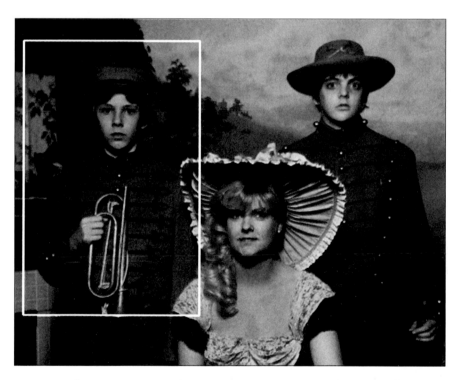

Figure 4-21: Can we create a portrait of the bugle boy alone? Unfortunately, his mom's hat and shoulder intrude into the picture.

To use the Clone Stamp, follow these steps, which are quite similar to the steps for the Healing Brush and Patch tool combined. I use Photoshop Elements here:

1. **Verify the layer you're in, making sure that the layer containing the content you want to clone is highlighted in the Layer palette.**

   You can switch to another layer later when you stamp the content onto the image.

2. **Click the Clone Stamp tool in the Tool palette to activate it.**

   The Options bar (shown in Figure 4-22) appears, offering several settings that you can tweak to control how the tool is applied, including

   - *Brush:* This pop-up palette on the left side of the Options bar contains the brush styles you set for painting, erasing, or using any brush-applied tool. Pick a brush from the palette based on your target area, going for a size that's just a bit smaller than the area you want to stamp over. You don't want to leave an obvious edge to a single stamping of content. With two or more stamps in the area, you can avoid a clumsily pasted look.

   - *Mode:* You can choose a mode to control how the pixels will be merged when the cloned content is pasted. The Mode controls were discussed earlier, in the section, "Finger painting to blend colors and textures." (This option is available only when the Smudge tool is active.) Normal works for most jobs, but you might want to experiment.

   - *Opacity:* If you want to see through your stamped content, reduce the opacity from the default 100%.

   - *Aligned:* This keeps the same distance/offset between the sampled spot and the stamped area. If you deselect this option, the tool returns to the original sampled spot as its source each time you release the mouse button and continue stamping.

   - *Use All Layers:* If you want your cloning and stamping to affect all the layers of your image, select this option. It's unchecked (off) by default, just so you don't make more of an impact on your entire image than you had intended.

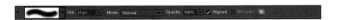

Figure 4-22: The Clone Stamp's Options bar.

   After you customize the tool, you're ready to clone and stamp.

3. **To clone the spot that will be used to cover unwanted content, hold down Alt (Option key on a Mac) while you click the spot that you want to clone.**

   The mouse pointer changes when you're in clone mode, and a cross hair appears in the center of your brush point.

   In this example image, I Alt-clicked in the bugle boy's sleeve to cover his mother's arm at the lower-right corner of the picture.

4. **Release the Alt or Option key and apply the cloned content by clicking to cover the unwanted content, as shown in Figure 4-23.**

   Here, multiple copies of the cloned content have been applied over a large area to cover the seated woman's shoulder and hat.

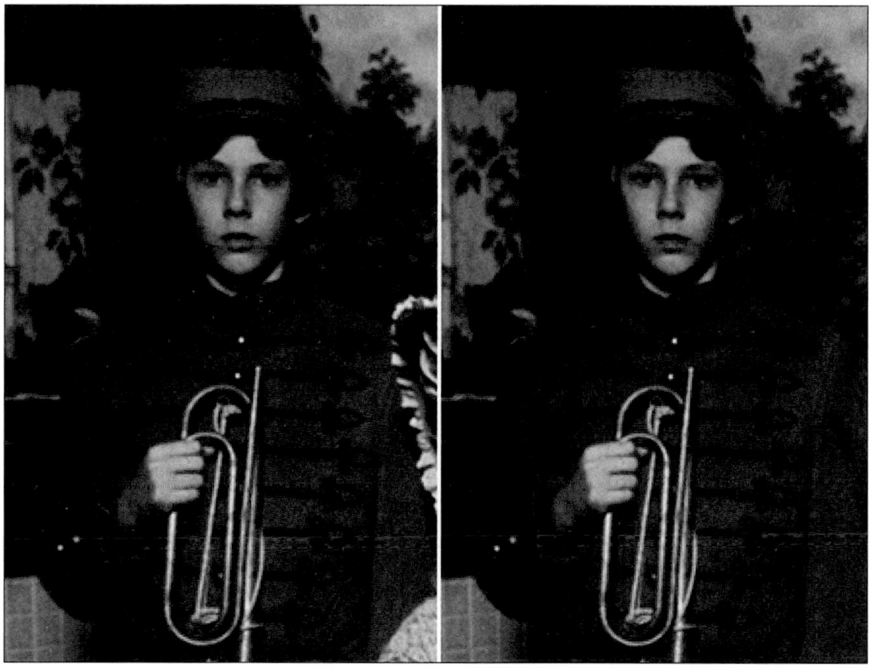

Figure 4-23: Remove the edge of the hat and shoulder with the Clone Stamp tool.

I've also used the Clone Stamp to remove some dust spots and other artifacts from the background and uniform.

As you gain skills with Photoshop CS4, you'll want to learn how to use the Clone Source palette, which can be chosen from the Window menu if it is not visible, shown in Figure 4-24. It makes cloning more accurate by providing a phantom image of the portion of the photo you are cloning from, and more flexible by allowing you to choose multiple origins and flip between them with a click.

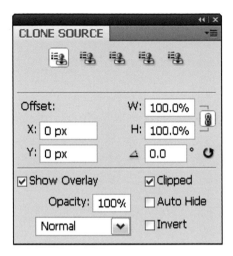

Figure 4-24: The Clone Source palette lets you preview your cloning effects — and much more.

Chapter 5: Correcting Faded, Funny, or Funky Colors and Tones

In This Chapter

✔ **Mastering the color balancing act**

✔ **Controlling the intensity of color**

✔ **Improving color quality overall**

✔ **Eliminating red-eyed demons**

*P*hotos displayed on a sunny wall or desk can fade from the exposure to sunshine, even if you live in a rainy climate. You'd be surprised how just a small amount of sunlight or fluorescent light can fade a photo if it's exposed long enough. Time, too, can fade photos printed from old negatives on old photo paper. You might also have photos that looked a bit odd from the start — perhaps there was too much red or green, or the colors looked washed out from the minute you had the photo developed or captured it with your digital camera.

Regardless of the cause, color photos present a whole host of color-balance, level, and quality issues, and Photoshop and Photoshop Elements are well prepared to deal with them. This is where Photoshop's status as the standard for photo retouching software kicks in. You can find several ways to manually and automatically adjust color levels and quality. Photoshop Elements has many of the same tools that Photoshop does, as well as a few of its own. This chapter focuses on the color and tonal adjustments you can make to bring your images up to snuff.

Using Automated Tools in Photoshop and Elements

Your first stop when attempting to correct your colors and tones is the automated tools built right into both Photoshop and Elements. These tools are training wheels of a sort that work well for some basic image problems, but they don't allow the kind of fine-tuning that you want to apply to really optimize your photos. Try these automatic tools first and then turn to some of the more advanced options described in the rest of this chapter.

Auto Correction in Photoshop

Your automated toolkit in Photoshop is located in the Adjustments submenu of the Image menu and includes these tools:

- **Auto Tone:** This command automatically examines the tonal values in your image, including the lightest tones (highlights), the middle tones, and the darkest tones (the shadows). Then it attempts to provide a balance among all those tones so that the lightest tones aren't washed out, the darkest shadows still have some detail, and the middle tones are right in the middle.

- **Auto Contrast:** This command looks at how many different tones are in your image. If only a few are present, your image could have excessive contrast. If the image information is spread evenly among hundreds of different tones, your image might be low in contrast. Photoshop attempts to redistribute the tones to provide a more pleasing picture.

- **Auto Color:** This command attempts to determine whether the color in your image is heavily biased toward one color or another and then removes excessive color to provide some correction.

   No image editor can *add* color that isn't there; colors can only be removed, leaving whatever other colors are present.

None of these commands have any options. You just invoke them and evaluate your results. If you don't care for the changes, press Ctrl+Z (Cmd+Z on the Mac) and go from there.

Auto Correction in Photoshop Elements

Elements has six automatic settings under the Enhance menu: Auto Smart Fix, Auto Levels, Auto Contrast, Auto Color Correction, Auto Sharpen, and Auto Red Eye FixAuto Smart Fix command that attempts to apply all the Auto Levels, Auto Contrast, and Auto Color Correction commands, as appropriate, simultaneously.

You can throttle back the amount of correction applied by Smart Fix by moving a slider in the Adjust Smart Fix dialog box. Choose Enhance⇨Adjust Smart Fix and move the Smart Fix slider from 0 percent (almost no correction) up to 200 percent (a whole lot of correction) until you get the effect you like. The current effect can be viewed in the original image's window as you adjust the slider.

Photoshop Elements also has a Quick Fix mode, shown in Figure 5-1, (select it by clicking the Quick Fix tab on the right side of the main window). It has an assortment of correction tools for general fixes, lighting and contrast, color, and sharpening. Each of these has an Auto button that you can click to apply the automatic version of that correction, as well as sliders for applying the fixes manually. Read more about manual fixes in the next sections. Always remember to return to the Full Edit mode when you want to apply separate tools or applications.

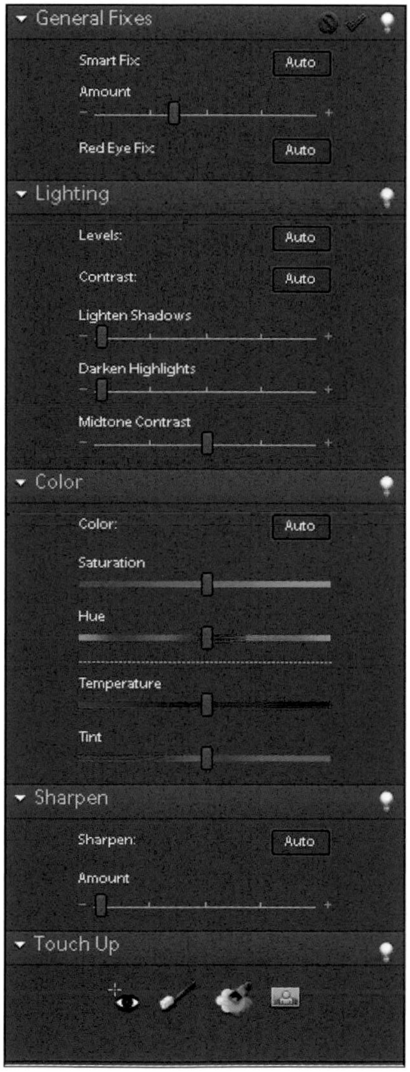

Figure 5-1: Elements' Quick Fix mode gives you fast access to automated and manual correction tools.

Adjusting Color Balance

Say a photo has too much red or yellow, or the whole picture is too dark or too light. These problems — problems you might think would require multiple tools and several steps to solve — could just be a couple of clicks away from their solutions. With automatic color and lighting adjustment tools, commands that address specific color levels, and Photoshop's Channels palette, you have the power to make sweeping changes to your photos or sections thereof, significantly shortening the amount of time that you spend editing and improving your photos.

Adjusting levels

Both Photoshop and Photoshop Elements offer a Levels command. In Elements, it's squirreled away under the Enhance⇨Adjust Lighting submenu; in Photoshop, you can find it on the Image⇨Adjustments menu. Or just press Ctrl/⌘+L to bring up the dialog box directly.

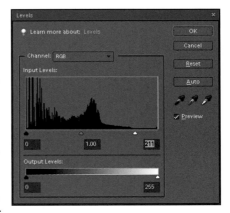

Figure 5-2: Adjust shadow, midtone, and highlight levels.

The Levels command in either application allows you to set the highlights and shadows in an image by dragging three Input Levels sliders (in this case, a set of three black, gray, and white triangles along the slider axis) to adjust the Levels histogram. A *histogram* is a visual representation of quantities — in this case, levels of tones. The sliders, as shown in Figure 5-2, allow you to adjust levels of shadows, midtones, and highlights.

While in Levels, double-click each of the Eyedroppers in turn to open the Color Picker so that you can choose new colors for these three levels (Shadows, Midtones, and Highlights). Alternatively, you can choose new color levels by clicking existing shades within the image. As you make your selections (using the Color Picker or the image itself) and okay them, you see the results in your image.

You can find more about working with the Levels command in *Photoshop CS4 All-in-One Desk Reference For Dummies,* by Barbara Obermeier (Wiley).

Using the Variations dialog box

The Variations command (Color Variations in Elements 7) is a useful feature found on the Image⇨Adjustments submenu in Photoshop and on the Enhance⇨Adjust Color submenu in Photoshop Elements.

The Variations/Color Variations command enables you to view a series of thumbnails, each showing a different color or contrast effect. As you can see in Figure 5-3, clicking the Darker thumbnail shows you how adding more black to the image will affect it. If color adjustment is your goal, you can see what will happen if you bump up the Blue component just by clicking More Blue (in Photoshop) or Increase, under the blue-tinted thumbnail (in Photoshop Elements). Earlier versions of Elements spelled out these changes (Increase Blue, Increase Red, and so forth), but the color references have been dropped for Elements 7. You'll need to pick out the hue you want to change visually.

While you're experimenting by clicking the Variations thumbnails, you can always click the Original thumbnail to return all the thumbnails to their default states. You can view the effects of multiple changes, such as making the image lighter, adding more of one or more colors, or switching between the Midtones, Shadows, Highlights, and Saturation radio buttons. No matter what variations you're considering, Photoshop lets you see your results in a Current Pick thumbnail, and Photoshop Elements shows an after version of the image, as shown in Figure 5-4.

Equalizing colors

The Equalize command has been christened with a name that clearly tells you what it does. Choose Image⇨Adjustments in Photoshop or Filter⇨Adjustments in Elements. The command evenly distributes color over the range of brightness levels throughout your image (or in a selected area) from 0 to 255. When the Equalize command is issued, Photoshop or Elements locates the brightest and darkest pixels, and the rest of the colors are adjusted, making white the brightest value and black the darkest. Then all the colored pixels that fall between these two extremes are *equalized,* or made to fall between the two extreme shades.

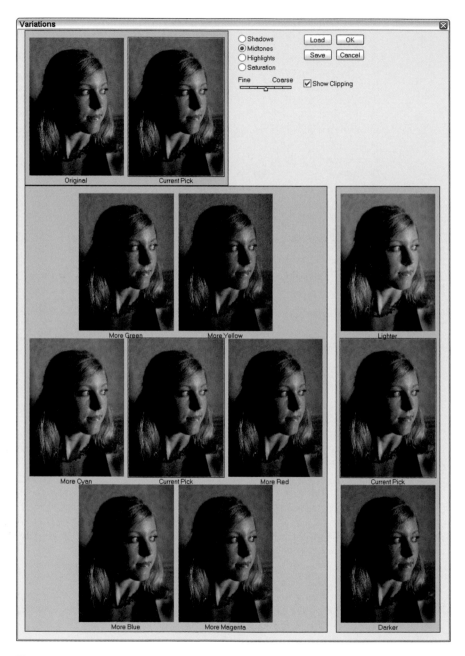

Figure 5-3: Photoshop's Variations dialog box lets you see your results in the Current Pick version of the image.

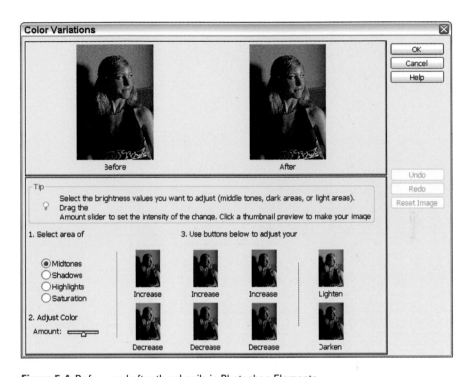

Figure 5-4: Before and after thumbnails in Photoshop Elements.

If you don't select part of your image before issuing the Equalize command, no dialog box appears; the changes just take place automatically over the entire image. If you do make a selection first, a dialog box appears, as shown in Figure 5-5.

Use this dialog box to indicate whether you want to equalize a selected area only or equalize the entire image based on the selected area. In Figure 5-6, only part of the image is equalized, and it's easy to spot it. Therefore, be careful that you don't make the rest of your image look shabby by improving just a small section so drastically.

The Equalize command affects each image differently. The effect depends on how damaged, faded, and light or dark the image was to begin with. Don't assume that if equalization was a big problem solver in one photo, it will be as successful with another.

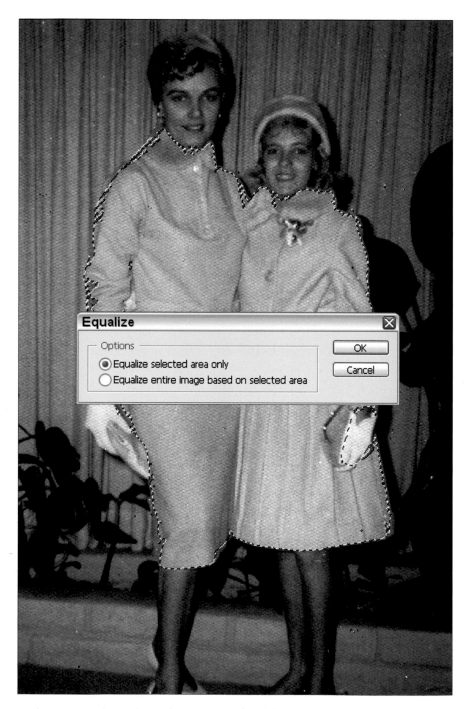

Figure 5-5: Indicate how you want to use a selection to equalize colors.

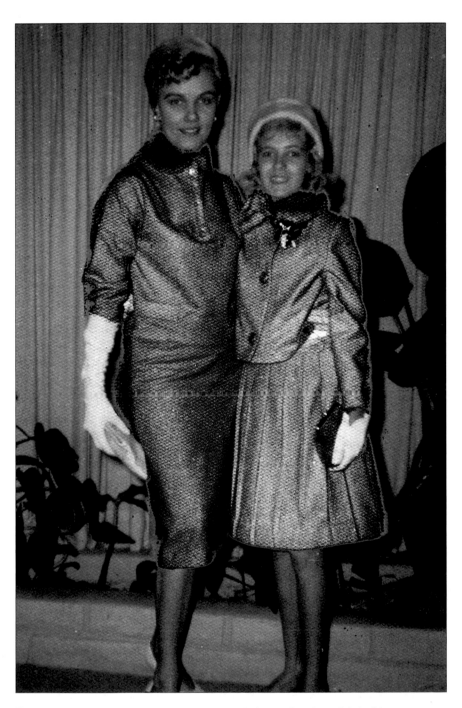

Figure 5-6: Equalizing just part of your image might be too drastic, as it is in this case.

Fixing a color cast

A *color cast* is a tinge — a shade of red or maybe yellow — that discolors your image in whole or in part. Casts occur for a variety of reasons, including the age of the photo, the quality of your scanner (if you scanned a printed original), the print from which you scanned the image, or the film used to take the picture. If a cast appears in an image captured with a digital camera, you need to reset something on the camera (what you change and how you change it varies by the camera). A digital camera is rarely the culprit, however. Your cast probably came from a print, film, or age problem instead.

To get rid of a cast, use Photoshop Elements' Color Cast command (Photoshop doesn't have it) to rid an image of any unpleasant preponderance of a single color. Just follow these steps:

1. **Open the image with the unwanted color cast.**

2. **From the main menu, choose Enhance⇨Adjust Color⇨Remove Color Cast.**

   The Remove Color Cast dialog box opens, as shown in Figure 5-7, offering instructions.

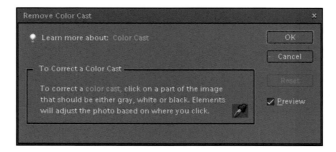

Figure 5-7: Correct a color cast and get rid of any dominant shade.

3. **Click on the Eyedropper to activate the tool, and then use the dialog box's Eyedropper tool (already activated within the dialog box) to click the gray, and then white, and then black points in the image.**

   As you click in the image (about three times — one for gray, one for white, and one for black), the color cast in the photo changes.

   You can keep clicking different spots until you like the results or bail out entirely by clicking Cancel.

Make sure that you leave the Preview option on in the Remove Color Cast dialog box. Most Photoshop and Elements tools and applications offer a Preview capability in dialog boxes that adjust visual elements. Leaving it on means that you don't have to apply the changes just to see them in your image. If you do apply them by clicking OK and then decide you don't like the change, choose Edit⇨Undo from the main menu.

Displaying and using channels

Channels are the different individual color layers that make up your image. Most photos are either in RGB (red/green/blue) or CMYK (cyan/magenta/yellow/black) modes, and photos in those modes have either three (in the case of RGB) or four (in the case of CMYK) channels.

Photoshop's Channels palette (not found in Elements) allows you to view the individual channels for your photo, as shown in Figure 5-8. If the Channels palette is not visible, you can display it by choosing Window⇨Channels.

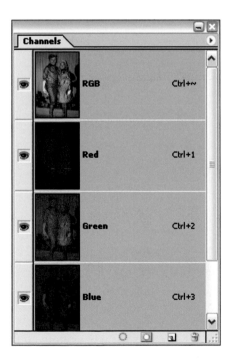

Figure 5-8: Photoshop's Channels palette lets you view an image's basic color components.

The channel that includes all the colors (the RGB or CMYK channel) is displayed when all the individual channels are showing in the photo, and it turns off (the eye disappears from that channel in the palette) if any one of the channels is hidden. (Show or hide a channel by clicking on the eye symbol.)

Use the Channels palette to focus your editing efforts on a single color channel's content or on a combination of two or more channels. For example, if you want to make changes only to the red portions of an image, you can edit the Red channel alone without disturbing the Green or Blue channels. You can edit any channel that's visible. When you hide all but one channel, your edits affect only the channel that's active. To edit a single channel, keep these rules in mind:

- White applies the selected channel color at 100 percent intensity.
- Black wipes out the channel's color wherever you paint or draw it.
- Use a shade of gray to apply the channel's color at a lower intensity.

To display a channel, make sure that the eye appears next to the channel in the Channels palette. If you want to hide a channel, click the eye to the left of the channel. You can't turn off the RGB or CMYK channel directly; it's visible only if all the other channels are visible, too. Using Channels is a complex topic, and I recommend checking out *Photoshop CS4 All-in-One Desk Reference For Dummies,* by Barbara Obermeier (Wiley), for more information.

Working with Color Intensity and Quality

Automatic tools that ask nothing — or ask just a few questions and then make global corrections to color and light — can fail you. In these situations, Photoshop and Photoshop Elements can help. These applications provide targeted tools that you can apply manually to adjust color, lighting, brightness, and contrast. Whatever your photo's color difficulty is, however, chances are that these tools offer a quick and easy solution:

- The Sponge tool for saturating and desaturating color
- The Brightness/Contrast dialog box
- The Curve dialog box, for adjusting individual colors

Increasing and decreasing color intensity

Found in both Photoshop and Photoshop Elements, the Sponge tool adds color (in Saturate mode) or removes color (in Desaturate mode), depending on how you set up the tool.

The Sponge tool can come in handy if you added too much color in a previous editing session and the edit can't be undone. Or perhaps you simply want a subtler, more faded look to some or all of an image. New photos are often faded to look vintage or in preparation for the use of an artistic filter that will make the photo look like a drawing or painting.

Regardless of your motivation, the Sponge tool is very simple to use. To saturate or desaturate color in either Photoshop or Photoshop Elements, follow these steps:

1. **Click the tool in the Tool palette to activate it.**

   The Sponge shares a space on the Tool palette with the Dodge and the Burn tools. Hold down the Shift key and press O to cycle through the three tools until the Sponge is active. (Elements versions prior to 3.0 gave the Sponge tool its own spot.)

2. **Choose Saturate or Desaturate mode, using the tool's Options bar, as shown in Figure 5-9.**

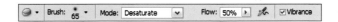

Figure 5-9: The Sponge tool's Options bar.

   Adjust the *flow* — how much saturation or desaturation occurs — by using the Flow drop-down menu.

4. **Use the Brush drop-down menu and choose the right brush size for the area to be sponged.**

   A small brush can give you undesirable results when used in a large area, and a big brush can go too far. Choose one that lets you fix the problem area with the least number of clicks or brush strokes.

5. **Apply the Sponge to the image by clicking and/or dragging to add or remove color where desired.**

   Passing over the same spot more than once intensifies the sponge effect. You add or wash out more color on each successive pass, as shown in Figure 5-10, where too much color has been sponged away.

Tinkering with brightness and contrast

Although automatic tools can correct brightness and contrast, you might want to control these levels manually. To do so, you can use the Brightness and Contrast command found in the Image⇨Adjustments submenu in Photoshop or the Enhance⇨Adjust Lighting ⇨Brightness/Contrast submenu in Photoshop Elements. In either application, the command opens a dialog box, shown in Figure 5-11, that offers two sliders. One adjusts the brightness, and the other adjusts the contrast.

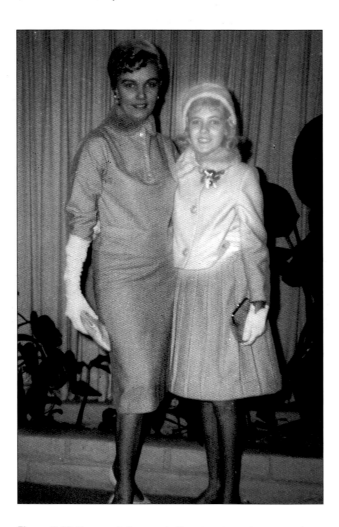

Figure 5-10: Too much Sponge in Desaturate mode can wash away all your colors.

Although the Brightness/Contrast controls are tempting for the beginner, most of the time, they are the *worst* choice for making corrections to your photos. That's because they provide uniform changes in brightness or contrast to *all* the pixels in your image or selection. That might work out in some cases, but most of the time, the results will be terrible. If you bump up brightness to lighten shadows, you'll find that your highlights are now completely washed out. Darken highlights, and your shadows will turn black. And rarely will any photograph need adjustment in contrast over its entire image. I recommend using the Levels command (discussed earlier in this chapter) and Curves (discussed next) as your Photoshop or Elements proficiency increases. Each of these commands deserves most of a chapter of its own,

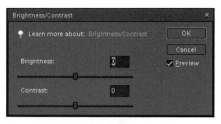

Figure 5-11: Adjust brightness and/or contrast with this handy dialog box.

and that's what you'll find in the companion books to this one, *Photoshop CS4 All-in-One Desk Reference For Dummies,* by Barbara Obermeier, or *Photoshop Elements 7 For Dummies,* by Barbara Obermeier and Ted Padova (both by Wiley).

Riding the curves

Another way to adjust the tones in your image is to work with the Curves dialog box, available in Photoshop (but not in Photoshop Elements) by choosing Image⇨Adjustments⇨Curves. You can use this box (see Figure 5-12) to adjust the entire range of colors in your image. To adjust the tones and color balance, drag the curved line up, down, left, or right, and watch the Preview to see how the adjustments affect your image. You'll also want to use the set of three eyedroppers to set the shadow, midtone, and highlight samples from within the image and then readjust the curve.

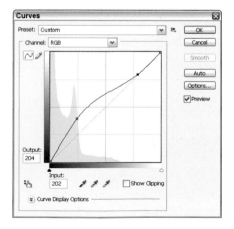

Figure 5-12: Drag the curve to adjust color balance and to get rid of uneven tones.

If you want to change only certain color levels in the image, choose which color channel you want to adjust by selecting that channel within the Channels palette. If you want to adjust multiple (but not all) channels, hold down the Shift key as you click to select more than one channel.

Removing Red-Eye

Another tool that originated with Photoshop Elements and migrated to Photoshop is the Red Eye Removal tool (called simply the Red Eye tool in Photoshop). This tool allows you to literally click or paint away those glowing pupils that affect children or anyone else wide-eyed and close enough to the camera and its overzealous flash. Figure 5-13 shows an image in dire need of red-eye treatment.

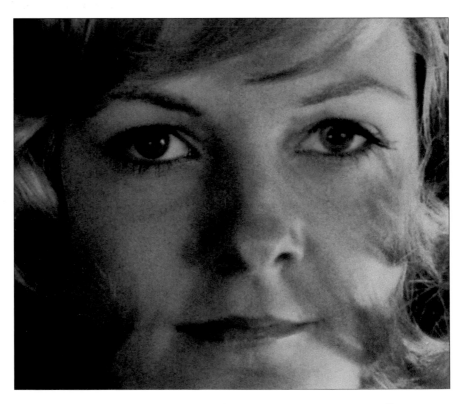

Figure 5-13: Have some demonic eyes to fix? Use the Red Eye Removal tool in Elements 7.

Using the Red Eye Removal tool requires using the Options bar, shown in Figure 5-14; Photoshop's Red Eye tool has a similar Options bar, but without the Auto button. To use the Red Eye Removal tool, follow these steps to customize the tool's effects and apply them to the glowing eyes in question. In Elements, you can also click the Auto button and let the tool find and fix the red eyes without your help (it does a fairly good job).

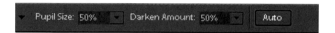

Figure 5-14: Elements (but not Photoshop) has an Auto button in the Red Eye tool's Options bar that can be clicked to automatically zap red eyes.

1. **Make sure that the layer with the demonic eyes is in fact the active layer in the Layers palette.**

2. **Click the Red Eye Removal tool in the Tool palette to activate it; then consider the following options:**

   - *Pupil Size:* The size of the brush you'll use to paint over the red-eye.

   - *Darken Amount:* The degree you want the red eyes darkened.

3. **Click in the area that includes the red-eye effect. The tool cursor becomes a cross hair symbol.**

   The tool automatically seeks out the red tone and darkens it, creating more natural-looking eyes.

4. **If both eyes are glowing (they usually are), you can repeat this process for the second eye.**

   Figure 5-15 shows both eyes exorcised, with no glow remaining.

The current version of the Red Eye Removal tool does not work with the similar yellow- or green-eye effect produced in animals. Try using the Color Replacement tool instead.

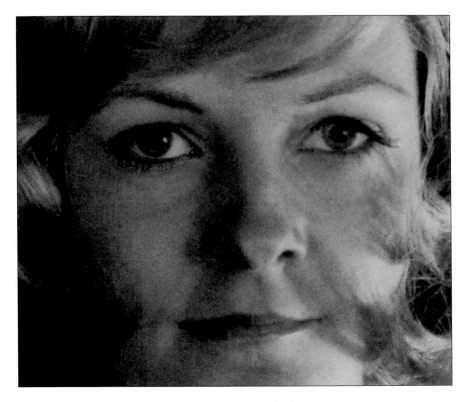

Figure 5-15: The glowing-eyed demon has been exorcised.

Chapter 6: Enhancing Photos with Filters and Special Effects

In This Chapter

✔ Understanding how filters work and what they do

✔ Using Photoshop Elements' special effects for images and text

*F*ilters allow you to apply groups of effects and formats to your images, whether to a specific selected area or to the entire image on one or more of its layers. You can use filters to add or change the color and texture of your images or to add patterns. Each of the filters in Photoshop CS4 and Photoshop Elements 7 enables you to control how the filter affects your image, and most filters give you a preview so that you don't have to formally apply the filter to your image until you see how it will look.

Telling you everything you need to know about using filters is beyond the scope of this book. After all, Photoshop and Elements each include more than 100 different filters that span a broad range of special effects. But this chapter certainly gets you started using these fascinating tools. For more detailed information on using filters, check out *Photoshop CS4 All-in-One Desk Reference For Dummies*, by Barbara Obermeier (Wiley).

The main thing to remember when using filters is to experiment and have fun with them. Several of the illustrations in this chapter are not simply digital photos with a filter applied to them. Some of them are digital creations in their own right, using a combination of digital photos cut and pasted together, special editing techniques, and a bit of filter special effects magic.

Working with Photoshop's and Photoshop Elements' Filters

Both applications provide most of the same filter categories, shown in the Photoshop Elements menu in Figure 6-1. Photoshop's Filter menu is similar, with Sharpen tools (found in Elements' Enhance menu), plus Extract, Liquify (located in the Distort menu in Elements), and Vanishing Point commands added for good measure. Photoshop CS4 also has the additional capability of using Smart Filters, which are actually just filters you can adjust after they are applied because you used the Convert for Smart Filters command to change the current layer you are working with to a Smart Object.

You can read more about this advanced capability in *Photoshop CS4 For Dummies*.

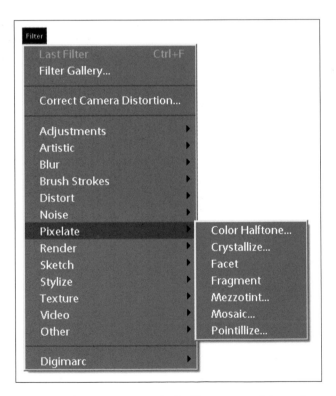

Figure 6-1: Choose a category in the Filter menu and then select a filter from the submenu.

Filters can be used for many different purposes, including creating original works of art from scratch. However, for the purposes of this discussion on editing digital photos, the filters I discuss fall into three categories: corrective, artistic, and special effects. These are the kinds of filters that you're likely to use to retouch photos for personal or professional use. As for those filters that fall outside these categories, you can take your newly found knowledge of the filters that I actually cover and apply it when you experiment with other filters. And just think of the fun you'll have with the trial-and-error process!

Understanding how filters work

When you open the Filter menu, you see all the filter categories, each followed by a right-pointing triangle that spawns a submenu. Most of the categories have at least four filters in their submenus, and many of them have even more to choose from.

Just about all the Filter commands work through either a dialog box or the Filter Gallery found in both Photoshop and Elements. Either mode enables you to both preview and customize the filter's effect. Figure 6-2 shows a stand-alone filter dialog box for the Surface Blur effect.

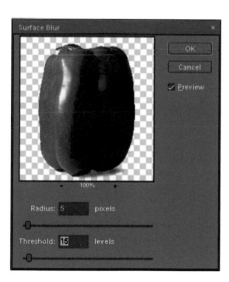

Figure 6-2: The stand-alone Surface Blur filter dialog box and preview pane.

You access other filters through the Filter Gallery, which presents you with a large number of filters, all of which can be quickly tried out from within the Gallery. You can even add several filters together, change their order, and preview the results of the combination before you apply the effects. Figure 6-3 shows the Filter Gallery in Photoshop Elements 7. Elements also has other effects in the Effects palette, which I describe later in the chapter.

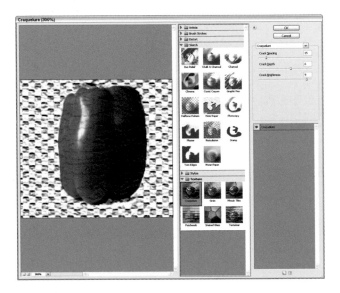

Figure 6-3: Photoshop Elements 7's Filter Gallery is similar to the one found in Photoshop CS4.

Before I discuss individual filters, consider these important filtering tips:

- ✔ Filters can be applied only to the active layer, and only if that layer is visible. If your photo has only one layer, this is a moot point.

- ✔ You can limit the filter's effects to a selection by using the various selection tools before applying a filter.

- ✔ If you don't make a selection before you apply a filter, the filter is applied to the entire active layer.

- ✔ Certain filters work only with certain file types. If your file type doesn't support a certain filter, the filter command is dimmed in the submenu.

Not all filters have a dialog box or appear in the Filter Gallery. Some of them, called *single step filters,* have no options to bother with and are applied the instant you click the command in the Filter menu within a particular category's submenu. The downside? You have no control over the effects, although you can select a section of your image beforehand. If you don't like the results, though, you can easily use the Undo command or the History palette to get rid of the effect.

Fixing flaws with corrective filters

Corrective filters are those that improve the quality of the image without distorting it, changing the content significantly, or applying any stylized effect. The three filters that are most appropriate for a discussion of digital photos fall into three Filter menu categories: Blur, Sharpen, and Noise.

These three categories contain several filters, each performing a relatively subtle effect, depending on the settings that you employ in the available dialog boxes.

Blur filters

Use the Blur filters (Blur, Blur More, Gaussian Blur, Motion Blur, Radial Blur, Smart Blur, and Surface Blur) to soften the content of your image. The Motion and Radial blurs do a bit more than soften. They actually give the appearance of circular movement (Radial) or movement through space (Motion). The Blur and Blur More filters don't have dialog boxes; the commands automatically apply a modicum of blurring to your image in its entirety or to a selection made before issuing the command.

Use the Blur and Blur More filters instead of the Blur tool when you want uniform results. When you use the Blur tool, your mouse has the greatest effect on the results. You might be able to see the strokes that you used to apply the blur, or you might miss some spots or apply the effect unevenly. If you use the filter, the same amount of blurring is applied everywhere, with no strokes or places that are blurred more or less than somewhere else.

In Photoshop and Elements, the last filter you used is repeated at the top of the Filter menu so that you can access the filter quickly if you want to use it again in the current session. In both applications, the keyboard shortcut to reapply the most recently used filter is Ctrl+F (⌘+F on a Mac).

The specialized Blur filters — Gaussian, Motion, Radial, Smart, and Surface — have their own dialog boxes where you can choose the degree of blurring. You'll use the Gaussian Blur filter most often because it allows a high degree of control over the amount and type of blur applied. Figure 6-4 shows a Gaussian Blur applied to the background part of an image to make the foreground stand out.

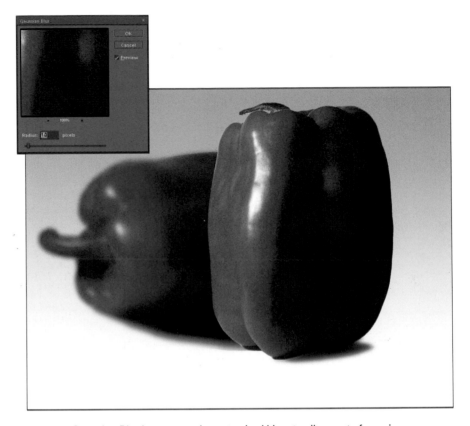

Figure 6-4: Gaussian Blur lets you apply customized blurs to all or part of your image.

For the Motion blur, you can also choose the direction in which the object is supposed to be moving. Figure 6-5 shows the Motion Blur filter applied to an image created in Photoshop using actual photos blended together in a creative way.

The Radial blur completely distorts everything to which it's applied. If you want to create a background that appears to be spinning around or behind parts of the image, select the content that will remain static and copy it to a new layer. Then apply the Radial Blur to the original layer, which should be placed behind the static content layer. Voilà! Your objects are in the center of a hurricane, but they've not moved a bit. Figure 6-6 shows a fanciful image created in Photoshop from an actual vacation photo I took in London, with the addition of some type and special filter effects.

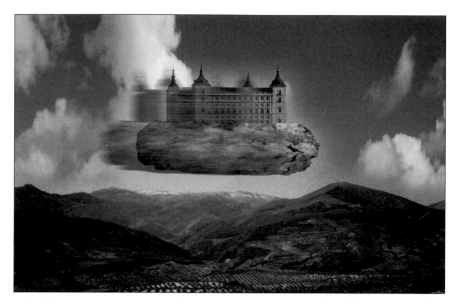

Figure 6-5: Zoom! The Motion Blur filter makes your image take off.

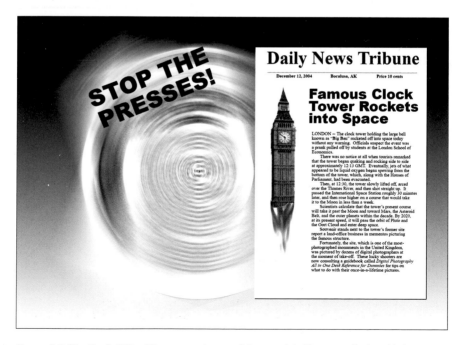

Figure 6-6: The Radial Blur filter was only one of the special effects applied to this image.

Sharpen filters

Just as the Blur and Sharpen tools are opposites, so are the Blur and Sharpen filters. They're the same in one respect, though — the filters apply the effect in a uniform way, whereas the tools are entirely dependent on your brush size, mouse movements, and selection to control them. Elements has an Unsharp Mask and Adjust Sharpness filters, located in the Enhance menu. Photoshop has five main Sharpen filters:

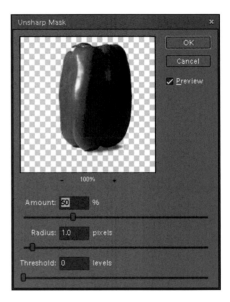

- ✔ **Sharpen:** This filter has no dialog box. Just choose the command, and a uniform, subtle sharpening effect is automatically applied. You might want to repeat it two or more times if you need more sharpening than it manages to apply in one pass.

- ✔ **Sharpen More:** This is Sharpen on steroids. The filter applies more sharpening in one fell swoop than the Sharpen filter.

- ✔ **Sharpen Edges:** This makes the edges, determined by a group of pixels varying in color and light levels from an adjoining group, stand out by sharpening the connecting pixels. If you have content in your image that just fades into its surroundings, this might be the filter for you.

Figure 6-7: The Unsharp Mask filter can refine the detail of any photo.

- ✔ **Smart Sharpen:** This filter is similar to Unsharp Mask (described next), but has options for removing Gaussian Blur, Lens Blur, and Motion blur if they appear in your image.

- ✔ **Unsharp Mask:** Despite its confusing name, this filter *sharpens* images. Very similar to Sharpen Edges, this filter adjusts the contrast of edges, with a dialog box, shown in Figure 6-7, which you use to control the effects.

Noise filters

Among the Noise filters, the Despeckle and Dust & Scratches filters are the ones you use to retouch photos. You use them to deal with artifacts, such as dust spots or scratches that are distracting or that obscure parts of an image.

The Despeckle filter finds the edges in an image and blurs everything but those edges. Although this sounds overly destructive, it can create an interesting effect that blends together parts of an image despite differences in color and texture that existed in the original. It's also a good tool for minimizing the halftone screen effects of photos scanned from newspapers or magazines.

The Reduce Noise filter is a welcome addition to the Photoshop and Elements repertoire, with helpful tools for removing multi-colored speckles created by long exposures or high ISO settings in your images.

The Dust & Scratches filter eliminates much of the noise (dust, scratches, small spots) by making pixels that are very different from their surroundings more similar. You can use the Dust & Scratches dialog box (shown in Figure 6-8) to adjust the Radius and the Threshold settings, which determine the scope and degree of the effects, respectively. Figure 6-9 shows the result of adjusting these settings.

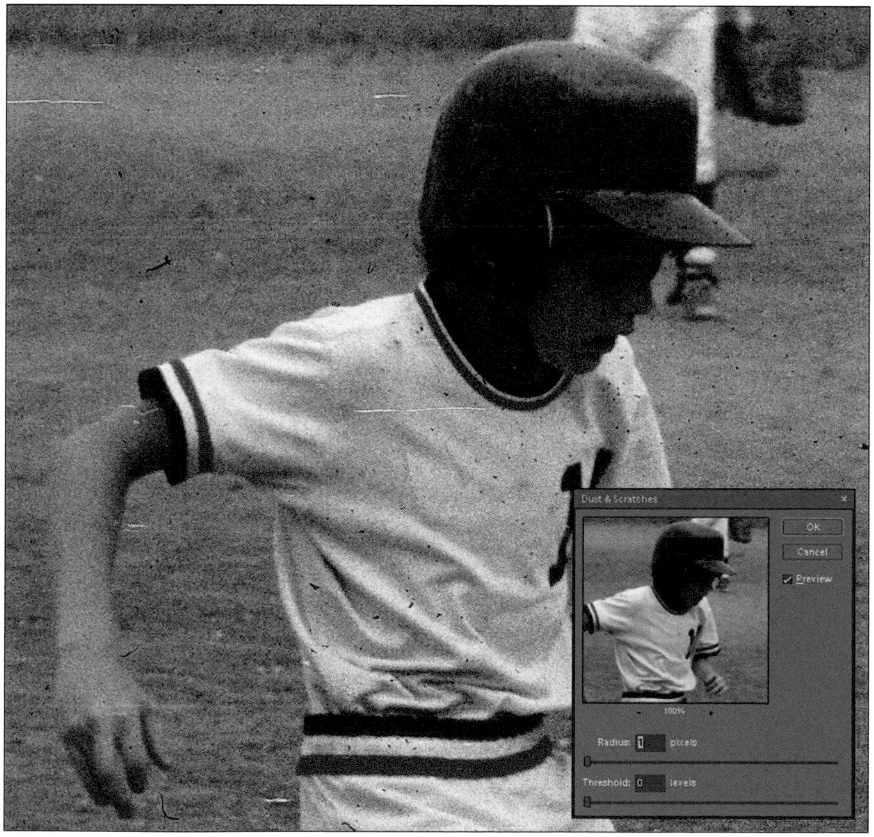

Figure 6-8: This photo needs the Dust & Scratches filter in a big way!

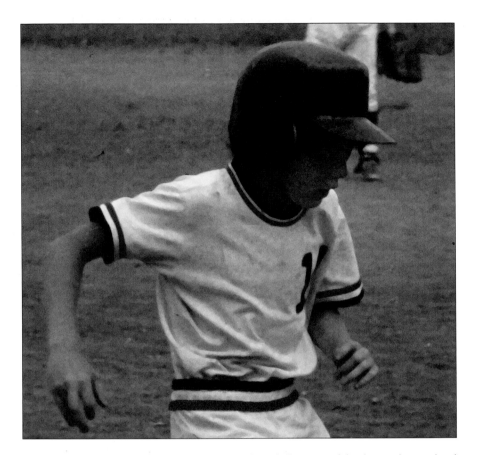

Figure 6-9: Although some details have been softened, the worst of the dust and scratches has been removed.

The steps for using this filter are pretty simple:

1. **Choose Filter⇨Noise⇨Dust & Scratches from the main menu to open the filter's dialog box.**

2. **Zoom in on the area with the greatest degree of dust and scratch damage by using the Hand tool and the + button.**

The Hand tool appears when you mouse over the preview. Examining the image preview helps you determine whether your settings are doing the job.

3. **Adjust the Threshold setting by dragging the slider.**

   Watch the preview for the desired result to appear.

4. **Adjust the Radius, again by dragging the slider.**

   Don't go too far with your Radius adjustment. The image can become so blurry that any details in the photo are indistinguishable.

5. **Click OK to apply the filter.**

Turning photos into paintings with artistic filters

The filters found in three of the Filter menu's categories — Artistic, Brush Strokes, and Sketch — are not truly restorative or retouching filters, at least not traditionally. However, as more people are either capturing images digitally or scanning prints, their needs and desires with regard to those pictures have become more sophisticated and complex. It isn't good enough to just scan a wedding photo and enlarge it for a framed copy on the piano. You might want to make the photo look like a drawing done with pastels or a painting created with oils.

For gifts, cards, Web graphics, and interesting marketing materials, you can turn any photo into an apparent work of hand-done art, as shown in Figure 6-10. Here, a photo has been filtered to look like a painting, with soft shapes and a slight texture that mirrors the weave of watercolor paper. I used the Ink Outlines and the Accented Edges filters, followed by a heavy-duty application of the Unsharp Mask filter.

Using artistic filters also performs another important role. If your image is simply beyond repair or beyond your skills or interest level to repair, you can hide a multitude of sins with the right filter. If your image is scuffed and scratched and you don't feel like dealing with each individual injury, just clean up the most offensive or extreme of the marks with the Clone Stamp and then apply a filter such as Colored Pencil or Dry Brush. This way, you create something entirely new while still preserving the content and history of the original image by hiding the damage that would have normally relegated the image to a drawer rather than a frame.

When you use these filters, you always get a dialog box, such as the one shown in Figure 6-11. Through the dialog boxes, you can customize how the artistic effect is applied — the thickness of the brush or pencil strokes, the frequency of them, how detailed the effect is, the intensity of the effect, and so on. You can select an area before using the filter to restrict the amount of the photo that's affected, or you can apply the filter to the whole image.

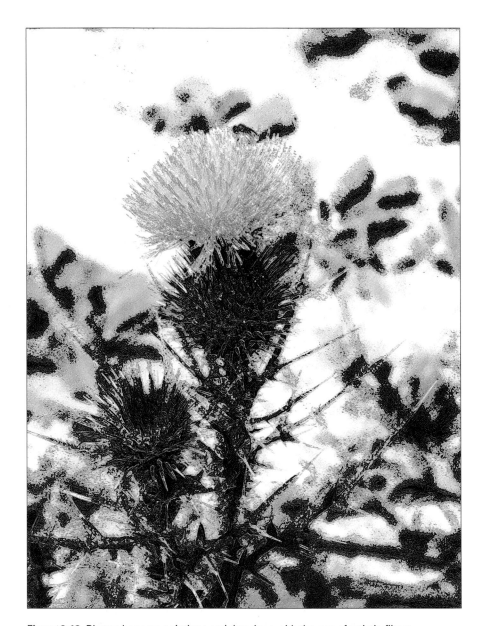

Figure 6-10: Photos become paintings and drawings with the use of artistic filters.

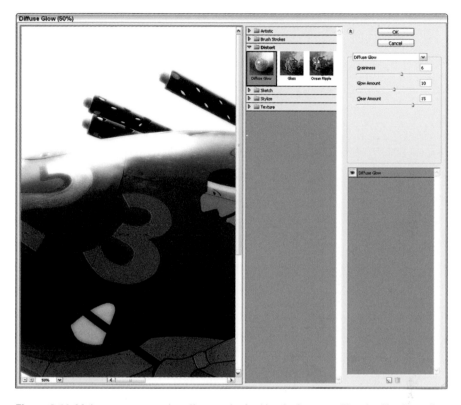

Figure 6-11: Make sure you get the effect you're looking for by controlling the filter's attributes.

Going a little crazy with special effects filters

The Distort, Liquify, and Stylize filters (found in both Photoshop and Photoshop Elements, although Liquify is tucked away in the Distort menu in Elements) are the least conservative effects. These unusual effects change the appearance of some or all of your image by stretching, pulling, or pinching or by mimicking textures and overlays, such as rippled water, glass, or by appearing to be ripped apart by a strong wind.

You might be wondering how on Earth you'd use these filters to restore or retouch a photo. Well, you wouldn't. However, you might use them to create an interesting piece of digital art, using one or more of your photos — or to achieve a symbolic look that's suggested, but not artistically realized, in a photograph you've restored traditionally. For example, if you have a photo of someone's boat, it might be interesting to apply the Ocean Ripple filter to the water in the image and the Wind filter to the boat's sails. That's a bit literal, but you get the idea.

As you work with these filters, their dialog boxes help you control how the filters work their special effects magic. You can change the size of the tiles or cracks in an image, choose which texture to apply, and adjust the degree of pinching or twirling to use. Figure 6-12 shows the Emboss filter dialog box (one of the Stylize filters) and the settings you can adjust to create a very interesting relief map of your drawing. Check the preview window as you drag sliders and enter values. When you like the results, click OK, and they are applied to your image or to a selection within it.

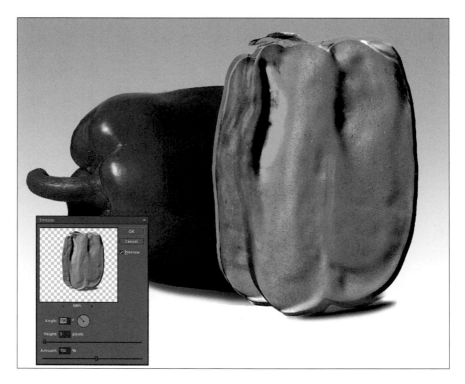

Figure 6-12: Emboss is one of the filters that provide a 3-D effect.

For a brief description of the more creative filters, check out the following:

✔ **Texture filters:** These filters apply artificial textures to your image. Figure 6-13 shows Stained Glass (top), Craquelure (middle), and Grain (bottom) applied to different sections of a single image, purely for demonstrative purposes.

TIP

Use the Texturizer filter (found in the Texture category) to apply textures, such as Canvas, Sandstone, and Burlap to your photo. These textures make a photo look like it's printed on very textured paper or some sort of fabric.

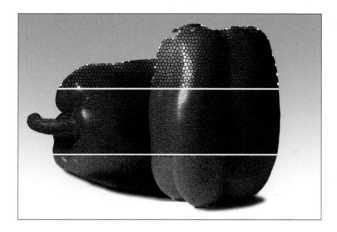

Figure 6-13: Stained Glass (top), Craquelure (middle), and Grain filters (bottom).

✓ **Distorting filters:** These filters manipulate the apparent shape of your image content, as shown in Figures 6-14, 6-15, and 6-16, in which the Ocean Ripple, Pinch, and Glass filters have been applied to the same photo. By creating an apparent shape to the surface of the image, the content looks as though it's being viewed through some sort of distorting lens, or as though the photo exists within a substance and not simply on paper or a computer screen.

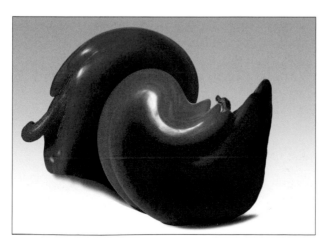

Figure 6-14: Ocean Ripple filter applied to an image.

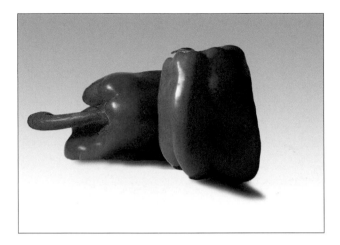

Figure 6-15: Pinch filter applied to the same image.

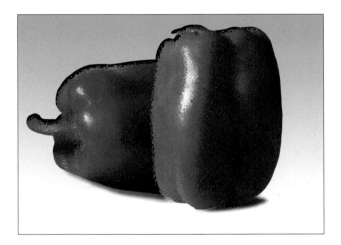

Figure 6-16: Yet another variation using the Canvas option of the Glass filter.

✔ **Stylize filters:** This category is sort of a hodgepodge of filters that don't really fit anywhere else. With names like Emboss, Glowing Edges, Solarize, and Wind, you'd be hard-pressed to find a more descriptive yet nondescript name for them. In Figure 6-17, I applied the Wind filter to the pepper on the left and Glowing Edges to the pepper on the right. The results are extreme and might go beyond your intentions for dealing with digital photos. On the other hand, these examples might inspire you to create something unique.

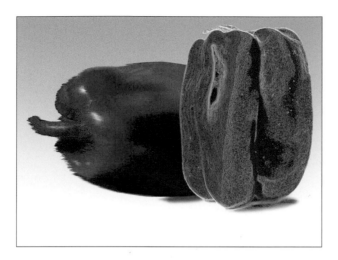

Figure 6-17: Here are the Wind filter (left) and Glowing Edges filter (right).

↙ **Liquify:** This is a command on Photoshop's Filter menu and is found in the Filter⇨Distort menu in Elements (see Figure 6-18), but it isn't simply a filter. Instead, it's a miniprogram of its own that gives you a full set of distortion and manipulation tools for pinching, twisting, scrunching, pulling, bloating, shrinking, or doing just about anything that sounds like some form of torture to your image. Figure 6-18 shows the Liquify window and some distortion in progress.

Don't hesitate to mix and match with filters. Apply one, then another, then another after that. Stacking their effects can give you unexpected and often quite beautiful results. Don't be afraid to experiment with different combinations!

The Photoshop Elements Effects Palette

The Effects Palette brings a host of special effects into a common interface, with a line of icons (which you can see in Figure 6-19) for (left to right) Filters, Layer Styles, Photo Effects, or All. Click each icon, located at the top of the menu under the Effects tab, and then select the effect you want from the drop-down list to the right of the icons, or scroll through the preview thumbnails to find the effect you want. These effects can be applied to a selection or to your entire image similar to the way you apply filters. Some of the Effects are actually canned applications of Elements' filters using a predetermined series of steps, much like a macro. Watch the status bar at the bottom of the screen as an Effect is applied to see the names of the filters used as they are added in turn.

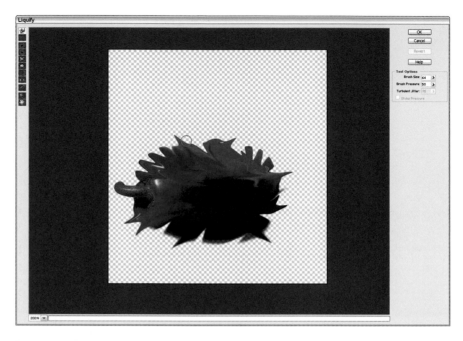

Figure 6-18: Turn your image to a liquid-like substance and then stir it up with the Liquify tools in this dialog box.

Displaying and moving the tab

The Effects palette is normally docked on the right side of the Photoshop Elements window when the Palette Bin is visible; if you click the tab, you can display the palette with its top still docked. If you want to move the palette around, you can simply drag it away from the Palette Bin by grabbing the tab with your mouse. You can move it anywhere on the workspace, and even minimize it in place by clicking the Minimize (–) button to shrink it to just a title bar. When you want to use it again, click the Maximize (X) button. You can also close the palette by clicking the triangle on the left side of the tab.

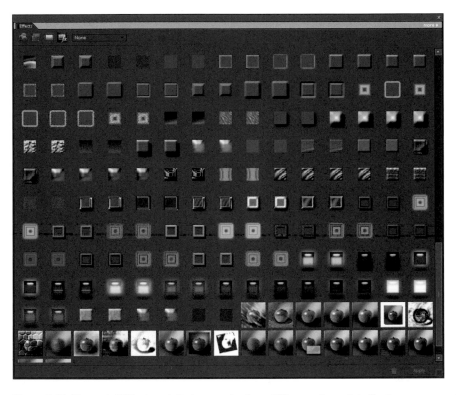

Figure 6-19: Elements' Effects palette has a selection of filters and special effects you can apply.

Applying an effect

After you understand how to see either the thumbnails or list of effects, and you
know how to manipulate the Effects palette (see the preceding sections), you
can apply these cool effects to your photos and text. Just follow these steps:

1. **Select the portion of your image to which you want the effect to apply.**

2. **Display the Effects palette.**

3. **Find the Effect you want by choosing one of the category icons, or by
   clicking the All icon.**

4. If you want to apply an effect to your image, drag the desired thumbnail onto your image.

After a delay — how long a delay depends on your available system resources — the effect is applied to the image. If you have part of your image selected, drag the thumbnail into that selected area. You'll get an effect like the one shown in Figure 6-20, in which I applied Psychedelic Strings to the background.

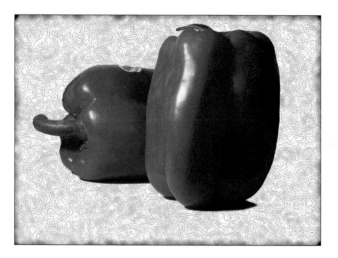

Figure 6-20: Photoshop Elements' Effects are an easy way to apply canned filter transformations.

Click the drop-down list in the upper-left corner of the Effects palette, to the right of the icons, to choose from different effect groups — Textures, Frames, Text Effects, Image Effects — to be displayed alone. The default setting for this drop-down list is All, which shows all the available effects. Choosing one of the groups in the drop-down list distills the displayed set down to just that group.

Book VI
Restoring Old Photos

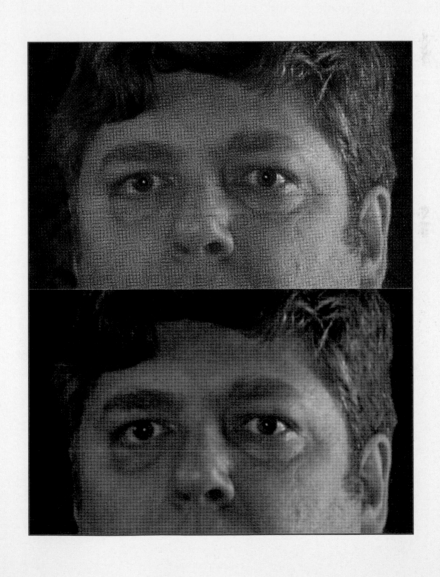

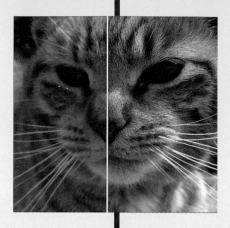

erhaps you've mastered digital photography and now take only flawless pictures that need so little further improvement that most of your image-editing efforts are just minor tweaks. Fortunately, becoming a paragon of photographic prowess leaves you that much more time to tackle that wretched shoebox full of old photos you've inherited, each infected by tears, speckles, stains, faded spots, and, in a few cases, some vexing content (such as a tree) growing out of the top of some poor soul's cranium.

In this book, I show you how to use a scanner to capture those vintage prints, negatives, and transparencies, and then mend them using Photoshop and Elements. I explain how to brighten dark shadows, sharpen blurry images, correct and enrich faded colors, and replace torn or missing content. If you're waxing nostalgic, I even demonstrate some easy techniques for adding sepia tones to a photo. This book helps you restore vigor to even the most lifeless photos.

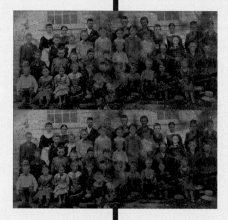

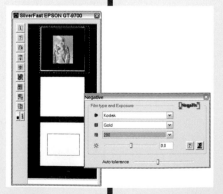

Chapter 1: Scanning Old Photos

In This Chapter

✓ **Preparing your originals**

✓ **Selecting resolution**

✓ **Choosing other scanner controls**

S canning old prints so you can retouch and edit them digitally has been easy and fast, and a popular option for those making the transition from film to the digital age. Capturing images from all those trays of slides that have piled up in the closet was a little trickier for many years. But with the introduction of $200–$300 (and up) scanners designed especially for film, slide and negative scanning has finally come of age. If you have a collection of 35mm slides or discover a treasure trove of family negatives, you can now bring them into the digital realm as easily as you would prints. There's no reason why you can't enjoy working with your film-originated photos in your image editor.

Scanning old photos, slides, and negatives is a great way to preserve and share your family history, especially when you restore the images using the techniques described in the next chapter and elsewhere in this book. Your great-great-great-grandchildren will love you for it!

Of course, scanning prints and other opaque documents (or *reflective originals*) is far more common than scanning film *(transparent)* originals, such as slides and negatives. In fact, most scanners can't handle anything but reflective originals. Sometimes, however, your only copy of an image is a transparency or negative. Other times, you might have both a hard copy reflective original and a transparency or negative film version, but the film is a better choice for scanning because film is usually in better condition and contains all the information originally captured.

You basically have three ways of scanning a color or black-and-white print into your computer: You can do it quickly, you can do it easily, or you can produce a high-quality digital image. If you're new to scanning, you can probably choose the fast route and do things the easy way or tediously create the best quality scan you can. If you want your scanning experience to be all three (fast, easy, and aesthetically satisfying), you need to read this chapter.

Modern scanning software helps you make the right decisions as you capture images from prints, but you still need to know what you're doing and what questions to ask yourself before you start. For example, what resolution should you use to scan a particular image? What other settings do you need to adjust? How can you scan problem prints with stains, scratches, bad color, or other defects?

Scan Film or Prints?

If you have good quality prints, scanning them is probably your fastest and easiest alternative. All flatbed scanners — even the least expensive models — can capture images from prints. Prepping prints for scanning involves little more than, possibly, cleaning off dust or marks. You can take a print, pop it in your scanner, and have an image in minutes.

But there are good reasons to scan film originals, such as negatives or slides. Perhaps it's the only form of an image you have. You might not have a print at all, or the print you do have might be too small or might have suffered some damage. And scanning even a well-made 4 x 5" print won't yield the same detail you can get from a high-quality scan of an original negative or slide. The original always has more information than a second-generation copy, such as a print.

If you still shoot film regularly, you'll find lots of good reasons to shoot either slide film or print film and then scan the respective positives/negatives. Slide film — for the creative control it offers you — is the choice of professionals for a reason. What you shoot is what you get. When you shoot color negative film, the prints you get might vary significantly from what you saw through your viewfinder. For example, if you deliberately underexpose a shot to produce a silhouette effect, the automated printing system at your photofinisher will try to thwart your creative efforts by pumping extra light on your print. Instead of a silhouette, you get a washed-out image with highlights that are too bright. Figure 1-1 shows a typical image that has suffered these vagaries. Because the lab printed for the dark shadows, they are rendered lighter, while washing out the sunset. Scan the negative and make a print yourself, and you can optimize the image for the dramatic sunset, as shown in the right half of Figure 1-1.

Or maybe you took a picture at sunset and are surprised when the reddish colors you remember are printed a little bluer than you'd like by the automated machinery. And try as hard as you like, Kentucky bluegrass is going to come out green.

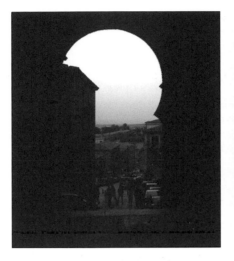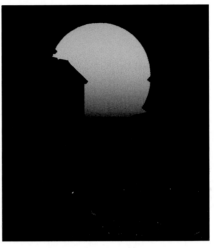

Figure 1-1: Your photofinisher might give you a washed-out image, but you can scan and adjust your print to get the dramatic rendition you really want.

However, when you shoot slide film, what you see is what you get. If the film is processed well and if you were using the proper film for the lighting conditions, your image appears exactly as you composed and focused it. You can then scan your slide and get the exact picture you visualized.

All this fuss probably makes you realize exactly how great digital photography is: You can take pictures the way you want them and never have to worry about your photofinisher messing with your vision. In one sense, slide film is the closest thing to digital imaging available. Transparencies can make a valuable complement to digital cameras for photographers who want the most versatility in their image-capturing options.

Scanning Options

If you want to scan prints, the choice is easy: Almost any flatbed scanner will do a good job. But if you want to scan transparencies or negatives, you have four primary options (ignoring the truly professional alternatives, such as drum scanners, which aren't available to the amateur digital photographer). I list them in order of descending quality.

Let the pros do it

Your photofinisher is equipped with high-resolution scanners that can convert your slides or negatives to a digital format. They can deliver the finished product to you on a CD or DVD. Going this route is a good idea for several reasons:

✔ **No equipment to buy:** If you have an archive of film originals to convert and don't plan to scan slides or negatives on a regular basis, you'll find it economical to use your photofinisher's equipment and personnel instead.

✔ **Better quality:** The pros have better equipment than you're likely to purchase and can give you better overall quality.

✔ **Less time:** I scan slides and negatives all the time. It's time-consuming. After you've spent most of an afternoon scanning 30 or 40 slides, you'll wonder why you wanted to do the job yourself.

✔ **Lower cost:** Unless you have a ton of film originals to scan on a continuing basis, it will take you a very, very long time to amortize the cost of a good slide scanner compared with the small fee your finisher will charge for each scan.

Buy a slide scanner

Dedicated slide scanners are high-resolution devices designed specifically for scanning slides, transparencies, and negatives. With the new breed of inexpensive film scanners, just about anyone can justify one of these beasts. There are some advantages to choosing this method, too:

✔ **Customized quality:** Although your photofinisher will give you standardized results that look good, you might want to scan a particular original in a particular way to produce the exact image you want. Perhaps the information in the highlights is most important, and you don't care whether the shadows go black. Perhaps you want to scan only a particular portion of the original. If you have your own slide scanner, you can customize your scan to meet your own creative needs.

✔ **Quicker turnaround time:** I tell colleagues that I scan my own transparencies because of the turnaround time. My scanner sits on a table behind me, so all I have to do is turn around. I can have a scan on my screen in five minutes; if I used a photofinisher, I'd probably have to wait a week to get my results. If you're in a hurry, making your own scans is definitely faster.

✔ **Lower cost for higher volumes:** If you do your own scans, your biggest costs are the scanner and your own time. If you make many scans of slides and negatives over time, your in-house capability will eventually pay for itself if you factor in the time you expend running to the photofinisher. It takes a lot of scans to pay for a dedicated scanner, but serious amateurs and professionals can justify their expenditure more quickly than they realize. (Don't forget the fun factor, too.)

Use a transparency-capable flatbed

Many flatbed scanners come with a slide-scanning attachment (chiefly a light source to *transilluminate* [shine light through] the originals) and have sufficient resolution and dynamic range to do a decent job scanning slides. This option has a few advantages:

- **Lower cost:** There's no expensive dedicated slide scanner to buy. You can find flatbed scanners that can grab decent film images for $200 or even less. Or, if you have lots of film to scan, go for a high-end model like the Microtek ArtixScan.

- **Acceptable quality:** If "good enough" is good enough, you'll find that flatbeds do give you enough quality to work with. You can still do some of the same customization steps with your scanner that make the dedicated slide scanner attractive. Hey, it beats paying a gazillion dollars for a slide scanner, doesn't it?

- **Quicker turnaround:** Again, just turn around and scan your slide or negative. No running to the photofinisher.

Figure 1-2 shows a typical scanner with a built-in transparency light source.

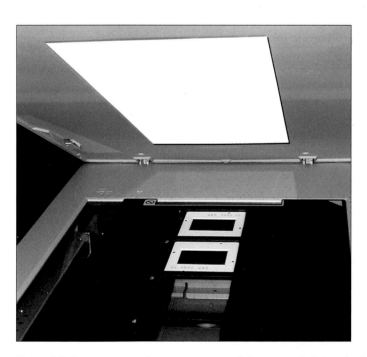

Figure 1-2: Some scanners have transparency light sources built into the lid.

Do-it-yourself limitations

You'll probably run into some limitations when scanning film using an inexpensive slide and negative scanner or when using your flatbed scanner. Here are a few things to keep in mind:

✔ **35mm only:** The least expensive dedicated film scanners handle only 35mm and smaller film formats. If you have 620/120 roll film or sheet film, like those used in old box-and-view cameras, twin-lens reflexes, or even press cameras, you won't be able to scan it yourself. Dedicated film scanners that work with larger sizes typically cost $1,000 or more.

✔ **Size limitations:** Even flatbed scanners that can capture film can probably scan only limited sizes. Perhaps your unit can accommodate up to ¼" wide film (6cm) but no larger. If you're lucky, you have a flatbed that works with 4 x 5" or 5 x 7" sheet film.

✔ **Dust busting limitations:** More expensive scanners use a sophisticated feature called Digital ICE to remove dust from film. This hardware/software combination is actually able to discern dust spots on film and remove them without degrading the rest of the image. Lower-cost scanners might have some sort of software dust brush that actually blurs the image a bit.

Examining Different Types of Originals

To successfully scan photographic originals, you need to understand the differences among prints, negatives, slides, and transparencies. I summarize them in this section.

Prints

Prints consist of color dyes (or a black-and-white emulsion in the case of monochrome prints) coated on a substrate of paper or plastic. You view prints by the light that passes through the dyes or emulsion and reflects back to your eyes. Scanners capture images of prints in much the same manner, using sensors instead of eyeballs.

Every print has light areas, dark areas, and tones in between.

✔ The lightest areas with detail (minimum density, called *Dmin* by the techies) can be no lighter than the whiteness of the paper itself. For that reason, photographic manufacturers are constantly looking for ways to produce whiter and brighter papers.

✔ The very darkest areas with detail (maximum density, called *Dmax)* are determined by how much light the dyes or emulsion can absorb. The better the Dmax, the darker the dark areas of a print look.

✔ The difference between the very lightest areas and very darkest areas is the *dynamic range,* or tonal range, of the photo.

Even the best photographic papers don't have whites that reflect all the light back to our eyes (only a mirror can do that) or blacks that absorb all the light (only a black hole does that). Thus, the dynamic range of a print is fairly limited, so any scanner should be able to capture a full range of tones from a print.

Transparent originals

Transparent media are lit from behind *(transilluminated)* and viewed by the light that passes through them.

The dynamic range of a transparent original is likely to be much, much greater than that of a print. You can easily find detail in the lightest areas of the slide as well as detail in the darkest areas. That presents a challenge to the scanner: It must have an extended dynamic range that's capable of registering both those bright details and dark details.

Slides

The term *slide* is usually applied to a 35mm transparency that has been cut from the film strip and placed in a mount so that it can be inserted in a slide projector. Larger film sizes can also be mounted and projected this way, but they usually aren't (except in the case of large overhead transparencies used in schools and businesses).

Of course, a slide can be projected onto a screen and viewed by the light that reflects off the screen, but that's another matter. You can view any slide quite well by shining a diffuse (soft, non-directional) light through it and viewing it directly, as shown in Figure 1-3.

The limitations of the substrate don't apply to slides. That is, where a very white piece of paper might reflect 75–80 percent of the light striking it, a slide can easily pass almost 100 percent of the illumination (in the clear or almost-clear areas).

Transparencies

In one sense, color transparencies are nothing more than color slides without the slide mount. You can even ask your photofinisher to process your 35mm slide film but not mount it, if you want, giving you long strips of 24mm x 36mm transparencies.

Transparencies come in other sizes, too. The most common roll film sizes are $2^1/_4$ x $2^1/_4$ inches (now more commonly referred to as 6 x 6 cm), $2^1/_4$ x $2^3/_4$ inches (6 x 7 cm), $2^1/_4$ x $3^1/_2$ inches (6 x 9 cm), and so forth. Transparencies also are available as sheets of film in 4 x 5", 5 x 7", 8 x 10", and 11 x 14" sizes (among others).

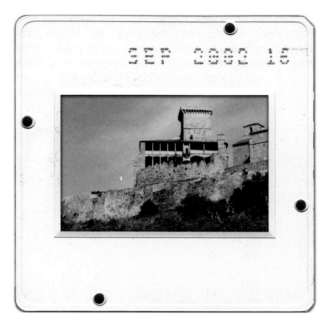

Figure 1-3: View any transparency just by shining light through it.

You see very large transparencies used for advertising displays in large light boxes, up to the mammoth 60-foot-wide Kodak Colorama ("The World's Largest Photograph"), which graced the east balcony inside Grand Central Station in New York City from 1950 to 1990.

Black-and-white or color negatives

Negatives are the film that can be used to make prints (and also film positives, including slides, if you want to go that way). They have a reversed image, with the dark areas of the subject appearing light in the negative, and vice versa. In a color negative, the colors are also reversed, so blues appear to be yellow, reds appear to be cyan, and greens appear to be magenta.

There's an additional complication in the orange mask that overlays all color negative films, which exists to provide better separation of the colors when printed on photographic paper. Because a scanner doesn't respond to the light passing through a color negative the way color paper does, there's no need for the mask, which has to be removed during the scan. Things get interesting because different vendors' color films have different types of orange masks. Photofinishers compensate for these by using filter packs designed for a particular type of film. Any negative-capable scanner has settings to accomplish the same thing. You'll be offered a choice of color negative types; select the type of film you are scanning, and the software will automatically compensate for the orange mask.

Exotica

As your reputation for old photo restoration magic grows, you'll be called upon to scan and fix up some really old, faded pictures of a rather exotic (for our 21st-century eyes) nature. These can include old daguerreotypes, silver prints, 19th-century glass plates, or even tintypes like the one shown in a wretched, unrestored version at top in Figure 1-4, and a wretched, partially restored version at bottom.

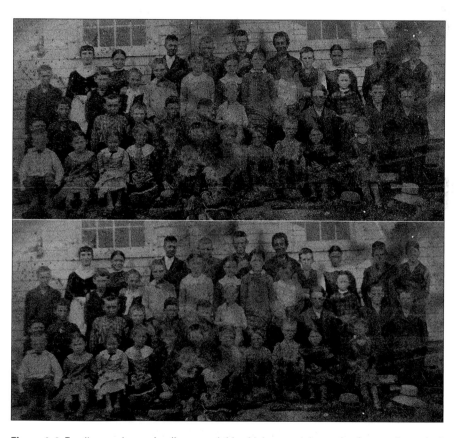

Figure 1-4: Family members who discovered this old damaged tintype (top) were pleased when even a small amount of the picture information was able to be restored.

Although these old photos were captured using different technologies, they all share some common attributes:

✓ **They may be housed in folders, glued to cardboard, or tucked away in frames.** You'll need to be very careful when removing them for scanning to avoid damaging the picture.

✓ **It's very likely that the old pictures will be faded, dark, or low in contrast.**

Increase the contrast and sharpness in your scanner's controls, if possible, because the improvements you make can sometimes be even better than what you could achieve later in your image editor. That's because the scanner is working with the original material.

✓ **Your old photos probably have dust spots, pits, mottling, and other defects that can't be removed by scanning alone.** Your best bet is to try to correct these problems in your image editor.

It's a good idea to scan the photo several times using different tonality settings. You'll end up with several versions, each with different details brought out. You can combine the best portions of each to create one finished photo.

Scanning Prints

The first thing to do before scanning is to prep your original. Although you might not have a lot of control over the artwork you need to scan, you can still prepare ahead of time to improve your chances of success. Here are a few tips:

✓ **Start with the best available original.** Don't use a copy print if you can avoid it. Use a print that was made recently from the original negative. Older prints usually have some scratches, or their colors might have aged over the years. However, as long as you're scanning from a print, use the newest and best print you can find.

If the print is housed in an album, frame, or cardboard display, carefully remove it before scanning unless removal will damage the picture.

✓ **Start with the largest print that fits on your scanner.** If you can choose between a 4 x 6" print and a 5 x 7" print, use the larger print. Because of the grain of the color emulsion in the print, a larger version is likely to be sharper and, more importantly, to have a larger *tonal range* — the range of colors from lightest to darkest. An 8 x 10" print might be even better, but there is a point of diminishing returns. An 8 x 10 might not be any sharper or better; it might simply show the grain of the film in a larger form, particularly if the print was made from a 35mm negative taken with an inexpensive camera. In addition, some scanners are known for having uneven illumination at the edges of the scanning area. A 5 x 7" print centered in the scanning glass won't suffer from this defect; an 8 x 10" print can't avoid it.

✓ **Clean the print and your scanner glass before you scan.** If you scan a dusty print, like the one shown in Figure 1-5, or if dust covers the glass platen or scanning bed of your scanner, you end up with an image that has dust spots that you must remove in your image editor. Dust the print carefully with a cloth and use Windex and compressed air on your scanner's bed.

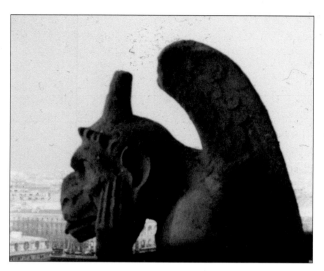

Figure 1-5: Dust off your prints before scanning!

✓ **Make sure the image is aligned properly on the scanner glass.** If you scan a print that's rotated slightly, you can always straighten it in your image editor. Of course, you lose some quality, particularly when straightening horizontal and vertical lines that could have been scanned with proper alignment in the first place. Some scanner software actually can straighten skewed pictures for you, but you want to avoid that feature when possible. The straightening uses the edges of the photo for reference, and that might not coincide with the correct orientation of the image (if the picture itself was printed skewed, for example).

Lining up images when they're face down on the scanner glass is tricky. Sometimes I hold the print up to the light and draw a straight line with a pencil on the back of the print. Then I can make sure the line is parallel to the top edge of the scanner glass so that the image in the photo is perpendicular to the direction of the scan. Hewlett-Packard has helped this problem by introducing a scanner with a transparent lid: You can see exactly how the print is aligned when you close the top. The latest versions of Photoshop Elements have a tool that can straighten scanned images at the click of a mouse.

Working with Scanner Settings

When you're ready to scan an image, you'll find an array of settings, and this section is here to guide you through them. Setting the resolution probably gets the most attention, but your scanner likely has other settings — such as interpolation, sharpening, blurring/descreening, and halftone — that might also help you get the best possible scan. Read on to find out what these settings do, when they're useful, and how to set them.

Choosing a resolution

What's the best resolution to use for a particular scan? Note that this is very different from the question, "What's the top resolution I want for my scanner?" The thing is, the top resolution available in any scanner is unlikely to be of much use to you, and the figures the vendors provide don't really tell you much about the image quality you get at a given resolution, anyway.

Even so, particular tasks have recommended resolutions. Unless you're working with a special image, you probably want to keep within the guidelines that I lay out in the following sections.

Why not simply use the highest resolution of your scanner at all times and be done with it? Here are a few reasons why this is a dumb idea:

✔ **Too much resolution wastes valuable hard drive space.** A 4 x 5" image scanned at 200 samples per inch *(spi* — the number of points in the image captured per linear inch) has 800,000 pixels and can be up to 6.4MB in size. (With the image compression provided by file formats such as TIFF and JPEG, the actual size on your hard drive is likely to be smaller.) Scan the same image at 2400 spi, and you can end up with a 76.8MB file! It wouldn't take long to fill up a hard drive with those babies; even if you archived them to a CD, you'd be able to fit only ten images on the CD and perhaps only 70 on a DVD. At 200 spi, you can pack 125 images on the same CD.

Printers measure resolution in dots per inch, and scanners measure it in samples per inch.

✔ **High-resolution (hi-res) images take a long time to scan.** Depending on your scanner model, you might be able to scan that 200 spi image in ten seconds or so, but you're sure to wait for two or three minutes when scanning the same photo at 2400 spi.

✔ **High-resolution scans of prints don't contain any more useful information.** This is the most important consideration, when you get right down to it. When you scan at a resolution higher than you need, all you're capturing is the grain of the paper (see Figure 1-6) or perhaps the film used to make the print. You're also getting beautiful close-up details of any scratches and dust on the original film plus any dust you forgot to remove before you scanned.

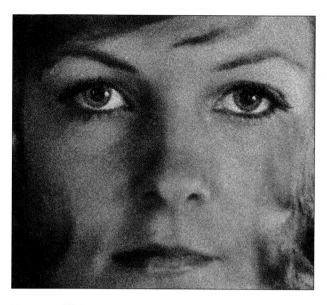

Figure 1-6: High resolution can just highlight the grain.

You actually need to consider three different resolutions:

- ✓ **The resolution of the scanner that captures the image:** I cover scanner resolution in this chapter.

- ✓ **The resolution of the display device that shows the image in your image editor:** Display resolution isn't something that you can do much about. You're probably working with a 17–19" color monitor and have the display resolution set to anywhere from 1024 x 768 pixels to (in my case) 1920 x 1440 or thereabouts.

- ✓ **The resolution of the output device, such as a printer that you'll use to reproduce the image:** The resolution of the output device, such as a 600 dpi laser printer, a 1440 dpi inkjet, or a high-resolution image setter, can affect the resolution you scan at. The higher the resolution of the output device, the more of your scanner's resolution that you can actually put to work.

Here are some guidelines for choosing a resolution for the two most common kinds of scanning tasks.

Line art

Line art includes black-and-white or color drawings comprising only solid lines, dots, or other strokes, with no shading. Artwork that has already been printed, such as photos clipped from publications, also qualifies as line art;

although such images might look like photographs, they're composed of black and white halftone dots.

Line art can usually be scanned effectively at the same resolution that you'll use to print the image, or a fraction of it. If a 600 dpi laser printer outputs an image, use 600 spi. If you'll be using a 1440 dpi inkjet, consider using 720 spi (or something close). Doing this allows a 1:1 (or 4:1, if you halve the output device's resolution to make your scan) correlation between scanned pixels and printed dots. This reduces the chance of the stair-step effect known as *jaggies*. A 3200 spi scan is shown in Figure 1-7.

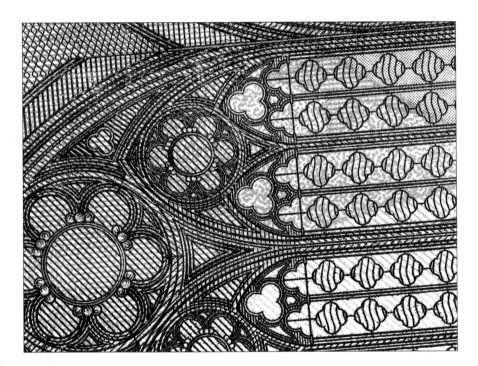

Figure 1-7: High-res scans of line art can provide sharp images.

Why not use 1440 spi when outputting to an inkjet printer? You'll find that the extra detail isn't needed, your image file is four times as large (compared with a lower resolution), and your file takes longer to print. However, if you're scanning something that really does have fine details and is so small that you can avoid mega-file sizes (postage stamps and other small engravings are the classic example), you can use the higher resolution.

Black-and-white and color photos

Black-and-white and color photos are known as *continuous tone* images because they contain a full range of tones from very light to very dark as well as all the shades in between. Photographs are a whole different ballgame than line art.

As you scan photos, choose a resolution based on two factors:

- ✔ What you plan to do with the photo and whether you'll be manipulating it in an image editor
- ✔ Whether you plan to enlarge it

For example, a print destined for a Web page might look just fine scanned at 75 spi because 75 spi is all you need for screen resolution. The same original scanned for reproduction using a printer should be scanned at around 150–200 spi. If you intend to manipulate the photo in your image editor or reproduce it at a size that's larger than the picture's original dimensions, use a higher resolution: perhaps 300 spi. Notice that none of these recommendations approaches the 1200–2400 spi top resolution of most scanners. High resolutions simply aren't required for photographic prints.

Most books about image editing, and even some scanning books, provide you with arcane formulas that you can use to calculate scanning resolutions for photos. These are usually based on the *halftone frequency* (the number of lines of halftone dots per inch in the screen used to create the halftoned version of your photograph). These formulas are needlessly complex. Who, other than professional photographers and other professional graphics workers, actually knows whether a photograph will be printed using an 85-line screen or a 133-line screen or some other frequency?

Today, digital photographers don't have to worry about these details. The halftoning is automatically handled by the printer driver that resides in your computer, and you don't need to know much about what's happening. If you scan a photo at 150–200 spi (or up to 300 spi if enlarging it), you'll get good results most of the time. The real pitfall is scanning at too high a resolution, which wastes your time and hard drive space. Your concern will probably focus more on how to remove moiré effects, discussed in the Blurring/descreening section, later in this chapter.

Many newer scanners can actually calculate an optimal resolution for you. You tell the scanner software what type of destination your image is intended for (Web page, laser printer, imagesetter, and so forth) and select a size for the image (50%, 100%, and so forth). Based on this information, the scanner then chooses the right resolution for you.

Book VI Chapter 1

Scanning Old Photos

Interpolate, schmerpolate

Questions about scanner interpolation are the second most common queries (after resolution) that I have received in the last decade.

Interpolation isn't limited to scanners, of course. You would think so only because scanner vendors like to trumpet their products' interpolation prowess in their specifications lists. *Interpolation* is a process used to create new pixels any time an image is made larger or smaller or changed to a color depth other than the one at which it was captured.

Photoshop uses interpolation all the time. If you enlarge or reduce an image, Photoshop has to create more pixels (when you enlarge) or fewer pixels (when you reduce) to represent the same image. Photoshop or Elements also needs to come up with a new set of pixels when you change an image from, say, 24 bits at full color to 8 bits and 256 colors. Within Photoshop or Elements, interpolation is almost always a bad thing (even if it's a necessary thing) because you always lose some quality when your image editor obliterates real, actual pixels and replaces them with best-guess estimates. You should, therefore, try to retain your image at its original resolution (such as the resolution it was taken at with your digital camera) until you absolutely have to resize it. And always keep an unedited version of the file to fall back on, should you need to!

Sometimes, the term *interpolation* is reserved for making larger images from a given resolution. You'll see the term *downsampling* to describe the type of interpolation used to produce a smaller image. I'm not particularly fussy about terminology that's not often used correctly anyway, so I use *interpolation* to mean both enlarging and reducing images or scans.

When scanning, interpolation isn't quite as evil because the scanner is working with the original image and can avoid some of the quality loss that plagues your image editor.

Scanner interpolation takes place whenever you scan at anything other than the native resolution of the scanner. That means if you're using a 1200 spi scanner and scan at 2400 spi, the scanner actually captures 1200 samples per inch but creates 1200 new pixels to make the resolution seem higher. The same scanner at 300 spi must figure out which 300 pixels per inch best represent the full 1200 spi scan.

Actually, when scanning in even fractions or increments of the scanner's optical resolution, the results are usually quite good. The problems start when you try to scan at odd resolutions like 5000 spi or 332 spi.

As the scanner interpolates an image, it doesn't simply duplicate pixels (say, doubling all the pixels in a 1200 spi scan to produce a 2400 spi image) or throw away pixels (to create a 600 spi scan). Instead, the interpolation algorithm examines the pixels surrounding the new pixel and produces one with characteristics that closely match the transition between the pixels. That is, if one pixel is dark tone and the next pixel is light tone, a medium-tone pixel is created to insert between them, as shown in Figure 1-8.

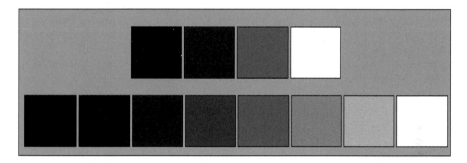

Figure 1-8: Interpolation examines the pixels in the top line and creates the new pixels in the bottom line.

**Book VI
Chapter 1**

Scanning Old
Photos

Interpolation is not all smoke and mirrors. A good interpolation algorithm can accurately calculate the pixels that would have been captured by the scanner if it had been able to scan at the interpolated resolution used. That is, you do get additional information through interpolation. However, there are diminishing returns. A 9600 x 9600 spi interpolated image is not eight times as sharp as one scanned at a true 1200 spi resolution.

Sharpening

You might think of sharpening as a way to increase the resolution of an image without boosting its file size. That's not exactly true. All scanners include optional sharpening routines to enhance images as they are scanned. (In most cases, leaving this feature turned on is a good idea.) Sharpening actually only increases the apparent resolution of an image by increasing the contrast between pixels, but it works very well.

In use, a scanner's sharpening routines examine squares of pixels that are, say, five pixels on a side. Depending on the values of the other 24 pixels in the square, the scanner might (or might not) darken or lighten the center pixel to increase the contrast between that pixel and its neighbors. If the scanner determines that there is a significant difference in contrast between the center pixel and its neighbors, it can increase the contrast even further, making the pixel look sharper, at least in relation to its neighbors. The sharpening algorithms look at every pixel in an image as it relates to its neighboring pixels and increase the contrast as appropriate to enhance the sharpness. Pixels that are included in edges in your image are lightened or darkened to make them more distinct, as shown in Figure 1-9.

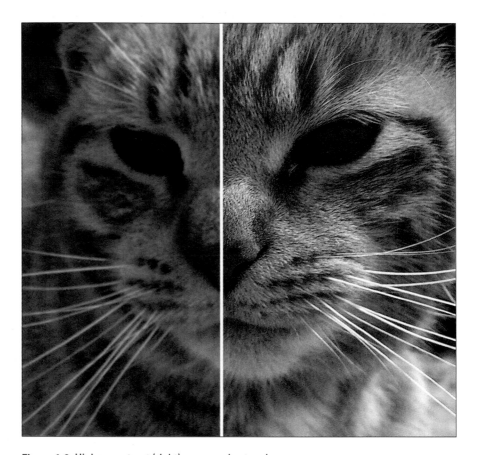

Figure 1-9: Higher contrast (right) can equal extra sharpness.

Because sharpening brings out details that are present in an image but that the scanner can't see otherwise, sharpening really can enhance the apparent resolution of the final image. That's why sharpening in the scanner is probably useful when making most scans. Don't overuse it with photographs, however, because the extra contrast can be objectionable, reducing the number of tones in the image and making highlights too bright and/or shadows too dark. If you sharpen an image, and the contrast is too high, undo the step and try again with a lower sharpening setting.

Blurring/descreening

The opposite side of the sharpening coin is a common scanner feature called *descreening*. Descreening is used when you scan an image that has already been printed and contains halftone dots, such as those found in newspapers, magazines, yearbooks, and other publications. The process blurs the image slightly by reducing the contrast between the edges (in this case, the dots) and tends to make the halftone dots merge.

I've found that descreening settings in most scanners tend to overdo the blurring, and you can get much better scans of halftones by doing the blur yourself in Photoshop or another image editor, as shown in Figure 1-10. Descreening can also help you avoid the *moiré effect* (an objectionable pattern caused by interference between the arrangement of the original halftone screen and the pixels in the scanned image).

Knowing when to halftone

Scanners sometimes have a halftone setting that lets you apply the halftone dots at the time the scan is made. If you know what size your printed image will be and what device will print the image, you can specify a halftone pattern that the scanner can apply.

This is generally not a good idea, and most scanners don't support this feature anymore. Because all the continuous-tone information is lost, you can't edit the image or scale it to a different size.

You can also apply the halftone dots in your image editor. Photoshop lets you apply various dot and dithering schemes, and this might be the choice of sophisticated users who know exactly what they want and need. This was even a good idea back when printers could reproduce only 300 dpi.

Usually, letting your printer apply the halftone dots is best. Laser printers today usually have resolutions of 600 dpi and up, and they have a lot more dots to work with when creating halftone dots (360,000 per square inch with a 600 dpi printer versus a mere 90,000 dots per square inch with a 300 dpi printer).

Other scanner controls

When you're scanning prints, other controls at your disposal might include automatic and manual exposure controls, fancy charts called *histograms* that let you compensate for tonal variations in your photos, color-correcting tools, or even a *densitometer* that lets you measure precisely the lightness, darkness, and color values of your image before you scan. Which of these should you be concerned with? Some controls actually duplicate similar features found in your image editor.

How can you decide? Here are some guidelines:

✔ If you're in a big hurry and need to scan only a couple photos, use your scanner's automatic features and don't worry about fine-tuning your scan. You can do that later in your image editor.

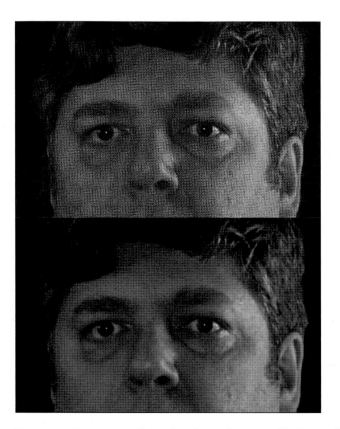

Figure 1-10: You can usually produce better descreened halftones, like the one at the bottom, in your image editor.

- ✓ If your original image is good, your scanner's auto settings will work well. You might not even need to make corrections in your image editor.

- ✓ If quality is very important and your original is a difficult one, use your scanner's controls to get the best original image possible because a good scan enables you to get better results. For example, color correction in an image editor can't add colors that are missing from the scan. However, you might be able to make adjustments with the scanner to grab those colors when the image is captured.

- ✓ If you're scanning a group of images with the same problems, it often makes sense to use your scanner's controls to correct the problem once and then scan each successive image using the same settings. Applying the same tonal or color corrections to a large group of images in an image editor can be tedious.

✔ Your scanner might have controls not found in your image editor. For example, my scanning software has Image Type controls that I can use to precisely set the exact type of image being scanned. My choices include Evening, Landscape, Skin Tones, Night, Snow, and Shadow. The scanner has built-in settings for those types of photos, and I can choose an appropriate image type to apply the settings before I ever make a scan.

✔ You want to use automated features that make your scans go faster. For example, my scanning software has choices for output resolution that include Newspaper, Magazine, Art Print, Photo Print, and others. I can choose a destination and let the software choose the resolution for the scan.

A great deal of your flexibility depends on the scanning software you use. Some scanning applications are fully automated, which means they collect information during a prescan and then determine the kind of image (that is, a color photo, grayscale photo, or line art), the proper exposure, and even what resolution to use. Other software lets you make these settings yourself.

I like to use automation when it is likely to give me a good scan as long as I can use manual settings when I need to. For example, my favorite scanning software lets me choose a color filter to scan through. That's a great tool for removing stains from a spoiled black-and-white photograph.

For example, if there's a greenish stain on the photo (who knows where *that* came from?), I can choose to scan through a light-green filter. The green stain is invisible to the scanner through the green filter, so the stain fades away. (The filter is simulated by manipulating the red, green, and blue information of a full-color scan.) Meanwhile, the details in red and blue are made darker and more visible. This works because the light-green filter blocks only some of the red and blue. (If it really let only green light through, the red and blue tones would appear as black.)

Or I might have a page with blue ledger lines and faded reddish text, as shown in Figure 1-11. I can use a light-blue filter to make the lines vanish, simultaneously making the reddish text darker because the blue filter passes all the blue light but blocks some of the red (and green). This technique is great for scanning legal and family records, deeds, and similar documents.

Scanning Film

Scanning film is only a little more complicated than scanning prints. But you must have a film-capable scanner, of course. You'll need to refer to the instruction manual for your scanner and the slide scanning software for the exact steps to follow, but here are some general tips.

Prepping the film

You absolutely must make sure the film is clean, particularly if you are scanning a 35mm slide or negative. Sometimes dust settles on the film when it's still wet and becomes embedded in the emulsion side; sometimes film just gets plain dusty. Because small film images are enlarged many times as you work with them, you magnify the size of the dust or other artifacts at the same time. For example, a 24mm x 36mm transparency enlarged to 5 x 7 inches is blown up to roughly five times its original size — and each tiny dust mote is visible when magnified that much.

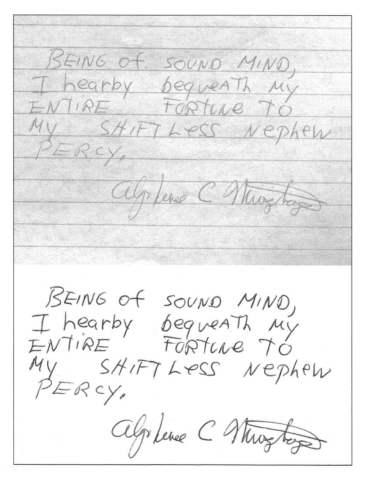

Figure 1-11: The blue lines are diminished while the reddish text is darkened in the bottom version.

Dust on either transparencies or negatives appears as dark black dots when scanned, of course, because the dots block the light from passing through to the sensor. However, when scanning a negative, you reverse the negative image to create a positive, turning the dust spot into a white speck. Tiny white specks can blend in with lighter areas of your image a little and are fairly easy to retouch out of the dark areas. (That's not to imply that you can go ahead and scan dusty negatives.) Dust on transparencies shows up as dark spots that are very visible and unsightly, so you should take extra care to make sure your transparencies are extremely clean when you scan them.

Clean dust from either a transparency or negative with a soft brush, an ear syringe, or a blast of canned air. Be careful not to allow the residual dust to scratch your soft film as you remove it. That's why soft brushes and air are your best tools. Figure 1-12 shows a typical slide scanner's film carriage. Dust off the film after you mount it in the carrier.

**Book VI
Chapter 1**

Scanning Old
Photos

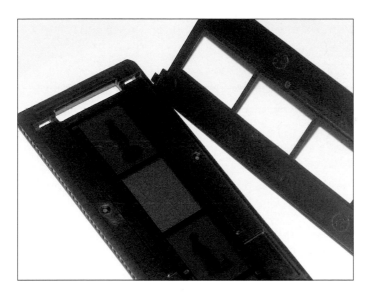

Figure 1-12: Dust off your film after inserting it in the scanner's carrier.

Film always has two sides: an emulsion side (where the image information is stored) and a base side. The emulsion side is usually dull-looking when compared with the shiny base side. If you're somewhere that is fully lit, you can tell which is which by holding the film sideways and looking across the film. If you view a strip of negatives, the film curls toward the emulsion side. If you plan to scan a Kodachrome slide, the emulsion side appears to be etched.

There is another way to tell which side is the emulsion side, and it works even in total darkness, but you're not going to like it. Back in my darkroom days, when I wanted to know which was the emulsion side of a piece of film or photographic paper, I'd put an edge between my lips. The emulsion side sticks to your lip. If you want to test this out, don't slobber all over the image area of an important image.

You can sometimes remove stubborn artifacts by soaking the film in distilled water. However, this works only if the dust hasn't replaced some of the image-forming part of the emulsion. In addition, the water removes the protective chemical applied to color film as a last step (black-and-white film is simply washed and allowed to dry after processing), so you need some of that solution if you want your film to last after cleaning. As you might guess, washing film should be done only as a last resort and only by those who know what they're doing.

In the old days, photographers used to do crazy things with film to make it printable, like soaking it in oil to mask scratches and printing it wet.

Performing the scan

When your film is clean and you're ready to start scanning, here are the steps to follow:

1. **Place the film on or in the scanner (depending on whether you're using a flatbed scanner or a dedicated film scanner) in a holder designed for it.**

   The holder masks the areas outside the image portion of the film. This is an important step that reduces the possibility of stray light striking the sensor, thus reducing the contrast in your image.

2. **Insert the film in the holder so that the emulsion side of the film is facing the sensor.**

   You want the light to pass through the film's base side and leave through the emulsion side. If you do the reverse, the light passes through the emulsion and is then diffused by the base side, giving you an image that is less sharp than it might be.

3. **Make sure you've done whatever is necessary to turn on your flatbed scanner's transparency light source.**

   Usually, this step is performed in the scanning software. If you're scanning a color negative, your scanning software has a dialog box, like the one shown in Figure 1-13, that lets you specify what brand and type of color film is being scanned. That ensures that the orange mask and other characteristics of that particular color negative film are dialed into the scanning software. You'll find the brand name of the film printed along the edge of the film itself.

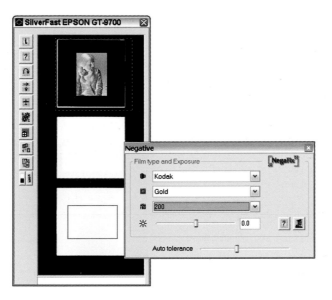

Figure 1-13: Choose your film brand and type to optimize the scan.

4. **Do a** *prescan,* **which is the step that all scanner software provides to let you capture a preview image before doing the main scan.**

   While you're viewing the prescanned image, your scanning software might offer various controls that let you choose black points and white points (the darkest and lightest areas of the image that contain image information).

5. **Make any corrections that are appropriate by using the dust removal, sharpening, brightness, contrast, and tonal controls of your scanner software.**

   The options vary widely from program to program.

6. **Set the black points and white points and then choose your resolution.**

   If you're making an important scan, you'll want to choose the highest optical resolution your flatbed scanner provides, typically 1200 to 2400 spi. A dedicated film scanner has resolution choices in the 2700 to 4000 spi range (and up). You can choose the setting recommended for the size of film you're scanning.

   Be prepared for a long wait while the scanner captures all that detail, and for the size of the file you end up with. A good scan of a transparency is a beautiful thing to behold, so it's worth the wait!

Book VII
Printing and Sharing Your Digital Images

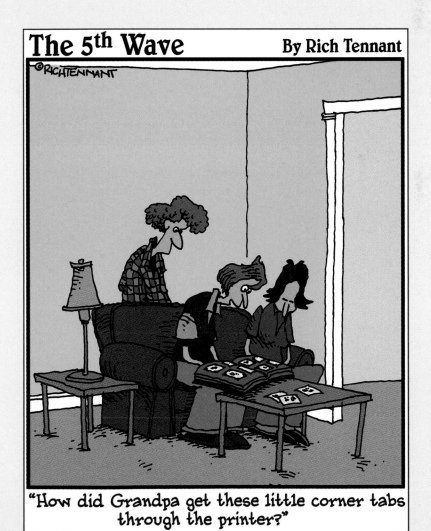

The 5th Wave   By Rich Tennant

"How did Grandpa get these little corner tabs through the printer?"

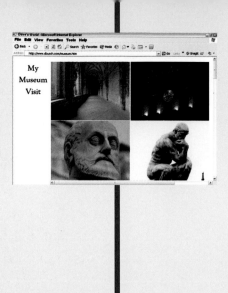

The best part about taking great digital photos is sharing them with your family and friends. In this book, I show you all the different ways you can make prints to pass around and techniques for sharing your best shots over the Internet.

After all, you can do a lot more with good photos than just admire them from afar. I also provide tips for setting up online galleries so friends, family, and colleagues can enjoy the results of your photographic efforts from the comfort of their own computers.

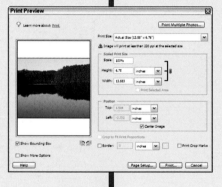

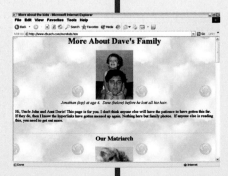

Chapter 1: Printing Your Final Result

In This Chapter

✔ Figuring out if and when you need to print your photos

✔ Choosing the right printer for the job

✔ Understanding the printing process

✔ Hiring a professional printing company or service bureau

Digitally captured and retouched photos live on your computer. That's where they came to life, whether you captured them with a digital camera or scanned a printed original. It's also where they may have been doctored for any number of purposes — to make them smaller for e-mail to friends and family, to make them safe for use on a Web page, or to make them picture-perfect for printing.

However, unless you deal only in Web images or on-screen presentations, you probably need lots and lots of prints of your photos. In this chapter, you discover when and how to print your photos, which printers do what kind of job, and how to create the best-quality print of your digital images.

Why Do You Need Prints?

The reasons you might need to print your photos are as numerous as the photos themselves. Look for your own reasons among these:

✔ You need to create a suitable-for-framing version of a photo that was too small or too damaged to be framed before you edited it. You can transform that wallet-sized photo into a framed picture for the top of your grand piano. Or, perhaps, a picture has wrinkles or tears you can fix with your image editor before making a pristine, new print. See Book VII for tips on restoring damaged photos.

- You want to create a backup print of a very precious photo in case something happens to the original. Better yet, display the duplicate and keep the precious original in a safer place, such as a safety-deposit box. Put a disc containing the digital version of the original in the box, too, so you won't have to duplicate your editing efforts.

- You're building a portfolio of your digital artwork, and you need a printed copy to show to possible employers or clients. Make as many prints as you want economically, and distribute far and wide.

- You need a *proof*, or printed evaluation image, that you can submit to someone who can't view the image online for his or her approval. You can fiddle with the proof print to make sure it's an accurate representation so the person passing judgment on it will have the best copy possible to approve.

- You require an evaluation proof for comparing the digital image with the hard copy original, and just viewing the file electronically won't provide the necessary information about print quality. The proof of the pudding, in this case, is in the viewing.

- Your photo is for printed marketing materials, such as ads, brochures, or flyers, and you need to create camera-ready art that a professional printer can use to create the finished materials. Although many professional printers today can work with digital files, some cannot. You need a print for the print shop's use.

- You'll often need prints for holiday greeting cards or birth announcements and other special events.

- When I prepare publicity pictures for my local newspaper, I always provide the original photo on CD. But I also include a print so the editor can decide whether the photo is worth using without having to pop the CD in a drive and dig down into it to view the picture.

Although this chapter's title is "Printing Your Final Result," you may also want to print versions of your image as you go along in the editing process. Because computer monitors aren't capable of displaying colors exactly as they print, you may want to print at least one in-progress version of your image so that you can check for color, clarity, and other qualities before you commit the final version to that sheet of expensive photo paper. You can purchase lower-priced photo paper for your test prints (because printing on plain old inkjet paper may be misleading) and then use the good stuff for your final printout.

Why does the same photo look different if you print it on plain inkjet paper than it does on photographic paper? The porous nature of regular inkjet paper absorbs more of the ink, and this affects the reflective quality of the colors. Images look darker, contrast is lost, and overall quality is diminished if you print on porous paper. If you print on glossy or matte photographic paper, where a coating on the paper prevents absorption, your photo's color and content stand on their own, unaffected by the paper. No details, color, or contrast is lost.

Evaluating Your Printing Options

After you know that you need to print your photo, it's time to decide how to print it. If you have only one printer and no money for or access to another printer, then the decision is already made — you'll use your one and only printer. If you have the cash for the perfect printer for your particular photo, that's great. If you don't have the cash but have access to a variety of printers, that's great, too. With the assumption that you have some choices available to you, consider the list of printing possibilities found in Table 1-1.

Table 1-1	Printer Options	
Type of Printer	*Price Range*	*Comments*
Inkjet	$50–$250	Great for color prints; good text quality, too
Laser	$300–$3,000	Fast, economical for text; not the best choice for images
Dye-Sublimation	$150–$500 (and up)	Best color print quality, but can't handle text

Inkjet printers

The name *inkjet* gives you an idea of how the inkjet printer works — assuming that the word *jet* makes you think of the water jets on a whirlpool bath or spa. The way these printers work is rather simple. *Piezoelectric crystals* make the ink cartridges vibrate (the crystals are sandwiched between two electrodes, which make the crystals dance). Different levels of voltage cause the crystals to vibrate differently, which adjusts the colors and the amount of color sprayed through a nozzle onto the paper.

Color inkjet printers can create photo-quality images, assuming you use good-quality photo paper for the output. Price isn't necessarily an indication of print quality, and you should print a test page before making a purchase or go on the recommendation of someone who owns the same model.

Laser printers

Laser printers work very much like photocopiers. A laser beam is aimed at a photoelectric belt or drum, building up an electrical charge. This happens four times, once for each of the four colors used to make all the colors in your image — cyan, magenta, yellow, and black. The electric charge makes the colored toner stick to the belt, and then the belt transfers the toner to the drum. The paper rolls along the drum as it moves through the printer, which transfers the toner from the drum to the paper. Then, either pressure or heat (or both) makes the toner stick to the paper.

Color laser printers are more expensive than inkjets and black-and-white laser printers and are more expensive to operate. Indeed, now that the prices for color laser printers have dipped down to affordable levels, many users are complaining that they easily spend more on toner in the first few months they own these devices than they spent on the printers themselves!

Dye-sublimation printers

Here, the name of the printer doesn't tell you much about the way the printer works. Despite their cryptic name, dye-sublimation printers work in a relatively straightforward way. A strip of plastic film, called a transfer ribbon, is coated with cyan, magenta, and yellow dye. When a print job is sent to the printer, a thermal print head heats up the paper-sized (4-x-6-inch or 8 1/2-x-10-inch) panel of plastic transfer ribbon. Variations in temperature control what colors and the amount of color that are applied to the paper. Because the paper has a special coating on it, the dye sticks.

Dye-sublimation printers produce an excellent image, especially for color photos. The subtle results are great for professional designers, artists, and photographers. The expense for full-sized dye-sub printers may be prohibitive for small businesses and home users, but the lower-priced models that produce only snapshot-sized prints and cost less than $150 (plus about 30 cents per print for paper and ribbon) may be within reach. There are only a few dye-sub printers on the market these days, but many are used by photographers who snap photos at special events and make pro-quality prints for sale on the spot.

Touring the Print Process

Regardless of the photo-editing and retouching software that you're using to process your photographs, some aspects of the image-printing process are the same. With most image editors, the print process consists of the following options:

✔ You get to choose which printer to print to. If you have a black-and-white laser and a color inkjet, for example, you can choose to output to the color inkjet.

✔ You can choose how many copies to print.

✔ You can choose to print only part of the image by choosing the Selection option. This assumes you made a selection before issuing the Print command.

✔ You can adjust your printer's properties to print at different levels of quality, assuming the printout is the final version.

✔ You can choose to print crop marks, which can help you or a professional printer cut along the edges of the printout. If you want to frame a 5-x-7-inch photo, for example, and you're printing it on 8½-x-11-inch paper (letter size), the crop marks can help you cut the paper to fit inside the frame and mat you're using.

Preventing surprises with Print Preview

Before you actually commit your image to paper, you may want to see a smaller view of an image in the context of a sheet of the currently set paper size, just to make sure everything is okay. This prevents nasty surprises such as printing your favorite portrait in horizontal format and cutting your subject in half. In virtually all software programs, you choose File⇨Print Preview (or just File⇨Print, depending on which program you're using) to see how the printout will look. Figure 1-1 shows the Print Preview window in Photoshop Elements. If you're happy with what you see, you go ahead and issue the Print command (File⇨Print or Ctrl+P) to open the Print dialog box.

Understanding your output options

In the Print Preview window, you can print the image by clicking the Print button, and you can also change the scale (size) and location of the image on the paper. With some image editors, a Show More Options check box opens an extension of the original dialog box. Options here may include applying a caption to your image or turning on crop marks. You may even be able to apply a background color and a border, which can be helpful if you're printing an image for framing and don't have a mat for the frame.

The Page Setup dialog box, which you open by clicking the Page Setup button in the Print Preview dialog box, lets you change the printer you're sending the job to and view your printer's properties. (See Figure 1-2.) It's also another place to choose the Background, Border, and Corner Crop Marks options. In many packages, the Page Setup dialog box also allows you to change the paper size and orientation.

Book VII Chapter 1

Printing Your Final Result

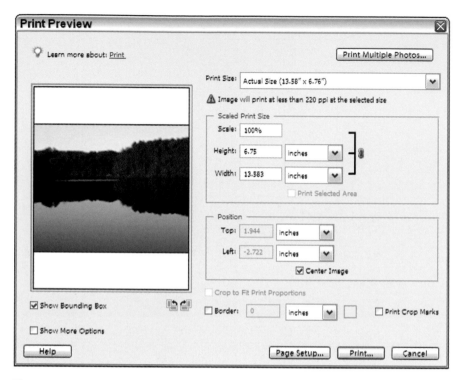

Figure 1-1: A Print Preview window shows how your image will look on paper.

Printing your photos

When you're ready to print your work, choose File⇨Print (or choose Print from the Print Preview window) and use the Print dialog box to take advantage of your printing options — which printer to use, how many copies to print, and so forth.

If the software you're using offers a drastically different set of options through its Print dialog box, you can press the F1 key (in Windows) to open the software's help files. (Mac users can click the Help button in the dialog box.) If that doesn't work (although it should because most applications support this feature), use the Help menu and look for articles about printing. The software may have also come with a *Read Me* file — a file that came with the software if you downloaded it from the Web — or a printed manual that you can refer to.

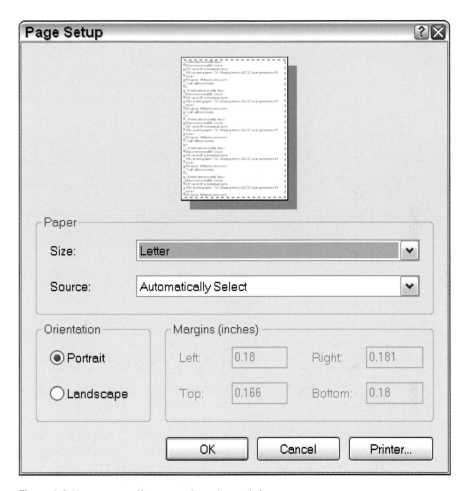

Figure 1-2: You can specify paper orientation and size.

Before you click the Print or OK button to begin the print job, you'll want to make sure the right paper is in the printer and be sure how your particular printer wants the paper fed — good-side down, the proper end in first, and so on:

✔ The printer should come with instructions, if not in a printed manual then right on the printer trays themselves, through little pictures of paper with arrows to show you how and where to insert the paper.

✔ Most photographic paper has a *good side,* which has the image-enhancing coating on it, and a repeated brand name on the back, making it easier to tell which side you want to print on. If you're not sure, though, do a test print first. In the worst case, you'll print on the wrong side and have to do it again, wasting a single sheet of paper. If you're planning to print several copies of the image, it's better to waste a single sheet than to print all ten copies on the wrong side of the paper!

Using Professional Printing Services

Also known as a *service bureau,* a professional printing firm offers services to graphic artists, photographers, fine artists, businesses (for business cards, brochures, and so on), and the public. Chains (such as FedEx Kinko's, AlphaGraphics, and Kwik Kopy stores) offer such services, and some office supply stores print your graphic files for a fee. You can also find small, privately owned printing services, which may charge more than the chains do, but you get personalized service and may find the staff more willing to help you if you're not entirely sure what you need to provide in order for them to do a job for you.

I used service bureaus for many years, back when laser printers could output text at no more than 300 dpi. Service bureaus were an economical way to produce black-and-white camera-ready pages (which can be photographed by the printer to make printing plates) without the need to purchase a high-resolution printer or *imagesetter* (a high-resolution printer especially suited for images). Those can be costly. Today, most laser printers have 600 dpi or better resolution, so the need for service bureaus for text output is reduced. They are still a good idea for making full-color prints from your digital photos if you don't own a color printer that provides sufficient quality.

Choosing a service bureau

Not sure who to call when you're ready to shop for a service bureau/printing service? You can always check the Yellow Pages online or in print, or you can ask friends and business associates for referrals. The best people to ask are graphic artists or people who work for an ad agency; they're likely to use service bureaus pretty extensively, and their recommendations would be valuable.

Before you hire a service bureau to print your photos, you want to ask the folks there a few questions:

✔ What do they charge and how do they determine their prices? Do they have minimum fees?

✔ When can they finish the job? Most service bureaus will want to fit your job into their normal queue of projects. They may charge extra for rush jobs. Find out what constitutes a rush job — is that overnight service, or anything less than a week?

✔ What file formats do they support (so you know the format in which you should save your photo after editing it)? At one time, service bureaus could handle only Macintosh files and common Macintosh formats, such as TIFF or PICT. Today, most service bureaus support all platforms and all image file formats. It doesn't hurt to check, though.

✔ Can you view a sample of the printout before paying for the final copies? It can be helpful to view a proof or evaluation copy, even if you have to pay extra.

✔ Is the kind of output you're looking for something they've done before and done frequently?

With answers to these questions in hand, you can choose the right service bureau for your needs.

If the person you're working with isn't open and cooperative with you, *run, don't walk,* to another company. I've worked with both kinds of service bureaus — the kind where the staff assumes you should know everything and doesn't want to be bothered explaining things, and the kind where folks are more than willing to help and answer any question, no matter how simple it is. Obviously, the former type of company doesn't deserve your business, and the latter type of company is best.

Tell them what you want, what you really, really want

After choosing a service bureau to work with, you need to discuss your exact printing needs. When you tell the person helping you how you plan to use the print, he or she should

✔ Suggest the type of paper for the print.

✔ Tell you what file format you need to use (a `.psd` file created in Photoshop, a `.tif` file, and so on) and whether you need to provide printed, camera-ready art.

If you need to provide camera-ready art, ask whether you need to provide *color separations* (each color within your image printed on a separate sheet of paper) and what kind of paper the bureau prefers you print to. If you have only an inkjet printer, the serviceperson may balk at your using it to create the camera-ready art. In general, though, any good service bureau prefers to get the image as an electronic file so that the staff can work with the image as needed to give you the printout you require.

Book VII Chapter 1

Printing Your Final Result

Knowing when you need a service bureau

In the end, the choice as to whether to work with a service bureau will come down to money. Time is money, and money buys quality if you shop carefully for printing services and/or your own printer:

✔ If you need a perfect, absolutely beautiful print of the photo and can't afford a high-end printer of your own (or don't know anyone who has one you can use), you need to spend the money to have a service bureau create the print for you.

✔ If you need a high-quality print and have a quality dye-sublimation or color laser printer at your disposal, you may be able to do the printing on your own.

If I sound as though I'm disregarding the role of inkjets in the printing process, I'm not. I've printed many photos with an inkjet printer and given them as gifts, used them as camera-ready art for brochures and business cards, and so forth. Some of my original artwork has also been printed on an inkjet, and the items look just fine in a portfolio. The printer you use depends on the print quality you need and whether the printer you have is capable of providing it. You might love the output that your inkjet generates, and if so, that's great. You've saved some money, and you have a quick and easy way to create your prints!

Chapter 2: Sharing Pictures on the Web

In This Chapter

✓ **Sharing your digital photo masterpieces with friends and family**

✓ **Showing off your business online**

✓ **Using commercial sites to share your pictures**

✓ **Creating your own Web page for displaying pictures**

*O*f course you can e-mail your photos to personal and business contacts, but most people are pretty tired of getting images attached to e-mail messages. They have to download the images in order to open and view them, and if they're on a dial-up connection to the Internet (as a surprising number of folks still are), that can be a pain. And after the download is (finally) complete, what do they do with the pictures? If they don't need the image or if the subject of the photo isn't near or dear to them, they either throw it out (into the Trash or Recycle Bin) or squirrel the image away in a folder they'll never open again. I have a folder on my desktop called Other People's Images where I drag all the pictures that I would feel bad tossing but have no use for.

So if e-mail isn't the best way to share pictures with people who need or want to see them, what is? You have several options, including posting them on your own Web site or using one of the many image-sharing services. In this chapter, you discover what Web sharing tools are available, how to pick the one that's right for you, and how to get busy sharing photos on the Web.

Appreciating the Advantages of Web Sharing

By using the Web to share images, you eliminate the other person's need to save or throw out the images you've sent. He or she can view them, say,

"Aw, isn't that cute!" or "Wow! Cool car!" and that's it. No need to download, save, throw out, or do anything with the image other than just look at it. If people want to save or print the image after they view it, that's up to them, but it isn't required or even firmly suggested. Figure 2-1 shows a page of images posted to a Web site. All people have to do to see the pictures is type the Web address into their browsers and voilà! There are the photos.

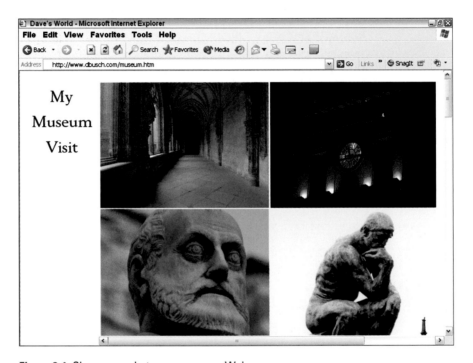

Figure 2-1: Share your photos on your own Web page.

By using the Web to share pictures, you're saving your image recipients' time, hard drive space, and aggravation by creating a single repository for all the images you want to share. You're also making it easier for yourself to keep up-to-date images available to all who want to see them.

Before you share a batch of photos with the world (the Internet is international!), check the photos for anything you'd regret sharing with the rest of the population. Avoid sharing identifying features, such as addresses and people's last names, which enable strangers to make undesired contact with you. Also check for embarrassing content. Going over the images with a discriminating eye before you share them will pay off in the long run.

Sharing personal photos with family and friends

The benefits of using the Web to share personal photos are obvious. You can share vacation photos, school pictures, shots of your new house, pool, car, bathroom tile — whatever. Through your pictures online, you can share all the stuff that you'd tell people about in a holiday newsletter. Think of the savings in postage alone! Instead of enclosing that extra sheet (or sheets) of paper, just write inside your holiday card the Web address where your photos can be found. If most of your friends and family have e-mail, you can alert them that way and save your wrist the strain of writing a Web address 50 times. Figure 2-2 shows an e-mail containing a Web address set up as a link. Recipients need only click the link in the e-mail and they're taken directly to your photos, wherever they're stored.

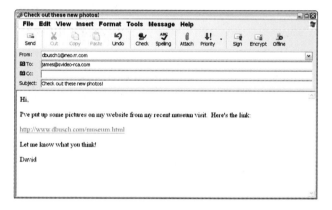

Figure 2-2: E-mail your picture link to a friend for point-and-click access.

Many e-mail programs will create such a *hot link* for you. For example, if you type anything that begins with `http://` into recent versions of Windows Mail, Outlook, Outlook Express, or America Online's mail system, the e-mail software automatically converts the address into a hot link, colors it blue, and supplies an underline that lets the recipient know the link is live.

The recipient must also have the HTML option active for your link to be hot when the message is received. If not, the recipient can still jump to your Web page by highlighting the link, copying it (usually by pressing Ctrl+C, or ⌘+C on a Mac), and then pasting the link into a browser's address bar (press Ctrl+V, or ⌘+V on a Mac).

Of course, some sharing is very targeted. If you want only your friends from college to see one batch and your family to see another, and you don't necessarily want the two camps to see each other's photos, how can you control it? By only telling certain people about certain images. Other than someone deliberately searching for your photos online, people will go and look only at the photos you direct them to, and by controlling whom you tell, you control who sees your images. If you want everyone and anyone to see all of your photos, you can store them all in the same place and use your name to identify them, so anyone can find them by searching the Web.

So where are these Web sites where your pictures can be found? They're everywhere. These sites are easy to use, easy to access, and make sharing your photos with whomever you want very simple.

Sharing images with business associates

Opened a new warehouse or have a new product to offer? Don't print up thousands of brochures or product information sheets, and certainly don't skimp and print up black-and-white flyers because printing in color is so expensive. Color is cheap online, and the cost (if any) of sharing your images online is just a tiny fraction of the cost of printing. You can even promote your goods and services with pictures, as shown in Figure 2-3.

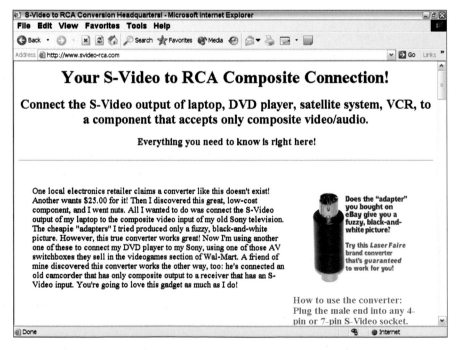

Figure 2-3: One reason for posting your photos online is to sell your company's goods or services.

You can put color images on your company Web site, or if you don't have one yet, you can usually get some free Web space from the people you're already paying to provide your e-mail and Internet connection — your ISP (Internet service provider). You can take advantage of the free Web space allocated to each customer. Although you probably don't have a lot of space, it might be just enough to share a bunch of photos because photos saved for the Web (in GIF or JPG format) are much smaller in file size than photos shared in other formats. You can get a lot of photos in 10MB of space.

To find out if your ISP offers free Web space, call its support phone number or go to its Web site. Most ISPs offer either online or phone support to coach you through the process. The folks at most ISPs assume that, if you're using their free space rather than registering a domain of your own, you're probably not a full-fledged Web designer. Using Earthlink as an example, going to www.earthlink.net/membercenter/benefits/webspace/ takes you to a page where you can click a link and put together a 10MB Web site. In fact, Earthlink's Free Webspace page has as one of its suggestions a recommendation for using the space to create a photo album.

Choosing a Free Sharing System

There are really too many free Web page hosting sites to list, and it's hard to tell which ones will remain active during the life of this book. I listed some in earlier editions and they were nearly *all* defunct or had changed within 12 to 18 months. Kodak, in particular, has changed the name of its photo-sharing site three or four times in the last few years, the most recent revisions from Picture Center to Kodak EasyShare Gallery to just plain Kodak Gallery. You'll find an up-to-date guide to free or nearly free hosting services at www.clickherefree.com. Of course, I'm hoping *that* service won't become defunct soon, too. (But it has hung around for a couple versions of this book, and it was still there when I worked in this fourth edition!)

Book VII
Chapter 2

Sharing Pictures
on the Web

Your best bet is your ISP or big operations like MSN, Kodak, and others, which are likely to be with us over the long haul. Of course, longevity may not be important to you. After all, when one service pulls up stakes and packs up its tent, you can always switch to another, newer free service. As a bonus, you don't have to worry about erasing all your outdated photos on the old service. They'll do it for you when they close up the shop.

You have a lot of choices. You can use an online sharing system to display your images. Most of these systems offer the space for free. You can build your own Web site in the free space that your ISP offers, or you can register your own domain and set up your own space on a host's Web server. In this case, a host offers space on its computer for you to store your pages, usually for a monthly or annual fee. You can also set up your own *Web server* (a computer that serves up Web pages to people on the Internet), but I wouldn't recommend it solely to store your images.

The best option for you depends on what you want, how much you're willing to pay, and how much time you want to devote to setting up your images online. From simple and set up in no time to slightly complex and completely customized, your choices run the entire spectrum.

Using commercial sharing sites and services

Commercial normally means *for a fee,* right? Well, not necessarily. Many of your sharing options are free, with additional options available if you pay a nominal amount. Flickr, for example, (see Figure 2-4) offers no-cost memberships that limit you to 100MB of uploads a month, which may be plenty of space if you want to add a few dozen photos to your display every 30 days. For a $24.95 annual fee, you can sign up for a Flickr Pro account with unlimited uploads.

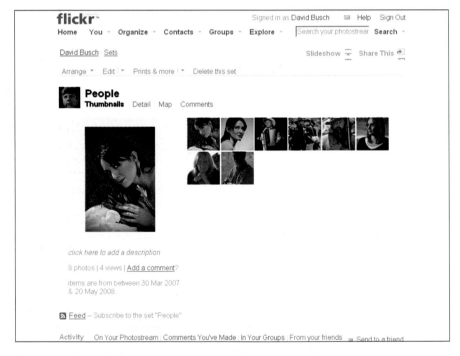

Figure 2-4: Flickr offers free and paid versions of its photo-sharing services.

Other commercial sharing services — Web sites known as *online galleries* — allow you to post your images for free in exchange for making you look at ads around the periphery of the Web page that displays your images. The thinking is that, by exposing you (and those you send to the site to see your photos) to the ads, the gallery's advertising partners gain exposure. Others provide free space simply because they want to be nice or to perpetuate an interest in photography. Some sell software, which they offer you throughout their site, enticing you to buy their image-editing and/or photo album application. You don't have to buy, but the companies figure that many people will.

Many services are available. Type *Online Galleries* or similar keywords into an Internet search engine to find free or low-fee services.

If you're willing to pay to store and display your pictures, you might be better off with a service like Flickr's Pro option, SmugMug, or PBase (www.smugmug.com and www.pbase.com). They offer versatile photo sharing without many of the limitations of the free services.

For example, SmugMug offers three levels of service: Standard, Power User, and Pro, for (at this writing) $39.95, $59.95, and $149.95 per year. Each service offers unlimited capacity and uses an interface that makes it easy to upload hundreds of photos quickly. With the basic service, you can track visits to your gallery, password-protect your images, organize your photos by keyword tags, and convert your images to prints and gifts. The Power User service lets you add video clips and choose your own colors and fonts for your gallery and allows much higher levels of traffic to your gallery, just in case you become hugely popular. The Pro level galleries let you sell your prints through SmugMug and even make a profit from your work.

PBase offers similar features, and some bonuses, including a slick online magazine with gorgeous photos and useful articles. PBase charges $23 a year for 300MB of photo storage and $60 annually for 900MB of storage. You can add more storage in 300MB increments.

A new option is Adobe's Photoshop Express Web site (http://www.photoshop.com/express, which brings Photoshop Elements–like editing tools to an online photo-sharing service. (See Figure 2-5.) Other services to evaluate (all alive and kicking as I write this) include PhotoBucket, Snapfish, Kodak Gallery, and Shutterfly (at http://photobucket.com, www.snapfish.com, www.kodakgallery.com, and www.shutterfly.com).

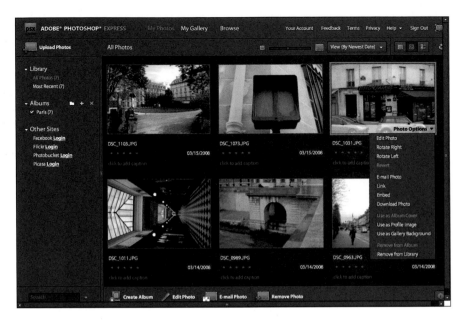

Figure 2-5: Photoshop Express offers basic image-editing tools.

Displaying images on your Web space

Whether your ISP provides the space for free or you enlist a paid host to provide space, you can use your Web space to store and display photos that you want to share with friends, family, customers, and business associates. Putting the images online requires a series of simple steps:

1. **Prepare your photos for use on the Web by opening them in a photo-editing package, such as Photoshop Elements, and saving them in a Web-safe format.**

   The two formats that all Web browsers (notably Internet Explorer, Firefox, Safari, and Opera) can deal with are .gif and .jpg. The best for photos is .jpg because it supports the multitude of colors and shading within the images.

2. **Set up the Web page where the images will be displayed.**

   You can use a variety of graphical tools to design the page (including Microsoft FrontPage) or you can create a page by writing HTML (HyperText Markup Language) code. If you're using an ISP's free Web space, the ISP gives you step-by-step procedures for creating a Web page, and the software does most of the work for you.

3. **Upload the Web page and the images.**

This is typically done with FTP (File Transfer Protocol) software; if you're using your ISP, it may provide an Upload page that loads both the Web page you set up and the images you want to display.

You can find free or low-cost FTP software online from sites such as www.tucows.com and www.hotfiles.com. You can also do a search for Free FTP Software at Google (www.google.com). Venerable oldies like WSFTP LE, shown in Figure 2-6, are very popular. Newbies (new online users) may prefer a program like FTP Explorer, which has a Windows Explorer–like interface, while Mac users like Transmit.

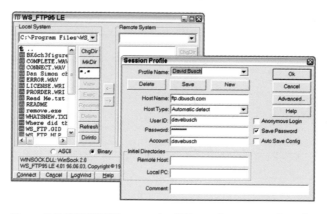

Figure 2-6: WSFTP LE is a popular FTP transfer program for uploading Web pages.

4. **Visit the page online to see how it looks.**

   You always want to check your page online to see if it's okay before you send people there to see your images. With any luck, it won't look like my page, shown in Figure 2-7.

   If you want to make changes, open the Web page file on your computer, make the changes, and upload it again.

If you check your page online and you see red Xs (in Internet Explorer) or gray icons with a question mark (in Netscape Navigator) where images should be, then the browser can't locate the image that's supposed to be there. Check your Web page settings to make sure that you have the right pictures in the right places, and check to see that you've uploaded all the images to your host's Web server!

As time goes by, you can always expand and improve your Web pages:

✔ **Refreshing content:** Edit your Web pages and add new pictures. Or take down the old ones entirely and replace them with your latest shots. As you become more proficient in setting up images and designing Web pages, your site can grow with you.

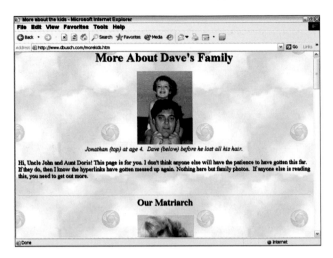

Figure 2-7: Family Web pages are popular — with families!

- ✔ **Organizing pictures:** Set up multiple Web pages and categorize your images. Set up a Vacations page, a Baby Pictures page, or a Graduation Ceremony page. Any category or special topic can have its own page.

- ✔ **Adding links:** Create links on your Web pages that take visitors to other people's sites or to online galleries where you have other pictures stored. If you're a real photography bug, you may have some of your more artistic shots stored on a gallery site. Through a link on your page, you can direct people to your works of art.

- ✔ **Letting others join in:** Set up a family Web site and have each branch of your extended family post their images to individual pages. This can help distant members of the family stay in touch (add e-mail links to the pages so people can view the images and then immediately write an e-mail to talk about them), and let everyone in the family know about new arrivals and special events like family reunions.

- ✔ **Advertising your business:** Use the space to show pictures of your products, services, staff, locations — anything that will enhance your customer's interest in your business. Like a family site with individual pages for branches of the family or types of pictures, businesses can also categorize their images and set up individual pages to house each group.

If you thought your only goal for that box of old photos was to put them in an album, you can now see that you can do so many more things with your images. The Internet lets you share pictures with anyone, anywhere, and it won't cost you much money or take up much of your time. Have fun!

Index

C